RAF Bomber command Striking Back

RAF BOMBER COMMAND STRIKING BACK

OPERATIONS OF A HALIFAX CREW

ALAN MEASURES

Whittles Publishing

Published by
Whittles Publishing Ltd.,
Dunbeath,
Caithness, KW6 6EG,
Scotland, UK

www.whittlespublishing.com

ISBN 978-184995-456-3

© 2020 Alan Measures

This book catalogues the stories of six young men drawn from all corners of the globe, all united in their desire to strike back against the rapacious aims of a ruthless dictatorship in the dark skies over Europe. Their destiny was to serve in RAF Bomber Command, from which a total of 55,573 equally committed and highly trained young men would die.

The incredible courage shown by these men is especially poignant for me, as one of them, Len Starbuck, was a relative of mine.

In dedicating this book to their memory, I also look forward and dedicate this book to my children, Phoebe and Abbie, that they may know of such heroism so that it may inspire them, and their generation, to tackle the challenges faced by a new age with the same courage and determination.

CONTENTS

ACKNOWLEDGEMENTS

There are many people and organisations I should like to thank for having contributed to this book, particularly:

Photographs*

Barnsley War Memorials Project
Ed Coates Collection
Deutsches Bundesarchiv
Chris Goss Collection
The Imperial War Museum
Leicester City Football Club's archives
The National Archive
F. Albert Schwartz

Ed Cooke
The Fernie family
John Hutchinson
Jane Lewis
Catherine Michel-Guevel
RAF Museum Hendon
Yorkshire Air Museum and Allied Air Forces Memorial

* All photographs credited individually except the contemporary aircrew map from RAF Museum Hendon, which has been reproduced with different overlays by the author.

Key Individual Contributors

Mark Beswick
Ed Cooke
Hendrik Eusterbarkey
Chris Harper
David Layne
Bas Maathuis
Andrea Meier
Frau Carina Notzke
Gill Richardson
Nicola Wheatley

Theo Boiten
John Coote MBE
Peter Fernie
Keith Janes
Gordon Leith
Yvonne Mather
Bill Napier
Duncan Payne
Tim Rowntree
Philip Winter

Nancy Bowers
Linzee Duncan
Sue Fernie
Frau Christin Kiner
Caroline Louth
Dee Matthews
Mark Napier
Nicolas Rasmussen
Eric Verdon-Roe

Principal Organisations

Das Bundesarchiv Militärarchiv, Freiburg; The National Archive, Kew; RAF Disclosures, Cranwell; RAF Museum, Hendon; Yorkshire Air Museum and Allied Air Forces Memorial, Elvington.

I am indebted to the late Ed Cooke, who kindly shared his experiences with me over a number of months before he was sadly lost to us on 10 November 2013. In July 1942 Ed completed his tour. He attested that he was only the third WOp/AG to complete his tour with A Flight since joining 102 Squadron in May 1941.

This project would also never have come to fruition were it not for the support and guidance of Chris Goss, to whom I am most grateful.

Thanks are also due to Graham Mannassi for proof reading and Caroline Petherick, for copy editing.

To all, thank you for contributing the individual pieces that combine to tell the story of one crew's fight to survive against the odds.

NOTES

Unless stated otherwise, crew records have been taken from the relevant Form 540 Operations Records Books (ORBs) listed in the References and Bibliography by squadron and date.

Entries from official documents such as ORBs have been included where appropriate, including spelling mistakes such as in the names of the crewmen. This is to ensure that similar names have not been mistakenly aggregated. Typographical errors in locations have been corrected as being self-evident, but where aircraft numbers or times have been incorrectly listed the correction is identified in a footnote.

The names of towns and cities targeted/referenced have been spelled as they appear in official British documents; usually this is the English spelling, but on occasions the German equivalent prevails. For example, although the name Nuremberg was in common English usage, official documents refer to the German spelling of Nürnberg; conversely the same documents usually refer to the city of Cologne using the English spelling, although in a minority of cases they revert to the German spelling of Köln. To avoid confusion, I have adopted a consistent approach on a city-by-city basis, based upon the most widely used official terminology.

Throughout this work I have sought to use primary source data wherever possible. In some areas where I have not found primary data, I have researched widely across available secondary data. Nevertheless, it has become apparent that even reputable secondary sources appear on occasion to be contradictory, so I have had to take a decision as to which version is the most credible. I realise of course that different schools of thought will persist.

FOREWORD

In 1995, I published *It's Suicide but It's Fun*, the story of 102 (Ceylon) Squadron from 1917 to 1956. Why? A dear friend of my wife and myself, a Flight Engineer on the Squadron, was shot down and taken prisoner in October 1943, and when I was researching his loss, I got to know more about 102, and what I learned was tragic: the third heaviest losses in Bomber Command in the Second World War; the highest losses for the Group in which it flew; and the highest percentage losses for all of the Armstrong Whitworth Whitley squadrons. As a result of my research, I contacted the 102 Sqn Association and was fortunate to attend a number of memorable reunions, the most memorable being the one when my book was launched. Sadly nearly all the Squadron veterans, including our friend who got me started, are no longer with us, although the Association still exists, members now being mostly relatives.

When Alan Measures contacted me a few years ago asking for my help with his book, I was only too willing to help. The results of his research, a labour of love over many years, were intended as a tribute to a relative and his crew lost in uncertain circumstances on operations in 1942. He and I discussed many times the best way to present the book and its format, and after much blood, sweat and tears what you see here is the result of his hard work. Alan was tempted to give up a number of times, and to his credit he has at long last published what he had hoped for. My congratulations are heartfelt, because I know what he has gone through.

Wg Cdr Chris Goss MA RAF Ret'd, Marlow, 2020

PREFACE

In 2011, I was handed a piece of paper by a relative who said that it contained information that may be of use in helping compile my family tree which we were researching at the time, with an added postscript that I might find it interesting. When I unfolded the paper, I found that it was from the Commonwealth War Graves Commission and bore the name of my father's cousin and best friend, Len Starbuck, growing up together during the 1920s and 1930s. Also on this notice was a squadron number 102 Squadron, and a date; 26 June 1942.

Interest piqued, I set about researching the fate of Len, but soon came to realise that the more I found out, the more I didn't know, not just about him but also the conduct of the air offensive over Europe during the period 1941–42 as the tide was beginning to turn in favour of the Allies.

This led to years of painstaking research at the National Archives, the RAF Museum, the Bundesarchiv Militärarchiv and the Yorkshire Air Museum and Allied Air Forces Memorial. I was also very lucky to get support from a number of veterans who had served alongside Len on the squadron and kindly shared their memories, helping to uncover a treasure trove of anecdotes and operational information that would otherwise have been lost to time. As I began to put together these disparate pieces of information, I found myself challenging some of the perceived wisdom about this period. This enabled me to reconstruct in much greater clarity the life and times of not only my cousin but also the fellow crewmen he flew with against the deadly reality of night time operations, stripping bare the glamour of wearing the uniform of RAF aircrew.

This book does more than simply answer the question of what happened to my cousin Len, but opens a door onto the strategic planning and night-by-night tactical execution of these plans, as well as counting the human cost of carrying them through.

Whether you approach this book from the perspective of military history or human interest, I hope you will enjoy it and find something to spur you on in your own reading or research.

Alan Measures

PROLOGUE

BREMEN, APPROACHING 0230 HRS

'Bombs gone!'

The Canadian accent of the navigator, P/O Richard Bradbury, was heard over the intercom as Handley Page Halifax, serial number W7654 carrying the callsign DY-Q for Queenie, released her payload of three 1,000 lb bombs and mixed incendiaries over the flaming maelstrom of Bremen, 14,000 feet below.

The crew had left their base at RAF Topcliffe in Yorkshire over two and a half hours earlier, and had joined the tail end of a bomber stream comprising 1,006 aircraft from Bomber Command, Coastal Command and Army Co-Operation Command making their way to the Dutch coastal village of Egmond aan Zee. Totally unaware of their significance as a turning point for the bombers taking part in this, the third Thousand Bomber Raid, the villagers would have heard a constant procession of aircraft overhead lasting for over an hour before their skies returned to normal. From here the bombers turned eastwards towards the inland port city of Bremen, facing a 179-mile run across the occupied Netherlands and Lower Saxony as flak and night fighters picked off some of their less fortunate colleagues around them at random.

The attack had started at 0120 hrs and when Q for Queenie arrived it was already an hour old. By this time the town, docks and industrial areas were all well alight.

At 20 years old, Pilot F/Lt Kenneth Wright was the youngest but most senior ranking of the six-man crew. Richard Bradbury's confirmation was almost superfluous to him, as he felt the aeroplane lift with the release of 6,840 lb ordnance, but still he held to his course, knowing that they carried a camera and were expected to bring back pictures from their sortie. Precious seconds ticked down, everyone holding their breath in their common discomfort at being exposed and vulnerable to the flak crews below and the night fighters flying unseen around them.

In the bulbous mid-upper turret, American-born Sgt Jack Fernie quartered the night sky, looking out for enemy night fighters with his two 0.303" Browning machine guns. Meanwhile in the rear turret Sgt Ernest Taxeira de Mattos from British Malaya was maintaining a similar vigil, with four guns for company.

The oldest member of the crew, 26-year-old Wireless Operator / Air Gunner Sgt Leonard 'Len' Starbuck, was approaching the end of his tour of operations. He was kneeling by the flare tube with a photo flash in his hand, timer primed, when he too heard Bradbury's message.

On that cue, he counted down seven seconds, then dropped the photo flash and waited for the timer to wind down. When the flash went off and with the picture taken, Kenneth Wright was finally free to pull them sharply onto a heading due north, descending steeply in an effort to prevent opportunist night fighters from getting underneath them.

Released from his bomb-aiming responsibilities, Bradbury extricated himself from the confines of the bomb aimer's position and made his way back to the navigator's table to plot the course to the next turning point. As they started to draw away from the target, Ernest de Mattos would have finally been given his first view of the sea of flames that they and the other crews had left in their wake.

A little over three minutes later Kenneth Wright turned left again, this time onto a heading of 300 degrees, which they were to follow to a featureless reference point above the stormy North Sea 177 miles away. From this lonely and anonymous point they were to fly due west to safety at their base in Yorkshire, to cross off one more operation and to lament the loss of friends and colleagues who had not been as lucky as them.

As the Bolivian-born air engineer, F/Sgt Ivor Lewis, made adjustments to the engines in preparation for this next hour's leg, Q for Queenie thundered along a route that took her low over the Lower Saxony countryside, avoiding flak concentrations to the south around Oldenburg and to the north around Wilhelmshaven, as she aimed for the channel between the islands of Juist and Norderney. She would shortly have completed the overland portion of her sortie as she made for the German coast just north of the town of Norden.

Closing unseen in the darkness was the sleek shape of a Bf 110 night fighter. Aboard, the German pilot, taking cues from his wireless operator, was straining in the inky blackness to see the shape of the large four-engined bomber emerge from the protection of the night. As he scanned for the first sign of his quarry, he was planning his next move, hoping that he would be able to carry out his attack before he was spotted.

1

ONE MAN'S WAR BEGINS

12 JULY 1941

Six novice crewmen arrived at RAF Topcliffe to join 102 Squadron; among them was Sgt Leonard, 'Len', Starbuck. As he stood facing the gates for the first time, he would have realised he was now at the culmination of an intensive period of training that had started almost a year earlier. He was 100 miles north of his home in Burton on Trent, but in terms of his personal development he was so much further away than he could have ever imagined when he had signed up: he had traded the security of his family, his friends and his job to fly as aircrew on one of the RAF's heavy bomber squadrons. As he stood there, he must have felt a degree of trepidation.

Ten miles south-east of Burton on Trent lies the village of Measham, which retained a historical coalmining heritage in addition to attracting industries such as brick making and cotton milling. The productivity of this industrious village was realised through its connection to neighbouring towns by both the Ashby Canal and the Ashby and Nuneaton Joint Railway (ANJR), which had been built to service the Leicestershire coalfields.

Florrie Meaden was one of five children whose parents ran the Bird in Hand public house, located

Alex Meaden with Elsie, Annie and Florrie at the Bird in Hand (Author)

1

prominently on the High Street. In practice it was her mother who ran the establishment; her father spent little time there as he was working as a traveller, possibly for the brewery, much of his time being on the Isle of Man. Even when he was at home, he chose not to get in the way of running the pub and liked instead to indulge in being driven around by a chauffeur with a peaked cap.

Just around the corner from the Bird in Hand lived Jonathan (Jonty) Starbuck, with his three brothers, his sister and his parents. The family trade was butchery, but Jonty was a gifted footballer with a particular talent for goalkeeping. He played initially for Measham United as captain, famously representing Leicestershire against Lancashire in 1905, when he was 21. From there he went on to play professionally for second division Burton United, making a total of 74 appearances, ending in 1907 when the club was relegated from the football league. Just as his final season at Burton United drew to a close, Jonty's mother Mary died, leaving his father a widower.

His two-year career with Burton United over, Jonty was signed up to play for another second division club, Leicester Fosse[1] ('The Fossils'). He was to start his first season as reserve goalkeeper to Horace Bailey; Horace played 33 of the matches whilst Jonty played 5 in a momentous season that saw the club promoted to the first division for the first time in their history.

In 1908 Horace played in goal for Great Britain in the summer Olympics held in London. Great Britain got through to the final where they beat Denmark 2–0, earning gold medals. Throughout the whole tournament Great Britain conceded only one goal, that being to Sweden in the quarter final during their 12–1 victory. This astonishing feat put Horace at the top of the table for best goalkeeping during the tournament, making him arguably the best goalkeeper in the world at that time. Jonty clearly had a highly capable mentor, but irrespective of his own talent it would be difficult for him to emerge from the shadow of his brilliant teammate.

Jonty Starbuck at Leicester Fosse 1911/12 (John Hutchinson)

In the 1908/09 season in the first division, Jonty and Horace split their appearances evenly, facing the best teams in the country. They tried their best, Jonty conceding 16 fewer goals than Horace in league matches, but ultimately the team were not able to retain their grasp on their new status, and so the club returned to the second division next season. During the 1909/10 season the two men again split their appearances and this time Jonty conceded only 19 goals from 18 matches while Horace let in 25 from 15 appearances before transferring to Derby County on 23 April 1910 and finishing the last three games of the season with them.

In the summer of 1910, Jonty married Florrie, and just over a year later their first son, George, arrived.

Jonty made his last appearance for Leicester Fosse on 8 April 1912, at the age of 28, after a career with them that had spanned five years, during which he had played a total of 77 league matches and 12 FA Cup matches. In total, he had conceded 83 goals in 59 second division appearances, 43 goals in 18 first division appearances and 16 goals in 12 FA cup matches.

Jonty and Florrie then moved to Horninglow, to run the Plough Inn, located prominently on the Horninglow Road North in Burton on Trent, opposite the village green. Jonty still retained a keen interest in football and joined Ilkeston United, which had just been accepted into the newly formed Central Alliance, playing his first match for them on 8 March 1913. He played for the rest of the season, making 13 appearances in total, the team finishing sixth in the table. However, the season overall had been disappointing and big changes were made during summer 1913 with a number of players leaving, including Jonty. After this, he went to play for Burton All Saints.

Five years after George's birth, Jonty and Florrie's second son, Leonard, was born, on 21 March 1916. It would have been challenge for his parents to have run the business as well as taking care of the needs of their two boys, especially as the majority of their extended family lived in Measham, 14 miles away by road. Fortunately the ANJR ran a regular rail service which linked Measham into the main rail network, and the main Burton on Trent railway station was only a mile and a half away from the Plough Inn. This provided an ideal arrangement, and Len was free to travel back regularly, not only maintaining links with his family but also cultivating a circle of friends in the village.

In 1927 Len followed his brother into Burton Grammar School, where he would study for seven years. But on 13 April 1931, when he had just turned 15, the London, Midland and Scottish (LMS) railway withdrew its timetabled passenger service on the ANJR. This now denied Len the convenience of the point-to-point carrier that had allowed him to travel both ways in a day, and so he made longer visits to Measham, and stayed over with relatives.

When he left school in 1934 he went to work as a forwarding clerk for Tutbury Glassworks in Ludgate Street, Tutbury, three miles away from his home. The factory had originally been set up to service the demand from public houses for glass jugs and tumblers, but expanded into the market for fine decorated lead crystal glassware. This heralded a period of rapid expansion to meet increasing demand, and Len's future was assured.

Len's father, the legendary footballer, local hero and latterly publican, died on 18 April 1939, just as a new house was being completed for the family on Tutbury Road. The grief felt by his widow Florrie would have been compounded by the fear of further loss when her younger son, Len, applied to join the RAF. The formation of its Volunteer Reserve had caused a surge of interest, especially as applications were now also being sought actively from those in reserved occupations, and there would be delays as large numbers of volunteers were fed into the system.

Having applied to join up, Len would have been called forward for evaluation. This involved sitting an examination in mathematics and English. Whilst the papers were being marked, he would have undergone a medical examination, following which he would have been called

Young Len Starbuck (Jane Lewis)

forward to an airman sitting behind a desk whose duty it was to inform the applicants whether they had been successful or not. Len passed and, in recognition of having been accepted onto aircrew training, was sworn in and given a badge to wear, following which he would have been sent home and told to await a call.

During this wait, Len's maternal grandfather Alexander died, on 2 April 1940. Florrie, having lost her husband only a year previously, had now lost her father and must have felt a rising sense of foreboding for the safety of her younger son.

When the anticipated call arrived three months later, Len was directed to report to No.10 (Signals) Recruits Centre at Blackpool on 26 July 1940, whereupon he assumed the rank of aircraftsman second class (AC2) as an aircraft hand wireless operator (ACH/WOp). During his time there he was introduced to military life, especially marching and arms drills, and more importantly initial wireless training.

Whilst at Blackpool Len wrote home asking for family to knit socks for him and his fellow recruits, due to the shortcomings of the officially issued garments. As his course drew to a close 12 weeks later, Len would have been examined to demonstrate that he had mastered Morse code to a threshold of at least 10 words per minute (wpm) on the wireless.

Len's next posting was on 18 October 1940, to No.2 Wing No.2 Signals School at RAF Yatesbury in Wiltshire, for advanced training. His training here was to last for 10 weeks, and was arranged as half a day getting up to speed with Morse code and the other half learning the technical aspects of the R1082 / T1083 wireless that was standard equipment on the bombers at that time. In addition, he also had to learn competence at signalling Morse code using the Aldis lamp. Towards the end of the course, he could have been given flights to gain a little practical experience of air-to-ground signalling. Upon completion of the course on 23 December 1940, he sat a final exam covering the technical syllabus and had to demonstrate Morse code on the wireless to a pass-out standard of 18 wpm and on the Aldis lamp of 8 wpm. Len scraped past this exam at 40 per cent, but this was just enough to give him his wireless operator's badge and earn him the new title of wireless operator under training air gunner (WOp ut AG).

By this stage, the unreliable R1082/T1083 wireless sets that the recruits had learned on were being superseded by new Marconi T1154/R1155 equipment. For a brief window whilst the advanced training at RAF Yatesbury caught up, the recruits had to be sent to learn about the new wireless equipment that they would be expected to use on the squadrons. To this end, a number of venues across the country ran bridging courses. Consequently, having had four days off for Christmas, Len was posted to RAF Pembroke Dock in South Wales for nine weeks, commencing on 28 December 1940. It was generally recognised and appreciated that the new wireless equipment was much more user friendly than that which it had succeeded, and as an added bonus Len was now capable of operating either the new or the old equipment.

On 1 March 1941, Len was able finally to move on to the gunnery aspects of his training and was posted to No.7 Bombing and Gunnery School (B&GS), RAF Stormy Down, in South Wales. To signify the start of this part of his training, he was now referred to as aircraft hand wireless operator air gunner (ACH/WOp/AG). As with his time at RAF Yatesbury, the tuition was to be split into differing morning and afternoon sessions.

The two machine guns taught on this course were the Birmingham Small Arms Company Ltd (BSA) or Vickers Armstrong-manufactured belt-fed 0.303" Browning Mk.II, the standard defensive armament for British bombers of the time, and the pan-fed 0.303" Vickers Armstrong K Gas Operated (GO) machine gun, which still remained in service. Both were capable of delivering a rate of fire of up to 1,200 rounds per minute, but although the Browning was belt-fed, the magazine on the Vickers K was limited to either 60 or 100 rounds, which meant that even the larger magazine could be expended within 5 seconds.

The students would have to complete the course by amassing a detailed knowledge of weapon husbandry, aircraft recognition and deflexion theory, and achieving a 7 per cent hit ratio marksmanship threshold.

Given the fact that Bomber Command was being operated as a night-time force, it was necessary for the students to be able to strip and rebuild their guns in darkness, resolving anything from a jam to more serious problems within the shortest possible time. This metric was tested by regular blindfolded strip-and-rebuild exercises within a target time of 2 minutes.

Principles of deflexion fire also had to be thoroughly understood, subject areas including:[2]

- Bullet trail, where the bullet appears to trail behind the line of aim
- Range estimation, based on knowing the wingspans of typical single- and twin-engined fighter aircraft
- Curve of pursuit, projecting the path of the fighter relative to the bomber
- Zone allowances, for fighters aiming fixed guns, given the different crossing speeds of the fighter across the bomber's stern
- Gravity drop, including sight harmonisation.

Practice was vital, but ammunition and air time for training were both scarce, so the students started on the ground by familiarising themselves with a variety of fully functioning aircraft turrets mounted on an array of wheeled contraptions capable of being relocated at short notice. They learned to fire firstly against static targets, then built up their expertise on plywood models moving along rails as their knowledge of deflexion fire improved.

Given the rate at which the guns consumed ammunition, students had to be taught the importance of firing in short accurate bursts rather than more wasteful 'hosepiping' techniques. Precious ammunition was sometimes further conserved during training by limiting the number of machine guns enabled in a turret to one, even though in practice an operational turret might have been be fitted with two, or even four. Sometimes, however, even one machine gun was too many, and it would be replaced by a shotgun.

After three weeks on this course, the students were halfway through. By now they were expected to be up to speed with theory and capable of demonstrating an acceptable level of expertise on the ground. At this point, as Len started the aerial gunnery aspects of his training, he was promoted to leading aircraftsman (LAC).

To gain experience of firing a Vickers GO gun mounted on a Scarff ring, the students flew first in the Fairey Battle. This aircraft was cramped, and only two students could fly on any given sortie, swapping over halfway through.

Drogue or flag targets would be towed behind an aerial tug such as another Fairey Battle, which would fly increasingly difficult engagement profiles as the students became more adept. Once the firing detail had been concluded the target would be dropped over the aerodrome and the strikes counted.

One student would have been issued with standard ammunition whilst the other would have fired bullets painted in a coloured wax that would, in theory at least, leave a stain around the bullet hole to provide clear discrimination between students' efforts, although this sometimes proved contentious in practice.[3]

Having mastered the Scarff ring, the students then progressed to an Armstrong Whitworth Whitley, which was much more representative of what they would be likely to encounter on operational squadrons. This aircraft could accommodate six students at a time, and was also equipped with the refinement of gun cameras, avoiding the problems of wax-coated bullets. Students would start by gaining familiarity in the front turret and then proceed to the rear turret.

The culmination of Len's course was marked by two days of exams, on 10–11 April 1941, which he passed at 72.5 per cent. This earned him his air gunner's brevet and promotion to temporary sergeant, which he was awarded the next day. He was now a wireless operator / air gunner (WOp/AG).

On 19 April 1941 he went to RAF Marham in Norfolk for a week, after which he was ready to be posted to an operational training unit (OTU). At this time, there were two heavy night bomber OTUs; 19 OTU at RAF Kinloss in Morayshire, and 10 OTU at RAF Abingdon in Oxfordshire. Len received his posting to 10 OTU with effect from 26 April 1941. He was now finally able to fly as a crewman respected and trusted by his peers, who were themselves emerging from their own respective training regimes, eager to prove themselves in a flying environment.

On this course, the novice crewmen would have spent half their time mastering the specific nuances of their particular flight disciplines and the other half flying as part of a crew, putting into practice their skills in increasingly demanding scenarios. Sometimes low-risk front line operations could even be conducted, such as dropping propaganda leaflets ('nickelling') or dropping mines ('gardening').

Here Len would have built upon the basic skills he had learned, and come to recognise the important role he played as a member of the crew, his primary function being to assist the navigator by using the loop antenna to secure reliable bearings from fixed ground stations. He was also responsible for rolling out the trailing aerial, which could then be used to get a fix by transmitting the aircraft's callsign to the appropriate ground station(s) to confirm its position.

The WOp could also directly assist the pilot by cueing him to a beacon, perhaps one conveniently located near their home base. In this case, the WOp would pick out the appropriate beacon, tune it in, set the loop antenna to 0 and switch the signal to the radio direction finding (RDF) meter. This gave the pilot an immediate visual reference as to whether he was homing to the beacon, since the needles had to cross on the centre line; if they crossed to one side, then he would have to correct his course to fly in that direction until the needles crossed on the centre line once again. Further, a temporary heading update could be achieved by requesting base to clamp their key down for a short time, and homing to that signal.

Another role with which Len would have to become familiar was to work with both the navigator and the pilot to provide evidence of a successful bombing run over the target; this was part of a new initiative being handed down to aircrews. When the navigator took up the bomb aimer's position in the nose, the WOp would take a photo flash, insert it in the flare tube, set the timer, hook the cord to the safety pin and wait. During the run to the target, the aircraft would be flown straight and level as the navigator provided the necessary last-minute corrections to ensure most accurate bomb release over the target; once it was in the optimum position he would release the payload and call 'bombs gone'. If the crew had been detailed to be one of those carrying a camera, the aircraft would then have to continue flying straight and level as the WOp counted a delay from the navigator's mark before releasing the flash. If the delay was correct, then the flash would go off at the right moment to capture the bomb bursts in the picture that would be analysed on their return to confirm the accuracy of their night's work. Only once the picture had been taken was the pilot finally clear to turn and head for home, whereupon the WOp would return to the wireless and transmit the 'bombs gone' signal and the time.

Now that Len was flying operations more representative of those that he would be called upon to support when on a front line squadron, he would have become aware as both WOp and air gunner that Armstrong Whitworth had not fully taken into account the low temperatures in which sorties would be flown. Temperatures as low as -32°C had been recorded operationally, which had led to systems failures such as the freezing of the oxygen system, the turret controls, the guns and even the wireless,[4] in addition to more fundamental issues such as an uncontrollable build-up of ice on wings and controls. Although the Whitley Mk.V had seen the introduction of de-icing boots, its flight controls could still be jammed by ice accretion, and there was still inadequate heating inside the fuselage. The effects were felt worst in the rear turret, and several air gunners actually lost fingers through frostbite.

On 23 May 1941, whilst Len was still under training, 10 OTU hosted a royal visit by the King and Queen, Princess Elizabeth and Princess Margaret Rose, accompanied by: Air Marshal Sir Richard Peirse, Commander-in-Chief Bomber Command; Mr Arthur Loyd, Lord Lieutenant of Berkshire; and Commander Legge, Chief Constable of Berkshire. This occasion was marked with a flypast of some of the more rare and exotic aircraft in Bomber Command's Order of Battle (ORBAT), some of which would have been familiar to the audience only from photographs in popular aviation periodicals at best. The royal party performed a half-hour inspection of the aircraft and then retired to the balcony on the regional control office for a privileged view of the two-way flypast, comprising:

1. Wellington Mk.II (this aircraft was carrying a 4,000 lb High Capacity (HC) bomb, which necessitated modifications to the bomb bay and removal of the central bomb bay doors[5])

2. Manchester

3. Halifax

4. Stirling

5. Lancaster (as this type was still unfamiliar, it was described as 'like a Manchester but with 4 Merlin engines')

6. Boeing B-17C Fortress I (this was only just going through acceptance into RAF service)

7. Martin Model 167 Maryland (these had been in service with the RAF since 1940 and were operating in the Mediterranean and Middle East).

This flypast highlighted not only Bomber Command's rapid transition away from its antiquated biplane designs, such as the Handley Page Heyford, which had been in front-line service as recently as 2 September 1939, but also the advent of a new class of weapon, the High Capacity (HC) bomb. Unlike the General Purpose (GP) bombs, which had a streamlined profile with a solid metal nose to deliver penetrative effects onto the target, these HC bombs were little more than thin-walled containers filled with explosive, raising the charge/weight ratio from around 15 per cent (in the case of the smaller GP bombs) to over 70 per cent.

The 4,000 lb HC bomb, known as 'Cookie', had a diameter of 30" and a length of 110" with a 5/16" cast steel casing, containing typically an AMATOL[6] fill. This bomb had first been used on 31 March / 1 April 1941 against the shipyards at Emden, the official report of the event quoting that 'masses of debris flying through the air were outlined against the glow of fires and the results appeared to be devastating'; one of the pilots was moved to observe that 'houses took to the air.'[7] However, before long these bombs would earn a reputation for being unstable, as they could detonate simply by being dropped during ground handling. Further, they could also detonate on release just by being exposed to the fast-moving airflow under the bomber, the pressure of the wind on the fuze being sufficient to cause the bomb to detonate, whether dropped live or safe.

June 1941 saw an increase in 10 OTU being called upon to conduct nickelling operations over the Paris and Orleans areas. As Len was coming towards the end of his course he would have been ideally placed to participate in these comparatively low-risk operations. When July came, Len was standing at the culmination of 50 weeks of training, and so when he received his posting to 102 Squadron he was finally ready for front-line operations.

Since November 1940 102 Squadron had been based at RAF Topcliffe, which, in common with other aerodromes of the time, did not have paved runways. Instead, the squadron's operations centred around a 'bombing circle' located amid 200 acres of prepared grass. This bombing circle could be configured to support operations from single bombing lanes or parallel dual ones, according to need.

The aerodrome was also home to 77 Squadron, and from late 1939/early 1940 both squadrons were operating the Whitley Mk.V, which was capable of carrying a 7,000 lb payload of bombs – 50 per cent more than the next heaviest twin-engined bomber, the Wellington. Further, the Whitley was the only aircraft in Bomber Command's ORBAT at the outbreak of war that had been purpose-designed as a night bomber, and as such it had played a pivotal role in taking the war to the enemy. The introduction of the new four-engined heavy bombers from August 1940 had, however, started to make the Whitley look outdated, but there was still plenty of work for it to do before being pensioned off.

The only appreciable difference between the aircraft was that those allocated to 102 Squadron carried the squadron code letters DY whilst those from 77 Squadron were identified by KN. During the time they were located at RAF Topcliffe, both squadrons ran combined

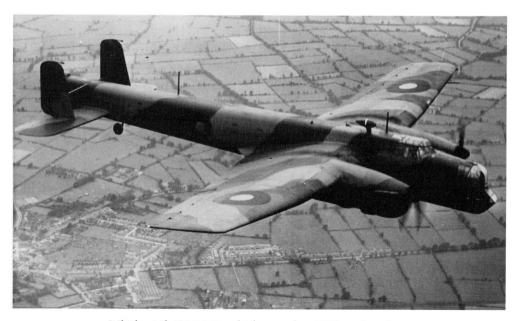

Whitley Mk.V N1352, which served on 77 Squadron from
September 1939 to April 1940 (Ed Coates Collection)

operations to the same targets and would line up together as two narrowly separated strands of the same fighting unit.

One of the most striking features of the Whitley was its distinctive nose-down attitude in flight. This characteristic was due to flaps having been omitted from the original design, and the mainplane thus being set at a high 8½-degree angle of incidence to provide stability during take-off and landing, even though this configuration would cause drag in flight. Hydraulic flaps were subsequently introduced prior to the completion of the prototype and were fitted to all production versions, but the mainplane angle of incidence, and thus the nose-down attitude, remained.

Although few would call the Whitley beautiful, the design won over crews through its qualities such as sturdiness and docility, one pilot stating:[8] 'The Whitley, like the old lady she was, never quite did as she was told to do, but the things that she did were for the most part reasonable and comfortable.'

Philip Winter, who trained as a pilot on the Whitley Mk.III at 10 OTU before being posted to 102 Squadron to fly the Whitley Mk.V, confirmed that although she flew with that unique nose-down attitude, the anomaly was never apparent in flight, and the configuration permitted good visibility with 'not a lot of nose to see over'. In fact, the design was considered to be good for its time, not least because it was capable of taking a lot of punishment.

For all of its strengths, the Whitley had a very stately cruising speed of 120 mph, although this was sometimes mistakenly misquoted. When Ed Cooke, survivor of 19 Whitley operations on 102 Squadron, was made aware that faster speeds such as 165 mph or even 185 mph were being quoted, he commented drily: 'Lucky to get 120 mph cruising speed; maybe they meant straight down at full throttle.'

The Whitley was designed to be operated by a crew of four, compromising captain, navigator, wireless operator (WOp) and air gunner. Of these, the navigator was expected to subsume into his duties the roles of bomb aimer and air gunner in the front turret as required. In practice, it was accepted custom and practice that the WOp would man the front turret, and thus the role of WOp/AG had been adopted. Aircraft on 102 Squadron were also routinely flown with a fifth crewman, a 2nd pilot, which was generally accepted as being a training position, allowing a novice pilot to gain familiarity with the aircraft on the safer legs of a sortie so that the captain could be fresh for the more arduous aspects of flying over enemy territory. Given that some of the longer sorties, such as Berlin, Nürnberg or Stettin, could extend to over ten hours, the importance of a fresh pilot was self-evident.

The payloads carried by the bombers operating from this aerodrome were generally either General Purpose (GP) or Fire Raisers. In both cases this meant a mix of 250 lb, 500 lb and 1,000 lb GP bombs supplemented by Small Bomb Containers (SBC); the difference was that the Fire Raisers carried two fewer 500 lb bombs and four more SBCs. Although these were fuzed either instantaneous or with 0.025 seconds delay, a 250 lb bomb with a random Mixed Long Delay (MLD) measured in hours could also be added into the bomb load. All these permutations of bomb load were allocated a specific number so that the armourers could readily bomb-up the aircraft without ambiguity; No.1 and No.3 were GP, whilst No.5 and

No.6 were Fire Raisers. There was also a No.12 bomb load: 250 lb and 500 lb Semi Armour Piercing (SAP) bombs designed to penetrate the decks of a ship, with a fuzing delay extended to 0.12 seconds to allow the bomb time to pass through to the lower decks before detonating.

During combined operations, 77 Squadron would generally carry the Fire Raisers and leave first. This would give the fire a chance to take hold of the target before 102 Squadron aircraft arrived to release its GP bombs with their High Explosive (HE) filling, creating blast effects that would spread the burning debris over a wider area.

Not all payloads were lethal; sometimes nickels were carried, the more durable examples being known as nickel cards. A few packets would frequently be released over the target area to accompany a full payload of bombs, but crews would sometimes be called upon to undertake dedicated nickelling operations. The message on the nickels would be changed on a regular basis, each tailored to deliver a specific message in the language of the people over whom they were to be dropped.

Delivering the nickels on target required different aiming principles from dropping bombs, and involved the aircraft being positioned upwind of the target area. When the aircraft was in position, a packet of nickels tied with string was placed into the flare chute, at which point the string would be cut, allowing the nickels to flutter down in a cloud. Cutting the string before the nickels were in the flare chute would result in a blizzard of paper throughout the aircraft, and was a mistake which once made was never forgotten.

Occasionally, 102 Squadron was also tasked with dropping morale-boosting gifts over occupied Holland en route to their targets, sometimes necessitating a slight deviation from the planned route. One such gift that kept appearing on the manifest was 'dockers', a term long lost from common usage, which referred to a type of tobacco product;[9] it was dropped to raise the spirits of the subjugated Dutch people.

Although known unofficially as 'Morecambe's Own', 102 Squadron was at the forefront of overseas recruitment, and would come to enjoy a rich mixture of personalities drawn from across the world.

There were two operational flights, A and B, both of which were run by S/Ldr flight commanders. Unusually, the squadron operated at least in part a flexible crewing system whereby novice crewmen were rotated one or two at a time amongst experienced crews wherever possible, to gain their first taste of combat from within a relatively supportive environment. This would have fostered a feeling of being part of a 'big family' the size of the flight, and would have simplified making up a crew, as all crewmen would have thus known each other to some degree. On the downside, any losses from within the flight would have been felt more closely by all crewmen on the flight rather than if they had been operating as fixed crews, as was more widely accepted practice.

The flexible system also meant that members of a crew would all have different experience levels, and thus finish their respective tours at different times. This could result in those finishing before their peers leaving with a sense of unfulfilled loyalty, feeling an obligation to stay and support their colleagues; but applications to stay on would be refused, even during these times of chronic shortage.

Some informal guidelines appear to have been observed. For example, a novice WOp/AG would serve in the rear turret for his first few sorties and only be allowed to operate the wireless once he had proven his worth. Even then he would only be serving in the interim position of 2nd WOp, learning his trade from an established WOp. Analysis of crew compositions on operations suggests that whilst 2nd pilots could stay with their captains, novice crewmen from the other flight disciplines might well change crews after their first operation, presumably to preclude the creation of any 'halo effect' around a particular crew or captain, which could compromise the novice crewman's ability to work effectively within another crew.

This is not to say that all crews on the squadron operated this way; some crews appear to have coalesced particularly well, although there was still room for manoeuvre rather than ring-fencing a crew from the outset. In addition to this, crewmen could be transferred across flights on an 'as needed' basis if specific aircrew disciplines were required to make up crews, sometimes for one operation, sometimes for a few more before returning.

On 15 August 1940, while the squadron had been based at RAF Driffield in Yorkshire, the aerodrome had been bombed by German aircraft. This had set the precedent that aircrew could no longer live on station, and so when they moved to RAF Topcliffe they were billeted in the nearby Skellfield House (or 'Skeleton House' as some crews would come to know it due to the dead mice and rats found in the building). This had previously been a private girls' school, and accommodation for the airmen could be either on the ground floor in a large room that held sixteen, or upstairs, where crewmen were accommodated two or three to a bedroom. Philip Winter gave a pointer to the former credentials of this imposing building in the following recollection: 'It was rumoured that in some bathrooms were bell pushes signed "Ring for Mistress" but I failed to find one.'

To provide improved protection against future attacks, Cold Kirby was established 7 miles ENE from RAF Topcliffe, becoming operational on 13 March 1940 as a K-type decoy airfield. This meant that it was laid out to represent an operational aerodrome in the hope of deceiving enemy daytime reconnaissance flights. All features of an operational aerodrome were modelled as realistically as possible, even to the extent of creating fresh taxi marks leading to the dummy Whitley bombers. On 19 June 1940 it was upgraded to a Q-type decoy airfield, with lights to simulate an operational aerodrome at night.

Although living off station was a minor inconvenience, this policy was seen to be vindicated when this aerodrome too was bombed:[10]

- 16 February 1941 – RAF Topcliffe was bombed by enemy aircraft at 0137 hrs as bombers returned from operations. The ordnance dropped comprised 3× 100 kg HE bombs and a hundred incendiaries near dispersal 500 yards east of the bomb dump. One was delayed action, detonating at 1230 hrs with no damage.
- 1 April 1941 – RAF Topcliffe was attacked by two enemy aircraft at 1522 hrs which proceeded to make an attack with machine gun fire on personnel at the bomb dump. There were no injuries and no bombs were dropped. The attackers were chased off by the arrival of RAF fighters.

A bus service was provided from Skellfield House to take the men to the Officers' and Sergeants' Messes in the mornings, and another to return them after dinner, with additional services laid on as they were needed.

Ed Cooke, who had recently joined as a WOp/AG, recalled:

> A typical day was seven days a week except that aircrew got 14 days leave every three months. Catching the bus to the Mess for breakfast, 77 Squadron was also with us so there was two sittings for every meal which was poor to say the least, sitting in the lounge reading the paper if one was lucky enough to get one, then off to the flights for 0900 hrs. Sitting around, playing various games until it was time for lunch, after sitting in the lounge waiting for the BBC time signal to check our watches, listen to the news and then back to the flights until dinner time. After dinner catch a bus to Skellfield House, where people went their different ways; some to change and go out drinking at the various pubs from the two in the village to as far away as Harrogate or just sit around reading, writing letters etc. The house was in a very nice setting, alongside the River Swale with nice gardens in about 80 acres of meadowland.
>
> Very occasionally our days would be interrupted in a morning by the word 'OPS ON', which meant we would board transport to our aircraft the other side of the field in their various dispersal points, check our aircraft and flight test them. In summer time after lunch we would go out to Skellfield House try to sleep a little or just generally laze around. Back to the Mess for dinner and about 1900 hrs off to briefing where we sat as crews waiting for them to pull the rope so that we could see the map and just where they were sending us, briefed by all from Met [Meteorological Officer] to Signals, WOps got the lists of timetables frequencies etc. written on rice paper[11] which we were supposed to eat in event of being captured. Back to the Mess for a Flying Supper, bacon and egg then sit around until time to go to the Flights where one began the process of kitting up by first emptying our pockets and donning our flight gear. On our return did things in reverse order then off to interrogation to tell our stories plus a hot cup of tea and a packet of cigarettes from one of the colonies, then catch the bus back to our billets and sleep.

Philip Winter explained 'when an operation was scrubbed too late for an evening out, we gathered in the huge kitchen at Skellfield, drinking cocoa and making dripping toast at the kitchen range'. On such occasions, he recalled, 'talk was of ops completed and how many more to go, what went wrong, what went well, a happy and convivial atmosphere'.

At this time 102 Squadron was feeling the shortage of aircrews due to losses and the delay in replacements graduating through training at the OTUs. Ed Cooke provides an anecdote supporting this state of affairs by recollecting that on one of the flights 'there were by this time only four Navigators left' but adds with dry humour 'morale during the summer of 1941 was quite good even though every day we saw the results as our chances of getting a seat in the lounge after lunch increased'. Certainly, towards the end of June the squadron was routinely despatching its Whitleys on operations up to eight hours long without a 2nd pilot.

Among recent losses had been B Flight's commander, S/Ldr William McArthur, on 27/28 June, followed less than a week later, on 3/4 July, by the loss of A Flight's commander,

S/Ldr Oswald Moseley, leaving both flights without commanders. Relief would arrive shortly as a tranche of 54 new crewmen started to arrive during July 1941. Within a brief period, the Sergeants' and Officers' Messes were suddenly going to become stretched to capacity with the arrival of new crews, and as Ed Cooke recounted wryly, 'it was no longer quite so easy to get a chair'.

To fill the gap left by the recent near-simultaneous loss of both its flight commanders, 102 Squadron appointed two replacements on 7 July 1941. B Flight was to receive experienced Whitley pilot S/Ldr Eric Verdon-Roe, who was already an established flight commander on 77 Squadron. He was the eldest son of aviation pioneer Sir Edwin Alliott Verdon-Roe, founder of Avro aircraft in 1910 and latterly Saunders-Roe in 1929. Meanwhile on A Flight, the duty of flight commander fell to the most senior ranking pilot currently serving on that flight, F/Lt James Walker. He had only just landed from completing his first operational sortie as captain (known as his 'freshman' operation) at 0514 hrs that morning. Given the prevailing loss rate of flight commanders and his relative inexperience, James Walker had his flying hours restricted to one operation in three.

As part of the relief effort to replenish aircrews, Len arrived on 12 July 1941 in the company of five other novice crewmen:

Pilots: P/O IPB Denton, Sgt Philip Eyre and Sgt BR Wilde

Navigator: Sgt WV Atkinson

WOp/AG: Sgt PJ Jennings.

Upon reporting in, Len was allocated to B Flight, where, having reported in again, he was allocated a locker in the crew room for his flying gear. As a WOp/AG he would next have gone to see the signals officer, who would have interviewed him and asked him to demonstrate his skill operating the new Marconi T1154 / R1155 equipment, now the standard wireless fits on the squadron.

As they settled in, Len and his fellow novices would have doubtless been regaled with stories of recent near misses, such as Sgt Allan Davis and his crew returning from Essen only a week earlier, desperately low on fuel, making a wheels-up landing on what appeared to be a straight road but turned out to be a dyke near Bacton, Cromer. Following a successful crash-landing, the crew were able to see that the dyke they had landed on was a mere 30 feet wide, only one third the wingspan of the Whitley!

14 JULY 1941

Churchill made a rousing speech containing the following text, 'From now on we shall bomb Germany on an ever-increasing scale, month by month, year by year, until the Nazi regime has either been exterminated by us or – better still – torn to pieces by the German people themselves.'

Len was to be part of this offensive, starting that very night.

Target[12]	Aircraft on target	Types
Bremen:		
(i) Aim point A east of old town	19	Whitley
(ii) Aim point B goods station	47	Wellington
(iii) Aim point C east of shipyards at Atlas Works	31	Wellington
Hanover:		
(i) Aim point A main station	66	44 Hampden 14 Halifax 6 Stirling 2 Wellington
(ii) GS152 Continental Gummiwerke AG rubber factory	19	Wellington
CC42 Rotterdam	9	Wellington
Minelaying:		
(i) Frisian Islands (Nectarine)	5	Hampden
(ii) Off the Elbe (Eglantine)	5	Hampden

Primary target: Bremen (old town).
Alternative: Strategic and Military (S&M).
Last Resort: S&M.
Combined ops 19 aircraft:
    102 Sqn operation C.139: 12 aircraft, operational call sign Q9J.
    77 Sqn operation C.152: 7 aircraft, operational call sign 8GT.
Bomb load:
    102 Sqn: No.1 or No.3 fuzed 0.025 and 1× 250 lb MLD to be included in each bomb load.
    77 Sqn: No.5 or No.6 fuzed 0.025 and 1× 250 lb MLD to be included in each bomb load.
Route: Base – Bridlington – Texel – Dümmer See – Bremen – Vlieland – Bridlington – Base.
Time Off: 2215 hrs.
Weather: Low cloud slight haze.
Opposition: Light and heavy flak intense, searchlights numerous.

Only two days after arriving, Len was flying in a bombing operation comprising 19 aircraft across the two squadrons bound for Bremen. He had been allocated to a crew in A Flight, led by the experienced P/O Kenneth Whisken, who retained two of his previous experienced crewmen with him, Sgt Anthony Holmes as navigator and Sgt Leslie Netherclift as WOp, and completed his crew by claiming another July starter as his 2nd pilot. In keeping with the custom and practice evolved on the squadron, Len, in common with all novice WOp/AGs on the squadron before him, would be starting his combat career in the cold and the isolation of the rear turret. The crew was also scheduled to drop dockers over Holland on the night's operation.

Following a check flight in the afternoon, Len would have unwound a little and maybe written a letter before going in for his bacon and egg Flying Supper. After this, he would have retired to B Flight and as the departure time drew closer he would have put on his flying clothes. Although the rear air gunner was unique amongst his crewmates in that he was issued with an electrically heated suit, the rear turret was still the coldest crew position in the aircraft,

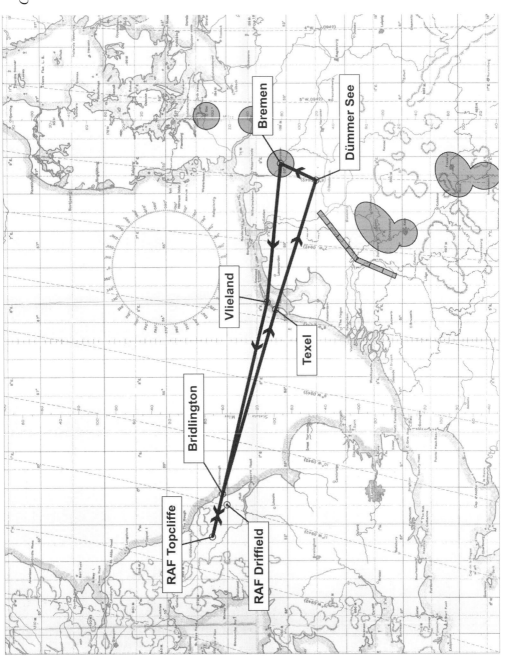

Operation C.139
to Bremen,
14 July 1941

so he may have brought along an extra sweater to help keep him warm. His remaining flying clothing would have consisted of his silk socks, woollen stockings and lambswool lined flying boots. Next, he would have put on his Irvine jacket containing his Mae West, and picked up his flying helmet with its oxygen mask, and the last item of safety equipment, his chest-type parachute. He was also issued with flight rations, which would typically contain a few biscuits, an apple or orange, a bar of chocolate, barley sugar, chewing gum, raisins and a thermos of tea or coffee. Stimulants known as 'wakey-wakey pills' containing the amphetamine Benzedrine were also available as required.

Once dropped off at their aircraft, the cockpit crew could climb a ladder up through the forward emergency hatch, or, more usually, all crew would enter by the crew door midway between the trailing edge of the port wing and the tailplane. Len would have climbed in through the crew door and turned right, to man his position in the rear turret.

He would then have worked his way down aft and clipped his parachute to hooks on the starboard side of the fuselage just outside the

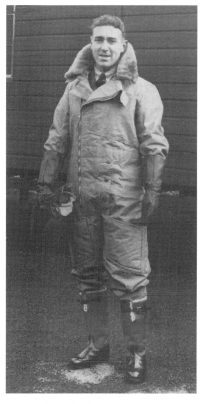

Sgt Len Starbuck (Jane Lewis)

turret, then squeezed into the cramped space between four machine guns, closing the turret's double doors behind him. As he settled in, he would have plugged in his electrically heated suit, oxygen supply and intercom.

The Nash & Thompson turret was state of the art, benefiting from hydraulic power and four 0.303" Browning Mk.II machine guns, giving a combined output of 4,800 rounds per minute. However, this capability had been granted at the expense of space, and it was a very cramped environment. Nearing the end of a long sortie, air gunners would always be tired, aching and stiff, but few would dare leave the turret just in case that was the moment when a night fighter might appear. Crews had become aware of the Luftwaffe's intruder operations, and knew that nobody was safe until they had landed and disembarked.

Not only was the turret cramped but it was so cold that the view from it was often impeded by mist and frost forming on the perspex. Consequently, it was not uncommon practice for air gunners to remove the perspex front panel to ensure good visibility, in spite of the added discomfort this would cause. Furthermore, seated in his position at the extreme end of the fuselage, the air gunner felt completely isolated; he would not be able to see any other part of the aircraft unless he turned the turret fully to one side. Several air gunners have recounted the eeriness of hurtling across the sky backwards, completely alone.

In the event of receiving the order to bale out, the air gunner had the choice of escape routes. In both cases, he would centre the turret and open the turret doors behind him to retrieve his parachute. Having clipped on his parachute, he could either choose to re-enter the turret, rotate through 90° and then fall out backwards, or alternatively he could go forward and escape through the crew door.

When the pilot was ready, Len's mind would have become sharply focused as the 1,280 horse power V12 engine on the starboard wing was kicked into life. The aircraft shook and surged a little on her oleo legs as the engine settled into its rhythm, and then the port engine spluttered into life.

Once the engines had settled into a steady rhythm, he would have next heard the flaps being cycled down and up again to test the engine-driven hydraulic pump, and used this as his cue to test the hydraulic controls in his turret.

Whilst the engines warmed up Whisken continued running through his checklist, and at some point Len would have seen the call lamp light up and heard him over the intercom to confirm his ability to hear and be heard, as well as confirming that he could operate the call lamp light from his end. Once up to temperature, the engines were put through a series of tests; the constant speed units, the magneto drops and then finally the full throttle checks before settling back and waiting for the signal to go.

The engines picked up just a little and the brakes were released, allowing the aircraft to move forward, then it paused momentarily as the pilot checked the brakes once more. Then it moved forward again, slowly, purposefully, as it took its place midway along one of the two lanes that tailed back from the parallel flare paths. Right on time, at 2215, hrs the first aircraft at the head of each line throttled up and began their take-off runs side by side, Sgt Robert Wheatley from 77 Squadron and Sgt WJ Wilson from 102 Squadron matching pace during the take-off run, both eventually struggling into the air with five souls on board apiece.

The aircraft took off in pairs at intervals of 1 minute 15 seconds and at 2220 hrs, Kenneth Whisken saw the green Aldis lamp from the chequered caravan at the beginning of the flare path indicating the way clear for him to proceed. In response, he opened both throttles and it was their turn to surge forward down the runway, building speed a bit at a time. Abeam of them was Sgt C Hildred from A Flight in Z6821, the DY-D lettering emblazoned prominently on the side of the fuselage.

The individual lights of the flare path marched past in pairs either side, almost imperceptibly breaking into a jog and then into a run. Len, in his turret, would have felt the bumps on the grass coming faster as the aircraft built up speed, then stopping altogether as the tail lifted, gently raising his position and giving him a better view of those still behind him, waiting their turn. The Whitley took an age to build up speed, and once the pilot was finally satisfied that they had safely achieved their unstick speed he eased back gently on the control column, and at the other end of the aircraft the elevators lifted a fraction in response. Just then, Len's stomach felt that familiar dropping sensation as they lifted off. Shortly afterwards there would have followed two loud clonks in succession as the undercarriage locked up into place, and they were on their way.

As they passed 1,000 ft they turned towards their objective, their route leading them 50 miles eastwards over the Yorkshire countryside to Bridlington, from where they would continue climbing out over the North Sea. In his turret, Len would have watched the last traces of his homeland disappear abruptly as they climbed into cloud. There may have been occasional gaps in the cloud affording teasing glimpses of the ridings of Yorkshire as they struggled on towards Flamborough Head and his last sight of England. After that, any hope of seeing anything familiar would have been replaced by a featureless new landscape beneath him comprising vast swathes of sea, accompanied by the realisation that next landfall would be over occupied territory. A call from the pilot would have come through the intercom inviting Len to test his guns, at which he would have fired a handful of the 2,500 0.303" rounds from each of his four Browning machine guns. This was not like training; this was for real, with real risks waiting for him from searchlights, flak and possibly even night fighters. On facing this prospect he may have allowed a shudder to pass through him momentarily, and then covered it by the realisation that it was becoming quite cold in the turret as they continued to climb through the night sky.

Len would have only witnessed their arrival over Texel once the aircraft was well over the Ijsselmeer and about to make landfall over mainland Holland. After that it would not have been long before the first of the night's flak shells would have been seen, heard and felt around the aircraft; fireflies in red and orange rising slowly from the ground and speeding up as they got closer, the men they were targeting hoping none would find their mark. The sight of them would have been hypnotic and almost beautiful were it not accompanied by the realisation of murderous intent from those who were firing from their flak batteries below. As the aircraft passed, Len would have just started to see the searchlights that they had crossed, brilliant spears of light in the dark summer sky. The sight would have been unreal but compelling for him, all the time fearing the moment when his world might come crashing down about him.

At around 0150 hrs, after about three and a half hours' flying time, the bomb bay doors opened, increasing the buffeting whilst the aircraft stayed on her dead straight course, irrespective of the pandemonium being wreaked all around. After what seemed like an eternity, he would have heard 'bombs gone' and felt the aircraft lift as she released her payload, followed by a sharp turn to port as Kenneth Whisken headed for home. From Len's vantage point at the rear of the aircraft, he would have looked through the haze and been rewarded by seeing bomb bursts 11,500 ft below, enabling him to report positively at the debriefing.

Now it was time to run the same gauntlet again: more flak, more searchlights, but this time from an enemy alerted to their presence. Every second would bring him closer to home and his ability to relax and breathe safely again – but how those seconds dragged by. Tonight, all the crews had been ordered to land away, probably due to bad weather over Topcliffe, and so when barely over the Yorkshire coast they descended towards RAF Driffield.

As they made their approach towards the flare path standing out against the darkness, crewmen in the cockpit may have glimpsed S/Ldr Dickenson from 77 Squadron landing just before them, whilst Len may have caught sight of P/O Norman Roscoe, who had joined immediately behind them. Len watched from his rearward-facing perspective as he saw the Chance light come into view, marking the threshold of the runway and the start of the parallel lines of the flare path as they settled down on the grass of the aerodrome, the main wheels touching down with gentle bumps. As the aircraft lost speed, Len's turret sank down slowly until finally the tailwheel touched the ground and he once more felt the bumps from the grass beneath. Then the aircraft taxied off to an appropriate spot to shut down, the men waiting for the engines to stop before recovering their belongings and exiting through the crew door.

As it turned out Whisken's was one of the first back; Sgt Wilson, who had led 102 Squadron into the air at the start of this operation, had landed 15 minutes earlier. Through a seething turmoil of emotions Len had completed his first operation and he was now back on British soil; he had fulfilled his role and defended the aircraft and its crew.

Whitley Z6494 (DY-M)

Bremen.

Takeoff 2220 hrs.

One stick released over primary target from 11,500 ft.

Landed 0500 hrs at RAF Driffield.

Operational combat time 6 hrs 40 mins.

P/O KD Whisken

Sgt SEH Morgan

Sgt AR Holmes

Sgt L Netherclift

Sgt L Starbuck   1st operation; combat time 6 hrs 40 mins

The remaining 102 and 77 Squadron aircraft followed them in at irregular intervals. Shortly, word would have spread that Sgt HG Benfield had crash-landed at RAF Docking in Norfolk over an hour earlier. This aircraft would have to undergo major repairs and would not fly with the squadron again, but fortunately there were no reported casualties. It turned out that the 2nd pilot, P/O Peter Gaskell, who had been at the squadron for less than a week, was on his second operation and had been at the controls during the landing. He had attempted the procedure on one engine, overshot and run through a hedge. The accident report concluded that he should have used both engines, suggesting that both had been available to the pilots at that time.

Half an hour later, at 0533 hrs, 102 Squadron's P/O MR Griffiths, overshot and crashed through the perimeter fence. The crew were all unhurt, and the subsequent accident report passed down the judgement that instead of continuing with the landing he should have gone around again. The aircraft was not badly damaged and would return to operations in two months.

At 0600 hrs the ambulance rushed to meet F/Lt George Davies' aircraft, Z6820. She was holed in many places and the elevator controls were damaged, but Davies had still managed to bring her back for a safe landing. When she came to a stop, the ambulance crew recovered the body of Sgt Neil Stockdale, a novice air gunner on his first operation. It turned out that the aircraft had been coned in searchlights and hit by heavy flak during their bombing run

Whitley Z6820 port side damage
(Chris Goss Collection)

Whitley Z6820 rear turret
(Chris Goss Collection)

at 10,500 ft, and subsequently attacked by a night fighter at 0217 hrs. Stockdale had been shot through the head and killed at the commencement of the attack, leaving the rear of the aircraft undefended as the night fighter had pressed home his attack on the aircraft's tail flight controls. This had caused Davies to lose control and enter a spin, the aircraft falling some 7,000 ft before he succeeded in regaining control, whereupon they had been attacked by another night fighter, which he had also been able to evade. The aircraft would be in repair for three months, the damaged rear turret bearing graphic witness to the tragic events that had made this Neil Stockdale's first and last operation.

Shortly after, word would have arrived that P/O BAQ Wynward-Wright, captaining the last of the 102 Squadron aircraft, had crashed at RAF Anthorn near Kirkbride in Cumbria, 100 miles north-west of their base. He had attempted a landing whilst very low on fuel and had overshot, hitting trees. The accident report blamed the captain for having left it too late to get a wireless fix and consequently being very low on fuel upon arrival over Cumbria.

Len's first operation had allowed him to share, as an equal, in the solidarity of those engaged in the fight against a common enemy and against their inner demons; to recognise the possibility of errors of judgement by even experienced crewmen upon whom others trusted. Tragedy and heroism in equal measure: a heady mix of emotions to relive over and over once finally alone.

The training he had been through had been intensive; he had been taught how to fulfil the roles of air gunner and WOp to such a level that other crewmen could rely upon him, and he had enjoyed lots of flying, all within a relatively safe atmosphere of light-hearted camaraderie and friendly rivalry. It had all been a bit of a lark. The one element that had been missing from his training, though, had been any mention of his odds of survival. The thought of fellow air gunner Neil Stockdale, shot through the head on his first operation, would have brought him up short; this was never a game. People died.

The bare fact was that a continuous attrition rate of only 2.3 per cent over 30 operations would see each one of them with less than a 50 per cent chance of survival. Whilst this had probably never crossed Len's mind before, it was certain to have been more widely known amongst the more experienced hands on the squadron. With dreadful clarity, he would have come to realise that the odds were not on his side.

The reality of the air war had lost little time in visiting Len. For better or for worse, he would now be on the squadron until he had completed 200 flying hours or 30 operations, whichever came first. Based on this sortie, which had lasted 6 hours 40 minutes, the two criteria would be met at around the same time.

One down for Len, 29 to go.

20 JULY 1941

Target[13]	Aircraft on target	Types
Cologne:		
(i) Aim point B East Kalk station	49	46 Wellington 3 Stirling
(ii) Aim point D Geron railway marshalling yards	64	39 Hampden 25 Whitley
CC42 Rotterdam	24	15 Wellington 9 Whitley
Nickelling: Paris – Chalon	9	Wellington

Primary target: Cologne (marshalling yards).
Alternative: S&M.
Last Resort: S&M.
Combined ops 20 aircraft:
    102 Sqn operation C.140: 12 aircraft (including 5 freshmen), operational call sign N7Q.
    77 Sqn operation C.153: 8 aircraft (including 3 freshmen), operational call sign D6B.
Bomb load:
    102 Sqn and remaining 77 Sqn: No.1 or No.3 fuzed 0.025 and 1× 250 lb MLD to be included in each bomb load.
    77 Sqn aircraft D, J, M, W and T: No.5 or No.6 fuzed 0.025 and 1× 250 lb MLD to be included in each bomb load.
Route: Base – Orford Ness – Gravelines – Liège – Cologne and return.
Time Off: 2220 hrs.
Weather: 10/10 cloud 7,000 ft over target area.
Opposition: Scattered heavy flak, numerous searchlights.

Today would see the first official unveiling of a distinctive new paint scheme for B Flight aircraft.

This local initiative had emerged from a meeting chaired on 9 July by the commanding officer, W/Cdr 'Curly' Howes, who had summoned his two new flight commanders to discuss the recent heavy losses.[14] The principal outcome from this meeting was that B Flight would trial an all-over black paint scheme, whilst A Flight, by far the larger of the two flights, would retain the established temperate land paint scheme camouflage pattern, with upper surfaces painted dark earth and dark green.

Possibly in a drive to introduce a spirit of competition on the squadron through inter-flight rivalry, and in a move probably without precedent, whilst all the aircraft retained the designated DY squadron code, B Flight would from today be operating its own independent

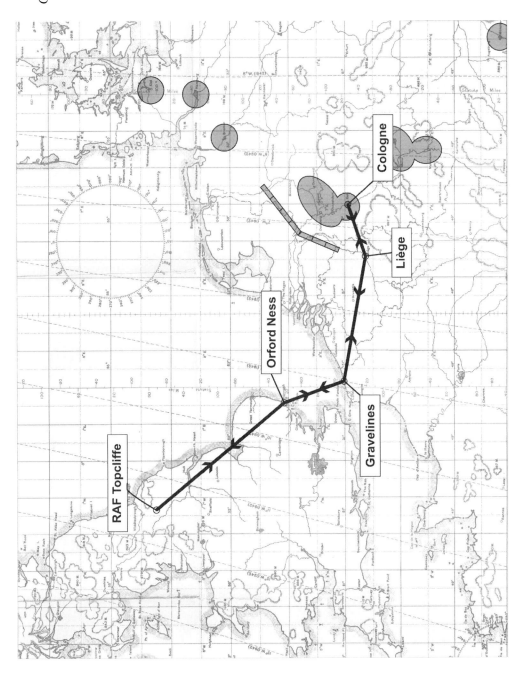

*Operation C.140
to Cologne,
20 July 1941*

sequence of callsigns, which was being allowed, possibly even encouraged, to overlap the historically established system still retained by A Flight. Hence from this night onwards there could be two aircraft on the same operation bearing the same callsign.

For this first operation under the new system, B Flight would be presenting four 'black bombers', identified as DY-Ā, DY-B̄, DY-C̄ and DY-Ē, laying claim to a sequence of letters at the beginning of the alphabet. To achieve this, existing squadron aircraft Z6574 and Z6798, which had last flown operationally on 14 July with callsigns DY-S and DY-T, had been called in to be repainted, emerging rechristened with their new callsigns, DY-B̄ and DY-Ē respectively. Those aircraft identified as DY-Ā and DY-C̄ were provided by painting up two newly delivered aircraft.

In a foretaste of what would follow in future operations, this evening saw two aircraft from the squadron both flying concurrently with the 'B for Beer' callsign:

- Sgt Gerald Powell, leading a crew from A Flight in Z6796, the existing DY-B,
- S/Ldr Joseph Reardon, leading a crew from B Flight in Z6574, the rechristened DY-B̄.

Instances of overlapping callsigns would occur on a routine basis from this date onwards as the squadron ran its two conflicting sequences of callsigns in parallel.

Having survived his first experience of combat, Len was placed back in B Flight, where he was introduced to a crew led by Sgt R Fisher in a newly delivered aircraft, Z6862. Sgt Fisher, who as 2nd pilot had been wounded in a night fighter attack on his last sortie only two weeks previously, was on his first operation as captain. His Whitley was to form part of a 20-aircraft contribution from both squadrons, which as before would be taking off in two lanes, and he would be taking up position almost at the tail end of the procession.

In accordance with the schedule, the first aircraft at the head of each lane were out at the allotted time and, as before, those following took off at intervals of just over a minute. When it finally came to the turn of Sgt Fisher to take off, at 2231 hrs, there was only one aircraft left behind him waiting to go. As Sgt Fisher began his take-off run, Len in the rear turret would have been able to focus on the solitude of the diminishing profile of the last remaining Whitley behind him, deepening his sense of isolation as the stark image brought home to him the true meaning of the expression 'tail end Charlie'.

Whitley Z6862 (DY-C̄)

Cologne.
Takeoff 2231 hrs.
One stick released over primary target from 11,500 ft.
Landed 0525 hrs.
Operational combat time 6 hrs 54 mins.
Sgt R Fisher
P/O EGN Anderson

Sgt TC Boyle

Sgt EA Hartle

Sgt L Starbuck   2nd operation; combat time 13 hrs 34 mins

Most crews found and attacked the primary target through the cloud, but there were exceptions. P/O DN Sampson was experiencing engine problems and losing height on his outward journey when he observed a flare path in the vicinity of Wevelgem, so dropped his bombs on it from an altitude of only 6,000 ft before turning for home. However, whilst Wevelgem-Bissegem was an operational aerodrome, there was also a decoy airfield 2½ miles WSW, identified as Wevelgem-Wezelhoek, and it is not known which P/O Sampson actually attacked.

A 77 Squadron freshman, Sgt Scott-Martin, got caught in searchlights and sighted lights at Keerbergen aerodrome, so aimed for it and dropped his bombs in two sticks, at least one of which was observed finding its mark. Sgt Scott-Martin's hand had been forced, but unfortunately Keerbergen was a decoy airfield.

Thick cloud over Cologne compromised targeting and the bombs had been widely dispersed; German reports[15] recorded only minor damage.

Sgt Fisher was the first of the aircraft back that had attacked the primary target, two others with unserviceabilities being back before him. As the morning wore on, a total of 15 aircraft would return to RAF Topcliffe, all five others landing away safely.

Endnotes

1   In 1919 Leicester Fosse was reformed as Leicester City Football Club.

2   Cooper, A.W. (2009) Air Gunner: The Men Who Manned the Turrets, ISBN 9781844158256, Pen and Sword, pp 26–27.

3   wallyswar.wordpress.com/gunnery-course.

4   Sweetman, J. (2005) Bomber Crew: Taking on the Reich, ISBN 0349117969, Abacus, p 29.

5   Wellingtons with the Type 423 modification were fitted with strengthened beams in the bomb bay, and the central bomb bay doors were removed to accommodate the new 4,000 lb HC bomb.

6   AMATOL is an explosive mixture of AMmonium nitrate And (trinitro)TOLuene; increasing the TNT content increases the explosive power, whilst increasing the ammonium nitrate reduces sensitivity.

7   Ministry of Information (1941) Bomber Command: The Air Ministry Account of Bomber Command's Offensive Against the Axis September 1939–July 1941, His Majesty's Stationery Office, p 114.

8   Green, W. (1960) Famous Bombers of the Second World War, MacDonald, p 27.

9   Obscure reference can still be found to a docker being a partially smoked cigarette.

10 AIR 28/851

11 Sometimes referred to as 'flimsies'.

12 AIR 14/2673

13 AIR 14/2673

14 Eric Verdon-Roe's personal diary.

15 Middlebrook, M. and Everitt, C. (1990) The Bomber Command War Diaries: An Operational Reference Book 1939–1945, ISBN 0140129367, Penguin, p 182.

2

GAINING EXPERIENCE

23 July 1941

Target[16]	Aircraft on target	Types
Mannheim aim point A industrial centre	51	Wellington
Frankfurt	33	Hampden
La Pallice, Vieljeux; Z381 Chantiers Navals Delmas shipyards (*Scharnhorst*)	30	Whitley
CC13 Ostend docks	5	Wellington
CC24 Le Havre docks	3	Wellington
Minelaying off the Frisian Islands (Nectarine)	1	Hampden
Nickelling: Paris – Rouen – Lille and aerodromes in occupied France	3	Wellington

Primary target: La Pallice (*Scharnhorst*), target code CC88.
Alternative: Any Invasion Port (AIP) except between Dieppe and Dunkirk.
Last Resort: AIP except between Dieppe and Dunkirk.
Combined ops 21 aircraft:
    102 Sqn operation C.141: 12 aircraft, operational call sign B9T.
    77 Sqn operation C.154: 9 aircraft (including 1 freshman), operational call sign HH8.
Bomb load:
    3× 500 lb GP TD 0.025 and 8× 250 lb GP TD 0.025, or 4× 500 lb GP TD 0.025 and 6× 250 lb TD 0.025.
Route: Base – Sywell – Bridport – St-Malo – La Pallice and return.
Time Off: 2145 hrs.
Weather: Clear over target very dark.
Opposition: Light flak slight, no heavy flak. Searchlights few.

Sister battleships *Scharnhorst* and *Gneisenau*, nicknamed 'Salmon and Gluckstein' after the contemporary London tobacconists, had been in the Atlantic since 23 January 1941, engaged on Unternehmen Berlin (Operation Berlin) with orders to sink allied merchantmen. They had enjoyed good hunting, capturing or sinking 21 ships totalling 107,582 tons from four different convoys that had departed Liverpool between 11 February and 5 March 1941. In addition to this they had reported the position of a Liverpool-bound convoy that had

Operation C.141 to La Pallice, 23 July 1941

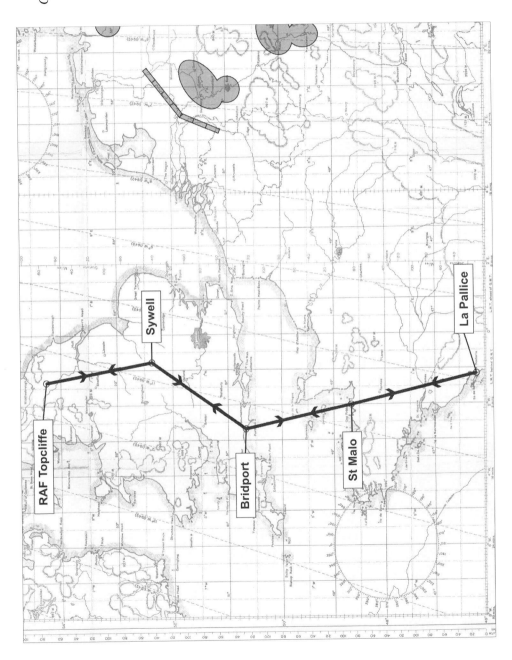

departed Freetown on 1 March 1941 to nearby U-boats, which sank five more ships, totalling a further 29,388 tons.

Scharnhorst and *Gneisenau* entered Brest on 22 March 1941, having avoided any direct confrontation, but *Scharnhorst* needed a permanent repair to her faulty superheaters. *Gneisenau* meanwhile had to go into dry dock for planned maintenance and minor refit to make her ready to accompany battleship *Bismarck* on Unternehmen Rheinübung (Operation Rhine Exercise) in the mid-Atlantic on a further anti-convoy patrol.

Recognising the vulnerability of these capital assets from the air, the defending forces disguised them as best they could with camouflage nets, and even rigged up an old French cruiser to look like *Scharnhorst*. They also disguised the dockyard buildings by creating a mock-up village across their roofs, the scene being completed with the deployment of fog generators.

Despite the excellent work performed in concealment, British Intelligence quickly identified the ships. Recognising they had been presented with something of a gift, having two of the most feared enemy battleships rendered at least temporarily immobile within reach of British aerodromes, Bomber Command was ordered to attack. They paid repeated visits to Brest to strike at these leviathans as they lay helpless, but the best result was to drop a bomb into the dock occupied by *Gneisenau* on the night of 4 April – which failed to explode.

On 6 April 1941, *Gneisenau* was refloated following her two-week spell in dry dock, and she was targeted swiftly by Coastal Command in an operation involving six Bristol Beauforts, three armed with mines to breach torpedo nets, to be followed by three more armed with torpedoes. In bad weather, F/O Kenneth Campbell from 22 Squadron was the only one to arrive, but still pressed home his attack 'with the utmost daring', dropping his torpedo 'at point-blank range' with such precision as to smash a propeller shaft, causing *Gneisenau* to return to dry dock. Campbell and his crew did not survive this attack, but he was awarded a posthumous Victoria Cross. *Gneisenau* would not now be joining *Bismarck* in the Atlantic, and would instead have to remain incarcerated uneasily within the range of Bomber Command for the foreseeable future.

On 1 June 1941 *Scharnhorst* and *Gneisenau* were joined by *Prinz Eugen,* which limped into Brest with serious defects in all three engines and a damaged propeller, following her return from supporting *Bismarck* during Unternehmen Rheinübung. This patrol had not gone as planned; they had run into a force of 10 Royal Navy ships led by battleship HMS *Prince of Wales* and battlecruiser HMS *Hood* in the Denmark Strait, resulting in the loss of HMS *Hood* and then *Bismarck* three days later. The concentration of all three capital ships in Brest presented an even more pressing target for Bomber Command, who were finally rewarded a month later on the night of 1/2 July when a bomb hit the bridge of *Prinz Eugen,* causing damage that would take a further six months to repair.

By 10 July 1941 Brest had been bombed 69 times, but Bomber Command and Coastal Command had inflicted only sufficient damage to delay the sailing of the three capital ships. Consequently, it was noon on 22 July that the inevitable news was relayed to London by a Coastal Command reconnaissance flight that *Scharnhorst* had gone; a tanker had been moored in her place and camouflage netting draped over the top. As this was unlikely to convince trained photographic interpreters for long, an oil slick had also been laid heading northwards away from the mooring.

At 0830 hrs the next morning, *Scharnhorst* was found at La Pallice, 240 miles south of Brest; she was now seaworthy and on the point of returning to her duties of harassing and sinking merchantmen in the Atlantic. Bomber Command lost no time in focusing its attentions in one last desperate attempt to sink this battleship before she broke out. Firstly, an evening attack with Stirlings was mounted immediately,

Gneisenau *in dry dock at Brest, 6 April 1941 (Catherine MICHEL-GUEVEL; Fichier* Gneisenau *drydock in Brest 060441.jpg / CC-BY-NC-ND)*

one reportedly scoring a hit with one bomb. This was to be followed by a night attack involving Whitleys in co-operation with aircraft from Coastal Command, and finally the next day would see a daytime attack with Halifaxes.

102 Squadron and 77 Squadron were called upon to support the second of these three operations, the night-time attack. This was scheduled to coincide with the onset of a new moon, meaning there would be no moonlight to assist navigation and targeting over this nine-hour operation. However, the urgency of attempting one last strike did not allow time to wait for better conditions; the job had to be done, and it had to be done immediately.

Sgt Fisher was called on to fly, and he fielded broadly the same crew as last time, including Len, but introducing a navigator on his second operation. This meant that Len was no longer the least experienced man on the crew. As they waited for their sortie to get under way, Len would have also reflected upon his forthcoming discomfort, as this sortie was scheduled to be two hours longer than the seven-hour stints he had served in the rear turret before; by the time they returned, he would have had more than enough of the intense cold in the rear turret.

This time all crews took off from a single lane, and to minimise delays the interval between aircraft was reduced to less than a minute. Sgt Fisher lined up eighth of 21 and got away without any problems. Sgt McLellen from 77 Squadron departed shortly after at 2157 hrs, but immediately experienced trouble with the Exactor airscrew pitch control[17] which prevented his selecting coarse pitch following take-off. This was one of the more regular failings on the squadron, second only to engine failures as the cause for aborted sorties. If the aircraft had to attempt cruise in fine pitch, the affected engine(s) would overspeed, and if operated in this condition for an extended period, would overheat, lose oil pressure, lose oil and eventually fail.

S/Ldr Eric Verdon-Roe described[18] suffering an Exactor failure during the outward leg of an earlier operation to Essen. Having chosen to continue, he recalled that the affected engine was run at 3,000–3,200 rpm with a temperature of 110°C and an oil pressure of 30 psi. To put this in context, the Merlin X engine in this application was designed to cruise at 2,200–2,600 rpm with an oil pressure of 60 psi and a maximum temperature of 100°C. In an emergency, it could be run for a maximum of 5 minutes not exceeding 3,000 rpm with an oil pressure of not below 45 psi, but in this case the overheated oil had thinned out catastrophically. Having given 'plenty of trouble on [the] way back, and cut completely over a convoy, but picked up again' the struggling engine had provided the crew with cause for mounting concern until they were able finally to land back at base. Subsequent examination revealed that the overstressed engine had burned and/or leaked 23 gallons of oil during the sortie, leaving only four gallons (less than 15 per cent) remaining.

Aware that this Exactor problem compromised his ability to complete the operation, Sgt McLellen flew a holding pattern away from the other aircraft as they took off, and after the last had departed at 2203 hrs, turned to land at 2208 hrs. He set off again at 2222 hrs and returned shortly thereafter at 2229 hrs with the same problem. Once more he set off at 2246 hrs and returned at 2248 hrs. This time his sortie was abandoned.

Tonight's operation marked a distinct change in what Len had seen previously, in that the target area was very dark and there was little opposition; a challenge for the novice navigator, but a respite from the attentions of flak and searchlights that accompanied their usual strategic land-based targets. Nonetheless, by the end of it he had still been in his turret for nine hours and would have been very glad to get home.

Whitley Z6862 (DY- C̄)

La Pallice.
Takeoff 2153 hrs.
One stick released over primary target from 8,000 ft.
Landed 0702 hrs.
Operational combat time 9 hrs 9 mins.
Sgt R Fisher
P/O EGN Anderson
Sgt WV Atkinson
Sgt EA Hartle
Sgt L Starbuck   3rd operation; combat time 22 hrs 43 mins

Sgt Fisher was one of the last to get down, landing 7 minutes after P/O David Delaney, who had lost control and crash-landed on his approach, accompanied by the undercarriage collapsing. His aircraft would be undergoing repairs for months and it would never again fly with the squadron. The subsequent accident report blamed the captain for having allowed the aircraft to get into a tail-down attitude. All 102 Squadron crews were back safely, but with a little touch of drama to round off the night's activities.

77 Squadron too had experienced some drama, as F/Lt Frederick Drury suffered a port engine failure and, after circling the beacon at RAF Upavon in Wiltshire, attempted a forced landing near Upper Upham, but he misjudged the sloping ground, resulting in injuries to all four crewmen.

Daylight brought with it the last chance for Bomber Command to stop *Scharnhorst*, and a series of coordinated attacks would be made against her and the two other capital ships. Firstly, *Gneisenau* and *Prinz Eugen* were targeted in Brest by a force of 100 bombers comprising Wellingtons, Hampdens and three new B-17C Fortresses, accompanied by three squadrons of Spitfires at their maximum range, whilst a diversionary raid of Blenheims and Spitfires attacked Cherbourg. Secondly, 15 Halifaxes went after *Scharnhorst* at La Pallice, but five would be lost as the target was beyond the range of fighter escorts.

During the intensive bombing operations from 23 to 24 July, *Scharnhorst* took five direct hits: two from 500 lb HE bombs and three from 1,000 lb SAP bombs in a line to starboard of her centreline. Whilst both 500 lb bombs detonated, all three 1,000 lb bombs passed through the ship without exploding, but they did cause damage to the ship's systems, and started flooding. Although the fatal blow so desperately sought had not been delivered, *Scharnhorst* developed an 8-degree list to starboard, taking on around 3,000 tons of water; she was saved only by controlled flooding on the port side, doubling the amount of water she was shipping and making her ride very low in the water. This rendered her unable to proceed with her scheduled return to operations, and she was forced to limp back to Brest for further repairs. The bombers had at least bought some time.

25 JULY 1941

Target[19]	Aircraft on target	Types
Hanover aim point A	55	30 Hampden 25 Whitley
Hamburg aim point B railway centre	43	Wellington
Berlin aim point B	9	7 Stirling 2 Halifax
Emden	2	Wellington

Primary target: Hanover (main post office and telegraph office).
Alternative: S&M.
Last Resort: S&M.
Combined ops 19 aircraft:
    102 Sqn operation C.142: 12 aircraft (including 1 freshman), operational call sign 7FV.
    77 Sqn operation C.155: 7 aircraft, operational call sign Y9P.
Bomb load: No.1 or No.3 TD 0.025. 1× 250 lb GP MLD to be included.
Route: Base – Bridlington – Vlieland – Hanover and return.
Time Off: 2220 hrs.
Weather: No cloud, ground haze.
Opposition: Moderate heavy flak, small amount of light flak, considerable searchlight activity.

This operation marked a breakthrough for the WOps, who up to now had been able to acquire fixes over enemy territory by securing direction finding (DF) loop bearings against a small number of transmitters such as radio beacons, communications or navigation devices that operated at known frequencies from known positions. For this operation, the signals officer briefed that they had been researching German high-speed Morse stations and gave the WOps a selection of three. One of these was known as DAN and, being based in Berlin, was ideal for the operation to Hanover; but the main problem was that this station did not send its call sign that often. When it did, it was sent quickly, at some 35 wpm, which meant that the WOp needed to be quick to get his DF loop fix; such was the gamble.

Len was becoming established as Sgt Fisher's air gunner, and for his fourth operation remained in the crew, as they were chosen to be one of 19 aircraft to attack Hanover. The crew would also be dropping dockers over Holland.

They lined up 15th with 77 Squadron leading, and at 2220 hrs the first of the aircraft got away exactly on time. Staying with taking off in a single lane, the crews once again managed to get airborne at less than 1-minute intervals. Sgt Fisher took his turn a full quarter-hour after the first aircraft had left, departing at 2235 hrs.

In his first two operations, Len had been insulated by cloud from the defenders on the ground, and for their attack on *Scharnhorst* the night had been pitch-black. But tonight there was a clear sky, and searchlights were plentiful. Any one of the high-powered beams sweeping soundlessly across the cloudless sky had the potential to point in their direction and cue retribution from flak – or worse, night fighters.

Whitley Z6862 (DY-C̄)

Hanover.

Takeoff 2235 hrs.

One stick released over primary target from 11,000 ft.

Landed 0609 hrs.

Operational combat time 7 hrs 34 mins.

Sgt R Fisher

P/O EGN Anderson

Sgt WV Atkinson

F/Sgt R Adams

Sgt L Starbuck   4th operation; combat time 30 hrs 17 mins

The Berlin-based DAN station had been obliging enough to send a series of identifiable transmissions, and those who had chosen to use it had done very well.

Sgt Fisher and his crew completed their sortie successfully and arrived home in the midst of the other returning crews. As time passed it started to become clear that although all 77 Squadron crews had returned, 102 Squadron had lost not one but two aircraft and crews. The first of these was Z6866, led by Sgt Benfield, which was hit by flak and crashed at Maurik, Culemborg, at 0235 hrs. The second was Z6576, captained by S/Ldr Eric Verdon-Roe, which had been shot down, possibly by Egmont Prinz zur Lippe-Weißenfeld of 4./NJG1, 10 km west of De Kooy aerodrome, Den Helder, at 0323 hrs. More than half of the crewmen missing were drawn from men who, like Len, had started during that month, and one had been on his first operation.

Operation
C.142 to
Hanover,
25 July 1941

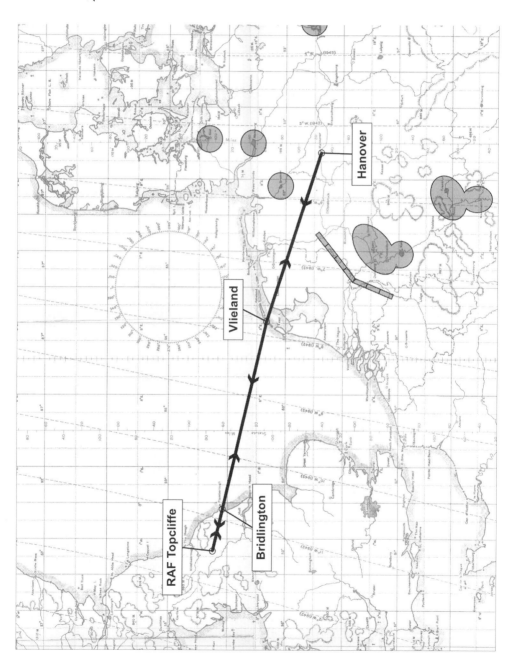

RAF Topcliffe

Bridlington

Vlieland

Hanover

On Eric Verdon-Roe's crew were WOp/AG Leslie Netherclift and navigator Anthony Holmes, with whom Len had flown on his first operation as he was eased gently into his role as aircrew, and to whom he would consequently have felt an unfulfilled debt of gratitude. Further, B Flight would be casting around for another new flight commander, Eric Verdon-Roe not having lasted three weeks.

At this point the reality of Len's task was laid bare before him; his first taste of losing people he knew had stripped away the immortality felt by all young men, and he must have now realised that he was in a race to beat the odds and survive to the end of his tour.

30 July 1941

Target[20]	Aircraft on target	Types
Cologne:		
(i) Aim point A industrial area	24	17 Wellington 7 Halifax
(ii) Aim point B East Kalk railway station	16	Wellington
(iii) Aim point C Köln West main railway station	34	29 Wellington 5 Stirling
(iv) Aim point D Geron railway marshalling yards	42	Hampden
CC29A Boulogne warehouses	12	Whitley

Nursery Operation

Primary target: Boulogne (docks and shipping).
Alternative: Dunkirk (docks and shipping).
Last Resort AIP.
Combined ops 4 aircraft (freshmen):
    102 Sqn: 3 aircraft, operational call sign X6F.
    77 Sqn operation C.156: 1 aircraft, operational call sign 9UZ.
Bomb load: No.1 or No.3 TD 0.025. 1× 250 lb GP MLD to be included.
Route: Base – Orford Ness – Boulogne and return.
Time Off: 0015 hrs.

Four novice pilots had just earned the right to fly as captain, faced for the first time with not just flying the aeroplane but also being personally responsible for taking command decisions based upon constant updates from the other crew members in a volatile and unpredictable situation that could lead easily to personal overload.

Formerly, novice captains would have graduated by being pitched without ceremony into flying deep strike operations alongside their battle-hardened colleagues, a true baptism of fire. But it had been decided that this was not always the best way of introducing the freshman captains to the difficulties of command, and that it might be better to ease them in a little more gently. Although any such exercise would have to be a genuine strategic operation in

Bf 110 from 5./NJG1 (Chris Goss Collection)

order to test their new captaincy skills, the targets chosen would all be close to home, to minimise risk. The obvious choices for these 'nursery' targets were docks and ports along the northern coastline of occupied France, and tonight the target for these particular four novices would be Boulogne.

The four crews were led out by P/O 'Hank' Iveson, the lone 77 Squadron freshman. On his take-off run he experienced boost problems and reached an altitude of only 100 ft before crashing in an adjacent field at 0025 hrs. The aircraft caught fire, but fortunately all crewmen escaped before the bombs exploded. Given the flaming spectacle facing the remaining three 102 Squadron crews, the operation was cancelled; all four pilots would have to wait for another opportunity to prove their readiness to command.

31 JULY 1941

Amongst the new starters on the squadron was a 6' 2" Canadian navigator with brown hair and brown eyes who had enrolled through the RCAF; Richard Forrest Bradbury, who had joined the squadron's B Flight from 10 OTU. He had been the beneficiary of a most unusual transatlantic lineage.

Richard was the son of Vernie and Horace Bradbury, who lived in Prince Rupert City, British Columbia. Vernie and her sister Hazel were of Native American extraction, and had been brought up as orphans on the Puyallup Reservation in Washington State at a time when the once numerous tribes were being concentrated down, pushed into a handful of reservations. Over the previous 50 years these tribal peoples had been progressively stripped of their lands by white settlers, and actively encouraged – or forced – to forsake their heritage.

By the time she was 8, Vernie and her older sister Hazel had been transported from the reservation to the United States Indian Training School at Chemawa, near Salem in Oregon, 160 miles to the south. Indian Training Schools had been founded on the stated objective to 'civilise' the Native Americans in line with Richard Pratt's philosophy to 'kill the Indian in him and save the man'. Whilst at this boarding school, the boys and girls were directed to conform to the culture of the white settlers, in a process that began immediately.

Lone Wolf of the Blackfeet recalls his experience upon arriving at one of these schools:[21]

> Once there our belongings were taken from us, even the little medicine bags our mothers had given to protect us from harm. Everything [including their clothes] was placed in a heap and set afire. Next was the long hair, the pride of all the Indians. The boys, one by one, would break down and cry when they saw their braids thrown on the floor.

Following this humiliation, the children were issued with Euro-American style clothing; the girls had to wear the long dresses of the period, whilst the boys were issued with military-style uniforms. Further, attendance at chapel was mandatory, as all students were encouraged to convert to Christianity. To enforce the break with their heritage during this assimilation, traditional tribal names were outlawed, traditional dancing, singing and drumming were banned. Further, under no circumstances were they allowed to speak in their native tongues, even amongst each other, a rule typically enforced harshly by use of the strap or more public spectacles of humiliation to deter others.

Here they received a rudimentary education and learned laundry, tailoring, sewing and pastry cooking, whilst boys studied blacksmithing, wagon making and shoemaking. Conditions were harsh, and allegations have emerged subsequently of abuse – broken bones not uncommon, rape[22] and even deaths:[23] 'At Chemawa, a cemetery contains headstones of 189 students who died at the school, and these represent only the ones whose bodies were not returned home for burial.'

Having survived Chemawa, the girls both returned northwards; Hazel took a job in a clothing factory in Seattle, whilst Vernie, now 17 years old, continued up into Canada in 1909. Her journey would see her trekking up the entire length of Canada's Pacific coastline before finally coming to settle on a reservation in Comox-Atlin, near Prince Rupert City. Her new home was only 30 miles from the Alaskan border, but 800 miles away from the start of her journey in Salem.

In 1917, Vernie married Horace Bradbury, a coalminer's son from Staffordshire who, along with three of his brothers, had set sail from Liverpool in 1908 to seek a new life in America, crossing the continent to establish an address in Prince Rupert City. In 1919 the couple had a daughter, Gertrude, who was followed on 1 August 1920 by a son whom they named Richard Forrest.

In February 1921, Vernie left her husband behind and travelled north by sea to Ketchikan to visit her sister Hazel, who had married one John Ahlers, a plumber from Illinois ten years her senior. He had been part of the migration northwards to the remote satellite port of Valdez in Alaska, which had been advertised to gold prospectors as a convenient staging post for the Klondike, a remote area that had seen the Gold Rush during 1896–99. He now worked for CW Young and Co,[24] a hardware and building materials store in Juneau, Alaska, where he and Hazel lived with their daughter, Juanita.

Vernie is listed as having taken her daughter Gertrude, who was one year old at the time, with her, but not Richard. This does not mean that he did not travel with her, but possibly because being less than a year old he was not entered on the ship's passenger list. By the time of the census in June, Vernie was back in Prince Rupert City with Richard and her nine-year-old niece Juanita, but there is no further mention of Gertrude.

Hazel's daughter Juanita died in her teens and was buried in Juneau on 31 December 1925, and in July 1926 Vernie made the journey northwards again to see her sister, taking Richard. The ship's passenger list records that Vernie was 5' 6" tall with dark hair, dark complexion and blue eyes, whilst Richard, who was now almost 6 years old, had a fair complexion, brown hair and blue eyes.

Although it must have been a sad visit, to console her sister over her recent loss, Vernie could not have failed to notice that Hazel's husband John had become a big success in the community, having left Marshall & Newman Co and formed a partnership with Oregon pioneer George Rice and his wife, Julia, to open the plumbing store Rice and Ahlers Inc. Their new business was busy catering for the demand of townspeople to fit oil furnaces into their homes, and was clearly a popular concern. Hazel's opportunity to enjoy this emerging success must have been short-lived, however, as on 14 April 1928 her husband John was remarried to another woman, Edna Baker, suggesting that Hazel had either died or become estranged.

In 1930, Horace and Vernie had another son, Jack Donald Bradbury, and on 18 September 1939, with the family now living in Victoria, almost on the border with America near Seattle, Richard signed up into the 5th (British Columbia) Field Artillery Regiment, Royal Canadian Artillery (RCA) Canadian Active Service Force (CASF). On 26 September 1939 he was given the rank of gunner and posted to the 56th Heavy Battery in Victoria. During his time with the militia he became a qualified gun layer and a chauffeur, earning promotion to lance bombardier on 3 December 1939.

No small degree of tragedy had been visited upon the Cliffe girls, and although Vernie would have been accepting of her eldest son playing his part in the local militia, it was quite another thing to open herself up to the uncertainty of giving approval to his joining up to fight a war half a world away. However, in March 1940 Richard applied to join RCAF, and then again on 3 May 1940 whilst the first application was still pending. He listed his sports as badminton, tennis, rugby, golf and swimming, adding that he had also passed the lifeguard test. His hobbies are listed as artistic, with his prime interest being the piano. Interestingly, given his ancestral links with Native Americans, he listed his religion as Christian Scientist. The statement from the officer commanding the recruiting centre reads:

This lad has been using political influence to effect his discharge and secure his enlistment in the RCAF. Has intelligence some military experience, is a reasonably good shot, and for his years had a lot of outdoor life travelling with his father. Is willing to serve in any position on air crew. Better suited as an air gunner than anything else.

So it was on 18 June 1940 that Richard enlisted as an air gunner at the rank of AC2, and was posted to No.1 Manning Depot (MD) Toronto, Ontario. On 30 June 1940 he received a posting to No.2 Initial Training School (ITS) at RCAF Regina, Saskatchewan, where he joined course No.4. After a month of training, he passed this course at 80.5 per cent, earning the comment that he was 'considered suitable as an alternative pilot'. It was clear that he was shaping up to be a proficient air gunner, but that he also had more to offer, and so was to be given a chance as a navigator / air observer as well.

From here he was posted to No.2 Air Observer's School (AOS) at RCAF Edmonton, Alberta, where he joined course No.6. During this three-month course, Richard flew 27 hours 50 minutes in an Avro Anson, of which 5 hours 45 minutes were at night, and 16 hours 05 minutes in a Lockheed,[25] of which 1 hour 45 minutes were at night. His proficiency as an observer was marked at 71 per cent; his ground training 78.8 per cent, and his qualities as an officer 84.7 per cent. Overall, he scored 77.7 per cent and was assessed as an average navigator, but an above average air observer.

Next, he got his posting to No.2 B&GS at RCAF Mossbank, Saskatchewan, on 24 November 1940, where he joined course No.2. During this five-week posting Richard learned bomb aiming and air gunnery from a Fairey Battle. He accrued 12 hours and 20 minutes of air time: 6 hours 30 minutes by day, 1 hour 35 minutes by night and the remainder as a passenger. In terms of bomb aiming, he achieved an average error across all exercises of 273 yards, with the average error of his best exercise being 143 yards. As an air gunner he managed to score (i) Beam test 10 per cent, (ii) Beam relative speed test 7 per cent, (iii) Under tail test 13 per cent. These scores gave him 62.3 per cent as a bomb aimer and 67 per cent as an air gunner, earning him a pass and the comment that he was an 'industrious average type'.

On 4 January 1941, he was awarded his air observer's badge and promotion to sergeant. In addition he was posted to No.1 Air Navigation School (ANS) at RCAF Rivers, Manitoba, where he joined Advanced Air Observers Training Course No.6. During this one-month course Richard accrued more flying hours in an Anson, giving him a total of 58 hours 20 minutes by day, 27 hours 25 minutes by night and 12 hours 20 minutes B&GS. In air navigation he was awarded 86 per cent, and in ground training he was awarded 77.6 per cent; overall, he scored 81.8 per cent and was assessed an excellent air navigator, graduating third in his class of 48. His final assessment took into account his marks from No.2 AOS, No.2 B&GS as well as No.1 ANS, and totalling 75.7 per cent, earning him a pass.

Richard took leave from 3 February to 11 March 1941, after which he was posted to the Embarkation Pool RCAF Debert, Nova Scotia. Following a brief stay in the military hospital he embarked on a troopship on 5 April 1941 and arrived in England two weeks later, reporting to No.3 Personnel Reception Centre (PRC) RAF Uxbridge in Middlesex. After a week, he was posted to 10 OTU on 26 April 1941, the same date as Len. (Len's course would finish first, though, and he would arrive on 102 Squadron three weeks before Richard joined, on 31 July 1941.) Upon arrival at RAF Uxbridge, Richard was taken on a check flight by B Flight's commander who signed him off as being a 'very good Air Observer'.

3 AUGUST 1941

Target[26]	Aircraft on target	Types
GH577 Frankfurt main railway centre	39	Whitley
Hanover aim point A railway centre	39	Wellington
CC37 Calais docks	7	Whitley

MAIN OPERATION

Primary target: Frankfurt (marshalling yards), target code GH577.
Alternative: S&M.
Last Resort: S&M.
Combined ops 20 aircraft:
    102 Sqn operation C.143: 10 aircraft, operational call sign 6OX.
    77 Sqn operation C.157: 10 aircraft, operational call sign XZ6.
Bomb load: No.1 or No.3 TD 0.025. 1× 250 lb GP MLD to be included.
Route: Base – Orford Ness – Gravelines – Frankfurt and return.
Time Off: 2200 hrs.
Weather: 10/10 cloud over Channel, haze and broken cloud to Koblenz. Very thick haze and cloud appearing to be 10/10
    with tops 7,000 ft over Frankfurt.
Opposition: Moderate accurate heavy flak. Searchlights fairly numerous ineffective through haze and cloud.

NURSERY OPERATION

Primary target: Calais (docks and shipping), target code CC37.
Alternative: AIP.
Last Resort AIP.
Combined ops 4 aircraft (freshmen):
    102 Sqn operation C.144: 3 aircraft, operational call sign 6OX.
    77 Sqn operation C157: 1 aircraft, operational call sign XZ6.
Bomb load: No.1 or No.3 TD 0.025. 1× 250 lb GP MLD to be included.
Route: Base – Orford Ness – Calais and return.
Time Off: 2230 hrs.
Weather: Clear over target.
Opposition: Heavy flak moderately intense and very accurate. Numerous searchlights.

Len started August with another operation under the command of Sgt Fisher. By now, Len had shown his calibre as an air gunner and was allowed to start demonstrating his worth on the wireless. To develop these skills in a combat situation, he was flying as 2nd WOp, creating a six-man crew. This time they formed part of a 20-aircraft combined detail to attack Frankfurt, and were also called upon to drop dockers over Maastricht, a task that would fall to Len for the first time.

Once the 20 aircraft on the main operation had gone, the freshmen from the spectacularly abortive nursery run of 30 July 1941 would be entitled to a second chance. However, this time the unfortunate P/O Hank Iveson would be the last to leave – just in case his jinx prevailed.

In a stirring and evocative sight, all 24 aircraft scheduled to go on operations lined up together, the 20 Frankfurt crews getting away exactly as scheduled at 2200 hrs in just under 1-minute intervals. Sgt Fisher lined up 17th and took off at 2215 hrs. The freshman crews waiting behind the aircraft on the main operation were held for a few minutes longer to ensure that the last of the Frankfurt crews was clear before being given their green light to go. The first departed a little before time, at 2226 hrs, and the others followed at double the interval of their Frankfurt-bound colleagues. All got away without incident, but unlucky Hank Iveson suffered a wireless failure and turned for home at 2312 hrs, returning at 0013 hrs.

Now Len had been promoted to the relative space and warmth of the cockpit, he was a dual-skilled WOp/AG flying as 2nd WOp, so in the event of night fighter attack he would be responsible for scrambling into the front turret to help defend the aircraft, whilst the more experienced WOp would remain at the wireless. Although the front turret looked impressive and enhanced crew morale, it was heavy and was regarded as serving little useful purpose other than shooting at enemy searchlights if the aircraft was low enough; head-on attacks by the enemy at night were considered unlikely, so it had earned the nickname of the 'scare gun'.

Whitley Z6862 (DY- C̄)

Frankfurt.

Takeoff 2215 hrs.

One stick released possibly over primary target from 11,000 ft.

Landed 0610 hrs.

Operational combat time 7 hrs 55 mins.

Sgt R Fisher

P/O EGN Anderson

Sgt WV Atkinson

Sgt EA Hartle

Sgt L Starbuck   5th operation; combat time 38 hrs 12 mins

Sgt M Humphrey

They were the first 102 Squadron crew to get back from Frankfurt, although three 77 Squadron aircraft had returned before them. After an hour, nine of the 102 Squadron Frankfurt crews had returned, and eventually word got through that the tenth, P/O MR Griffiths, had landed at Crail Aerodrome in Fifeshire with flak damage to his aircraft. One crew from 77 Squadron also landed away, P/O Jack Belton diverting to RAF Scampton in Lincolnshire. All crews from both sister squadrons had returned safely, even if two of the Frankfurt crews had landed away.

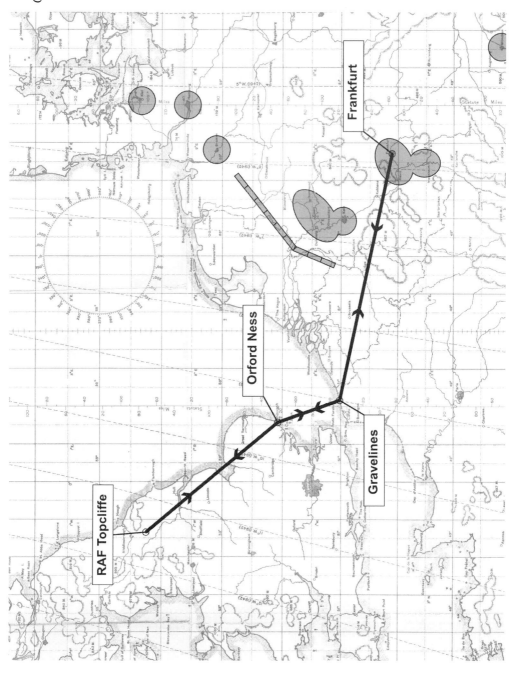

*Operation C.143
to Frankfurt,
3 August 1941*

Frankfurt

Orford Ness

RAF Topcliffe

Gravelines

5 August 1941

Target[27]	Aircraft on target	Types
Mannheim:		
(i) Aim point A (industrial targets)	36	Wellington
(ii) Aim point C (railway targets)	34	33 Hampden 1 Wellington
(iii) Aim point D (railway targets)	28	Wellington
GH378 Karlsruhe railway works	97	50 Hampden 18 Wellington 11 Halifax 8 Stirling
GH378 Karlsruhe 2,000 yards 295° post office	10	Wellington
Frankfurt:		
Aim point A (industrial targets)	48	46 Whitley 2 Wellington
Aim point B (railway targets)	20	Wellington
GH627 Aachen west railway marshalling yards	13	Wellington
CC29A Boulogne	8	Wellington
Minelaying:		
(i) Langeland Belt (Quince)	1	Hampden
(ii) Kiel (Forget-me-nots)	1	Hampden
(iii) Eckernförde (Melon)	1	Hampden
(iv) South entrance to Little Belt (Endives)	1	Hampden
(v) South entrance to Little Belt and Flensburg Fjord (Wallflower)	1	Hampden

Main Operation

Primary target: Frankfurt (Post Office), target code Sole A.
Alternative: S&M.
Last Resort: S&M.
Combined ops 23 aircraft:
    102 Sqn operation C.145: 12 aircraft, operational call sign TJ6.
    77 Sqn operation C.158: 11 aircraft, operational call sign S8W.
Bomb load: No.5 or No.6 TD 0.025. 1× 250 lb GP MLD to be included.
Route: Base – Orford Ness – Gravelines – Frankfurt and return.
Time Off: 2150 hrs.
Weather: Clear over target until latter part of attack.
Opposition: Heavy flak moderately intense and very accurate. Numerous cones of searchlights co-operating with flak.

NURSERY OPERATION

Primary target: Boulogne, target code CC29A (docks and shipping).
Alternative: Dieppe, target code CC31 (docks and shipping).
77 Squadron: 1 aircraft (freshman), operational call sign S8W (cancelled).
Bomb load: No.1 or No.3 TD 0.025. 1× 250 lb GP MLD to be included.
Route: Base – Orford Ness – target and return.
Time Off: 0030 hrs.

For this return visit to Frankfurt, Len remained with Sgt Fisher and continued his training as 2nd WOp. As with their last trip to Frankfurt two nights earlier, he would once more be tasked with dropping dockers over Maastricht.

The start of the operation was routine; the nearly full moon had risen just over an hour previously[28] as they took their position at 11th in the line of 23 Whitleys. The first aircraft took off exactly on time at 2150 hrs, and 10 minutes later Sgt Fisher took off in his turn.

Everything was normal until they approached Maastricht at 0050 hrs, at which point attention in the aircraft turned to dropping their dockers, when they were intercepted by a Bf 110 night fighter at 8,000 ft. Len, as 2nd WOp, would have had the responsibility for dropping the dockers, and at the precise moment when the attack began was probably engaged on this duty, away from both his post at the wireless and the front turret. Rushing forward quickly to assume his secondary duty in the nose turret, he and Canadian Sgt Morley Humphrey, the rear air gunner, would have worked closely with Sgt Fisher to evade the night fighter, but dependable Z6862 was 'badly damaged'. This was Len's first direct experience of German night fighters, and it would have brought home to him with sudden and frightening clarity the awful reality of the struggle between bomber and night fighter. With concerns about being able to continue to his primary target, Sgt Fisher abandoned the idea of proceeding to Frankfurt and made instead for the nearer city of Cologne, which he attacked from the unusually low altitude of 6,000 ft before turning for home.

Whitley Z6862 (DY- C̄)

Frankfurt.

Takeoff 2200 hrs.

One stick released over Cologne from 6,000 ft.

Landed 0530 hrs.

Operational combat time 7 hrs 30 mins.

Sgt R Fisher

Sgt NG Williams

Sgt WB Atkinson

Sgt EA Hartle

Sgt L Starbuck   6th operation; combat time 45 hrs 42 mins

Sgt M Humphrey

At 0530 hrs Sgt Fisher landed back at base, the shorter journey time from Cologne bringing him in before the other Frankfurt crews. Only one was down before them, an early returner with an engine problem.

At 0548 hrs, the first of those that had completed their attack on the primary target started to come back. One of the last back was Sgt Wilson, who had inadvertently dropped his bombs safe over the target, because in all the excitement of evasive manoeuvres during the bombing run his navigator had forgotten to fuze them. At 0844 hrs, the last of 102 Squadron's aircraft was down safely, one of their number having landed away 60 miles short, at RAF Hibaldstow in Lincolnshire.

77 Squadron had two of its number land away, but the last of its aircraft, captained by P/O Douglas Baber, had not returned. Having encountered bad weather en route, Baber elected to attack the alternative target of Koblenz rather than proceed to Frankfurt, a further 50 miles. On the return journey, his aircraft was hit by flak over Meulebeke, 6 km SSW of Tielt, at 0200 hrs. The port engine having been hit, the captain considered that the damage was sufficient to order the crew to bale out – after which the aircraft went on to make a perfect wheels-up landing in a meadow near Zegelsem in Belgium.[29]

The 2nd pilot, Sgt Albert Day, an American flying for the RCAF, landed near Lochristi, 5 miles north-east of Ghent. He walked through the town still wearing his flying clothing, but amazingly was not challenged, because he was believed to be a Luftwaffe crewman. When he approached the village of Leffinge on the outskirts of Ostend he made to cross the Plassendale-Nieuwpoort canal, unaware until too late that there was a German checkpoint on the bridge. Although he had no papers, he was the only one not stopped at the checkpoint, and passed through unchallenged.

On 15 August 1941 he arrived in Ostend but could not get a passage to Britain, so returned inland where he met up with a member of the Belgian Resistance, who took him by bicycle and train to Brussels, where he caught pneumonia and was put up at a series of safe houses. Four months later he was sent on an escape route through France and over the Pyrenees to Spain, from where he travelled to Britain via Gibraltar.

Meanwhile, Air Gunner Sgt Delaney went into hiding and was captured two weeks later, on 18 August 1941, when he crossed a road in Hundelgem.

Douglas Baber baled out between Meilegem and Beerlegem, landing in a tree and subsequently spraining his ankle whilst freeing himself. He improvised a walking stick and limped into Meilegem where he met the mayor, who directed him northwards to the Scheldt where he could find a boat that would give him a passage to Britain.

On the ferry across the Scheldt he introduced himself to the ferryman, François Rigaux,[30] whose family took him in and gave him a change of clothes. Rigaux's son, who lived in Brussels, had a neighbour who said he had a friend who could help British aircrew escape. Douglas Baber was then reunited with his navigator, P/O Ivan Kayes – and both were captured because this 'friend' turned out to be a collaborator. Whilst in captivity, Douglas Baber began to write of his experiences, and subsequently published them in a semi-autobiographical book, *Where Eagles Gather*.[31]

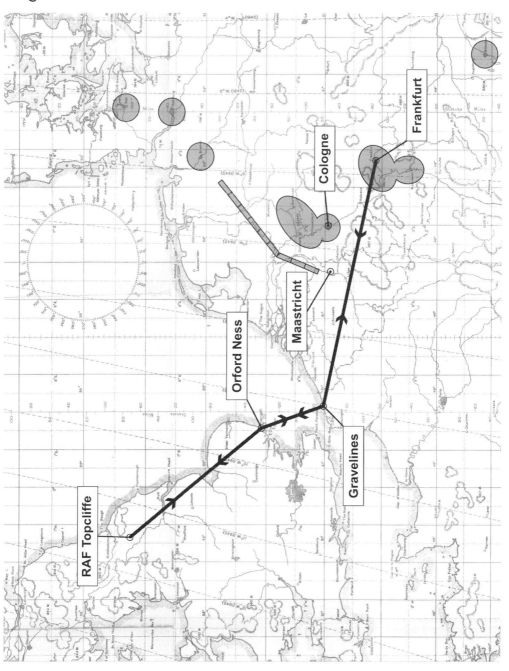

Operation C.145
to Frankfurt,
5 August 1941

RAF Topcliffe

Orford Ness

Gravelines

Maastricht

Cologne

Frankfurt

Sgt William Thuell, the WOp/AG, baled out over Zingem, and was taken in by the Moerman family, who sent him on to Sylvain Van De Velde in Sint-Maria-Latem. William Thuell was captured on 27 August, and his host, Van De Velde, was also arrested.[32]

Unlucky crewmen Navigator Ivan Kayes and WOp/AG William Thuell had been crewed together one week previously on a sortie to Bremen when their aircraft had been hit by flak and ditched 100 miles off Flamborough Head, after which they had spent two and a half uncomfortable days adrift at sea. They recovered from this ordeal only to end up in captivity on this Cologne run.

6 AUGUST 1941

Target[33]	Aircraft on target	Types
Frankfurt:		
(i) Aim point B	34	Whitley
(ii) GH577 Railway yards	19	Wellington
GH378 Karlsruhe railway workshops	38	Hampden
Mannheim aim point D railway workshops	38	Wellington
CC37 Calais	38	21 Hampden 11 Wellington 6 Whitley
Nickelling: Paris – Limoges and enemy aerodromes	2	Wellington

This was the squadron's third trip to Frankfurt in four nights, but the day started badly when P/O Alexander Ogston from 77 Squadron went on a cross country during the afternoon. During this training exercise an engine caught fire resulting in main spar failure, and the aircraft crashed at 1430 hrs near Alveston, Warwickshire, killing the five-man crew. No other 77 Squadron aircraft would take part in the night's operation.

Primary target: Frankfurt (railway station), target code Sole B.
Alternative: S&M.
Last Resort: S&M.
102 Sqn operation C.146: 5 aircraft, operational call sign K8R.
Bomb load: No.1 or No.3 TD 0.025. 1× 250 lb GP MLD to be included.
Route: Base – Orford Ness – Nieuport – Valenciennes – Frankfurt and return.
Time Off: 2200 hrs.
Weather: 10/10 cloud at 8,000 ft. Slight icing conditions and some electrical storms.
Opposition: Very slight owing to cloud conditions. flak opened up on aircraft that bombed below cloud.

This was to be the first operation that Len did not participate in since joining the squadron. The conditions were frankly unpleasant, crews reporting icing and electrical storms that took their toll on the aircraft. In addition to the usual problems of combat flying, the aircraft suffered ice build-up on the leading edges of wings so losing lift, on aerials so compromising the wireless capability, and in carburettors so losing power. Ice would also form on propeller blades, from where it would be thrown off, rattling against the fuselage accompanied by other alarming bumps and bangs as larger lumps of ice became detached. In parallel the electrical storms would have been causing disruption to the wireless and the compass.

Two aircraft returned with technical failures, leaving only three to press home the attack on the primary target; P/O David Delaney chose to bomb through cloud from 12,000 ft on ETA, whilst P/O DN Sampson dropped down below cloud level to 6,500 ft to confirm the target, a decision which presented the flak batteries with an attractive target. P/O MR Griffiths meanwhile reported that he had overshot the target by 120 miles and 'bombed what appeared to be a dam in the hills'.

7 AUGUST 1941

Target[34]	Aircraft on target	Types
GQ1838 Friedrich Krupp AG works coke oven batteries	106	54 Hampden 32 Wellington 9 Halifax 8 Stirling 3 Manchester
Hamm aim point B railway yards	46	45 Wellington 1 Stirling
Dortmund	40	20 Wellington 20 Whitley
CC29A Boulogne warehouses	6	Wellington
Minelaying:		
(i) Frisian Islands (Nectarine)	3	Hampden
(ii) Langeland Belt (Quince)	1	Hampden
(iii) Little Belt (Carrot)	1	Hampden
(iv) Great Belt (Broccoli)	1	Hampden
(v) Great Belt (Asparagus)	1	Hampden
(vi) Great Belt Seiro Revsnes (Pumpkin)	1	Hampden
Nickelling: Paris – Limoges - Vichy and attack aerodromes in occupied France	2	Wellington

Primary target: Dortmund (marshalling yards), target code Sprat.
Alternative: S&M.
Last Resort: S&M.
Combined ops 20 aircraft:
    102 Sqn operation C.147: 12 aircraft, operational call sign SR9.
    77 Sqn operation C.159: 8 aircraft (including 2 freshmen), operational call sign AG7.
Bomb load: No.1 or No.3 TD 0.025. 1× 250 lb GP MLD to be included.
Route: Base – Skegness – Cromer – Hague – Dortmund – Hague – Cromer – Finningley – Base.
Time Off: 2300 hrs.
Weather: 3/10 cloud from 0200 hrs onward. Haze.
Opposition: Very moderate flak. Few searchlights ineffective.

Aircrews chosen to support this operation to Dortmund were drawn from those who had not been involved in the previous night's operation to Frankfurt, with the exception of two trainee 2nd pilots, Sgt John Roe and Canadian Sgt Paul Carreau, who were building up their flying experience.

The crews left on time, led out by P/O Mill from 77 Squadron. Unusually, no aircraft turned back with technical faults, and they all pressed home an attack, most against Dortmund. Two of the crews were freshmen, one of whom was P/O Hank Iveson, who had been so badly fated on his two previous attempts at a nursery operation.

The only incident of the night was recorded by P/O Vannio Albrecht on 102 Squadron. His aircraft was attacked by a night fighter during the outward leg of the journey, and he did not proceed to Dortmund, but instead dropped his bombs on Hamborn, a town in the Ruhr 30 miles short of Dortmund. Following a safe return, the aircraft was withdrawn for repairs that would last a month.

9 AUGUST 1941

This was a momentous date for the German night fighting campaign; at 0025 hrs Oblt Ludwig Becker of 4./NJG1 became the first German night fighter pilot to be credited with an interception[35] using the new Lichtenstein Airborne Intercept (AI) radar.

This success demonstrated that the Luftwaffe's AI technology had been developed to a level that could prosecute an end-to-end interception *without the need for searchlights*. The range of the Lichtenstein B/C was short, however, and thus positive Ground Control Interception (GCI) tracking from the ground was crucial. It was delivered in much the same way as for Helle Nachtjagd Verfahren (HeNaJa, bright night fighting) intercepts;[36] clear commands from the Jägerleitoffizier (JLO – Fighter Control Officer) being essential to get the pilot close enough to facilitate the interception. This new radar-based GCI/AI combination would be known initially as Seeburg Lichtenstein Verfahren, and Oblt Becker would become one of its earliest exponents, accumulating six victories between 9 August and 30 September 1941 using the technique.

As this new technology became established, new purpose-built radar-controlled intercept zones designed from the outset not to use searchlights introduced a new term; Dunkel Nachtjagd (DuNaJa – dark night fighting). These DuNaJa zones started appearing principally along the German and Dutch coasts, thereby providing a second defensive belt through which bombers would have to cross on the way to their targets. In keeping with the system established by the Kombinierte Nachtjagd (KoNaJa, combined night fighting) zones,[37] they were also given code names, principally of birds and other animals.

Changing from a system that relied upon visual acuity to one that was driven by a novel non-visual technology demanded a period of acclimatisation. This transition was helped by the simultaneous availability of both systems, and afforded crews the opportunity to familiarise themselves with the DuNaJa concept whilst still being able to revert to a searchlight-based system if they needed. In spite of initial misgivings, once crews became familiar with the new

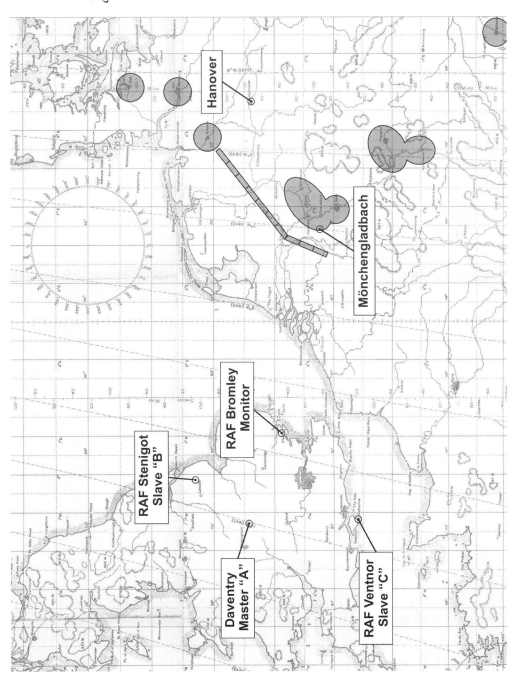

Transmitter and target locations for Eastern GEE chain trials in August 1941

Hanover

Mönchengladbach

RAF Bromley Monitor

RAF Stenigot Slave "B"

Daventry Master "A"

RAF Ventnor Slave "C"

system they found DuNaJa to be four or five times more effective than searchlights. It would now be possible to manage air intercepts even in bad weather and through cloud.

11 AUGUST 1941

Ten Wellingtons from 115 Squadron were despatched on an operation to attack railway sidings at Mönchengladbach, two of which were equipped with a new navigational device. Following a series of trials over the British Isles, this would be the first trial over enemy territory using the new system, known as GEE (G for Grid).[38]

It was no coincidence that the Wellington crews had been despatched to Mönchengladbach, because it lay on a line perpendicular to the locations of the transmitters, therefore benefiting from the strongest signal strength. It also lay at a distance of around 330 miles from the transmitters, roughly 75 per cent of the way towards the projected maximum range of the system, and therefore a good first test. When they returned, those crews charged with trialling the GEE equipment reported 'uncanny accuracy', which vindicated the system and seemed to provide an unambiguous steer for the future of the night bomber offensive.

12 AUGUST 1941

To offset the demographic of new and inexperienced crewmen being brought in from the OTUs, 102 Squadron started to take in numbers of established crewmen from other squadrons, thereby not only increasing aircrew numbers but also raising overall experience levels. Representative of this initiative, 78 Squadron posted one pilot and four WOp/AGs to help out, but the move was not entirely seamless. It would appear from the odd poorly judged comment that not all those who had arrived to enhance 102 Squadron's capability had been volunteers. Whether there was a genuinely justifiable criticism or not, this did highlight that aircrew movements between squadrons during a tour may not always have been well received, and any unbalancing of a delicate status quo may have resulted in the opposite effect from that intended.

115 Squadron flew the GEE equipment again, this time the two specially equipped aircraft flying to Hanover, at the 450–460-mile extreme limit of the GEE system. This target was on broadly the same heading as the night before, which also fell under the area best illuminated by the intersecting hyperbolae and made the next logical step in evaluating the system.

But this time their luck did not hold, and the GEE-equipped Wellington captained by Sgt John Wallace failed to return. The significance of this loss on strategic planning could not be overstated, the principal worry being that the new hardware could fall into enemy hands, or that the GEE lattice charts showing the locations of the transmitters would be found, or even that the crew might under interrogation reveal something that would compromise the system before it had even got into service. Opinions were split as to whether to hold off and wait until the new airborne sets could be prepared in sufficient numbers to support a massed raid, or alternatively to attack immediately with the few sets available before the Germans could work out how to jam it.

To inform the decision, eyewitness accounts were sought for all losses on that night to give an indication as to what could have happened to John Wallace and his crew. As luck would have it, there had been a number of accounts of aircraft going down in flames and exploding; there were enough independent sightings along his aircraft's planned route to support the conclusion that it 'seems most probable that the "GEE" aircraft crashed in flames and may have exploded'.[39] The cautious approach won out; Bomber Command would wait for more airborne GEE sets to be built before deploying it at the head of a significant force. Also, there would be no more flights with this equipment over enemy territory until that time.

Endnotes

16 AIR 14/2673

17 Hydraulic airscrew pitch controls made by the Exactor Control Company are frequently referenced incorrectly in ORBs as "extractors".

18 Eric Verdon-Roe's personal diary.

19 AIR 14/2673

20 AIR 14/2673

21 Readers Digest (1995) *Through Indian Eyes: The Untold Story of Native American Peoples*, ISBN 089577819X, Readers Digest, p 338.

22 *Seattle Times*, 3 February 2008

23 Marr, C.J. Assimilation Through Education: Indian Boarding Schools in the Pacific Northwest, content.lib. washington.edu/aipnw/marr.html.

24 1915–1916 Alaska-Yukon Gazetteer and Business Directory, p 299.

25 Type not specified, probably an Electra.

26 AIR 14/2673

27 AIR 14/2673

28 Moonrise over York (nearest datum point to RAF Topcliffe) 1828 + 2 hours correction for BDST.

29 luchtvaartgeschiedenis.be/content/whitley-z6826-te-zegelsem.

30 Rigaux and his family were arrested and interrogated by the Germans. Some of his family were released, but 76-year-old Rigaux would be sent to Esterwegen concentration camp, where he died.

31 Baber, D. (1954) *Where Eagles Gather*, Viking Press.

32 Van De Velde was imprisoned and executed.

33 AIR 14/2673

34 AIR 14/2673

35 Wellington T2625 from 301 Squadron brought down near Groningen.

36 Annex B

37 Annex B

38 Annex C

39 AIR 14/3256

3

UP TO STRENGTH

14 AUGUST 1941

Target[40]	Aircraft on target	Types
Hanover:		
(i) Aim point A north railway station	97	96 Wellington 1 Stirling
(ii) Aim point B south railway station	55	Whitley
Brunswick main railway station	81	Hampden
Magdeburg:		
(i) Aim point A railway centre	22	13 Wellington 9 Stirling
(ii) Aim point B north station	30	14 Wellington 9 Halifax 7 Manchester
CC29A Boulogne warehouses	13	Wellington
CC42 Rotterdam	9	6 Whitley 3 Wellington
CC25 Dunkirk	2	Wellington
Minelaying off the Frisian Islands (Nectarine)	1	Hampden

Primary target: Hanover (aircraft component factory).
Alternative: S&M.
Last Resort: S&M.
Combined ops 28 aircraft:
102 Sqn operation C.148: 18 aircraft, operational call sign 6OX.
77 Sqn operation C.160: 10 aircraft (including 1 freshman), operational call sign N6A.
Bomb load:
    102 Sqn: No.5 or No.6 TD 0.025. 1× 250 lb GP MLD to be included.
    77 Sqn: No.1 or No.3 TD 0.025. 1× 250 lb GP MLD to be included.
Route: Base – Vlieland – Hanover and return.
Time Off: 2150 hrs.
Weather: No cloud, some haze over target.
Opposition: Moderate heavy accurate flak and some light flak. Numerous searchlights concentrating into a cone over
    centre of town.

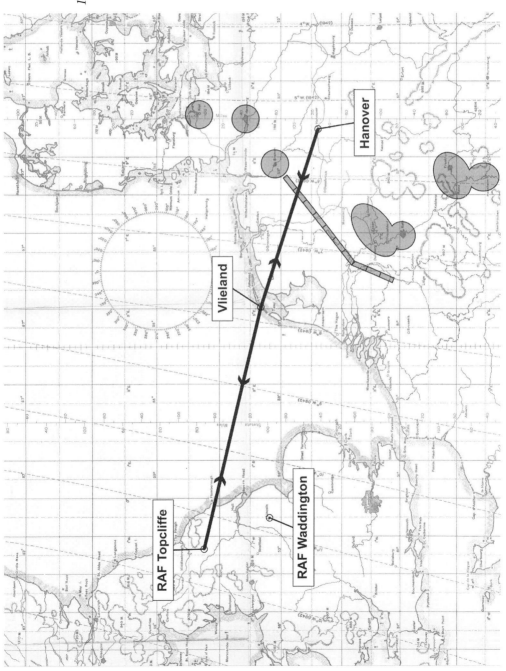

Operation C.148 to Hanover, 14 August 1941

Len had not flown operationally since tangling with a night fighter over Maastricht one week earlier. Whitley Z6862, in which he had flown for his last five operations under the captaincy of Sgt Fisher, was in for repairs, and his former captain now had another aircraft and a different crew. Having sat out the last two operations, Len was now introduced to a crew led by the experienced Sgt WJ Wilson. This would provide him with the opportunity to continue developing in his role as 2nd WOp, his mentor on this crew being WOp/AG Sgt Philip Brett, who had already been cited for his distinguished performance on the squadron.

For the first time in his flying career, Len would be flying a route that would take him over the feared defensive searchlight belt known as the Kammhuber Line[41] instead of around it in a dogleg, as had been previous form. No doubt he would have reflected on the clear skies of his previous operation one week earlier and how this had attracted a night fighter, wondering how much worse it would be to pass over this belt of searchlights in plain sight, with night fighters free to strike at will, if the skies were clear once more.

Meanwhile, recent arrival Sgt Richard Bradbury was assuming the role of navigator on his first operation. He was assigned to a crew led by P/O Edwin Anderson, who himself had only started in July 1941 and was now on his second operation as captain.

This combined operation demanded the participation of 28 aircraft. Up to this point 102 Squadron had been routinely providing a maximum of 10–12 aircraft in support of a night's operations, but tonight it was called upon to provide 18, its greatest mustering of effort to date.

Sgt Wilson lined up 18th within this combined force, taking off at 2208 hrs, whilst Edwin Anderson was last away, 13 minutes later.

Whitley Z6798 (DY- Ē)

Hanover.

Takeoff 2208 hrs.

One stick released over primary target from 12,500 ft.

Landed 0527 hrs.

Operational combat time 7 hrs 19 mins.

Sgt WJ Wilson

Sgt JR Roe

Sgt RH Adamson

Sgt PG Brett

Sgt L Starbuck   7th operation; combat time 53 hrs 1 min

Sgt W Nicholl

Whitley Z6837 (DY- Ṅ)

Hanover.

Takeoff 2221 hrs.

One stick released over primary target from 12,000 ft.

Landed 0510 hrs at RAF Waddington.

Operational combat time 6 hrs 49 mins.

P/O EGN Anderson

Sgt P Carreau

Sgt RF Bradbury   1st operation; combat time 6 hrs 49 mins

Sgt NC Carter

Sgt CS Neveu

As it turned out, the squadron was going to experience a night of drama and tragedy.

Having made a successful attack on the target, Sgt Wilson and his crew were intercepted by a night fighter on their return journey. This was the second consecutive operation when Len would have pitched into the front turret to tangle with a night fighter, and once again, the engagement was inconclusive as the bomber flew back to land safely; Len had been lucky for a second time.

As Sgt Wilson made his approach in limited visibility, he may not have been aware of a crashed Whitley at the end of the runway; Sgt John Reid had returned 26 minutes earlier and overshot on landing due to poor visibility, his aircraft now sitting forlornly with her undercarriage collapsed. As the hours passed it became apparent that five more crews from the squadron had failed to return. News came through that two of them had landed away, including P/O Edwin Anderson who had landed at RAF Waddington in Lincolnshire – but three other crews were still unaccounted for.

One of the missing aircraft was manned by five crewmen who had only arrived two days earlier; Z6877 was led by Sgt Alan Hawkes, an experienced captain, two WOp/AGs from 78 Squadron and two novices from the OTUs. Alan Hawkes takes up the story:[42]

> We planned getting into the searchlight belt at about 0050 hours but they got us after five minutes and held us so I put the propellers into coarse pitch and cut the motors. At 0115 hours I told the rear gunner to keep a look out for fighters but he replied he was unable to see because of the searchlights, about 100 of them by now. A couple of minutes afterwards as we were about to leave the belt, I noticed tracer [possibly from Uffz Wilhelm Benning of I./NJG3] through the top perspex.
>
> I did a diving turn to the left but as we turned, the intercom failed and there was a loud explosion in front of me. The observer reported that the front perspex had been blown away so I told him to jettison the bombs. Then the airspeed indicator dropped, the port exactor went unserviceable and the propeller went into fine pitch so I commenced the drill for single-engined flying. The wireless operator reported the rear turret was completely ablaze and the rear gunner burning. The wireless operator couldn't find the extinguisher so I told the second pilot, who seemed to be rather dazed and in a flat spin, to get the extinguisher from the front turret which he did and passed it back. The bombs had gone and we were losing height rapidly. The wireless operator put the fire out but couldn't get the gunner out as the turret was off centre and was also white hot.
>
> By now we were at 5,000 feet and I was just about able to fly level but the trim tabs were not working. I had great hopes to getting back but they were dashed to smithereens

when the port motor started to pack up, the oil pressure dropped and the temperature rose. I throttled right back but the plane juddered and started to lose height quite rapidly. Then the port engine caught fire so I pressed the fire extinguisher button – the flames go out for a second but the engine caught fire again and the flames got bigger. I now had to cut the petrol and the engine packed up altogether. We were now at 2,000 feet and descending. Fire had now got a good hold so unfortunately I had to inform the crew to prepare to bale out.

The aircraft crashed near Sögel, Meppen, at 0145 hrs, the four surviving crewmen escaping safely; but all were captured.

Another two 102 Squadron crews also failed to return; P/O DN Sampson in Z6842, shot down by Oblt Ludwig Becker of 4./NJG1 over Terwispel, Heerenveen, at 0117 hrs, and Sgt Gerald Powell in Z6829, shot down by Ofw Paul Gildner of 4./NJG1 over the Wattensee, south of Terschelling, at 0448 hrs. These two crews included three men who had started in July 1941 and three even less experienced August starters. By comparison, 77 Squadron had enjoyed a fairly unremarkable operation, though with some crews experiencing difficulties locating the primary target. The most significant event to befall them was a night fighter attack against P/O Norman Roscoe's crew on their return journey, but the engagement had been inconclusive.

17 AUGUST 1941

Target[43]	Aircraft on target	Types
Bremen aim point B centre goods station	59	39 Hampden 20 Whitley
Duisburg aim point B railway centre	41	Wellington
CC25A Dunkirk tidal basin and dock area	1	Wellington
Minelaying:		
(i) Frisian Islands (Nectarine)	7	Hampden
(ii) Aalborg (Krauts)	1	Hampden
(iii) Little Belt (Carrot)	1	Hampden
(iv) Great Belt (Broccoli)	1	Hampden
(v) Great Belt (Asparagus)	1	Hampden
(vi) Great Belt Seiro Revsnes (Pumpkin)	1	Hampden
Nickelling over Paris area and aerodromes in use in occupied France	6	Wellington

Primary target: Bremen (railway junction).
Alternative: S&M.
Last Resort: S&M.
Combined ops 20 aircraft:
    102 Sqn operation C.149: 12 aircraft, operational call sign 7XC.
    77 Sqn operation C.161: 8 aircraft, operational call sign 8FD.
Bomb load:
    102 Sqn: No.1 or No.3 TD 0.025. 1× 250 lb GP MLD to be included.

77 Sqn: 2 aircraft No.1 or No.3 TD 0.025. 1× 250 lb GP MLD to be included.
77 Sqn: 6 aircraft No.5 or No.6 TD 0.025. 1× 250 lb GP MLD to be included.
Route: Base – Cromer - Hague – Bremen and return.
Time Off: 2125 hrs.
Weather: 7/10 cloud thickening to 10/10 over target 3,000 ft to 4,000 ft. Ground haze.
Opposition: Moderate heavy flak and some light around Bremen. Intense flak west and southeast of target. Searchlights
numerous but ineffective due to cloud.

With the second aircraft he had served aboard now also in for repair courtesy of the Luftwaffe, Len was appointed to fly with a crew led by Sgt Fisher's former 2nd pilot, P/O Edwin Anderson, in Z6837. This was to be a memorable operation for Len, as this was the first time he would be performing as WOp in his own right, his probation now over. This crew also included Navigator Sgt Richard Bradbury on his second operation. In fact, Edwin Anderson's crew was broadly the same as it had been on the disastrous Hanover raid, but with Len relegating their previous WOp to the rear turret, where he in turn bumped Canadian Sgt Charles Neveu, their previous air gunner, off the crew.

This next operation was to be part of a 20-aircraft detail to attack Bremen. The crew, along with another four crews, also had an unusual secondary cargo to drop en route tonight; not the usual nickels or dockers, but sacks of tea for the subjugated Dutch people. The tea had been imported from Batavia in the East Indies, in the heart of the Dutch empire overseas; the drop served to show that not only were the Dutch colonies still free, but also that the Dutch people themselves had not been forgotten.

Sgt Fisher's aircraft lined up 12th out of 20 and took off at 2140 hrs. The night's activities should have followed a routine pattern, but instead of Bremen they bombed the railway line at Lathen, some 70 miles short of their intended target, and less than 10 miles inside the German border. This probably points to their having suffered some technical failure that limited their ability to proceed to the primary target. Having continued on their heading from Hague to Bremen, they waited until they had just crossed the border into enemy territory and sought out the nearest secondary target, railways and infrastructure being high on the list.

Further, on their return they recovered to RAF Acklington in Northumberland, miles away to the north, reinforcing the possibility of instrumentation / navigational malfunction. They stayed there for an hour before setting off to fly the 90 miles south to land at RAF Topcliffe, arriving home at around the same time as the other crews returning from Bremen.

Only one other crew landed away that night, and that was Sgt Wilson, whose aircraft had suffered starboard engine failure and returned early, crash-landing at RAF Bircham Newton in Norfolk. An accident report into this event advises that following the engine problem the fuselage was damaged during jettison of fuel and fuselage door. Clearly things had not gone well on this sortie.

Whitley Z6837 (DY-N̄)

Bremen.

Takeoff 2140 hrs.

One stick released over Lathen from 13,000 ft.

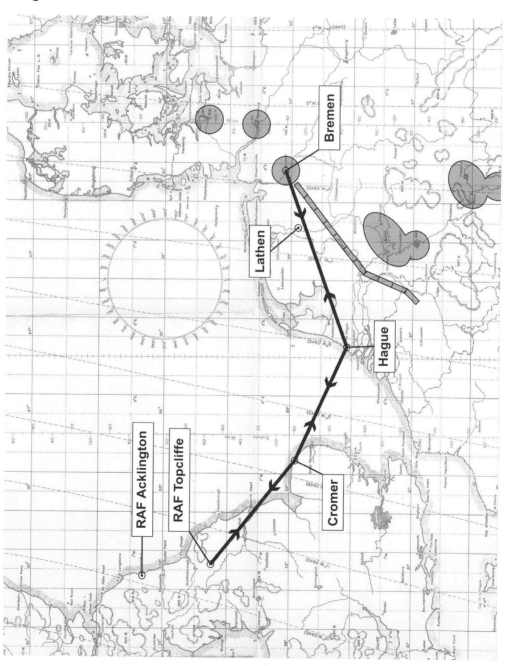

Operation C.149 to Bremen, 17 August 1941

Landed 0425 hrs at RAF Acklington. RTB 0620 hrs.

Operational combat time 6 hrs 45 mins.

P/O EGN Anderson

Sgt P Carreau

Sgt RF Bradbury   2nd operation; combat time 13 hrs 34 mins

Sgt L Starbuck   8th operation; combat time 59 hrs 46 mins

Sgt NC Carter

18 AUGUST 1941

Economist David Bensusan-Butt issued what was to become a milestone report[44] analysing the aerial photographs taken by the bomber crews during June and July 1941. He summarised his report in the following points:

1. Of those aircraft recorded as attacking their target, only one in three got within five miles.

2. Over the French ports, the proportion was two in three; over Germany as a whole, the proportion was one in four; over the Ruhr, it was only one in 10.

3. In the Full Moon, the proportion was two in five; in the new moon it was only one in 15.

4. In the absence of haze, the proportion is over one half, whereas over thick haze it is only one in 15.

5. An increase in the intensity of A.A. fire reduces the number of aircraft getting within five miles of their target in the ratio three to two.

6. All these figures relate only to aircraft recorded as **attacking** the target; the proportion of the **total sorties** which reached within five miles is less by one third.

Thus, for example, of the total sorties only one in five got within five miles of the target, i.e. within the 75 square miles surrounding the target.

The upper echelons were thus delivered shocking first-hand evidence of the problems associated with navigating at night. Specific objectives requiring pinpoint accuracy were routinely being handed out to the squadrons, and an unfounded optimism had allowed the decision makers to convince themselves of that success, although such confidence could now be seen to have been misplaced. Indeed, the Germans themselves would frequently be unaware of what the focus of a night's bombing operations had actually been, because in many cases it had been missed altogether.

Prosecuting precision targets at night had been shown not to be possible; something had to be done:

- Either the requirement for accuracy had to be relaxed, which in turn would mean abandoning any pretence of precision bombing in favour of larger targets that were easier to find, principally the area bombing of towns and cities with the associated ethical dilemmas of targeting civilian populations.

- Alternatively, there needed to be some breakthrough in navigation to allow the specific military, infrastructure and industrial targets to be attacked with confidence.

- Or both of the foregoing.

21 AUGUST 1941

Len's first regular ride, Whitley Z6862, in which he had completed five of his early operations with Sgt Fisher, was back in service for the first time since repairs following the attack by a night fighter. Sgt Ian Hay, an experienced Whitley pilot recently arrived from 58 Squadron, was allocated this aircraft for an air test. In his crew he had retained Air Gunner Sgt Charles Neveu from their last operation.

Shortly after taking off at 1445 hrs, the aircraft climbed so steeply that she stalled and crashed within the aerodrome perimeter. The impact was so severe as to kill all those in the front of the aircraft, but Charles Neveu in the rear turret survived, albeit with head injuries. This would have played on Len's mind, as it was Neveu whom he had moved on from P/O Edwin Anderson's crew just four days earlier, to accommodate him as their new WOp.

The accident report identified that the elevator trim tabs were wound fully back, and made the observation that the pilot had neglected to check.

26 AUGUST 1941

Target[45]	Aircraft on target	Types
Cologne:		
(i) Aim point A main square	19	Wellington
(ii) Aim point B East Kalk station	30	29 Hampden 1 Manchester
(iii) Aim point C Köln West main railway station	38	Wellington
(iv) Aim point D Geron railway marshalling yards	22	Whitley
(v) Searchlight suppression 10 miles west of Cologne	6	Hampden
CC24A Le Havre inner docks	29	15 Wellington 14 Whitley
CC29A Boulogne warehouses	16	14 Wellington 2 Stirling
Minelaying:		
(i) Frisian Islands (Nectarine)	12	Hampden
(ii) Aalborg (Krauts)	1	Hampden
(iii) Kiel Harbour (Forget-me-nots)	1	Hampden

Target	Aircraft on target	Types
(iv) Travemünde (Hollyhock)	1	Hampden
(v) Little Belt (Carrot)	1	Hampden
(vi) Langeland Belt (Quince)	1	Hampden

MAIN OPERATION

Primary target: Cologne (marshalling yards).
Alternative: S&M.
Last Resort: S&M.
Combined ops 15 aircraft:
    102 Sqn operation C.150: 7 aircraft, operational call sign LD8.
    77 Sqn operation C.162: 8 aircraft, operational call sign XR7.
Bomb load:
    102 Sqn: No.1 or No.3 TD 0.025. 1× 250 lb GP MLD to be included.
    77 Sqn: No.5 or No.6 TD 0.025. 1× 250 lb GP MLD to be included.
Route: Base – Orford Ness – Nieuport – Givet – Cologne and return.
Time Off: 2200 hrs.
Weather: 8/10 – 9/10 cloud in target area.
Opposition: Moderate heavy flak fairly accurate firing through cloud, numerous searchlights ineffective.

NURSERY OPERATION

Primary target: Le Havre (docks and shipping).
Alternative: AIP.
Last Resort: AIP.
102 Sqn operation C.151: 8 aircraft (freshmen), operational call sign LD8.
Bomb load: freshmen No.1 or No.3 TD 0.025. 1× 250 lb GP MLD to be included.
Route: Base – Grantham – Abingdon – Bognor – Le Havre and return.
Time Off: 2330 hrs.
Weather: 5/10 to 8/10 cloud over target.
Opposition: flak negligible. No searchlights over target.

It had been three weeks since the last nursery operation, but in that time three further freshmen had graduated by flying on deep strike operations. As there were now five more time-served 2nd pilots ready to accept the challenge, time had come for another nursery operation, this time to Le Havre.

Continuing the policy of introducing experienced crews from other squadrons, three seasoned Whitley pilots newly arrived from other squadrons were to join the nursery operation: P/O John Croucher and Sgt Derrick Riley from 58 Squadron, and P/O Bruce Roy from 78 Squadron. These experienced pilots were to participate not so much to familiarise themselves with operational flying, but more to become acquainted with the way 102 Squadron organised and supported operations. They had brought with them two WOp/AGs, and would take the opportunity to familiarise them at the same time.

By now the squadron was receiving new crewmen at such a rate that the big family training philosophy that had worked for so long was overloaded; it was now no longer possible to

*Operation
C.151 to
Le Havre,
26 August 1941*

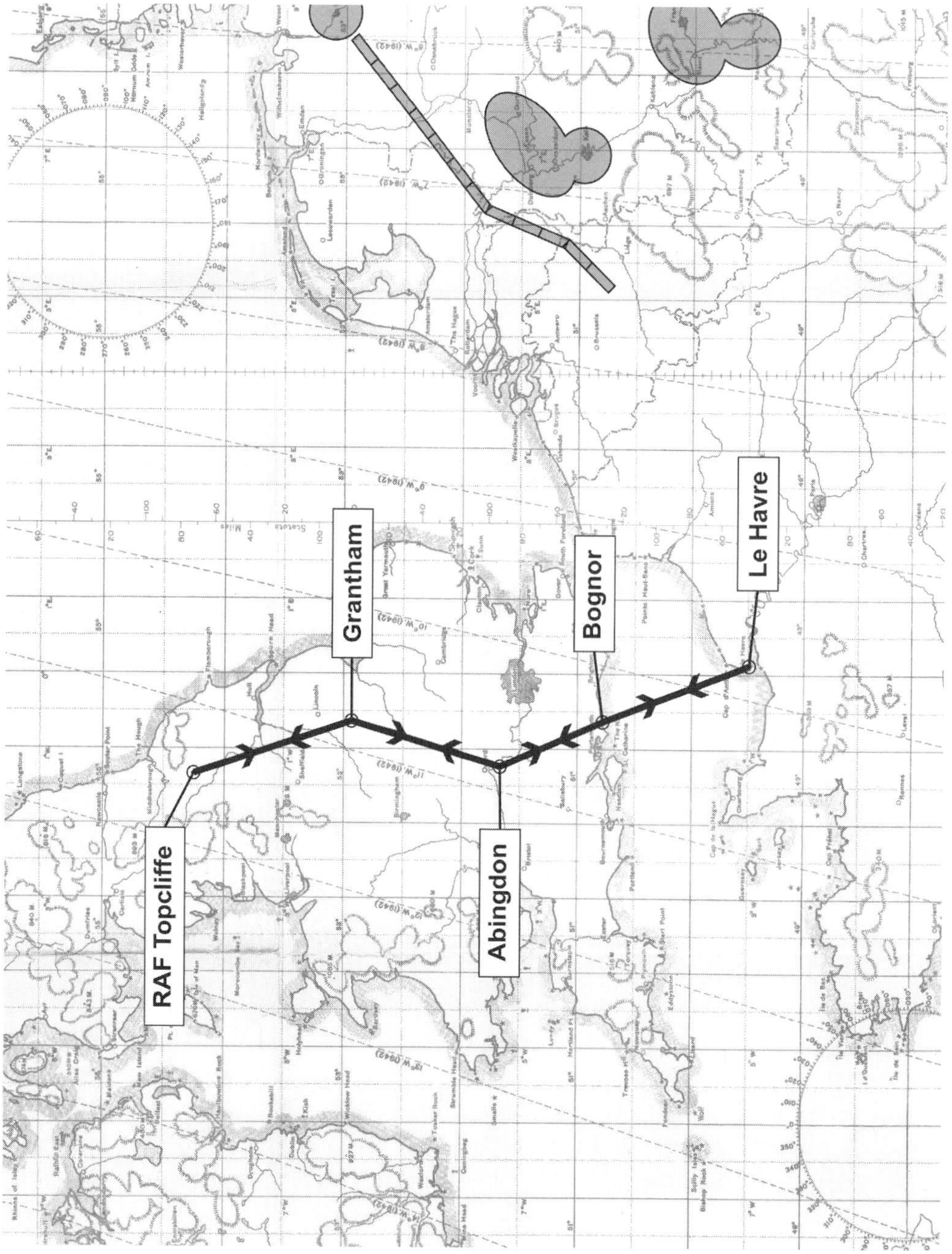

RAF Topcliffe

Grantham

Abingdon

Bognor

Le Havre

circulate one or two new crew members around experienced crews before pitching them into operations. Still recognising the fallibility of despatching nursery crews without any experience on operations, the squadron decided to take the opportunity afforded by the nursery operations and introduce novice crewmen into crews originally intended to be of sufficient experience to support the new captain on his first operation.

To ensure that the new captain had some battle-hardened experience with him on the flight deck, it was decided that there should as a minimum be an experienced WOp or navigator. As a consequence, the remaining crew members were this time selected on the basis of their inexperience, those chosen being typically on their first or second operations, with a smattering of experienced personnel across each of the crews. Indeed, this had become a training operation not just for qualifying 2nd pilots but for novice crewmen across all disciplines.

There was also a run to Cologne for the more experienced crews, who would be leaving first. Len had been fortunate, and his wireless experience had been called upon to support novice captain P/O Peter Gaskell aboard Z6949 on the easier of the two operations to Le Havre.

The Cologne crews would have been relieved that tonight they would not be crossing the Kammhuber Line on their way to the target; instead they would be skirting around it and running in from the west. Further, the bomber crews would be having the benefit of a handful of Hampdens flying searchlight suppression sorties 10 miles to the west of Cologne, on precisely the route they would be flying. These sorties involved strafing the searchlights at low level and dropping small bombs to deter their operators, thereby buying an opportunity for the bomber crews to pass over more safely.

The Cologne crews started taking off at 2150 hrs and with the last one gone at 2213 hrs a transitory silence descended as the clock ticked down to the arrival of the eight 102 Squadron Le Havre crews, readying themselves for their departure over an hour later. As Len reflected on the night's events and the twist of fate that had handed him the easier of the two operations, it may have crossed his mind that although he was the most experienced man on his crew tonight, everybody else upon whom he relied was less experienced. The Le Havre crews would have played at being relaxed, and then, following the example of the Cologne crews before them, gone to wake up their aircraft for the night's activities.

At 2335 hrs, former 58 Squadron Captain Sgt Derrick Riley headed the eight freshman crews out, 5 minutes late. Peter Gaskell followed as second in line fully some 7 minutes afterwards, suggesting some last-minute problems arising amongst his inexperienced crew. The other crews followed at an irregular pace, at anything between 1- and 4-minute intervals between aircraft.

Whitley Z6949 (DY-Ū)

Le Havre.

Takeoff 2342 hrs.

One stick released over primary target from 11,000 ft.

Landed 0540 hrs.

Operational combat time 5 hrs 58 mins.

P/O PR Gaskell

Sgt JR Roe

Sgt WV Atkinson

Sgt L Starbuck   9th operation; combat time 65 hrs 44 mins

Sgt AL Halsey

The aircraft from both operations returned to their base within the same time window, all but one of the Le Havre crews reporting having attacked their primary target, whilst the remaining crew brought back their bombs. All of the 102 Squadron Cologne crews reported having attacked their primary target and all returned safely in spite of the flak. The only incident of note arising was reported by P/O Vannio Albrecht, whose aircraft had been hit by flak and lost her compass, necessitating a diversion to RAF Bircham Newton on their return. 77 Squadron also managed a night without loss.

Poor weather over Cologne had once more hampered targeting; German reports[46] recorded that only 15 per cent of the bombs dropped had even landed within the city.

The night's operations had gone smoothly, which was all the more surprising considering the defences over Cologne; the link with the Hampden crews having flown their low-level searchlight suppression sorties was self-evident.

28 August 1941

Target[47]	Aircraft on target	Types
Duisburg:		
(i) Aim point B railway centre	82	60 Wellington 13 Stirling 9 Halifax
(ii) Aim point C railway centre	36	30 Hampden 6 Manchester
(iii) Searchlight suppression within 10 miles of Duisburg area	6	Hampden
CC13A Ostend dock area	14	13 Wellington 1 Hampden
CC25A Dunkirk tidal basin and dock area	10	Whitley
Nickelling over Paris area and attack enemy aerodromes within 20 miles of Paris	2	Wellington

Nursery Operation

Primary target: Dunkirk (docks and shipping).
Alternative: AIP.
Last Resort: AIP.
Combined ops 5 aircraft (freshmen):
    102 Sqn operation C.152: 1 aircraft, operational call sign 6UR.

77 Sqn operation C.163: 4 aircraft, operational call sign W6Z.
Bomb load: No.1 or No.3 TD 0.025.
Route: Base – Orford Ness – Dunkirk and return.
Time Off: 0115 hrs.
Weather: 1/10 cloud over target tops 2,000 ft.
Opposition: Negligible.

This was another nursery operation in line with that run successfully two nights previously to Le Havre. So it was that Sgt HW Wickham from 102 Squadron took up position behind the four 77 Squadron freshman crews whilst the rest of his squadron stood down. As with the last nursery operation, there was a slight delay in getting airborne. Four hours and 27 minutes later, Sgt Wickham, the last to depart, was the first to land, having successfully completed his sortie as the rest of the squadron slept. All the other aircraft followed in behind, having also successfully completed their first operation.

29 AUGUST 1941

Target[48]	Aircraft on target	Types
Frankfurt:		
(i) GH871 East Harbour (Osthafen)	76	73 Hampden 3 Manchester
(ii) Aim point B (railway targets)	67	62 Whitley 5 Halifax
Mannheim:		
(i) Aim point A (industrial targets)	25	Wellington
(ii) Aim point D (railway targets)	69	Wellington
CC24A Le Havre dock area	5	Wellington

Primary target: Frankfurt (main railway station).
Alternative: S&M.
Last Resort: S&M.
Combined ops 28 aircraft:
    102 Sqn operation C.153: 18 aircraft, operational call sign SY9.
    77 Sqn operation C.164: 10 aircraft, operational call sign KA9.
Bomb load: No.1 or No.3 TD 0.025. 1× 250 lb GP MLD to be included.
Route: Base – Orford Ness – Nieuport – Dinant – Frankfurt and return.
Time Off: 2100 hrs.
Weather: 9/10 cloud over target.
Opposition: Moderate heavy flak. Searchlights ineffective through cloud.

Another 28 aircraft had been detailed to attack Frankfurt, but Len would be sitting this one out. Two of these crews would not be returning. Firstly, S/Ldr John Lalor had sent a message at 0140 hrs advising that Z6863 had lost an engine and he was returning to base. This was followed at 0152 hrs with a fix, but shortly after that, the aircraft was shot down by flak near Macken, Boppard, killing the 2nd pilot and navigator. John Lalor suffered grievous injuries to his legs and was pulled clear of the wreckage by his WOp, Sgt Frederick Potts, and air gunner,

Sgt RC Watchorn, who took him to a nearby barn, where he died six hours later from his injuries.

Secondly, Sgt Paul Carreau, on his first operation since qualifying as captain, attempted landing at RAF Bircham Newton but crashed on a farm near the neighbouring RAF Docking at 0500 hrs. The only two survivors were the WOp, Sgt Frank Kuebler, and the air gunner, Sgt Cyril Higson, who were both injured and were rushed to Ely hospital. Frank Kuebler would not fly operationally with the squadron again for a further nine months. The accident report stated that their aircraft had lost flying speed during the circuit, stalled and crashed.

At 0630 hrs, 77 Squadron's Sgt Robert Wheatley was running out of fuel on his return, and put down 20 miles short of base in a field to the south of Rufforth, near York. This happened to be the site of the new RAF Rufforth, which was at that time under construction and would not become operational until June 1942, so at that point the ground would not have been prepared with either grass or paved runways, causing some inevitable damage to the aircraft.

By this time, only one more aircraft was not yet accounted for, and that was Sgt Stanley Morgan's from 102 Squadron, who landed a staggering 1 hour and 17 minutes later, at 0747 hrs, clocking up 10 hours and 41 minutes for his sortie.

Poor weather over Frankfurt had hindered targeting; German reports[49] recorded damage to a gasworks, a warehouse and a few houses.

31 August 1941

Target[50]	Aircraft on target	Types
Cologne:		
(i) Aim point A main square	51	45 Wellington 6 Stirling
(ii) Aim point B East Kalk station	45	39 Hampden 6 Manchester
(iii) Aim point C Köln West main railway station	7	Halifax
(iv) Searchlight suppression in Cologne area	6	Hampden
Essen; Friedrich Krupp AG works	71	43 Whitley 28 Wellington
Boulogne aim point A warehouses	6	Wellington
Minelaying:		
(i) Frisian Islands	7	Hampden
(ii) Travemünde	1	Hampden
(iii) Kiel Harbour	1	Hampden
(iv) Great Belt	1	Hampden
(v) South entrance to Little Belt	1	Hampden
(vi) Little Belt	1	Hampden

Primary target: Essen (Krupp works).
Alternative: S&M.
Last Resort: S&M.
Combined ops 30 aircraft:
    102 Sqn operation C.154: 18 aircraft, operational call sign Z7D.
    77 Sqn operation C.165: 12 aircraft, operational call sign WH8.
Bomb load:
    5 from 102 Sqn: No.1 or No.3 TD 0.025. 1× 250 lb GP MLD to be included.
    77 Sqn and 13 from 102 Sqn: No.5 or No.6 TD 0.025. 1× 250 lb GP MLD to be included.
Route: Base – Zandvoort– Essen and return.
Time Off: 1945 hrs.
Weather: 8/10–10/10 cloud over target.
Opposition: Moderate to intense heavy flak. Searchlights ineffective through cloud.

Len's former captain, Sgt Fisher, had been allocated Whitley Z6959 and required a WOp. Len had flown with him as both an air gunner and 2nd WOp, so would have been pleased to have the opportunity to demonstrate his skills as WOp to his previous mentor. Their target was the Krupp works at Essen, the main supplier of arms, most especially large-calibre guns, to the Wehrmacht.

For the second time in his career, Len would be flying over the feared Kammhuber Line. The last time he had survived an attack from a night fighter in the clear skies on a run to Hanover, but this time crews would have received the good news that a number of searchlight suppression sorties were being flown in the Cologne region. Not only that, but the forecast was for cloud, providing them with a further cloak of protection.

The massed departure of 30 aircraft was to be the biggest combined operation ever flown by the joint forces of the two sister squadrons. However, one of the 77 Squadron pilots reported sick, depleting the force by one. The remaining 29 aircraft assumed their positions in a dramatic spectacle of massed airpower, the first one leaving on time at 1945 hrs, whilst Sgt Fisher took off seventh, at 1952 hrs. As he was climbing out the excitement began; P/O Bruce Roy's aircraft was destroyed by a big explosion whilst preparing for take-off. The crew all escaped without injury, but the explosion killed Aircraftsman 1st Class (AC1) Keith Ward. The intensity of the explosion was such that it damaged a neighbouring aircraft, captained by P/O David Delaney, which was also unable to start. This would have given Canadian Sgt Isadore Stein, in Z6959's rear turret, an alarming view in the distance behind him as they climbed away.

Whitley Z6959 (DY-Ā)

Essen.

Takeoff 1952 hrs.

One stick released over primary target from 12,500 ft.

Landed 0203 hrs.

Operational combat time 6 hrs 11 mins.

Sgt R Fisher

Sgt TH Thorley

Sgt GAG Murray

Sgt L Starbuck   10th operation; combat time 71 hrs 55 mins

Sgt I Stein

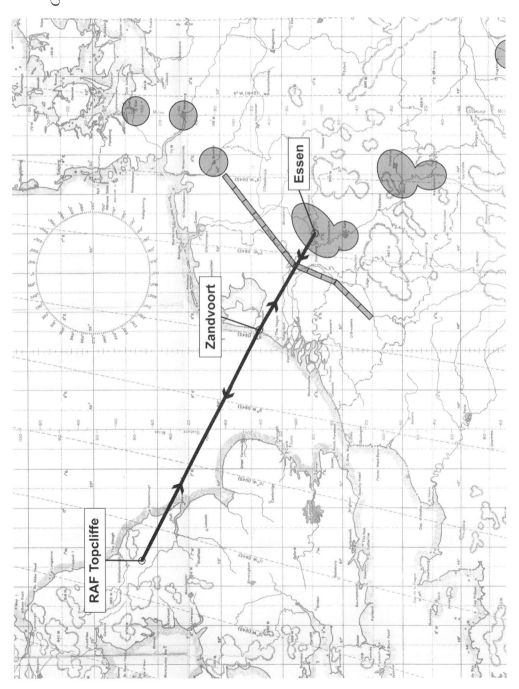

Operation
C.154 to Essen,
31 August
1941

Essen

Zandvoort

RAF Topcliffe

Four aircraft experienced technical faults and returned early. The remaining 23 that proceeded to target had been lucky that the fairly thick cloud had stayed mostly in place, taking some of the sting out of the searchlight-based defences over which they had to fly; however, where there were gaps the defending forces had been quick to capitalise.

Sgt Fisher completed his attack and returned after an uneventful sortie. Less fortunate was P/O Edwin Anderson, with whom Len had flown on four of his earliest operations. Anderson had been captain of Z6837, which had failed to return, believed shot down over Schaffen, Diest, at 0012hrs by Uffz Heinz Pähler 2./NJG1. Two 77 Squadron aircraft were also intercepted by night fighters, but both escaped with varying degrees of damage.

So in spite of the initial expectation of immunity being afforded by the searchlight suppression sorties, losses had still been suffered. This provided a reminder that there remained no room for complacency, especially in proximity of the Kammhuber Line.

Thick cloud over Essen had compromised targeting; German reports[51] recorded that only one house in the region had been damaged – poor reward for the 71 aircraft despatched.

2 SEPTEMBER 1941

Target[52]	Aircraft on target	Types
Frankfurt:		
(i) Aim point A industrial centre	21	Wellington
(ii) Aim point B main railway centre	44	Whitley
(iii) GH577 main railway marshalling yards	50	Wellington
(iv) GH871 Inland ports / East Harbour (Osthafen)	11	Hampden
Berlin:		
(i) Aim point B	13	7 Halifax 6 Stirling
(ii) Aim point C	36	32 Hampden 4 Manchester
Ostend:		
(i) CC13A	7	Wellington
(ii) CC13	3	Whitley
Minelaying:		
(i) Frisian Islands (Nectarine)	11	Hampden
(ii) South end of the Sound (Daffodil)	2	Hampden
(iii) Eckernförde (Melon)	1	Hampden
(iv) South end of Little Belt (Wallflower)	1	Hampden

MAIN OPERATION

Primary target: Frankfurt (main railway station).
Alternative: S&M.
Last Resort: S&M.
Combined ops 29 aircraft:
    102 Sqn operation C.155: 18 aircraft, operational call sign O9R.
    77 Sqn operation C.166: 11 aircraft, operational call sign C9S.
Bomb load:
    77 Sqn: No.5 or No.6 TD 0.025. 1× 250 lb GP MLD to be included where possible.
    102 Sqn: No.1 or No.3 TD 0.025. 1× 250 lb GP MLD to be included where possible.
Route: Base – Orford Ness – Nieuport – Dinant – Frankfurt and return.
Time Off: 2030 hrs.
All 77 Squadron aircraft to land at RAF Leeming.
Weather: 9/10 to 10/10 cloud over target.
Opposition: flak normal heavy accurate for height. Searchlights ineffective through cloud, numerous.

NURSERY OPERATION

Primary target: Ostend (docks and shipping).
Alternative: AIP (docks and shipping).
Last Resort: AIP (docks and shipping).
102 Sqn operation C.156: 1 aircraft (freshman), operational call sign O9R.
Bomb load: No.1 or No.3 TD 0.025.
Route: Base – Orford Ness – Ostend and return.
Time Off: 2000 hrs.
Weather: 10/10 cloud over target.
Opposition: Slight.

This was to be Len's second consecutive operation with Sgt Fisher in Z6959, reaffirming a successful relationship that had lasted for an unbroken sequence of five operations between 20 July and 5 August 1941. For this operation they were detailed to attack Frankfurt, and were once again called upon to drop dockers.

This was another intense night for the squadron, involving 18 of its own aircraft and a further 11 from 77 Squadron in their last joint operation. Bringing the total of aircraft on operations to a round 30 was Sgt BR Wilde, a lone freshman scheduled to depart half an hour before the main force on his nursery operation.

However, instead of this nursery operation being to a French coastal target as had become the accepted norm, Sgt Wilde was destined for the Belgian port of Ostend, and his departure was delayed by 9 minutes, until 2009 hrs. The main force, paradoxically, started 5 minutes ahead of schedule, just 16 minutes after the freshman; this would have been the most spectacular send-off for Sgt Wilde (who had started at the squadron on the same date as Len). Sgt Fisher lined up 22nd in the main force and took off at 2051 hrs.

Whitley Z6959 (DY-Ā)

Frankfurt.

Takeoff 2051 hrs.

One stick released over primary target from 12,000 ft.

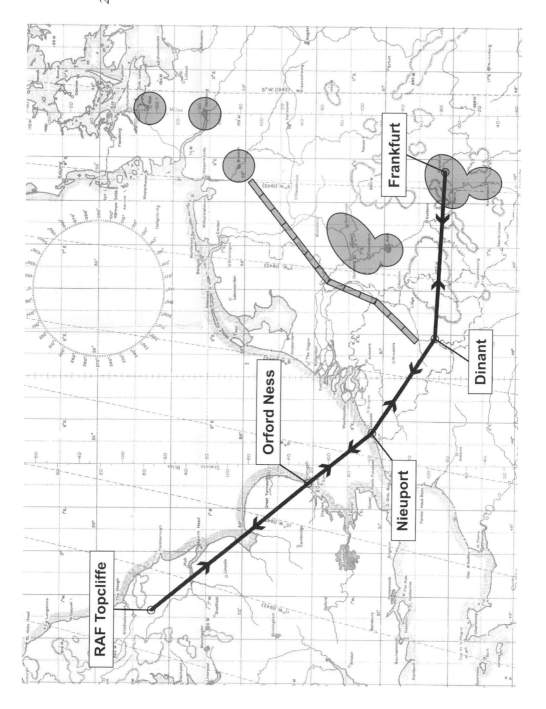

Operation
C.155 to
Frankfurt,
2 September
1941

Frankfurt

Dinant

Orford Ness

Nieuport

RAF Topcliffe

Landed 0544 hrs.

Operational combat time 8 hrs 53 mins.

Sgt R Fisher

Sgt GW McDonald

P/O AD Dobson

Sgt L Starbuck   11th operation; combat time 80 hrs 48 mins

Sgt I Stein

Sgt Wilde's nursery operation was conducted safely in spite of complete cloud cover over the target, which meant that he returned with his bombs at 0120 hrs. Four aircraft from the Frankfurt detail were struck by unserviceabilities on their way to the target, the most pressing of which was Sgt Wilson's, which suffered a seized port engine, causing him to jettison his bombs near the French/Belgian border. His WOp, Sgt Philip Brett, was once more credited with some adept wireless work, this time in facilitating their recovery to RAF Manston in Kent.

The long-term partnership enjoyed between 77 Squadron and 102 Squadron at RAF Topcliffe would start to be dissolved that night, the 77 Squadron crews being ordered to land at their new base 10 miles north-west at RAF Leeming. This parting of the ways was not to be a happy event for either squadron; one of the returning 77 Squadron crews crash-landed at Chellaston, Derbyshire, having run low on fuel at 0400 hrs, and worse was to come. At approximately the same time, the worst incident of the night occurred; Z6946 from 102 Squadron crashed, with the loss of all crew, at 0355 hrs. It would appear that Sgt Seward Modeland had been attempting a landing at RAF Nacton in Suffolk under conditions of heavy ground mist. In poor visibility, the aircraft hit electric power lines and crashed into two houses in Rectory Lane, Kirton, fracturing a water main and injuring the properties' occupants, including a four-year-old girl. Hindsight suggested that under such conditions the crew would have been better advised to abandon the aircraft.

6 SEPTEMBER 1941

Target[53]	Aircraft on target	Types
Marl; GS162 Hüls chemical factory	86	41 Whitley 27 Wellington 18 Hampden
Minelaying in Oslo Harbour (Onion)	24	Hampden

Primary target: Marl[54] (Hüls chemical factory).
Alternative: S&M.
Last Resort: S&M.
Operation C.157: 16 aircraft, operational call sign UL7.
Bomb load: No.1 or No.3 (preferably No.3) TD 0.025. 1× 250 lb GP MLD to be included.

Route: Base – Bridlington – Vlieland – Marl and return.
Time Off: 2020 hrs.
Weather: Clear over target.
Opposition: Moderate heavy flak in Haltern and Dorsten area. Searchlights few.

102 Squadron was next ordered to attack the Chemische Werke Hüls GmbH at Marl, near Duisburg, one of the most important producers of synthetic rubber in Germany. The operation demanded 16 aircraft, including that of Sgt Fisher, who would retain Len's services; this time, however, Len reverted to the role of air gunner whilst a new WOp was introduced. Once again, they were routed over the Kammhuber Line, and fingers would have been crossed that the met forecast for clear skies would be wrong, especially as no searchlight suppression sorties had been scheduled.

The aircraft had to marshal themselves for the night's operation in darkness, as the moon had not risen clear of the horizon.[55] During this time, P/O Bruce Roy got Z6871 stuck during taxiing, and in these conditions of limited visibility Sgt John Stell taxied Z6800 into another aircraft, believed to be Z6958 captained by Sgt Stanley Morgan, resulting in all three crews missing the night's operation. The combined effect of these mishaps was that all the crews were all delayed and large gaps appeared in the order as the aircraft following threaded their way carefully past their immobilised colleagues.

Sgt Fisher lined up second behind P/O John Croucher, who would lead the squadron out. They watched as he got the signal to go and throttled up then faded into the distance, building up speed. They did not know it then, but as they watched this Whitley ease gently into the air, they would be the last of their squadron colleagues to see John Croucher and his crew alive.

Sgt Fisher, with his mind firmly on the job in hand, followed on, and took off 1 minute later, at 2035 hrs. Thirteen aircraft did eventually get airborne, but in a process lasting no less than 45 minutes – unheard of until then. It was indeed fortunate that Sgt Fisher was so far up the order as this comedy of errors unfolded behind him.

Whitley Z6959 (DY-Ā)

Marl.

Takeoff 2035 hrs.

One stick released over primary target from 12,500 ft.

Landed 0303 hrs.

Operational combat time 6 hrs 28 mins.

Sgt R Fisher

Sgt GW McDonald

P/O AD Dobson

Sgt GE Sumpton

Sgt L Starbuck   12th operation; combat time 87 hrs 16 mins

*Operation
C.157 to Marl,
6 September
1941*

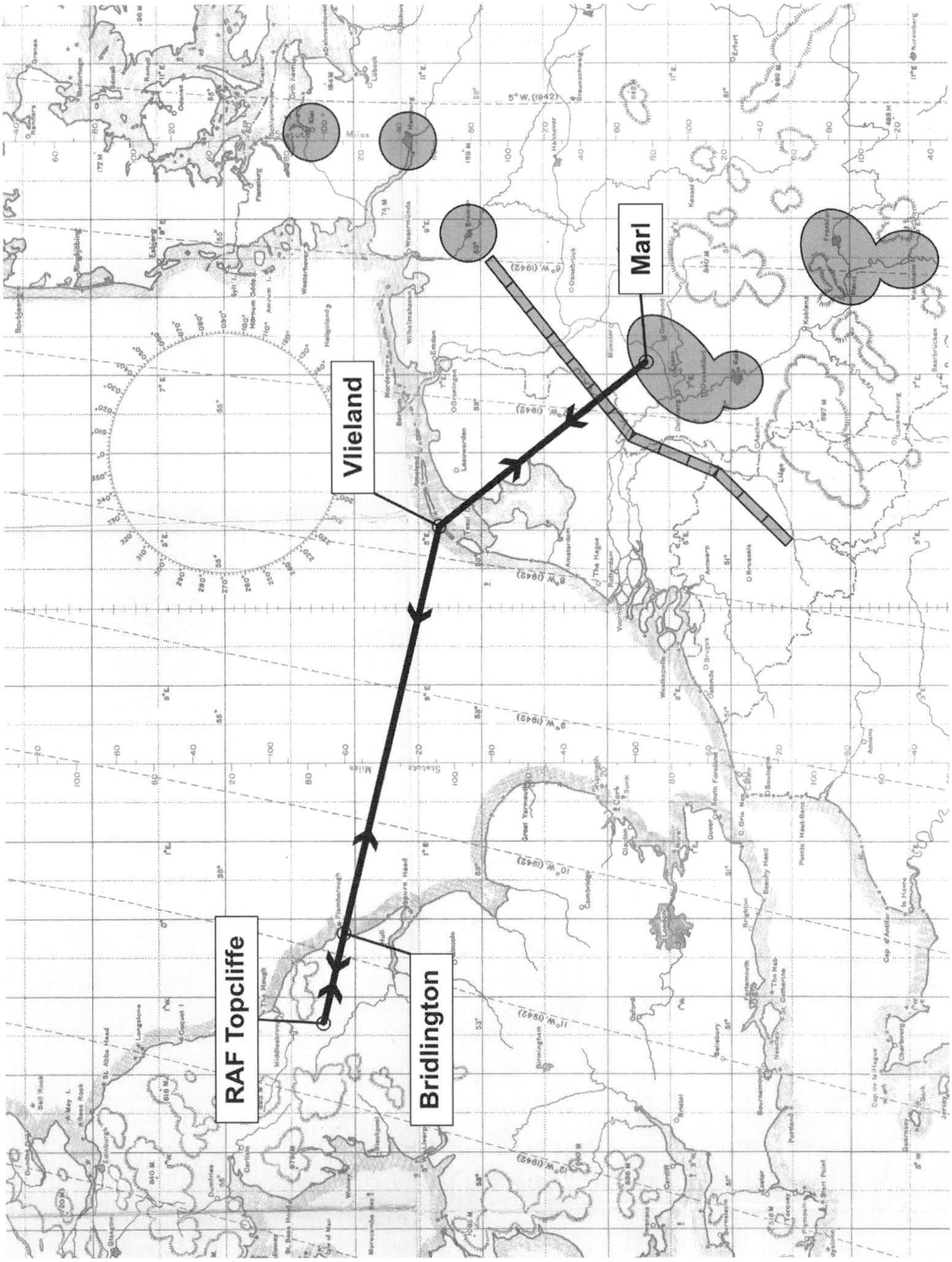

Marl

Vlieland

RAF Topcliffe

Bridlington

The met forecast proved to be correct, and the weather over the target was uncharacteristically clear, which would leave the crews very exposed not only over the target but also during their two consecutive passes over the Kammhuber Line, with its searchlights and waiting night fighters. The bomber crews had an unenviable run ahead of them.

Two aircraft returned early with faults and were on the ground when Sgt Fisher came back, the first of the successful crews to return from the night's action. As the morning wore on, it became apparent that two further crews had been lost. The first of these was Z6970, flown by Sgt Philip Eyre on his fourth operation as captain, shot down possibly by Ofw Wilhelm Schmale of III/NJG1 over Sambeek, Boxmeer, at 0107 hrs. Philip Eyre had joined the squadron on the same day as Len; of the six men who had started together on 12 July 1941, only eight weeks earlier, half had now been shot down.

The second aircraft lost was Z6574, captained by John Croucher. The crew had sent an SOS and followed this up with notification that they were going to ditch at a location 60 miles north-east of RAF Bircham Newton at 0137 hrs, a position to the south of their planned return route from Vlieland to Bridlington.

Concurrent with this, Uffz Heinz Grimm of 4./NJG1 is recorded as having engaged a Whitley 35 km north-west of Terschelling at 0200 hrs in his Bf 110. The Marl operation was routed over Vlieland and there were no other operations being flown anywhere near. The prevailing one-hour time difference between British Summer Time (BST) and Mitteleuropäischen Sommerzeit (MESZ) suggests that Uffz Grimm conducted his engagement at around 0100 hrs BST, linking these two sorties.

During the ensuing exchange of fire, Uffz Grimm's aircraft received serious damage and he was shot in the thigh, prompting his disengagement as both he and his wireless operator baled out over the sea. With his attacker now gone, John Croucher had an opportunity to focus on nursing his damaged aircraft home.

The two positions given by Uffz Grimm and RAF Bircham Newton confirm that John Croucher had abandoned his planned WNW course to cross the coast at Bridlington, and had instead steered a more westerly course to get over land more quickly. This shows how things were starting to go wrong on board, and indeed by the time he radioed his intention to ditch at 0137 hrs, the fatally damaged Z6574 had covered around 130 miles following her interception

Bf 110 from 6./NJG1 (Chris Goss Collection)

before finally succumbing. Uffz Grimm would be recovered, and following recuperation would go on to amass 24 victories, whereas following a search no trace of John Croucher's crew would be found.

In as far as it was possible to find anything positive amongst such losses, there was some cause for celebration in A Flight, as WOp/AG Sgt Frederick 'Junior' Braybrook had completed his tour. As a result he would be awarded a DFM, but more importantly for Len this was some-one on the squadron of the same discipline as himself who had completed his tour.

7 September 1941

Target[56]	Aircraft on target	Types
Berlin:		
(i) Aim point A	47	43 Hampden 4 Manchester
(ii) Aim point B	98	88 Wellington 10 Stirling
(iii) Aim point C	52	31 Whitley 15 Wellington 6 Halifax
GR3588 Kiel (Deutsche Werke shipyards)	51	30 Wellington 18 Hampden 3 Stirling
CC29A Boulogne warehouses	47	38 Wellington 9 Whitley
Minelaying off the Frisian Islands (Nectarine)	8	Hampden

Primary target: Berlin (Schlesischer railway station).
Operation C.158: 6 aircraft, operational call sign R8F.
Bomb load: No.5 or No.6 (preferably No.6) TD 0.025. 1× 250 lb GP MLD to be included.
    50 lb incendiaries up to 25%.
Route: Base – Flamborough – Meldorf –Travemünde – Berlin and return.
Time Off: 2000 hrs.
Weather: Clear over target. Bright moonlight.
Opposition: Very intense flak. Searchlights normal ineffective owing to moonlight.

The flight to Berlin would be long and dangerous, and was sure to be unpopular with the crews destined to go there. Len was not called forward for this operation, but would not have to wait long for his turn at another deep strike operation with an equivalent flight time.

The weather was clear over the target, which should have left the aircraft very exposed to the defending forces, but the moon was so bright that it rendered the searchlights ineffective. Although the flak was intense only P/O Vannio Albrecht reported any damage, and all crews returned safely, having reported bombing either their primary target or another nearby.

Clear skies over Berlin had supported accurate bombing; German reports[57] confirmed that most bombs had fallen on suburbs to the east and north of the city centre, causing significant damage to war industry factories, transport, public utilities and housing. Berliners would come to rue this night, as a number of bombers from other squadrons had carried the new 4,000 lb Cookie HC bombs, which exploded with such devastating effect as to cause many cases of burst lung.

8 September 1941

Target[58]	Aircraft on target	Types
Kassel:		
(i) GN3819 Henschel und Sohn land armaments	68	41 Wellington 27 Hampden
(ii) GH525 Henschel railway locomotive workshops	27	16 Whitley 11 Wellington
CC16A Cherbourg docks	7	Wellington
Minelaying:		
(i) Frisian Islands (Nectarine)	1	Hampden
(ii) Copenhagen (Verbena)	1	Hampden
(iii) Eckernförde (Melon)	1	Hampden
(iv) Flensburg Fjord (Wallflower)	1	Hampden
(v) Langeland Belt (Quince)	1	Hampden
(vi) Great Belt (Asparagus)	1	Hampden

Primary target: Kassel (railway workshops).
Alternative: S&M.
Last Resort: S&M.
Operation C.159: 9 aircraft, operational call sign M7M.
Bomb load: No.5 or No.6 (preferably No.6) TD 0.025. 1× 250 lb GP MLD to be included.
Route: Base – Finningley Beacon – Orford Ness – Nieuport – St-Hubert – Kassel and return.
Time Off: 2000 hrs.
Weather: Clear in target area.
Opposition: Slight light flak. Very few searchlights.

Nine aircraft were ordered onto the next deep strike, this time to the Henschel railway locomotive workshops in Kassel, which were being used to build tanks. The route would avoid the Kammhuber Line, but at the expense of taking a long diversion round southern Belgium, increasing significantly the duration of the operation. Because the flight time was broadly the same nine to ten hours' hard slog as the Berlin crews had faced the night before, all those who had done the Berlin run were stood down.

Sgt Fisher was to present an aircraft with no crew changes from the previous operation, a situation most unusual when rotating crewmen was the norm. That meant that Len would be called upon to protect the aircraft from his position in the rear turret once more. As an additional duty, the crew had been ordered to drop nickels.

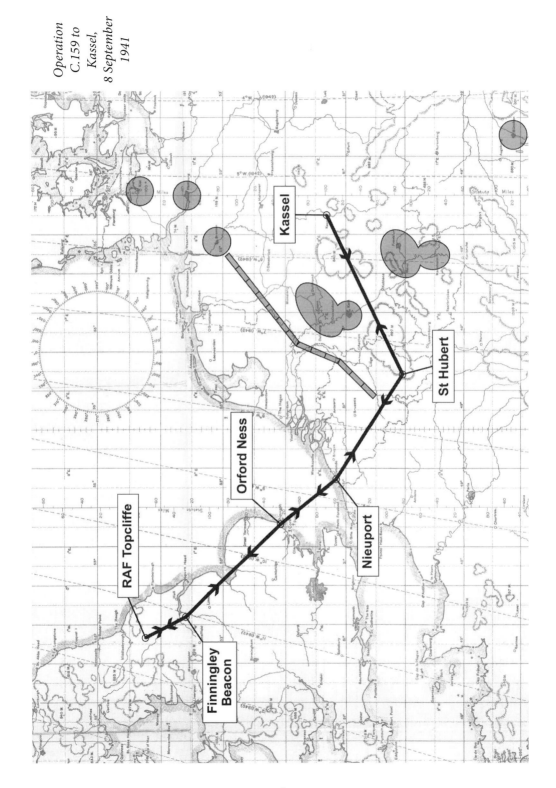

Operation C.159 to Kassel, 8 September 1941

Kassel

St Hubert

Orford Ness

Nieuport

RAF Topcliffe

Finningley Beacon

They lined up fifth out of nine, and after a few minutes' delay at the front took off at 2009 hrs. This was a very long sortie, lasting almost 10 hours, which was bad enough when trying to retain concentration in the cockpit, but doubly difficult in the cold rear turret. This would be the longest sortie that Len would ever undertake.

Whitley Z6959 (DY-Ā)

Kassel.

Takeoff 2009 hrs.

One stick released over primary target from 12,000 ft.

Landed 0559 hrs.

Operational combat time 9 hrs 50 mins.

Sgt R Fisher

Sgt GW McDonald

P/O AD Dobson

Sgt JE Sumpton

Sgt L Starbuck   13th operation; combat time 97 hrs 6 mins

The weather was once again clear over the target, but with fewer searchlights and less flak than the Berlin crews had experienced. Indeed, this turned out to be the less uncomfortable of the two operations, but conversely with more tragic consequences.

Sgt Fisher's was the fifth aircraft to land back at base, and the last to land, four others having landed away. Of these, one had returned early; Sgt EP Pike had been intercepted by a night fighter on the way out but had managed to escape, although the crew's freedom had been bought in no small part by the sacrifice of their air gunner, Sgt Frederick Wrigley. Aborting his sortie, Sgt Pike did not continue to target, but instead returned and put down at RAF Waterbeach in Cambridgeshire, 150 miles nearer than RAF Topcliffe so his air gunner could receive more immediate medical attention. Sadly, this gesture was to be of no consequence for Frederick Wrigley, who had been killed in the action.

Clear skies over Kassel had facilitated accurate bombing; German reports[59] confirmed that serious damage had been caused to a railway works and an optical instrument factory,

Tank production in the Henschel railway locomotive workshops in Kassel (Deutsches Bundesarchiv, Bild 146-1972-064-61 / CC-BY-SA)

in addition to which the main railway station, along with other public buildings, had been damaged, and around 90 houses had been damaged or destroyed.

11 SEPTEMBER 1941

S/Ldr Joseph Reardon had not flown an operational sortie on the squadron since becoming B Flight's commander following the loss of S/Ldr Eric Verdon-Roe on 26 July 1941. On this evening he took up a novice crew on a training flight in Z6870. The aircraft made a bad approach, with flaps and undercarriage down, and attempted to go around but climbed steeply, stalled and crashed, bursting into flames on impact at 2250 hrs. Only two of the five-man crew survived, the navigator suffering serious injuries whilst his air gunner[60] escaped without physical injury.

12 SEPTEMBER 1941

Target[61]	Aircraft on target	Types
Frankfurt:		
(i) Aim point A industrial centre	37	19 Wellington 18 Whitley
(ii) Aim point B railway centre	61	52 Wellington 9 Stirling
(iii) GH577 main railway marshalling yards	32	Hampden
CC16A Cherbourg docks	21	18 Wellington 3 Whitley
Minelaying:		
(i) Frisian Islands (Nectarine)	5	Hampden
(ii) North entrance to the Sound (Nasturtium)	1	Hampden
(iii) Fehmarn Channel (Radish)	1	Hampden
(iv) Travemünde (Hollyhock)	1	Hampden
(v) Great Belt (Broccoli)	1	Hampden
(vi) Great Belt (Asparagus)	1	Hampden

Primary target: Frankfurt (centre of town).
Alternative: S&M.
Last Resort: S&M.
Operation C.160: 12 aircraft, operational call sign Z7D.
Bomb load: No.1 or No.3 TD 0.025. 1× 250 lb GP MLD to be included.
Route: Base – Orford Ness – Nieuport – St-Hubert – Frankfurt and return.
Time Off: 2000 hrs.
Weather: 10/10 cloud over target tops at 8,000 ft.
Opposition: Normal heavy accurate flak. Searchlights ineffective through cloud.

Frankfurt was the next strategic target, and Sgt Fisher would once again be captaining Z6959, with Len as air gunner, on another long sortie. Once more, the crew would be tasked with dropping dockers.

During air test, P/O Harry Williams encountered long yellow flames from both cylinder banks on the starboard engine of his aircraft, Z6562, requiring a hasty last-minute substitution to enable the crew to participate in the night's operation. Sgt Fisher lined up 10th out of 12, and took off at 2010 hrs.

Whitley Z6959 (DY-Ā)

Frankfurt.

Takeoff 2010 hrs.

One stick released over primary target from 11,000 ft.

Landed 0511 hrs.

Operational combat time 9 hrs 1 min.

Sgt R Fisher

P/O lb Renolds

P/O AO Dobson

Sgt JE Sumpton

Sgt L Starbuck   14th operation; combat time 106 hrs 7 mins

That night spelled the end of the clear weather experienced over Germany, and the more familiar cloak of cloud cover returned, providing a measure of protection from searchlights, although the heavy flak still seemed to be as accurate as ever.

Three aircraft reported flak damage, and would be out of service for two to four weeks undergoing repairs, but there were no casualties, and all crews recovered to base, Sgt Fisher landing seventh. This was to be Len's last turn in the rear turret, which would probably have come as a relief to him as his last two air gunner sorties had both been over nine hours long, cramped and cold.

Thick cloud over Frankfurt had hampered targeting; German reports[62] recorded that around 75 HE bombs and 650 incendiaries had fallen jointly on the city and Offenbach, 4 miles to the east. Mainz, 20 miles to the south-west, also reported having been bombed. Aside from the destruction of a workshop in Offenbach, most of the damage had been inflicted on housing.

15 September 1941

Target[63]	Aircraft on target	Types
Hamburg:		
(i) Aim point A West Altona station	44	28 Wellington 10 Whitley 6 Halifax
(ii) Aim point C main railway station	60	52 Wellington 8 Stirling
(iii) Blohm und Voss shipyards	50	Hampden

(continued)

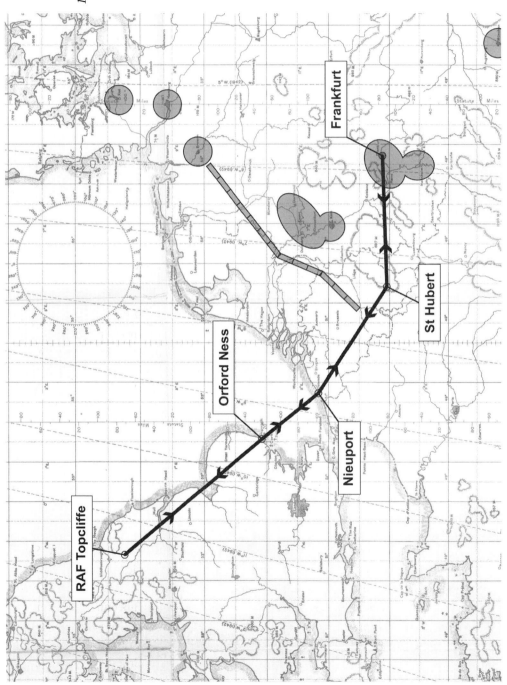

 Operation C.160 to Frankfurt, 12 September 1941

Frankfurt

St Hubert

Orford Ness

Nieuport

RAF Topcliffe

Target	Aircraft on target	Types
(iv) Aim point B East Berliner Tor station	5	Manchester
CC24A Le Havre docks	45	27 Wellington 11 Hampden 6 Whitley 1 Stirling
Minelaying:		
(i) Warnemünde (Jasmine)	3	Hampden
(ii) Fehmarn Channel (Radish)	2	Hampden

NURSERY OPERATION

Primary target: Le Havre (docks and shipping).
Alternative: AIP.
Last Resort: AIP.
Operation C.161: 4 aircraft (freshmen), operational call sign H7V.
Bomb load: No.1 or No.3 TD 0.025.
Route: Base – Sywell – Abingdon – Bognor – Le Havre and return.
Time Off: 1900 hrs.
Weather: Clear over target.
Opposition: Moderate heavy flak north of town some light flak round docks. Searchlights negligible.

On the next nursery operation, four aircraft were detailed to attack Le Havre. The weather had cleared up over the target, providing not only perfect bombing conditions for the inexperienced crews but also perfect visibility for anti-aircraft defences. The defenders had responded to the attack with moderate heavy flak, but all crews returned without incident within a half-hour of each other. Clear skies contributed to accurate bombing; local reports[64] confirmed that the harbour had been hit, but a number of the freshman crews had started fires in the town.

16 SEPTEMBER 1941

On this date, an air gunner with dark hair and brown eyes by the name of Ernest Ralph Taxeira de Mattos joined 102 Squadron from 10 OTU. He had come to Britain from British Malaya, and his background was unique.

Ernest Ralph was the son of Ernest Norman Taxeira de Mattos,[65] described variously as a merchant and a banker. He and his family were British, and resided in Penang, in the Straits Settlements, which formed part of British Malaya. The region was rich in natural resources, especially tin, rubber and timber. It was also of paramount strategic significance, in that it was located on the Malacca Straits, the most important sea lane connecting the Pacific and Indian Oceans.

Against the backdrop of revolutionary unrest spreading across the region during the 1920s and the Japanese refusal to renew the Anglo-Japanese Alliance, Ernest Norman took his family, comprising his wife Janet Louisa, their son Ernest Ralph, who was 4½ years old, and their daughter Yolanda Ottzen, who was 1½, to Britain, arriving on 1 July 1924. Four months later, Ernest Norman sailed home to British Malaya alone, and ten months after that Janet followed with the children.

Six years after their reunion in Malaya, Ernest Norman made a second visit to Britain, arriving on 10 August 1931. As many observers had predicted, Japan started flexing her military might against the disarrayed Chinese, and invaded Manchuria in September 1931 – only one month after Ernest Norman had arrived back in Britain.

On 24 February 1933 Japan withdrew from the singularly impotent League of Nations, swearing never to rejoin it, and prepared for full-scale invasion of China. With the advent of war with Japan now being a question of *when* rather than *if*, the natural assets that had once provided British Malaya with prosperity now became a prize for the taking by the increasingly avaricious and unchecked Japanese army. Recognising the dangerous situation confronting their homeland, Janet sold up and set off with the children to join their father and make a new life together in the relative stability of Britain, arriving on 3 April 1933.

Ernest Ralph settled into life in Great Britain and took up work as a motor fitter, but volunteered for service in the RAF as soon as war broke out. He enlisted on 16 September 1939, with a recommendation for training as an air gunner. His first posting was to No.3 Depot RAF Padgate in Lancashire, and two weeks later he was transferred to No.2 Wing RAF Padgate. Following four weeks of basic training, he was posted to No.7 AOS at RAF Stormy Down for a gunnery course, starting on 27 October 1939. During his two months there, Ernest would have come to grips with all the different guns in service with Bomber Command at that time, most notably the Browning Mk.II, the Vickers Armstrong K GO pan-fed machine gun and even the obsolescent Lewis gun.

Before completion of this course, Ernest was posted to No.3 Wing RAF Cosford in Shropshire on 1 February 1940, to learn about the Bristol Hercules and the Bristol Pegasus aero-engines. He took his fitter's exam on 7 June 1940, which he passed at 82 per cent, earning promotion to leading aircraftsman. With that very convincing pass mark, Ernest was next posted to the Aeroplane and Armament Experimental Establishment (A&AEE) Boscombe Down, where a very special assignment awaited him: L7605, the sole surviving prototype Short S.29 Stirling. This aircraft had first flown on 3 December 1939 and during the spring of 1940 had been transferred to A&AEE, where she was to spend a total of four months before, in August 1940, the first production Stirlings were to be delivered into RAF service. This radical new aircraft was powered by four Bristol Hercules engines of the type on which Ernest had freshly qualified. He provided support to this project, earning flying pay between October 1940 and April 1941; there is also evidence to suggest that during this time he had become familiar not only with the engines but also the Stirling's guns and turrets.

As his time at A&AEE drew to a close on 25 June 1941, Ernest was once again recommended for training as an air gunner, and his next posting on 5 July 1941 was to No.33 Air Gunner course at No.10 B&GS at RAF Dumfries in Dumfriesshire, which he passed at an astonishing 87.73 per cent. A skilled engine fitter and now a high-scoring air gunner, Ernest was next posted to 10 OTU as an air gunner[66] on 2 August 1941, from where he received his first posting to an operational squadron, with effect from 16 September 1941. Upon his arrival to 102 Squadron, Ernest was assigned to A Flight.

20 SEPTEMBER 1941

Target[67]	Aircraft on target	Types
Berlin:		
(i) Aim point B Alexanderplatz	46	26 Hampden 18 Whitley 2 Halifax
(ii) GU3897 Reichsluftfahrtministerium (Air Ministry)	31	Wellington
Frankfurt aim point A industrial centre	34	22 Wellington 12 Hampden
CC13A Ostend	28	17 Wellington 13 Whitley 4 Hampden

Primary target: Berlin (Alexanderplatz railway station).
Alternative: S&M.
Last Resort: S&M.
Operation C.162: 7 aircraft, operational call sign G9H.
Bomb load: No.1 or No.3 (preferably No.3) TD 0.025. 1× 250 lb GP MLD to be included.
Route: Base – Scarborough – Hooge – Fehmarn – Berlin and return.
Time Off: 1900 hrs.
Weather: 9/10 cloud.
Opposition: Slight except in vicinity of Rostock.

Len had been overlooked for the squadron's last trip to Berlin two weeks earlier, but tonight his time had come. Further, he was to be making the run as part of a six-man crew with whom he had only cursory experience, having flown only once with the pilot, Sgt Wilson, and once with the navigator, Richard Bradbury, who had been promoted to F/Sgt since his last operational sortie.

Not only was Len to be brought in from the cold of the rear turret for this 10-hour operation to resume duties at the wireless, but for the first time was to have the responsibility for a 2nd WOp. Canadian P/O Arthur Graham had flown four operations as air gunner and was now to be given his first taste of working the wireless under combat conditions. This would mean that if the front turret had to be manned, Len's place, for the first time, would be to stay at the wireless whilst others did the fighting.

Unfortunately the crew was one of two on the operation to be issued with a camera to record their bomb strikes, a task which would keep them in harm's way over the target area for much longer.

Sgt Wilson led the other crews out, taking off exactly on time at 1900 hrs. All was routine until they received a recall message at 2230 hrs, which had been issued due to deteriorating weather. The timing of the recall message was important, in that they had not yet crossed over the Kammhuber Line and could seek a target of opportunity that did not involve running the gauntlet of the focused German air defences.

The target they chose was the railway junction at Husum, near Schleswig, which they attacked, reporting only slight opposition. Husum-Narrenthal was a major enemy aerodrome, and to service the high demand for fuel and ammunition it had been provided with a dedicated railway spur. Possibly with this in mind, Sgt Wilson elected not to bomb the aerodrome but instead to inflict, possibly more significantly, greater disruption to enemy operations by bombing the railway junction.

Whitley Z6949 (DY-Ū)

Berlin.

Takeoff 1900 hrs.

All aircraft recalled 2230 hrs.

One stick released over Husum from 10,000 ft.

Landed 0236 hrs.

Operational combat time 7 hrs 36 mins.

Sgt WJ Wilson

P/O JM Hartley

F/Sgt[68] RF Bradbury   3rd operation; combat time 21 hrs 10 mins

P/O AJ Graham

Sgt L Starbuck   15th operation; combat time 113 hrs 43 mins

Sgt WA Gillies

First out was first back, and Sgt Wilson landed at least an hour before any of the other crews. Owing to the recall notice, his colleagues had struck at a variety of targets of opportunity, and thus their return times were more widely spread than usual. A mixture of one- and two-stick concentrations had been dropped on a variety of secondary targets, popular amongst which was the shipyard at the Baltic port of Flensburg.

Sgt Sidney Tackley was wounded on his run into Flensburg, and Sgt George McDonald, on his sixth operation as 2nd pilot, immediately took over the controls to continue the attack, following which he flew the 4½-hour return flight home, making his landing at RAF Topcliffe an hour and a half after Sgt Wilson.

One of the most spectacular stories came from Sgt K Clack, who had chosen to take a look at Schwerin aerodrome. He dropped a stick that happened to fall at just the same time as an enemy aircraft was landing. In response, the aerodrome lights were reported as having been 'extinguished immediately', giving the German crew a landing that they would remember for a long time.

Operation
C.162 to
Berlin,
20 September
1941

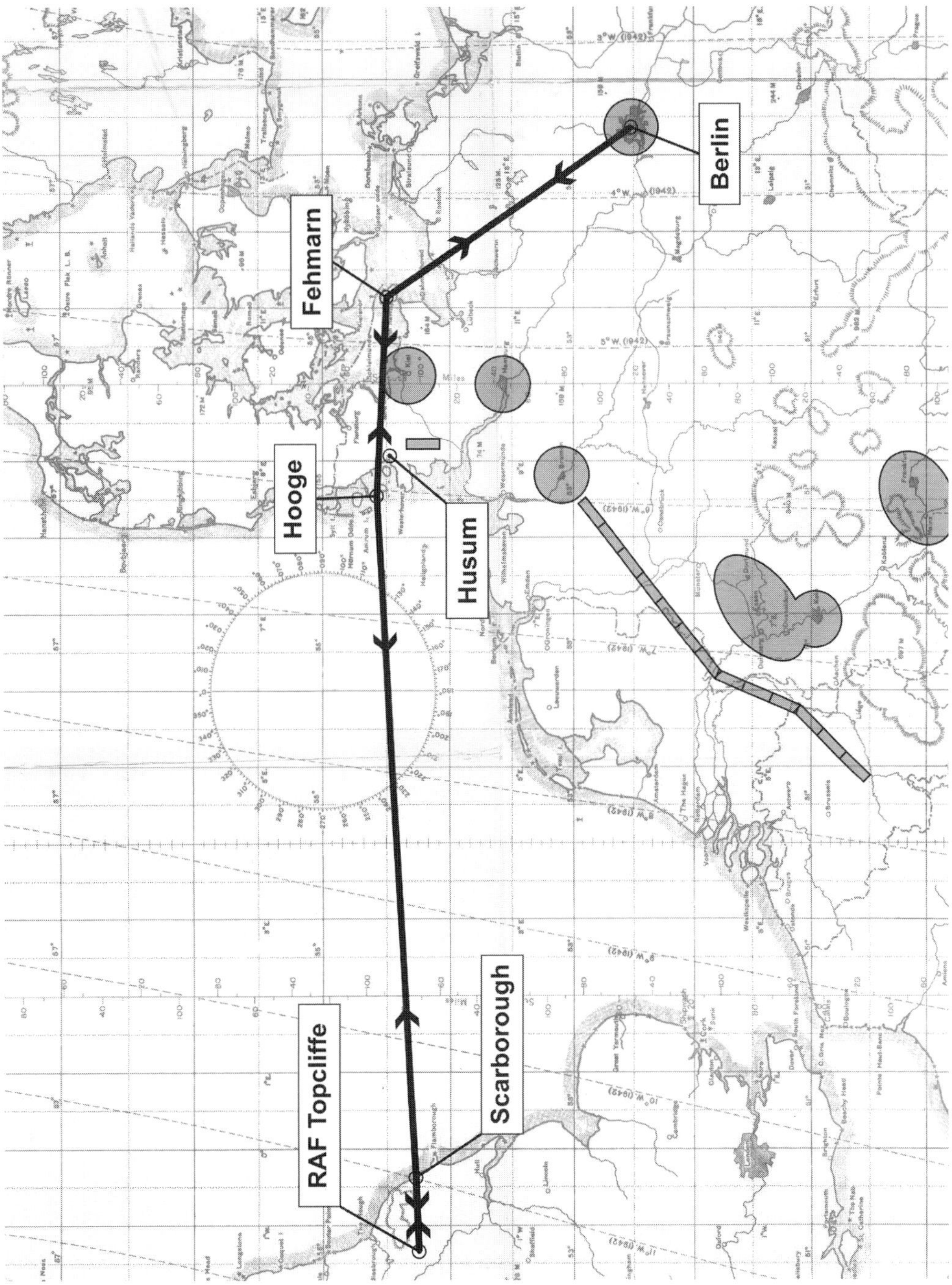

Bahnhof Alexanderplatz, Berlin (F. Albert Schwartz / public domain)

With 15 operations successfully completed, Len was halfway through his tour. Further, as the sorties he had been on were generally long, he had accrued 113 hours towards his objective of 200 hours. Better still, if he kept on building hours at this rate, he would complete his 200 hours after 27 operations, three less than he might have otherwise had to do.

This was an appropriate juncture for Len to stand down from flying for one month. He had experienced much since joining the squadron only 10 weeks earlier. During this time, he had seen faces come and go, and had quickly transitioned to be one of the seasoned old hands. He would take the opportunity of this month away to see his family again, always in the back of his mind was whether he would ever have the chance to see them again; how far could he continue to push his luck?

Endnotes

40 AIR 14/2673

41 Annex B

42 Goss, C. (1995) *It's Suicide but It's Fun: The Story of 102 (Ceylon) Squadron 1917–1956*, ISBN 0947554599, Crécy, pp 57–58.

43 AIR 14/2673

44 AIR 14/1218

45 AIR 14/2673

46 Middlebrook, M. and Everitt, C. (1990) *The Bomber Command War Diaries: An Operational Reference Book 1939–1945*, ISBN 0140129367, Penguin, p 196.

47 AIR 14/2673

48 AIR 14/2673

49 Middlebrook, M. and Everitt, C. (1990) *The Bomber Command War Diaries: An Operational Reference Book 1939–1945*, ISBN 0140129367, Penguin, p 197.

50 AIR 14/2673

51 Middlebrook, M. and Everitt, C. (1990) *The Bomber Command War Diaries: An Operational Reference Book 1939–1945*, ISBN 0140129367, Penguin, p 199.

52 AIR 14/2673

53 AIR 14/2673

54 This operation is frequently mistaken for being to the actual town of Hüls. The synthetic rubber producer, Hüls AG, was based in Marl which was the target for this operation. This can be confirmed by reference to 77 Squadron ORB; Whitley Z6956 reported having 'attacked a small town believed to be Horstman [Horstmar] about 25 miles north of the target'. Horstmar is 30 miles north of Marl, but 60 miles north-east of the town of Hüls.

55 Moonrise over York (nearest datum point to RAF Topcliffe) 1900 + 1 hour correction for BST.

56 AIR 14/2673

57 Middlebrook, M. and Everitt, C. (1990) *The Bomber Command War Diaries: An Operational Reference Book 1939–1945*, ISBN 0140129367, Penguin, p 200.

58 AIR 14/2673

59 Middlebrook, M. and Everitt, C. (1990) *The Bomber Command War Diaries: An Operational Reference Book 1939–1945*, ISBN 0140129367, Penguin, p 201.

60 Possibly Sgt Frampton

61 AIR 14/2673

62 Middlebrook, M. and Everitt, C. (1990) *The Bomber Command War Diaries: An Operational Reference Book 1939–1945*, ISBN 0140129367, Penguin, p 202.

63 AIR 14/2673

64 Middlebrook, M. and Everitt, C. (1990) *The Bomber Command War Diaries: An Operational Reference Book 1939–1945*, ISBN 0140129367, Penguin, p 203.

65 The full surname 'Taxeira de Mattos' is taken from the Commonwealth War Graves Commission (CWGC). For registering on shipping passenger lists, the family would remove the 'de Mattos' suffix for simplicity; further, Ernest Norman would always spell it 'Taxiera', whilst Janet would either spell it 'Taxeira' or even 'Teixeira'. The Squadron ORB lists his name as 'ER DeMattos' during Whitley operations in 1941 and then 'ERT De Mattos' during Halifax operations in 1942.

66 Not a WOp/AG, but a single discipline air gunner.

67 AIR 14/2673

68 Richard Bradbury had been promoted to F/Sgt on 1 September 1941. The ORB would continue to reflect incorrectly his rank as Sgt until 31 January 1942.

4

TIREDNESS: THE ENEMY WITHIN

26 September 1941

Target[69]	Aircraft on target	Types
Cologne:		
(i) Aim point B East Kalk railway station	14	Wellington
(ii) Aim point C Köln West main station	21	13 Wellington 8 Stirling
Genoa: Aim points A and B industrial centres to east and west of city	34	Wellington
Emden	18	16 Wellington 2 Stirling
Mannheim aim point D main railway station	17	Whitley

Primary target: Mannheim (railway station).
Alternative: S&M.
Last Resort: S&M.
Operation C.163: 6 aircraft, operational call sign YY9.
Bomb load: No.1 or No.3 TD 0.025.
Route: Base – Finningley – Orford Ness – Gravelines – Mannheim and return.
Time Off: 1830 hrs.
Diversion, aircraft will land at RAF Oakington.
Weather: 2/10 to 3/10 cloud, haze.
Opposition: n/a

Amongst the six crews selected for the operation to Mannheim was new arrival Sgt Ernest de Mattos, who was appointed to F/Lt George Davies. They lined up second and took off as planned, but all were recalled at 2030 hrs, two hours after getting airborne, due to worsening weather. Five of the six aircraft brought their bombs back and diverted to other aerodromes; meanwhile Davies, along with two other crews, landed away at RAF Oakington in Cambridgeshire as directed.

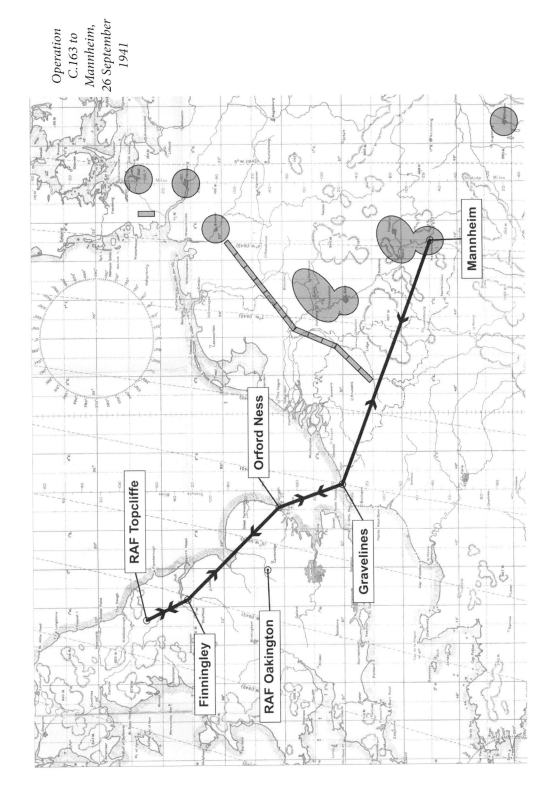

Operation
C.163 to
Mannheim,
26 September
1941

Mannheim

Orford Ness

RAF Topcliffe

Gravelines

Finningley

RAF Oakington

The only one of the six to do anything different was Z6749, captained by P/O William Welch with Australian S/Ldr Grant Lindeman as his 2nd pilot. They had found a way to attack Calais docks during their return journey, and were also the only crew to brave a landing at RAF Topcliffe.

Whitley Z6747 (DY-Q)

Mannheim.

Takeoff 1834 hrs.

Brought bombs back.

Landed 2229 hrs.

Operational combat time 3 hrs 55 mins.

F/Lt GG Davies

Sgt JW Ralston

Sgt FH Mylrea

Sgt K O'Connelley

Sgt CW Griffin

Sgt ER DeMattos   1st operation; combat time 3 hrs 55 mins

29 SEPTEMBER 1941

Target[70]	Aircraft on target	Types
Stettin:		
(i) Aim point A main railway station	73	56 Whitley 11 Wellington 6 Halifax
(ii) Aim point B	48	38 Wellington 10 Stirling
(iii) Aim point C	18	Wellington
Hamburg:		
(i) Aim point A West Altona station	23	14 Wellington 7 Whitley 2 Halifax
(ii) Aim point C main railway station	20	Wellington
(iii) GY4761 Osthalle; Blohm und Voss subsidiary aircraft factory	42	38 Hampden 4 Manchester
(iv) GR3587 Blohm und Voss shipbuilding yards	10	Hampden
CC24A Le Havre inner docks	6	5 Wellington 1 Stirling
CC16 Cherbourg	3	Whitley
Minelaying off Swinemünde (Geranium)	5	Manchester

MAIN OPERATION

Primary target: Stettin (railway station).
Alternative: S&M.
Last Resort: S&M.
Operation C.164: 10 aircraft, operational call sign B6M.
Bomb load: No.1 or No.3 TD 0.025. 1× 250 lb GP MLD to be included.
Route: Base – Scarborough – Amrum – Fehmarn – Darβ – Stettin and return.
Time Off: 1845 hrs.
Weather: Clear with ground haze.
Opposition: Moderate heavy flak. Searchlights few and ineffective.

NURSERY OPERATION

Primary target: Le Havre (shipping and docks).
Alternative: AIP.
Last Resort: AIP.
Operation C.165: 3 aircraft (freshmen), operational call sign B6M.
Bomb load: No.1 or No.3 TD 0.025.
Route: Base – Sywell – Abingdon – Bognor – Le Havre and return.
Time Off: 2330 hrs.
Weather: Clear over target deteriorating.
Opposition: Moderate heavy flak, few searchlights.

The railway station at Stettin was strategically important to supplying Wehrmacht forces during their invasion of Russia. However, this target lay east of Berlin, in the Prussian province of Pomerania, and promised a very long night ahead for the ten crews chosen to mount the attack. Given the duration of this operation, all ten were carrying a 2nd WOp – and 2nd pilots were equally in demand, but only nine were available; one captain was going to have to fly the entire sortie without relief.

Sgt Ernest de Mattos would be in action again, this time as part of P/O Vannio Albrecht's crew. Also in the air was F/Sgt Richard Bradbury, flying with Sgt WJ Wilson, the one captain who would have no 2nd pilot to support him on this long operation.

Three further aircraft were detailed to Le Havre on another nursery operation, but they would not be leaving until three hours after the Stettin crews had gone. These aircraft would all have dangerously inexperienced crews supporting novice captains, the only appreciable experience on any of the crews being provided by the WOps. Sadly, inexperience would prove telling as the night wore on and the weather closed in, causing all aircraft returning between 0107 hrs and 0533 hrs to be diverted to land away. This would prove too much of a challenge for two of the three freshman crews, with disastrous results.

Whitley Z6875 (DY-P)

Stettin.
Takeoff 1849 hrs.
One stick released over primary target from 11,000 ft.
Landed 0525 hrs at RAF Acklington.

Operational combat time 10 hrs 36 mins.

P/O VM Albrecht

Sgt CR Barr

Sgt JV Kirkwood

Sgt AM McLaren

Sgt K O'Connelly

Sgt ER DeMattos   2nd operation; combat time 14 hrs 31 mins

Whitley Z6494[71] (DY-R)

Stettin.

Takeoff 1845 hrs.

One stick released over primary target from 12,000 ft.

Overshot and crashed on landing at 0457 hrs.

Operational combat time 10 hrs 12 mins.

Sgt WJ Wilson

F/Sgt RF Bradbury   4th operation; combat time 31 hrs 22 mins

Sgt RC Perriam

Sgt JA Steeves

Sgt A Huddlestone

The Stettin operation started well, nine of the ten aircraft despatched making successful bombing runs as ordered. However, Sgt Clack's aircraft developed engine trouble, so he looked for a target of opportunity. As luck would have it, the turning point at Amrum was only 3 miles away from the island of Sylt, which was of strategic importance to the Luftwaffe, thus presenting itself as a most opportune secondary target. At this time there were three seaplane bases on this very narrow 24-mile-long island: List at the northern end, and Hörnum and Rantum at the southern. However, by far the most active base in the region was Westerland, equipped with three paved runways and situated in the middle of the island; at that time it was home to a number of flying units, presenting a prize for any bomber seeking a target of opportunity.

This was the second time in just over a week that Sgt Clack and his crew had found a valuable target of opportunity at short notice and pressed home an attack. However, aside from their inspired improvisation, things subsequently started to unravel for the crews returning from Stettin and Le Havre:

0355 hrs: P/O David Delaney in Z6871 (Stettin) is reported as having fallen asleep at the controls over the North Yorks Moors. He had recognised the nature of the terrain over which he was flying and initially climbed to 2,000 ft to provide a safe clearance over the highest ground in the area, which was Danby High Moor / Loose Howe at 1,417 ft above sea level. However, he had then drifted downwards, eventually impacting the top of a hill in the vicinity of Danby Head. The aircraft is reported as having bounced and then slid to a halt, during which 2nd Pilot

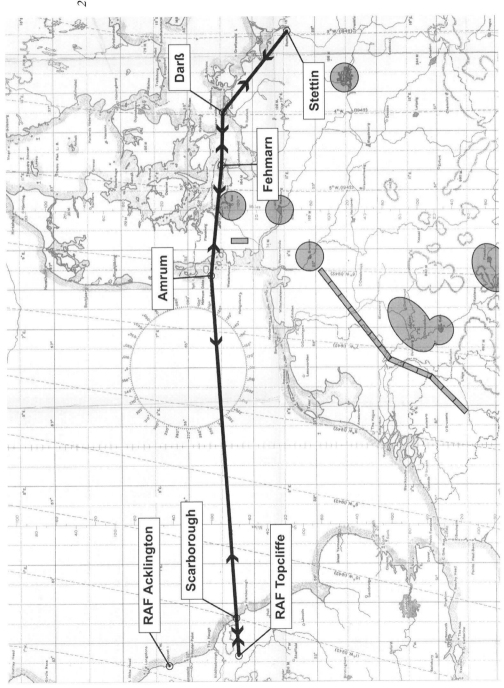

Operation
C.164 to
Stettin,
29 September
1941

Darß

Stettin

Fehmarn

Amrum

RAF Acklington

Scarborough

RAF Topcliffe

Stettin (Deutsches Bundesarchiv, Bild 196-02553 / CC-BY-SA)

Sgt Donald Kibbe, an American on his first operation, was killed and his body thrown clear. There was no fire, and the surviving crew escaped; David Delaney suffered a minor cut, whilst both WOps were more seriously injured. Because of the remoteness of the crash site it was not until late the next afternoon that the survivors arrived back at base, only to find that their lockers had already been cleared out by the 'vultures' in the belief that they would not be returning. The accident report went on to comment that as there were two pilots the captain should not have been tired.

0406 hrs: Sgt Reginald Matthews in Z6945 (Le Havre) overshot on landing at RAF Abingdon and swung to avoid obstacles in his path, causing the undercarriage to collapse. This aircraft was seriously damaged and would be undergoing repairs for months.

0457 hrs: Sgt Wilson in Z6494 (Stettin) crashed on landing at RAF Topcliffe in poor visibility. It was quite possible that the weather was starting to clear, but evidence shows that it wasn't until half an hour later, at 0533 hrs, that the first of two successful landings took place. Sgt Wilson had already been flying unaided for over ten hours due to unavailability of a 2nd pilot, and at the end of such a gruelling sortie found that he was unable to shut the throttle to the port engine on landing and was unable to go around, so overshot. This aircraft would be in for repairs for months to come.

0500 hrs: Sgt Pike in Z6935 (Stettin) ran out of fuel and ditched close to the Yorkshire coast, from where the crew were able to wade ashore; this was another aircraft beyond repair.

0500 hrs: P/O Lindsay Renolds in Z6949 (Le Havre) undershot and stalled attempting to land at RAF Upper Heyford in Oxfordshire. The aircraft crashed on approach and caught fire, resulting in injuries to all crewmen.

Of the thirteen aircraft the squadron had ordered to operations, three were struck off charge and two more were put in for major repairs in addition to which a number of crewmen suffered injuries or fatalities. Only four of the thirteen aircraft recovered to base, and one of those crashed. This was without doubt a catastrophic night for the squadron.

Given the disasters befalling so many of the other crews, Sgt Ernest de Mattos fared well, as Vannio Albrecht recovered without incident to RAF Acklington, whilst F/Sgt Richard Bradbury had a much less pleasant landing with Sgt Wilson, who had overshot and crashed at RAF Topcliffe.

1 October 1941

Target[72]	Aircraft on target	Types
Karlsruhe	45	44 Hampden 1 Wellington
Stuttgart	31	27 Whitley 4 Wellington
CC29A Boulogne dock area	7	4 Wellington 3 Whitley
Minelaying off the Frisian Islands (Nectarine)	2	Hampden

Main Operation

Primary target: Stuttgart (post office).
Alternative: S&M.
Last Resort: S&M.
Operation C.166: 5 aircraft, operational call sign XJ6.
Bomb load: No.1 or No.3 TD 0.025. 1× 250 lb GP MLD to be included.
Route: Base – Finningley – Orford Ness – Gravelines – Stuttgart and return.
Time Off: 1850 hrs.
Weather: 10/10 cloud over all.
Opposition: Nil.

Nursery Operation

Primary target: Boulogne (docks and shipping).
Alternative: AIP.
Last Resort: AIP.
Operation C.167: 1 aircraft (freshman), operational call sign FS7.
Bomb load: No.1 or No.3 TD 0.025.
Route: Base – Finningley – Orford Ness – Boulogne and return.
Time Off: 1845 hrs.
Weather: 10/10 cloud over whole area.
Opposition: Nil.

Once again a deep strike operation would be accompanied by a nursery run. On the last nursery operation, two of the three aircraft had crash-landed due to piloting errors precipitated by a combination of inexperienced crews, bad weather and landing at unknown aerodromes. For this next nursery operation, the qualifying captain had been allocated a 2nd pilot with a degree of experience behind him, helping to improve the odds.

Freshman Sgt Charles Anderson left 5 minutes before the five Stuttgart crews lined up behind him, the first of whom was P/O Vannio Albrecht, who retained Sgt Ernest de Mattos on his crew. He was not destined to be out for long, experiencing icing problems and returning early. The remaining Stuttgart crews encountered difficulties with the heavy cloud over the target. Of note was P/O William Welch, who had taken a route that passed

Operation C.166 to Stuttgart, 1 October 1941

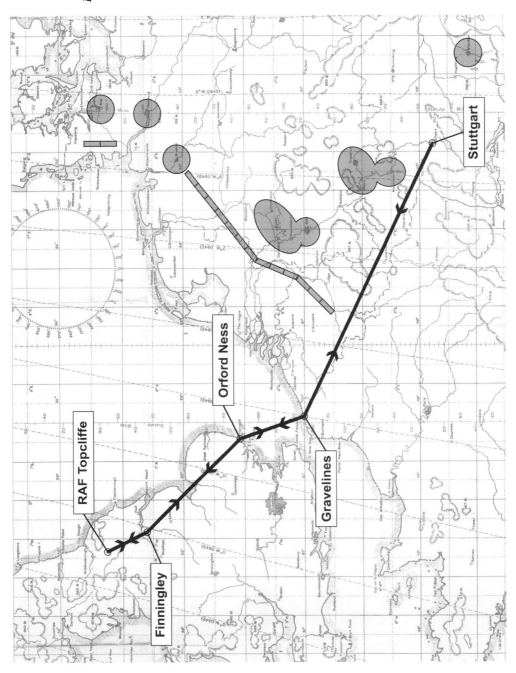

Stuttgart

Orford Ness

Gravelines

RAF Topcliffe

Finningley

over Geluwe in occupied Belgium immediately next to the French border, and dropped one of his 500 lb bombs on it before flying on. The nearest aerodrome to Geluwe was Wevelgem-Wezelhoek, the decoy airfield protecting Wevelgem-Bissegem, 2½ miles to the ENE, an aerodrome last attacked on behalf of the squadron by P/O DN Sampson, on 20/21 July 1941.

Meanwhile, the nursery operation was not a success either, as cloud also obscured the target, and the crew brought their bombs back. Then in an ominous rerun of the previous sorties two nights ago, the weather again closed in at RAF Topcliffe and the nursery crew was ordered to land away, but fortunately this time they were able to recover safely to RAF Linton-on-Ouse. By the time the four remaining Stuttgart crews began to arrive they all landed at their home base suggesting that the weather had improved.

Whitley Z6875 (DY-P)

Stuttgart.
Takeoff 1850 hrs.
Brought bombs back.
Landed 2359 hrs.
Operational combat time 5 hrs 9 mins.
P/O VM Albrecht
S/Ldr GM Lindeman
Sgt JV Kirkwood
Sgt AM McLaren
Sgt L Williams
Sgt ER DeMattos   3rd operation; combat time 19 hrs 40 mins

Thick cloud over Stuttgart had compromised targeting; German reports[73] recorded that the nearest the city had got to being hit was one load of bombs falling in nearby woods.

9 OCTOBER 1941

In preparation for a forthcoming long-distance operation, P/O Bruce Roy took the newly delivered Z9134 on an air test to acquaint himself with the aircraft's handling with extra tanks. During the sortie, he opened the throttles on go-around and climbed steeply, encountering a trim problem that resulted in a crash-landing. The problem had been brought about by the weight of the extra tanks taking the trim requirements beyond the range of the trim tabs. In future, flying in this configuration would require the provision of further trim adjustment; an expensive lesson had just been learned.

10 OCTOBER 1941

Target[74]	Aircraft on target	Types
Ruhr Valley:		
(i) GN3814 Essen; Friedrich Krupp AG works	83	46 Hampden 17 Whitley 10 Manchester 5 Halifax 5 Wellington
(ii) Cologne (railway targets)	69	63 Wellington 6 Stirling
(iii) Searchlight suppression in the Ruhr	6	Hampden
CC25 Dunkirk docks	23	Hampden
CC13 Ostend docks	22	18 Wellington 4 Whitley
Bordeaux:		
(i) Bassens port area	11	Wellington
(ii) Z420 Gare St-Jean railway marshalling yards	11	Wellington
CC42 Rotterdam docks	13	Wellington

NURSERY OPERATION

Primary target: Ostend (docks and shipping).
Alternative: AIP.
Last Resort: AIP.
Operation C.168: 3 aircraft (freshmen), operational call sign R9R.
Bomb load: No.3 TD 0.025.
Route: Base – Finningley – Orford Ness – Ostend and return.
Time Off: 1825 hrs.
Weather: Thick haze, patches of low cloud.
Opposition: Spasmodic heavy and light flak at intervals along coast. A few searchlight concentrations, did not hold aircraft.

Three more 2nd pilots were ready for their nursery operations, this time to Ostend. The visibility over the target was not good, and none of the crews was confident that they had found it even when they released their bombs. As a direct result the sorties could not be classed as successful, and so the novice captains would all have to conduct their freshman operations again.

12 OCTOBER 1941

Target[75]	Aircraft on target	Types
Nürnberg:		
(i) Nürnberg	85	78 Wellington 7 Stirling
(ii) GB3208 Siemens-Schuckert factory	67	54 Whitley 9 Halifax 4 Wellington

Target	Aircraft on target	Types
Bremen:		
(i) Bremen	79	72 Wellington 6 Whitley 1 Halifax
(ii) GR3586 Deschimag shipyards	20	Hampden
Ruhr Valley:		
(i) Marl; GS162 Hüls chemical factory	90	79 Hampden 11 Manchester
(ii) Searchlight suppression in the Ruhr	8	Hampden
CC29 Boulogne	24	23 Wellington 1 Whitley

Main Operation

Primary target: Nürnberg (engineering works).
Alternative: S&M.
Last Resort: S&M.
Operation C.169: 13 aircraft, operational call sign 6YU.
Bomb load: No.1 or No.3 TD 0.025. 1× 250 lb GP MLD to be included where applicable.
Route: Base – Orford Ness – Nieuport – Valenciennes – Nürnberg and return.
Time Off: 1840 hrs.
Weather: No cloud ground haze and smoke over target.
Opposition: Negligible over target.

Nursery Operation

Primary target: Boulogne (docks and shipping).
Alternative: AIP.
Last Resort: AIP.
Operation C.170: 2 aircraft (freshmen), operational call sign 8KO.
Bomb load: No.1 or No.3 TD 0.025.
Route: Base – Orford Ness – Boulogne and return.
Time Off: 1815 hrs.
Weather: Clear.
Opposition: Moderate heavy flak and active searchlight concentrations around town.

The main operation for the squadron tonight was another deep strike, this time to the heart of Bavaria. Their target was the Siemens-Schuckert electrical engineering works, which built aero-engines, especially the Bramo 323 that was fitted in a number of front-line aircraft, including the Do 17 and Fw 200. There was also an opportunity simultaneously to rerun the nursery operation of two nights earlier with two of the three freshman captains.

Amongst the Nürnberg crews were P/O Vannio Albrecht, who once more retained Sgt Ernest de Mattos, and Sgt Derrick Riley, who introduced F/Sgt Richard Bradbury onto his crew.

Whitley Z6973 (DY- B̄)

Nürnberg.
Takeoff 1844 hrs.

One stick released over primary target from 7,500 ft.

Landed 0516 hrs at RAF Swanton Morley.

Operational combat time 10 hrs 32 mins.

Sgt DN Riley

Sgt WG Caldwell

F/Sgt RF Bradbury   5th operation; combat time 41 hrs 54 mins

Sgt NW Haycock

P/O AJ Graham

Sgt D Boddy

Whitley Z6875 (DY-P)

Nürnberg.

Takeoff 1845 hrs.

One stick released possibly over Mainz from 12,000 ft.

Landed 0445 hrs at RAF Horsham St Faith.

Operational combat time 10 hrs 0 mins.

P/O VM Albrecht

Sgt EG Newell

Sgt JV Kirkwood

Sgt TB Nisbet

Sgt K O'Connelley

Sgt ER DeMattos   4th operation; combat time 29 hrs 40 mins

Firstly, it was the turn of the two freshman crews to get away, but one did not start, leaving Sgt Larry Carr to lead a solitary attack on Boulogne through clear skies with a dangerously inexperienced crew. They got lost on their return journey and could not find RAF Topcliffe, but recovered instead to RAF Leeming, where they made a heavy landing which burst the starboard tyre, followed by the undercarriage collapsing. This sortie was however sufficient to qualify Larry Carr, who was now accepted as a captain. 42 Maintenance Unit (MU) would get to work on this damaged aircraft and complete repairs inside the month.

One of the crews on the Nürnberg run did not start and another returned early, but 11 others proceeded to attack the target. None of the aircraft that pressed home their attack returned to base, all recovering to a scattering of secondary bases; Derrick Riley went to RAF Swanton Morley in Norfolk after attacking the primary target, whilst Vannio Albrecht landed at RAF Horsham St Faith in Norfolk, having attacked Mainz.

Whilst all the crews took in their alien surroundings, none would have been aware of the fate of their colleagues. All had returned, but Sgt John Stell had run out of fuel near Market Deeping at 0513 hrs. He ordered his crew to bale out and then remained aboard Z6761 to attempt a landing, but came in too fast, with undercarriage and flaps up. All of his crew landed safely except for his WOp Sgt Miller, who suffered a minor injury on landing

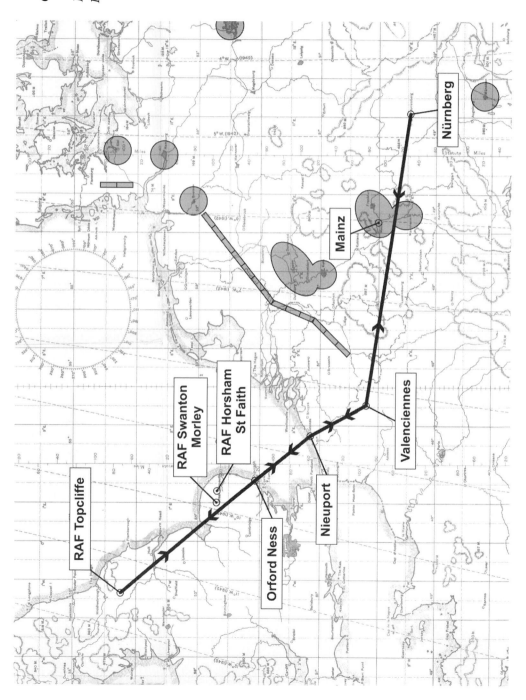

Operation C.169 to Nürnberg, 12 October 1941

heavily. The accident report blamed faulty navigation for having allowed the engines to run out of fuel.

Although clear skies over Nürnberg should have assisted with accurate targeting, this was not the case; German reports[76] recorded that only a few bombs had landed on the city. Instead, the force of the night's offensive had been directed onto housing in outlying towns and villages:

- Schwabach: 10 miles south of Nürnberg,
- Lauingen: 65 miles south-west of Nürnberg,
- Lauffen am Neckar: 90 miles west of Nürnberg.

Whilst the courage of the crews embarking on this operation could not be questioned, their sacrifice had once again been compromised by the inadequacy of the navigational technology available to them.

16 OCTOBER 1941

Target[77]	Aircraft on target	Types
Duisburg:		
(i) Duisburg	87	47 Wellington 26 Hampden 14 Whitley
(ii) Searchlight suppression 15 miles northeast of Bocholt	5	Hampden
CC25 Dunkirk docks	22	19 Wellington 3 Hampden
CC13 Ostend docks	15	Whitley

Primary target: Duisburg (railway station).
Alternative: S&M.
Last Resort: S&M.
Operation C.171: 14 aircraft, operational call sign PN8 (including 2 freshmen).
Bomb load: No.1 or No.3 TD 0.025. 1× 250 lb GP MLD to be included where applicable.
Route: Base – Flamborough – Dutch coast between Zandvoort and Katwijk – Duisburg and return.
Time Off: 0030 hrs.[78]
Weather: 10/10 cloud over Ruhr.
Opposition: Moderate heavy flak predicted through cloud. Searchlights ineffective.

The squadron was called upon to provide 14 aircraft to attack Duisburg, a city with a large industrial area fed by a main railway station only a mile away from its harbour, at that time the largest inland harbour in the world.

The crews chosen to fly included two 2nd pilots frustrated in their previous attempt to qualify as captains following the unsuccessful nursery operation of 10 October. Flying with experienced captains were F/Sgt Richard Bradbury and Sgt Ernest de Mattos, who were retained by Sgt Derrick Riley and P/O Vannio Albrecht respectively, as in their previous operation.

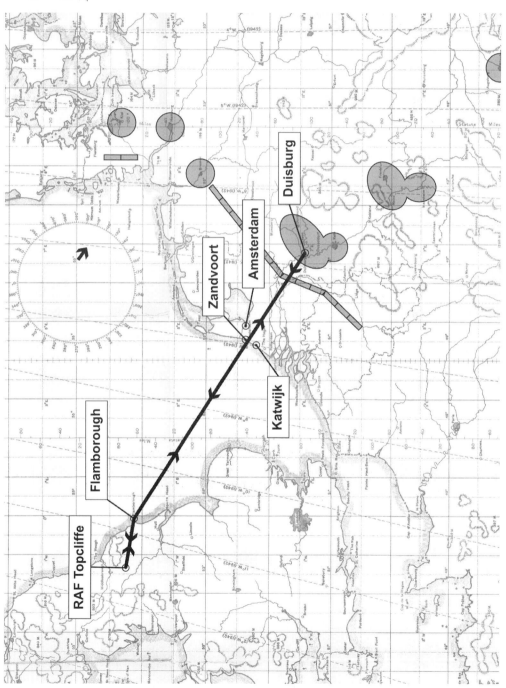

Operation C.171 to Duisburg, 16 October 1941

Duisburg

Amsterdam

Zandvoort

Katwijk

Flamborough

RAF Topcliffe

Meanwhile, A Flight's commander, S/Ldr James Walker, was leading a most unusual six-man flight crew. The sixth name on his crew was a passenger listed as being a medical officer (MO); not only that, but he was another squadron leader. This represented an unusually high value / high risk asset should anything go wrong, especially given the jinx that had prevailed with flight commanders over the summer months. Sometimes an MO would be seen on a check flight to evaluate a crew following a traumatising incident, but this provision was not extended to an operational sortie; in fact, the full extent of this particular MO's role may not have been disclosed even to the captain.

S/Ldr Roland Winfield was from the RAF's Physiological Laboratory, where he was studying the increasing use of the amphetamine Benzedrine. He had started his research in April 1941 with Coastal Command, which despatched crews in long-endurance aircraft to perform monotonous patrols over miles of featureless sea, the crews finding comfort in Benzedrine to keep them alert. He had experimented with different amphetamines, flying with the test crew to monitor their performance at first hand during 14 sorties that had finished that month. His conclusion was to endorse two 5 gram Benzedrine tablets on long flights, thereby providing official sanction for the use of the drug.

Whilst engaged on experiments with Coastal Command, he was also approached by Bomber Command, who sought his opinion on the applicability of Benzedrine for crews in high altitude combat, which subjected these crews to a combination of low oxygen, cold and stress, as distinct from the boredom experienced by Coastal Command crews. Consequently, he set out to evaluate the use of Benzedrine in this new environment, and performed a further tranche of experiments on Whitley and Stirling aircrews. Once again, he accompanied the crews on their sorties even though the operational environment was far from benign. He had been flying sorties with Bomber Command since August 1941, and his arrival on 102 Squadron followed the loss of Z6871 on Danby Head two weeks previously, when her captain had fallen asleep.

His professionalism for choosing to monitor his subjects first hand in clearly hazardous environments would draw him into danger not just from enemy action but also from crews' reactions to the medication. In the course of conducting his experiments, Rasmussen[79] recounts that Roland Winfield witnessed a number of effects:

> During an air raid against the Renault factory outside Paris … an air crew on Benzedrine swooped in at a tree-trimming 200 feet to strafe and kill an enemy anti-aircraft team with their ungainly bomber, impressing Winfield deeply.[80]

However, on the other side of the coin he reported that:

> On one occasion after flying through the night, poor visibility made it necessary to fly within fifty feet of the sea … the pilot flying the aircraft started to nod off and was roused only by a judicious nudge in the ribs.[81]

This latter event in particular had a certain chill of familiarity about it, especially when considering the recent events on Danby Head.

Duisburg harbour and port facilities (Deutsches Bundesarchiv, Bild 102-12562 / CC-BY-SA)

Roland Winfield was accredited as having been in possession of a 'keen taste for adventure', a penchant that he would be exercising that night by flying into the Ruhr Valley, a place where many went but few chose to go. One of the most dangerous phases of the forthcoming operation would be crossing the Kammhuber Line – but the Hampdens would be back once again, to mount the welcome searchlight suppression sorties for them.

Derrick Riley and Vannio Albrecht lined up ninth and tenth respectively, the first aircraft getting away only a minute past scheduled departure time at 0031 hrs. All aircraft departed at conservative intervals of almost 2 minutes from each other, with the exception of Sgt John Roe in Z9167,[82] who was delayed by 23 minutes after the penultimate aircraft had got into the air.

Whitley Z6973 (DY-B̄)

Duisburg.

Takeoff 0048 hrs.

One stick released over Amsterdam docks from 14,000 ft.

Landed 0707 hrs.

Operational combat time 6 hrs 19 mins.

Sgt DN Riley

Sgt WG Caldwell

F/Sgt RF Bradbury   6th operation; combat time 48 hrs 13 mins

Sgt NW Haycock

P/O AJ Graham

Sgt D Boddy

Whitley Z6875 (DY-P)

Duisburg.

Takeoff 0050 hrs.

One stick released over flak concentration in the Ruhr from 12,500 ft.

Landed 0737 hrs.

Operational combat time 6 hrs 47 mins.

P/O VM Albrecht

Sgt HE Batchelder

Sgt JV Kirkwood

Sgt T Nisbet

Sgt K O'Connelley

Sgt ER DeMattos   5th operation; combat time 36 hrs 27 mins

There had been unbroken cloud, and few had been able to find the target with any degree of accuracy, so most set about bombing flak concentrations through the cloud. S/Ldr James Walker, leading the amphetamine trial crew, attacked an 'unidentified town in the Ruhr'. Only Derrick Riley hung on to his bombs and waited for the cloud to clear on his return journey, being rewarded with a clear view of Amsterdam docks, which he attacked with greater certainty than any other crew that night.

Four aircraft reported being hit by flak, three of which had attacked flak concentrations, so their damage should not have come as much of a surprise; one of these was captained by Vannio Albrecht. The fourth aircraft suffering flak damage was captained by Derrick Riley, whose clear view of Amsterdam docks had the corollary of presenting himself as a clear target to defenders on the ground.

Greater drama befell Canadian Sgt Gordon Hoben and his crew, who got lost over the North Sea. They had been flying in a gale with a faulty compass, and were so far east of their return route that they were following a northerly track up the North Sea without making landfall. Fortunately, their WOp was the dependable Sgt Philip Brett, whose adept wireless work ensured their safe recovery to RAF Leuchars in Fifeshire with almost empty tanks, reinforcing Philip Brett's already glowing reputation.

19 OCTOBER 1941

All crewmen available were called upon to line up for the squadron photograph, and this included Len, recently returned from leave.

20 OCTOBER 1941

Target[83]	Aircraft on target	Types
Bremen:		
(i) Aim point A	63	48 Wellington 15 Stirling
(ii) Aim point B	90	82 Hampden 8 Manchester

(continued)

Detail of Sgt Len Starbuck (inset) from 102 Squadron Air Crews October 1941 (Ed Cooke)

Target	Aircraft on target	Types
Wilhelmshaven	47	40 Whitley 4 Wellington 3 Halifax
Emden:		
(i) Aim point A	33	Wellington
(ii) Aim point B	3	2 Wellington 1 Halifax
CC47 Antwerp docks	35	28 Wellington 5 Whitley 2 Stirling
Minelaying:		
(i) Frisian Islands (Nectarine)	5	Hampden
(ii) Sassnitz (Willow)	5	Manchester
Nickelling:		
(i) Paris area and aerodromes	6	Wellington
(ii) Caen – Tours – Le Mans and aerodromes	2	Whitley

Primary target: Wilhelmshaven (railway station).
Alternative: S&M.
Last Resort: S&M.
Operation C.172: 12 aircraft, operational call sign DJ9.
Bomb load: No.5 or No.6 TD 0.025. 1× 250 lb GP MLD to be included where applicable.
Route: Base – Filey Bay – Wangerooge – Wilhelmshaven and return.
Time Off: 1815 hrs.
Weather: 3/10 to 5/10 cloud tops to 7,000 ft, slight haze above.
Opposition: Intense light flak from dock area. Moderate heavy flak northeast and west of town. Searchlights in cones north and northeast **not** co-operating with flak, did not pick up aircraft.

Twelve crews were required to support the next strategic attack to Wilhelmshaven, amongst them S/Ldr JWB Richardson, newly appointed as B Flight's commander, undertaking his first operational sortie as 2nd pilot on the squadron. Others flying included Sgt Ernest de Mattos with P/O Albrecht, and F/Sgt Richard Bradbury with Sgt Derrick Riley who led the crews out on time at 1815 hrs.

Whitley Z6973 (DY- B)

Wilhelmshaven.

Takeoff 1815 hrs.

One stick released over primary target from 11,000 ft.

Landed 0115 hrs.

Operational combat time 7 hrs 0 mins.

Sgt DN Riley

Sgt WG Caldwell

F/Sgt RF Bradbury   7th operation; combat time 55 hrs 13 mins

Sgt MW Haycock

Operation C.172 to Wilhelmshaven, 20 October 1941

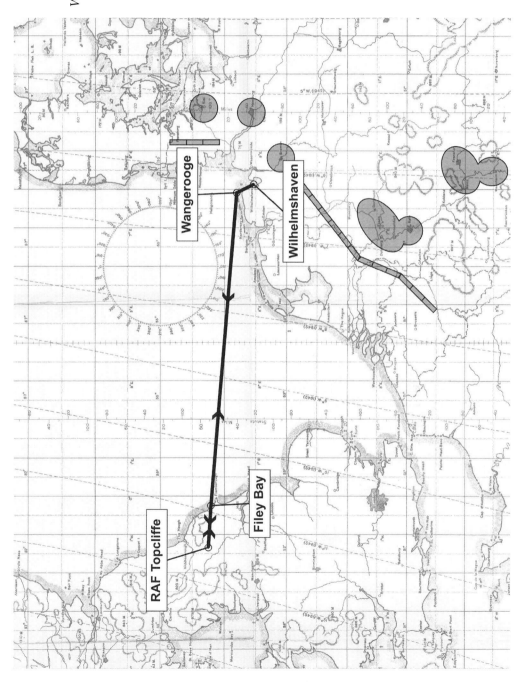

Wangerooge

Wilhelmshaven

Filey Bay

RAF Topcliffe

Air raid on Wilhelmshaven (Chris Goss Collection)

Sgt JA Steeves
Sgt JBT Smith

Whitley Z6875 (DY-P)

Wilhelmshaven.
Tail heavy, did not start.
P/O VM Albrecht
Sgt CR Barr
Sgt JV Kirkwood
Sgt K O'Connelley
Sgt IS Lloyd
Sgt ER DeMattos

Z6875 was found to be tail-heavy on test and was grounded for further investigation. This unusual failure meant that Vannio Albrecht and his crew, including Sgt Ernest de Mattos, would be stood down for the night. The crews that did proceed reported that the searchlights and flak, usually a deadly combination, were not co-operating, which minimised losses and contributed to all crews' safe return.

Limited visibility over Wilhelmshaven had hampered targeting; German reports[84] confirmed that only three loads of bombs had fallen on areas where there was any housing, but made no mention of the railway infrastructure.

22 OCTOBER 1941

Target[85]	Aircraft on target	Types
Mannheim:		
(i) Aim point A	60	54 Wellington 6 Halifax
(ii) Aim point C	28	22 Whitley 6 Wellington
(ii) Aim point D	45	Hampden
CC24A Le Havre docks	22	14 Wellington 7 Whitley 1 Stirling
Brest (*Scharnhorst* and *Gneisenau*)	6	Stirling

Primary target: Mannheim (railway station).
Alternative: S&M.
Last Resort: S&M.
Operation C.173: 12 aircraft, operational call sign 8FF.
Bomb load: No.1 or No.3 TD 0.025. 1× 250 lb GP MLD to be included where applicable.
Route: Base – Finningley – Orford Ness – Nieuport – Valenciennes – Mannheim and return.
Time Off: 1800 hrs.
Weather: 9/10 to 10/10 cloud over target area tops 11,000 ft to 14,000 ft.
Opposition: Moderate inaccurate heavy flak. Searchlights ineffective owing to cloud.

On his first operation following return from leave, Len was welcomed back by Sgt Fisher. This would be their twelfth operation together, and Len's sixth in Z6959. Len would be flying as WOp and mentoring Sgt Charles Neveu, recently reintroduced to operational flying following the disastrous crash on the aerodrome on 21 August 1941. Taking up the training role of 2nd WOp, Neveu would be assuming responsibility for dropping dockers once over Holland.

Sgt Derrick Riley was also in action again, retaining F/Sgt Richard Bradbury from their previous operation, although this time in a different aircraft. He was to line up eighth, with Sgt Fisher a little further back, in tenth. This time the departure process had been streamlined and the aircraft left in 1-minute intervals from 1800 hrs.

Whitley Z6959 (DY-Ā)

Mannheim.
Takeoff 1810 hrs.
Released one stick over primary target from 11,500 ft.
Landed 0250 hrs.
Operational combat time 8 hrs 40 mins.
Sgt R Fisher
P/O BGH Smith
P/O AO Dobson
Sgt L Starbuck   16th operation; combat time 122 hrs 23 mins
Sgt CS Nevue
Sgt WA Gillies

Operation C.173 to Mannheim, 22 October 1941

Mannheim

Valenciennes

Nieuport

Orford Ness

RAF Topcliffe

Finningley

Whitley Z9212 (DY-Ō)

Mannheim.

Takeoff 1808 hrs.

Released one stick over primary target from 10,000 ft.

Landed 0251 hrs[86] at RAF Dishforth.

Operational combat time 8 hrs 43 mins.

Sgt DN Riley

Sgt WG Caldwell

F/Sgt RF Bradbury   8th operation; combat time 63 hrs 56 mins

Sgt W Nicoll

Sgt D Smith

Two aircraft returned with the usual technical failures, but ten went on to attack the primary target. Two crews landed away, including Derrick Riley who landed at RAF Dishforth, only 5 miles to the south. Sgt Fisher, meanwhile, was fifth of the eight successful crews to land back at base.

Thick cloud over Mannheim had hindered targeting; German reports[87] recorded only 25 HE bombs and 30 incendiaries falling on the city, damaging around 40 houses.

1 November 1941

Target[88]	Aircraft on target	Types
Kiel:		
(i) Kiel	72	Wellington
(ii) GR3588 Deutsche Werke shipyards	62	32 Hampden 30 Whitley
Brest (*Scharnhorst* and *Gneisenau*)	17	9 Wellington 8 Stirling
CC24A Le Havre	13	10 Wellington 3 Whitley
Night-time coastal sweeps against enemy shipping from Texel to Wangerooge	4	Hampden
Minelaying:		
(i) Kiel (Forget-me-nots)	5	Hampden
(ii) Sassnitz (Willow)	2	Manchester
Nickelling over Paris area	3	Wellington

Primary target: Kiel (shipyards).
Alternative: S&M.
Last Resort: S&M.
Operation C.174: 11 aircraft, operational call sign 9BO.
Bomb load: No.1 or No.3 TD 0.025. 1× 250 lb GP MLD to be included where applicable.
Route: Base – Scarborough – Amrum – Kiel and return.

Time Off: 1730 hrs.
Weather: 10/10 cloud.
Opposition: Generally heavy flak moderately intense but ineffective.

Following the sinking of *Bismarck* on 27 May 1941, the largest battleship remaining available to the Kriegsmarine was *Tirpitz*, and she had so far been bottled up in the Baltic, guarding against a possible breakout of the Russian Fleet from Leningrad. Intelligence confirmed that she had steamed from Gotenhafen[89] to Kiel, where she now lay immobile in dry dock, presenting a window of opportunity to Bomber Command to stop her before she could head back to sea. Kiel was also a centre of ship and submarine building, so any bombs landing in the area would stand a higher than usual chance of causing damage to something supporting the Kriegsmarine's war effort.

Eleven aircraft were detailed to attack, and all departed from 1730 hrs, getting airborne at one-minute intervals. The cloud over the target made accuracy impossible, so most crews bombed on ETA. Two aircraft abandoned their attacks; Sgt Gordon Hoben reported being unable to see anything in the target area due to 10/10 cloud, and so focused on a target of opportunity on the strategic island of Sylt. Still presented with 10/10 cloud, he flew to the island on ETA, where he reported bombing flak installations.

P/O Vannio Albrecht in Z6749 radioed to confirm that he had also called off his attack on the primary target, but then nothing else was heard from him. It would appear that he had headed south to find a target of opportunity along the north German or Dutch coasts, and he had subsequently been intercepted. His successful attacker was Uffz Heinz Grimm, whose previous victory had been against P/O John Croucher on 7 September 1941, an encounter that resulted in Heinz Grimm being shot down by the Whitley's air gunners over the sea, with a bullet wound to his thigh. He had just transferred from 4./NJG1 at St. Trond to the newly formed 5./NJG2 at Leeuwarden, and his encounter with Albrecht provided the new Staffel with its first victory. The loss of Vannio Albrecht would have been felt by Sgt Ernest de Mattos, with whom he had been crewed for four of his five operations.

The blanketing cloud had been so thick as to shield completely their target. The squadron had been cheated of an opportunity to score any hits on *Tirpitz*; her fate would have to wait for another day.

3 November 1941

F/Sgt Richard Bradbury was admitted to RAF Hospital Rauceby in Lincolnshire. This facility was headed by plastic surgeon S/Ldr Fenton Braithwaite, and specialised in applying reconstructive techniques on severely burned aircrew. Richard Bradbury would remain there for four weeks.

7 November 1941

Target[90]	Aircraft on target	Types
Berlin:		
(i) Aim point C	152	101 Wellington 42 Whitley 9 Halifax
(ii) GU3897 Reichsluftfahrtministerium	17	Stirling
Cologne:		
(i) Aim point B	75	61 Hampden 14 Manchester
(ii) Knapsack; GO1237 RWE Goldenberg Werke power station	8	Hampden
Mannheim aim point D	55	53 Wellington 2 Stirling
CC13A Ostend docks	28	19 Wellington 5 Hampden 4 Stirling
Roving patrols over Essen area	24	12 Wellington 9 Whitley 3 Halifax
CC29A Boulogne docks	22	14 Wellington 4 Manchester 4 Whitley
Offensive patrols	6	Hampden
Minelaying off Oslo (Onion)	13	Hampden

MAIN OPERATION

Primary target: Berlin (Schlesischer railway station).
Alternative: S&M.
Last Resort: S&M.
Operation C.175: 12 aircraft, operational call sign MG7.
Bomb load: No.5 or No.6 TD 0.025. 1× 250 lb GP MLD to be included where applicable.
Route: Base – Scarborough – Meldorf – Müritz Lake – Berlin – Meldorf – 53°34'N 05°00'E – Southwold – Wattisham – Base.
Time Off: 2200 hrs.
Weather: 9/10 cloud and ground haze.
Opposition: Slight spasmodic heavy flak through cloud.

NURSERY OPERATION

Primary target: Boulogne (docks and shipping).
Alternative: AIP.
Last Resort: AIP.
Operation C.176: 3 aircraft (freshmen), operational call sign A6G.
Bomb load: No.1 or No.3 TD 0.025.
Route: Base – Finningley – Orford Ness – Boulogne and return.

Time Off: 2000 hrs.
Weather: Clear over target with small patches of cloud.
Opposition: Intense but very inaccurate. Searchlights active and working in cones.

The long run of bad weather and poor bombing results had spurred Air Marshal Sir Richard Peirse into mounting Bomber Command's largest raid to date against the German capital, allocating 252 aircraft to the task, from which 17 Stirlings were to be singled out to attack the Reichsluftfahrtministerium (RLM).

As warnings came in of storms, thick cloud, icing and hail, he persisted with the plan, even though Air Vice Marshal 'Jack' Slessor, AOC 5 Group, objected and withdrew his 69 Hampdens and 14 Manchesters in favour of an operation against Cologne. Events would shortly bear out whose choice was to constitute the better course of action.

Sgt Fisher was to lead one of the 12 aircraft on the Berlin run, and kept Len on his crew as WOp. Although Len had been detailed to bomb Berlin before, he had never got that far, his sortie of 20 September 1941 having been recalled. Now it seemed that his luck was finally on the turn.

Two hours before this operation could begin, three freshman crews would take off for Boulogne. The night started badly, as P/O SJB Hamilton, on his nursery operation, crashed the freshly received Z9219 on her maiden operation. The cockpit lighting failed during the take-off run, and as he reached forward in the darkness to turn it on again he caught one of the throttle levers, causing the aircraft to skid and the undercarriage to collapse. As things were to turn out, this incident was a bad omen.

The two other Boulogne-bound aircraft departed without further incident, one going on to attack the primary target in clear conditions, but P/O JM Hartley overshot his target and flew a further 5 minutes due south to attack the aerodrome at Le Touquet-Étaples. Because he overshot his primary target, he did not pass his nursery operation and would have to fly another one.

One crew cancelled from the Berlin operation, and so two hours after the departure of the freshman crews the remaining 11 Berlin crews were lining up for departure at 2200 hrs, when two aircraft went unserviceable and would not start, one of them Sgt Fisher's Z6959. As they would find out the next day, their reprieve had been timely; Len's luck had held out again, after all.

Whitley Z6959 (DY-Ā)

Berlin.
Did not start.
Sgt R Fisher
Sgt WE Davies
Sgt WG Butterworth
Sgt L Starbuck
Sgt WA Gillies

The remaining nine aircraft took off as scheduled, but two returned subsequently with equipment failures, leaving seven to continue the attack. The weather for those who continued was not kind, and severe icing and storms were reported. Presumably due to problems

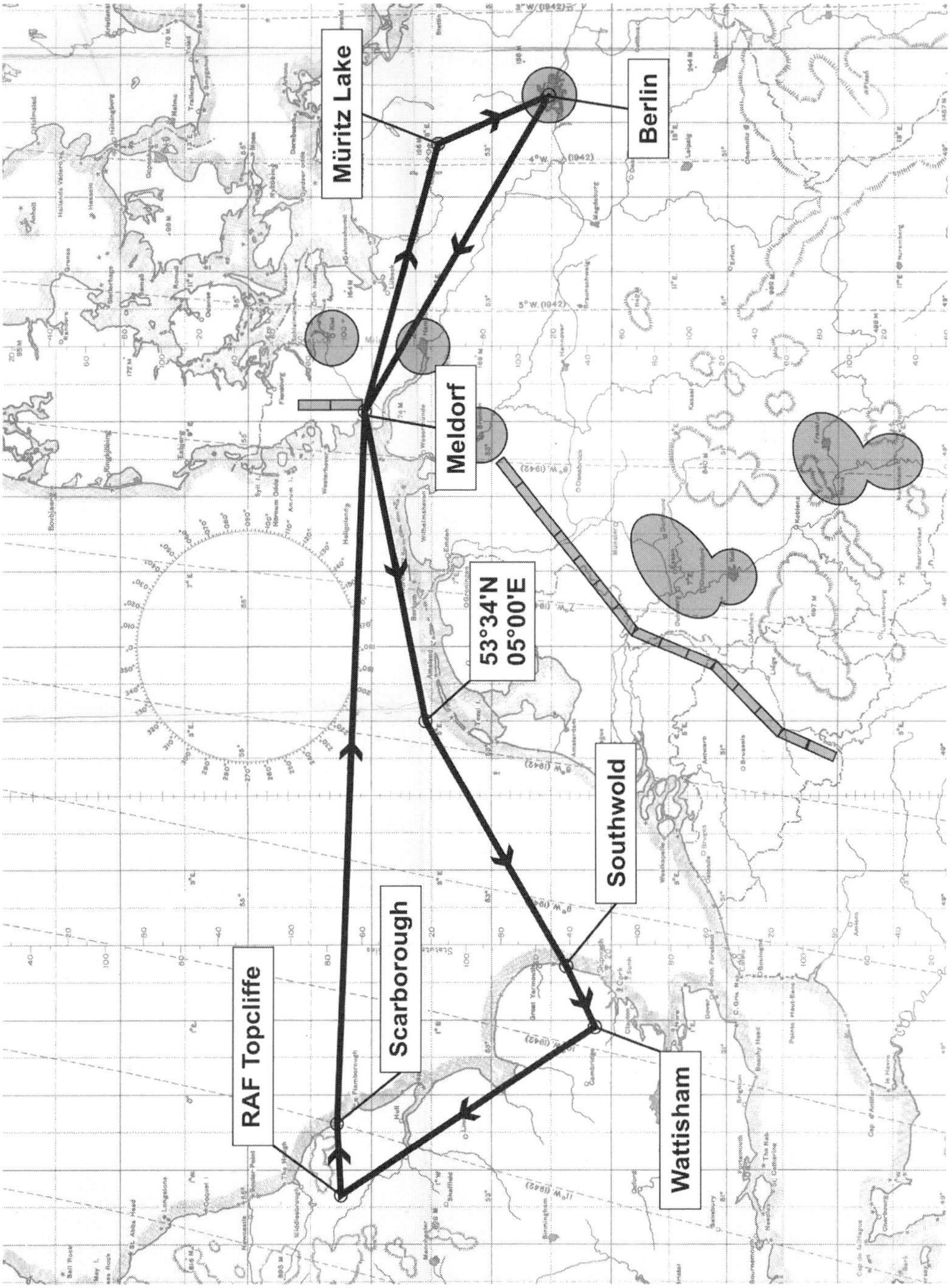

Operation C.175 to Berlin, 7 November 1941

Müritz Lake

Berlin

Meldorf

53°34'N 05°00'E

RAF Topcliffe

Scarborough

Southwold

Wattisham

experienced in the difficult conditions, Sgt Gordon Hoben elected to attack the nearer port of Kiel, where there was still unfinished business from the unsuccessful attack on *Tirpitz* the last time out. His attack was not successful, and now only six aircraft – half the intended force – were left to continue to Berlin.

Ironically the defences were less severe than expected, but the drama unfolded on the return journey when, one by one, crews radioed in to request navigational assistance to guide them home. The distance to Berlin was right on the range limit of the Whitley, so even slight changes in wind or navigational errors could increase the flying time to such an extent that they might be left with insufficient fuel to make a safe return.

First to make contact was Sgt Thomas Thorley in Z9128, who at 0642 hrs requested a fix which placed him 60 miles north of Borkum. It is believed that his aircraft may have been forced to ditch at around 0700 hrs. Next to call was Sgt Reginald Matthews in Z6796, who requested a bearing from Horsham St Faith at 0726 hrs. Finally, at 0743 hrs, an SOS was received from P/O Bruce Roy in Z6820.

The three crews that radioed for assistance – 50 per cent of the force that had got through to Berlin – were all lost without trace. The three surviving crews from the Berlin run recovered to bases in Norfolk, noticeably nearer than their home base for the returning bombers. This attests to the severity of the weather experienced en route, and provides a strong indicator as to the fate of those crews that had not returned. By the coming of morning, the aerodrome at RAF Topcliffe would have looked ominously sparse. This had without doubt been a very bad night for the squadron.

The cost of missing crews was being counted at other aerodromes too; in all, 21 aircraft had been lost on the Berlin operation, in contrast to the 5 Group squadrons, which had been redirected to Cologne, and lost none of their aircraft. Peirse's dogmatic pursuit of the Berlin operation in the face of bad weather forecasts and objections from AVM Slessor would come to weigh heavily on his future career.

The Reichsluftfahrtministerium on Wilhelmstraße in Berlin (Deutsches Bundesarchiv, Bild 146-1979-074-34A / CC-BY-SA)

Clear skies over Berlin had supported accurate bombing; German reports[91] confirmed scattered bombing across the city, with damage recorded to a handful of industrial, public and official premises as well as the railways. A number of houses were damaged and destroyed, the effects to buildings and Berliners alike being exacerbated by the renewed deployment of the

4,000 lb Cookie HC bombs by some of the other participating squadrons, following their earlier use against the capital on 7/8 September 1941. Although the cost of delivering the message had been high, the Reich Chancellery had received another clear notification of intent, and populace and leadership alike would have come to realise that they could be targeted in force at the whim of Bomber Command.

8 NOVEMBER 1941

Target[92]	Aircraft on target	Types
Essen:		
(i) GN3814 Friedrich Krupp AG works	54	27 Wellington 19 Hampden 8 Whitley
(ii) Searchlight suppression	6	Hampden
CC25 Dunkirk	18	10 Hampden 5 Manchester 3 Wellington
CC13 Ostend	8	Whitley

MAIN OPERATION

Primary target: Essen (Krupp works).
Alternative: S&M.
Last Resort: S&M.
Operation C.177: 2 aircraft, operational call sign D97.
Bomb load: No.1 or No.3 TD 0.025. Aircraft on main target to carry 1× 250 lb GP MLD where applicable.
Route: Base – Bridlington – Vlieland – Essen and return.
Time Off: 1730 hrs.
Weather: No cloud but thick ground haze.
Opposition: Intense heavy flak co-operating with searchlights.

NURSERY OPERATION

Primary target: Ostend (docks and shipping).
Alternative: AIP.
Last Resort: AIP.
Operation C.178: 1 aircraft (freshman), operational call sign 7GB.
Bomb load: No.1 or No.3 TD 0.025.
Route: Base – Finningley – Orford Ness – Ostend and return.
Time Off: 1750 hrs.
Weather: 10/10 cloud.
Opposition: Spasmodic flak. Searchlights ineffective.

Two aircraft were detailed to join an attack on Essen. Sgt Fisher was one of the pilots chosen, but having been spared the debacle of the previous night's operation to Berlin, his non-starting Z6959 was undergoing maintenance and would be unavailable, so he laid claim to the factory-fresh Z9289 destined for A Flight. His crew was almost the same as for the previous night, and this time his remit included carrying a camera to record bomb strikes. However, their task was made less hazardous by the Hampdens once more flying their searchlight suppression sorties in this high-risk area.

This was to be Sgt Fisher's last operation, and he lined up his brand-new aircraft behind Sgt George McDonald, who was flying the only other aircraft detailed for the attack. McDonald had flown three of his sorties as 2nd pilot under Sgt Fisher's tutelage, and similarly, all the crewmen chosen had connections with one or other of the two pilots. Len had flown with both, but none more so than Sgt Fisher, so he was an obvious choice to join his crew. Graciously, Sgt Fisher let his protégé, McDonald, lead them out at 1728 hrs, following along 2 minutes later.

Another 20 minutes later the third and final aircraft scheduled to fly that night took off. This was a nursery operation to Ostend, being flown by P/O JM Hartley, who was having a second attempt at qualifying, with the same crew as the night before except for Canadian air gunner Sgt Isadore Stein, who had left earlier with George McDonald on the Essen run for Sgt Fisher's farewell. This move was to cost Isadore Stein his life.

The nursery operation was completed as ordered, and P/O Hartley led his crew home to land successfully at 2209 hrs, his reprieve earned.

Sgt Fisher, relieved at completing his tour and in a celebratory mood, landed at 2358 hrs, noting only one aircraft having returned, this being Z9222 back from Ostend. Now Len was safely back on the ground, the completion of this sortie would have raised his spirits as it showed him that it was possible to beat the odds – but on the other hand the captain who had been his principal mentor, flying 13 of his 17 operations with him as he progressed through the ranks of air gunner, 2nd WOp and WOp, would now be moving on.

They would have waited for the return of George McDonald and his crew to join in the celebrations, but before long the awful truth would have sunk in that they would not be returning. As it turned out, Z9212 had been shot down by Ltn Fritz Carstens of 7./NJG1 over Wassenberg, Heinsberg, at 2039 hrs.

Len had remained lucky and survived the 50:50 odds to fight again – but would he finish his tour, like Sgt Fisher, or simply fail to return, as had so many of his colleagues?

Whitley Z9289 (DY-G)

Essen.

Takeoff 1730 hrs.

One stick released over primary target from 11,000 ft.

Landed 2358 hrs.

Operational combat time 6 hrs 28 mins.

Sgt R Fisher

P/O BGH Smith

Sgt GW Butterworth

Sgt L Starbuck   17th operation; combat time 128 hrs 51 mins

Sgt WA Gillies

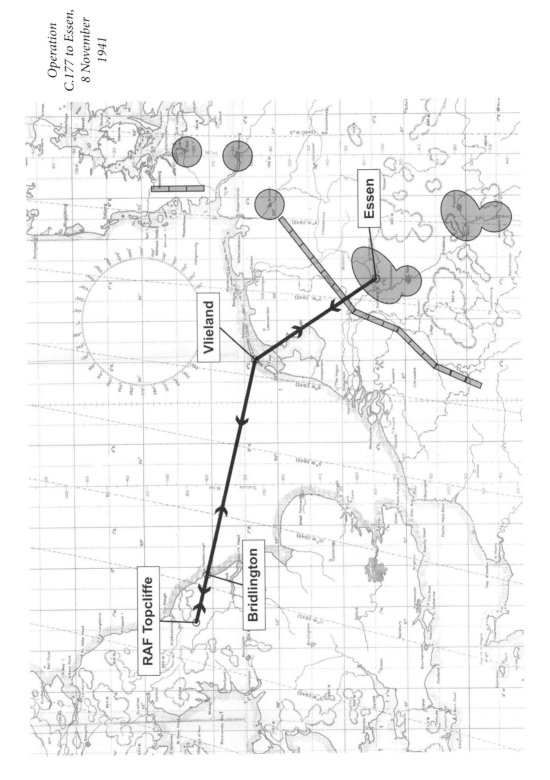

Operation
C.177 to Essen,
8 November
1941

Essen

Vlieland

RAF Topcliffe

Bridlington

15 November 1941

Target[93]	Aircraft on target	Types
Emden	49	26 Wellington 11 Hampden 6 Manchester 6 Whitley
Kiel:		
(i) Kiel	12	Whitley
(ii) GR3589 Friedrich Krupp Germaniawerft AG shipyards	35	29 Wellington 6 Stirling
CC29 Boulogne docks	9	Wellington
Minelaying off the Frisian Islands (Nectarine)	5	Hampden

Nursery Operation

Primary target: Emden (docks).
Alternative: AIP (docks and shipping).
Last Resort: AIP (docks and shipping).
Operation C.179: 1 aircraft (freshman), operational call sign UV8.
Bomb load: No.1 or No.3 TD 0.025.
Route: Base – Filey – Juist – Emden and return.
Time Off: 1700 hrs.
Weather: 10/10 cloud.
Opposition: Spasmodic flak. Searchlights ineffective.

S/Ldr Grant Lindeman was ready for his freshman operation. This time the destination was significantly further afield, and instead of it being a port facility in occupied French or Belgian territory, he would be flying to Emden. This demanded more concentration and greater precision than the previous nursery operations because of the increased over-water navigation requirement, but it was conducted without incident.

This would be the last operation carried out from RAF Topcliffe before hard runways were installed. The aerodrome that had served them since November 1940 would have to become more robust in order to take the greater loads of operating one of the new breed of heavy bombers. In the short term, flying operations from 102 Squadron would be interrupted whilst they moved on detachment to RAF Dalton, a satellite station 2 miles to the south.

RAF Dalton had been meadowland, cleared to provide a relief and dispersal landing ground for its parent station. Although it was in fact the closer of the two to the village of Topcliffe, it was instead named after the village of Dalton, to the east of the aerodrome. Concrete runways had already been laid and were arranged with the main 1,100-yard runway running north–south, the traditional triangular layout being completed with the addition of two 1,000-yard runways to the east, aligned 06/24 and 12/30. All three runways were linked by a perimeter track, attached to which were 36 dispersals.

17 NOVEMBER 1941

One of the first air tests conducted from RAF Dalton was captained by the freshly exonerated P/O JM Hartley. Unfortunately, his take-off run was marred by a swing to port which he overcorrected with a swing to starboard that saw his aircraft swing off the runway. The station commander's recommendation on the accident report was that this inexperienced pilot should be taken off heavy bombers. This would have been the second harsh blow in 10 days for the star-crossed P/O Hartley, and once again he would have to earn a reprieve to stay and continue operations.

30 NOVEMBER 1941

Target[94]	Aircraft on target	Types
Hamburg:		
(i) Hamburg	129	92 Wellington 24 Whitley 11 Halifax 2 Stirling
(ii) GR3587 Blohm und Voss shipyards	52	48 Hampden 4 Manchester
Emden	50	30 Wellington 14 Whitley 3 Stirling 2 Manchester 1 Hampden
CC13 Ostend docks	3	2 Whitley 1 Wellington
Minelaying:		
(i) Sassnitz (Willow)	4	Hampden
(ii) Warnemünde (Jasmine)	2	Hampden
(iii) Kiel Harbour (Forget-me-nots)	1	Hampden
(iv) North entrance to the Sound (Nasturtium)	1	Hampden
Nickelling: Orleans – Tours and aerodromes	4	Whitley

MAIN OPERATION

Primary target: Hamburg (railway station).
Alternative: S&M.
Last Resort: S&M.
Operation C.180: 8 aircraft, operational call sign V7Z.
Bomb load: No.1 or No.3 TD 0.025. Aircraft on main target to carry 1× 250 lb GP MLD where applicable.
Route: Base – Filey – Meldorf – Hamburg and return.
Time Off: 1640 hrs.
Weather: Clear, slight haze.
Opposition: Intense heavy flak co-operating with searchlights.

Nursery Operation

Primary target: Emden (docks and shipping).
Alternative: AIP.
Last Resort: AIP.
Operation C.181: 3 aircraft (freshmen), operational call sign YA6.
Bomb load: No.1 or No.3 TD 0.025.
Route: Base – Flamborough – Juist – Emden and return.
Time Off: 1650 hrs.
Weather: Clear, slight haze.
Opposition: Moderate light flak, very little heavy. No searchlights.

For its first operation from RAF Dalton, the squadron was tasked to support an attack on Hamburg, concurrently running a further nursery operation to Emden, following the precedent set by S/Ldr Grant Lindeman two weeks earlier. Unusually, this nursery operation was manned by experienced pilots, but the freshmen were other crew members, principally navigators.

Len was given the easier of the two operations, and with the departure of his friend Sgt Fisher was appointed to a crew led by Sgt Derrick Riley. He had arrived from 58 Squadron in August, when 102 Squadron had been drawing in experienced crewmen to offset the large numbers of inexperienced personnel arriving in from the OTUs at that time.

Tonight would mark the return of Len's most familiar and reliable ride, Z6959, which had only let him and Sgt Fisher down once, and that was three weeks earlier, on 7 November 1941, when she failed to start – and had thus spared her crew from going on the disastrous Berlin operation. The crew would also be dropping nickels on their sortie.

The 11 aircraft for both operations lined up together, the three Emden crews falling in behind those bound for Hamburg, all taking off sequentially. Derrick Riley lined up ninth, and led out the Emden crews, taking off just ahead of time at 1648 hrs.

Whitley Z6959 (DY-Ā)

Emden.
Takeoff 1648 hrs.
One stick released from 9,000 ft.
Landed 2331 hrs.
Operational combat time 6 hrs 43 mins.
Sgt DN Riley
Sgt WG Caldwell
P/O EM Lloyd
Sgt L Starbuck   18th operation; combat time 135 hrs 34 mins
F/Sgt JA Newbold

Two aircraft returned early from the Hamburg operation, reporting the usual crop of technical faults. Three and a half hours later the Emden crews started to return, having experienced uneventful sorties; Derrick Riley returned last of the three, almost an hour after the first had landed.

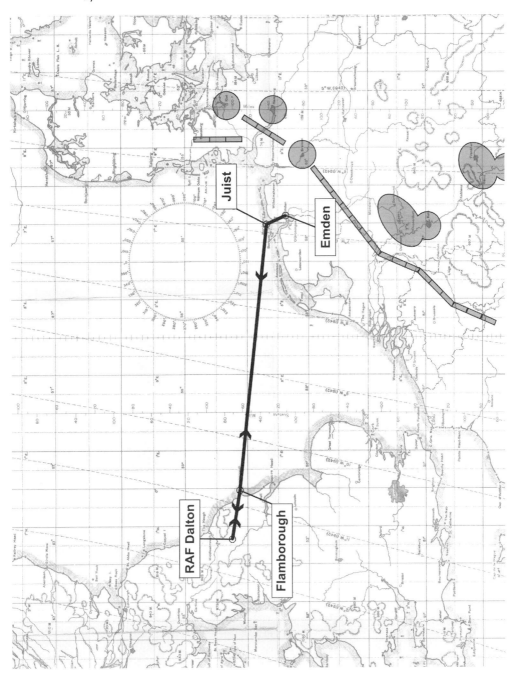

Operation C.181 to Emden, 30 November 1941

In contrast, two aircraft had been lost on the Hamburg run. A flight's commander, S/Ldr James Walker, had been shot down by flak over Kiel, and Z6800 had crashed in the Kiel Canal with its air gunner, ex-Metropolitan Policeman Sgt Jamie 'Big Jock' Williamson, the only survivor; having escaped through holes in the perspex of his rear turret. Kiel was about 50 miles north of their target in Hamburg, their lonely departure northwards from the scheduled route being put down at least partly to a defective compass.

Shortly after leaving Hamburg, Sgt Pike and his crew encountered an electrical storm and icing problems, the effects of which included the rare and beguiling St Elmo's fire, which sent sparks shooting off all points and created haloes around the propeller tips. However, far less aesthetic was the interference on the wireless and the effect on the compass, which deviated by some 15 degrees, causing them to become quite lost on their return.

When, hours later, they eventually saw a coastline, they had expected to see Flamborough Head, but in fact it was the unfamiliar coastline of Holy Isle by Arran in the Firth of Clyde, off the west coast of Scotland. In the hope of finding some familiar topographical feature, they executed a square search pattern and started to convince themselves they were over Eire. By the time their tanks registered empty they still had not been able to confirm their location, and baled out. By that point they were over Newton Stewart in Wigtownshire, and Z9281 finally came down at Springholm in Kirkcudbrightshire, a very long way away from home.

Emden harbour and port facilities (Deutsches Bundesarchiv, Bild 168-50-22 / Unknown / CC-BY-SA)

German reports confirmed that under clear moonlit skies 22 fires had been started in Hamburg and significant damage caused, especially to housing.

Tonight was also the final straw for one air gunner[95] still early in his career, whose actions would become a *cause célèbre*. He had been performing erratically on his last few sorties, delaying the departure of the aircraft, and reporting sick. Ed Cooke takes up the story:

> As usual on the way out the pilot would call the tail gunner to test his guns when clear of the coast. No reply so he sent the WOp back to check and he found the turret turned to the side and empty; the poor chap must have flipped and baled out. He landed on the coast and was returned to camp where he was court-martialled and given a sentence of five years hard labour. Now that did get things going and for a while there the people in charge were a little worried.

> It happened [during] the hours of darkness. [I] remember discussing it the next day how he really must have flipped to bale out in total darkness not knowing if he was over land.

> When word came through of his sentence things were really on the edge; it wouldn't have taken much for things to have got really ugly.

> Everyone thought that it was disgusting and echoed back to the dark ages, specially since all aircrew were volunteers.

There would be no operational flying for two weeks.

Endnotes

69 AIR 14/2673

70 AIR 14/2673

71 Listed erroneously in the ORB as Z6454. Z6454 was not a Whitley, it was a Blenheim.

72 AIR 14/2673

73 Middlebrook, M. and Everitt, C. (1990) *The Bomber Command War Diaries: An Operational Reference Book 1939–1945*, ISBN 0140129367, Penguin, p 207.

74 AIR 14/2673

75 AIR 14/2673

76 Middlebrook, M. and Everitt, C. (1990) *The Bomber Command War Diaries: An Operational Reference Book 1939–1945*, ISBN 0140129367, Penguin, p 209.

77 AIR 14/2673

78 The ORB lists the Duisburg operation C.171 as starting on 16 October, but with the time off being 0030 hrs this implies the night 15/16 October. However, the Night Bomb Raid Sheet specifies the operation as being planned for 16/17 October. As there was no operation against Duisburg on 15/16 October, the ORB is in error.

79 Rasmussen, N. (2008) *On Speed: The Many Lives of Amphetamine*, ISBN 0814776019, New York University Press, p 64.

80 Typical bombing heights were at least 10,000 feet if not significantly higher!

81 Rasmussen, N. (2008) *On Speed: The Many Lives of Amphetamine*, ISBN 0814776019, New York University Press, p 61.

82 The ORB lists Z6749 twice: once under the captaincy of Sgt HW Wickham, and again under Sgt JR Roe. It is believed that the entry for Sgt Wickham is correct, and that Sgt Roe actually flew Z9167 on this occasion, as he did on 12 October and 20 October, either side of this operation.

83 AIR 14/2673

84 Middlebrook, M. and Everitt, C. (1990) *The Bomber Command War Diaries: An Operational Reference Book 1939–1945*, ISBN 0140129367, Penguin, p 212.

85 AIR 14/2673

86 Listed erroneously in the official record as '25.10'; Author has assumed 0251 hrs because that aligns with the return times for the other aircraft which also attacked their targets successfully.

87 Middlebrook, M. and Everitt, C. (1990) *The Bomber Command War Diaries: An Operational Reference Book 1939–1945*, ISBN 0140129367, Penguin, pp 212–213.

88 AIR 14/2673

89 Now Gdynia in Poland.

90 AIR 14/2673

91 Middlebrook, M. and Everitt, C. (1990) *The Bomber Command War Diaries: An Operational Reference Book 1939–1945*, ISBN 0140129367, Penguin, pp 217–218.

92 AIR 14/2673

93 AIR 14/2673

94 AIR 14/2673

95 Name withheld.

5

TOWARDS A NEW DAWN

7 December 1941

Reports would have started to filter through during the evening that Japanese forces had launched an attack on British Malaya, followed shortly after by an invasion of neighbouring Thailand, sealing the fate of the region. Having been raised in British Malaya, Sgt Ernest de Mattos would have recognised that a battle of survival would now rage throughout the country he had once considered to be home. Had it not been the foresight of his father and the privileged opportunities afforded by him that had permitted their escape eight years previously, his whole family could now have been caught in the middle of this fight, watching as all they held dear was torn apart in front of them.

Hard on the heels of those reports came the news that a carrier-borne assault had begun on the United States Naval Base at Pearl Harbor, the single most significant action in the avaricious Japanese overture that would precipitate the start of war in the Pacific.

14 December 1941

S/Ldr Grant Lindeman was posted away on promotion to head up 455 Squadron RAAF, operating Hampdens out of RAF Swinderby in Lincolnshire, the first Australian squadron in Bomber Command.

On the same day, 102 Squadron took receipt of its first Handley Page Halifax, the new heavy bomber to which its crews were going to convert, and the driver behind the installation of paved runways at RAF Topcliffe. These new aircraft must have seemed awesome beside their Whitleys, and would have raised concerns among them about completing their last remaining operations in their obsolescent 'flying coffins'. Ed Cooke recalls that the Halifax was 'welcomed by all; a faster aircraft, more room inside etc'; in fact, a better package all round.

Conversion flying started straight away, with the assistance of experienced ground staff attached from 1652 Conversion Unit (CU) Marston Moor who had moved onto the site.

The first 102 Squadron pilot to gain experience on the new Halifax was F/Sgt Larry Carr, followed as the month wore on by F/Sgt Stanley Morgan, P/O Peter Gaskell and P/O David Delaney.

The paved runways at RAF Dalton would soon be found to be too short for the new bomber, and within a year they would have been extended, with 12/30 becoming the new main runway at 1,760 yards, supplemented by 06/24 at 1,430 yards and 18/36 at 1,395 yards.[96,97]

16 December 1941

Target[98]	Aircraft on target	Types
Wilhelmshaven	83	57 Wellington 14 Hampden 12 Whitley
CC13A Ostend docks	32	30 Wellington 2 Stirling
Brest (*Scharnhorst* and *Gneisenau*)	22	17 Wellington 5 Stirling
CC25A Dunkirk docks	14	8 Whitley 5 Hampden 1 Wellington
Minelaying off Brest (Jellyfish)	18	Hampden
Nickelling: Paris – Orleans and aerodromes	4	Whitley

Nursery Operation

Primary target: Dunkirk (docks and shipping).
Alternative: AIP.
Last Resort: AIP.
Operation C.182: 1 aircraft (freshman), operational call sign 6FL.
Bomb load: 12 × 250 GP TD 0.025.
Route: Base – Finningley – Orford Ness – Dunkirk and return.
Time Off: 1643 hrs.

Following a lull in operations, the squadron had developed another 2nd pilot ready to take on the role of captain. Instead of being given Emden, as had become the norm of late, Sgt Wilson Caldwell was given the much closer coastal target of Dunkirk. He took off with his crew in Z6973 at 1643 hrs but was not heard from again, having been hit by flak and crashing into the sea.

This served to highlight that although these nearby coastal targets had been selected for nursery operations to build up experience for novice crewmen, they were still well defended and were by no means safe.

17 December 1941

During the day, three more Halifaxes flew in. As the squadron's tired and patched-up Whitleys went about their business around them, the number of these imposing leviathans increased, raising an air of expectation amongst crews.

Target[99]	Aircraft on target	Types
Brest (*Scharnhorst* and *Gneisenau*)	121	72 Wellington 25 Hampden 24 Whitley
CC24 Le Havre	14	7 Wellington 4 Whitley 3 Hampden
Nickelling: Paris - Orleans area and enemy aerodromes	2	Whitley

Primary target: Brest (*Scharnhorst* and *Gneisenau*).
Alternative: AIP.
Last Resort: AIP.
Operation C.183: 6 aircraft, operational call sign D9C.
Bomb load: 4 × 500 lb SAP TD 0.12 and 4 × 250 lb GP TD 0.025.
Route: Base – Cottesmore – Bridport – Pointe de Pontusval – Brest and return.
Time Off: 1705 hrs.
Weather: 9/10 to 10/10 cloud, in target area with gaps, haze and smoke.
Opposition: Intense searchlight concentrations through gaps, with heavy and light flak in dock area.

As the unfamiliar lull in operations on the squadron continued, word was received that the battleships *Scharnhorst* and *Gneisenau* were once again ready for action, along with the heavy cruiser *Prinz Eugen*. All were berthed at Brest, and appeared to be ready to slip out once more and resume their duties harassing convoys. This spurred Bomber Command into action, sending in aircraft by both night and day.

102 Squadron provided six aircraft to support attacks during the night of 17/18 December 1941. Sgt Derrick Riley was one of those chosen for this operation, and he retained Len as WOp, leading the other crews out in Z6959 on time at 1705 hrs.

Whitley Z6959 (DY-Ā)

Brest.

Takeoff 1705 hrs.

Released one stick over primary target from 7,000 ft.

Landed 0057 hrs.

Operational combat time 7 hrs 52 mins.

Sgt DN Riley

Sgt WR Davies

Sgt DL Boyd

Sgt L Starbuck   19th operation; combat time 143 hrs 26 mins

F/Sgt JA Newbold

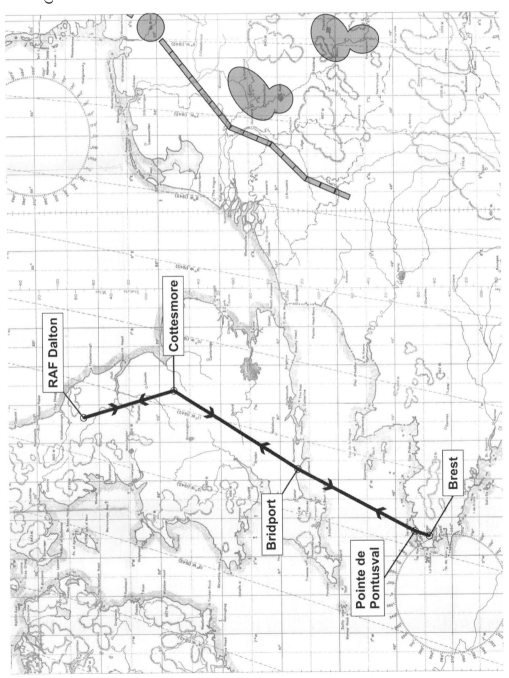

Operation C.183 to Brest, 17 December 1941

RAF Dalton

Cottesmore

Bridport

Pointe de Pontusval

Brest

Derrick Riley was fifth and last to land back at base, the sixth crew led by P/O JM Hartley landing away at RAF Bramcote in Warwickshire, 100 miles to the south. Five of the six pilots claimed they had bombed the primary target under difficult conditions, whilst the sixth had jettisoned his bombs. The next day, a daylight raid was massed, comprising a force of 18 Halifaxes, 18 Stirlings and 11 Manchesters, supported by fighter cover from Hurricanes and Spitfires. The next night, a further force of 19 Whitleys was despatched against the same targets. However, for all the intensity of these attacks not one crew had succeeded in delivering the sought-after killer blow – but crucially, the intense bombardment had damaged the lock gates behind which *Scharnhorst* lay impotently, sealed in until January 1942.

This was to be the squadron's last operation before Christmas, and Len's mind would have turned to how many more operations he would have to carry out on the obsolescent Whitleys before he could convert to the Halifax.

18 December 1941

A gale swept across RAF Dalton with such suddenness as to catch the squadron by surprise. Z6494, freshly repaired following a landing accident on 29 September, was caught in the open at dispersal before she could be tied down, and received further damage that would see her out of action for another three months.

21 December 1941

As the squadron headed towards conversion, it conducted its last few Whitley operations with reduced numbers. Crewmen found they were not flying operationally at the same pace as previously, and some slack appeared in their routines. Taking advantage of this opportunity,

Scharnhorst *in Brest (Chris Goss Collection)*

Sgt Ernest de Mattos was posted on a two-week detachment to 75 Squadron, which was just about to start converting from the Wellington Mk.Ic to the Wellington Mk.III. One of the upgrades to the Wellington Mk.III was the replacement of the twin-gun rear turret with the same four-gun turret as the one used on the Whitley and the Stirling, within which he had already proven himself so adept.

23 DECEMBER 1941

The forthcoming introduction of the Halifax heralded the need for further crewmen, especially an air engineer and another air gunner who would either man the beam guns or more typically the mid-upper turret. Among the influx of new personnel was F/Sgt Ivor Lewis, an air engineer. He was an experienced hand who had come from an eventful background and had already enjoyed a comprehensive service career before arriving at 102 Squadron.

He was of Welsh descent, his parents, Ivor John Lewis and Morfydd Bowen, hailing from a community that had seen a boom in coalmining, providing opportunities not only underground but also for all the support services being demanded by the rapidly expanding community. Morfydd came from a mining family in Aberrhondda and worked as a shop assistant, whilst Ivor John lived with his family in Pwllgwaun and started his career as a clerk in a furniture shop.

As they were coming to know each other, disaster struck the region: on 14 October 1913 there was an explosion underground at the Universal Colliery in Senghenydd, 2 miles to the east of Cilfynydd, which killed 439 miners, making it the worst ever mining disaster within Great Britain. This hit the community very hard, none more so than the Bowen family, who had originally lived in Cilfynydd and would have lost many close friends. The number of bodies recovered overwhelmed the local undertakers and churches, and it took over a month to conduct all the funerals, a sombre backdrop on the run-up to Christmas.

Two weeks later, just after sunset on 27 October 1913, a tornado with winds in excess of 160 mph tracked northwards up the Taff Valley through Treforest, Pontypridd, Cilfynydd and Abercynon, venting its indiscriminate fury on communities that were still reeling from the mining disaster and were not yet halfway through burying their dead. Accompanied by violent storms and even occurrences of ball lightning, the tornado caused massive damage and killed three more people, making this the deadliest tornado seen in Great Britain at that time.

A few months later, on Christmas Eve 1913, 18-year-old Morfydd boarded a ship at Liverpool to undertake a voyage to Chile. Such a journey to South America was not uncommon amongst Welsh families choosing to seek out better prospects overseas than faced them at home, and had become popular during the 19th century. What was so unusual was that at the tender age of 18 she was making the journey unaccompanied. The route took the pioneering Morfydd around Cape Horn, notorious as one of the most hazardous shipping routes in the world, so her passage was unlikely to have been smooth.

Seven months later, on 1 August 1914, Ivor sailed from Liverpool for Rio de Janeiro. He gave his occupation as a telegraphist, and confirmed his age as 21 when he was in fact nearer 23. Another pioneer was on his way. Three days later, Britain declared war on Germany.

Ivor John and Morfydd had made arrangements to meet up on an alien continent thousands of miles from home in Wales to start a new life together. However, before they could be reunited, Ivor John would have to have found his way across the width of South America. He may have joined a group of fellow countrymen heading for the popular Welsh settlements in Argentina to get him at least part of the way, then parted company as they went south and he went on to cross the Andes mountains.

The reunion would have been a particularly special event, as Morfydd had recently given birth to a baby girl, Gwynedd Mary. The timing of the birth suggests that the couple had only just had time to conceive their daughter before putting into motion their plans to emigrate. One possible reason to explain such hurried planning could have been that their union, once discovered, may not have been received with complete approval from the fire and brimstone preachers prevalent in Welsh communities, where strict interpretation of the Bible was the anchor. This could provide a clue as to the circumstances surrounding Morfydd's hasty exit from Wales.

The couple soon had another addition to the family, Illtyd Gad Ivor, born on 5 May 1916 in La Paz, Bolivia. Then, after the couple had increased their family by two more, they decided it was time to pay a return visit to their home country and show their children where they had come from. So it was that eight years after Ivor John and Morfydd had left Wales, the young family of six made the passage from their home in Peru to Cristóbal, Panama, where they boarded a ship for Avonmouth.

Each family member then proceeded to make four more transatlantic crossings between 1923 and 1929, splitting their time between two homes 6,000 miles apart. Ivor John would always travel alone, never spending more than a few weeks away from his job in Peru, while Morfydd stayed longer in Wales and would always accompany the children. By the time he was six years old, Illytd Gad Ivor had chosen to drop his first two names, to become known by his last forename, Ivor, like his father.

There was only a finite time remaining before the elder children would have to start paying adult fares, and although Morfydd had been exercising increasing creativity with the children's ages for ticketing purposes, a decision had to be reached as to where they would finally settle. In the end, when Morfydd returned to Peru on 31 July 1929 with their younger children, Ivor and his big sister were left behind in Wales to make their own lives.

Rising tensions in Peru stemming from long-running disputes with Colombia and Ecuador were ratcheting up, leading to fears of civil unrest or even war. A couple of months after Morfydd's return to Ivor John in South America, things started going badly wrong. The stock market crash of 29 October 1929 and the subsequent global depression hit Peru hard, leading to the overthrow of the government in a coup on 25 August 1930. This heralded a period of great turmoil in which there were five presidents in less than seven months, adding to the political instability.

The couple began sorting out their affairs, and Morfydd returned to Wales eight months later, with Ivor John following on 9 January 1932, their overseas adventures now finally behind them. Their departure had not been a moment too soon, because President Sánchez

Cerro survived an assassination attempt in March and another revolt in June, after which the country was plunged into war with both Ecuador and Colombia over land boundaries. In the same year, Peru's southern neighbour, Bolivia, went to war with Paraguay over border disputes. It seemed that the whole continent was descending into anarchy, and the family would have been able to reflect on their lucky escape.

In December of the same year, 16-year-old Ivor gained employment with Pontypridd Council, starting work as an office boy at the coal-fired generating station in Treforest, less than 2 miles from the family home in Ann Street. He was only there for one month, however, before he enlisted as an RAF Apprentice at No.2 Wing, RAF Halton in Buckinghamshire.

Ivor passed his general fitter's exam on 14 November 1935 with a mark of 71.6 per cent, and requested to be posted to a fighter base such as RAF Biggin Hill, RAF Hornchurch or RAF North Weald. Instead he was promoted to AC1, on 3 January 1936, and posted to 16 Squadron at RAF Old Sarum in Wiltshire, which was operating the Hawker Audax. This station was also concurrently hosting the RAF School of Army Co-operation, and had Avro 671 (Cierva C-30A) Rota autogyros. Whilst there, Ivor gained experience on the Audax and its Kestrel engine, but was also enrolled onto Rota course No.7, passing his fitter's exam at 78 per cent on 25 March 1936.

On 2 January 1937, Ivor was posted to No.9 Air Gunners course at the Temporary Armament Training Camp, RAF North Coates Fitties, in Lincolnshire. Six weeks later, on 13 February 1937, he passed at 74 per cent. From here he was posted back to 16 Squadron at RAF Old Sarum, where he started flying as air gunner, and on 11 February 1938 he was promoted to LAC.

Ivor's next posting was to 501 (B) Squadron Auxiliary Air Force at Bristol Aero Works, Filton, on 14 May 1938, where he completed a two-week course on the Mercury engine. Upon completion of this course he was awarded his Mercury engine certificate and posted once more back to 16 Squadron at Old Sarum, where it had just taken delivery of the Westland Lysander, which happened to be powered by a Mercury engine.

Ivor received his Good Conduct badge on 3 January 1939, and three months later, on 30 March 1939, he was recommended for training as an airman pilot. One month after this, 16 Squadron took delivery of the Lysander Mk.II, and Ivor earned promotion to corporal. On 14 June 1939 he was posted on a one-week detachment to Folly Gate Camp at RAF Okehampton in Devon, which was being used at that time by 13 Squadron and 16 Squadron with their Lysanders, after which he returned to 16 Squadron at RAF Old Sarum.

Now considered ready to serve on an operational squadron, Ivor was posted to 4 Squadron at RAF Odiham in Hampshire, on 5 September 1939. At that time it was operating both Lysander Mk.I and Lysander Mk.II aircraft, and preparing to deploy to France. On 22 September, the squadron took a bus to Hook station and caught a train to Southampton, where the men embarked on the Infantry Landing Ship SS *Maid of Orleans*, leaving Cowes Roads at midnight. Upon arrival in France, they disembarked at Cherbourg and caught a train at 1545 hrs, travelling 300 miles overnight to arrive at Péronne in Picardie, from where they went to their billets in Mons-en-Chaussée on 24 September.

Less than a fortnight later, on 5 October, they marched 2½ miles to the south-east, to arrive at Monchy-Lagache, where after settling in they set about embarking on flying duties. The ORB states that 4 Squadron had a 'steady demand from the Army for photographs', confirming reconnaissance operations to be their prime purpose. They also undertook a number of training sorties, including cross-countries, gunnery and bombing practice. Further, because of their forward location, the men of 4 Squadron found themselves hosting a number of high-profile visits. During this period, Ivor flew regularly as air gunner on operational sorties lasting between 20 minutes and 2½ hours, and on 9 February 1940 he was promoted to sergeant.

On the night of 9/10 May 1940, German troops invaded Luxembourg, Holland and Belgium, followed by the main thrust through the 'impenetrable' Ardennes into France. At 0430 hrs on the day of the invasion, a He 111 flew low over the village of Monchy-Lagache, but it was not fired on because no alarm had been sounded. At 1430 hrs an *alarme* was sounded as six He 111s appeared and were fired on; one was claimed as having been brought down in flames whilst another was expected to have carried out a forced landing. The war in France had shifted up a gear.

As the tempo of the war ratcheted up, 4 Squadron's Lysanders were in increasing demand to fulfil tactical and artillery reconnaissance sorties, operating from an Advanced Landing Ground (ALG) at Aspelare in Belgium, 90 miles north-east of Monchy-Lagache. During this period of intense operations, Ivor was again recommended for training as airman pilot.

On 15 May at 1135 hrs, Ivor took off in Lysander P1711 to fly to Aspelare with his pilot, P/O Stephen Hankey, but they crashed 2 miles away from the ALG, near the village of Outer, both crewmen escaping unhurt. The next day, news was received that German forces had penetrated the French line on the River Meuse, so at first light the squadron drew back 60 miles north, to Little Ronchin. As the German advance continued, the Lysander operations faced ever greater opposition from the advancing Heer forces on the ground and the increasingly confident Bf 109 and Bf 110 fighters in the air.

It was already clear that the British footprint in France was unsustainable, and 4 Squadron joined the retreat of other British fighting units towards Dunkirk. In the next step of its withdrawal, the squadron left Little Ronchin at 0300 hrs on 21 May and relocated to Clairmarais, 40 miles to the north-west. Next day at 0100 hrs, it began its final 10-mile journey north to Dunkirk. In parallel with this evacuation, all of the squadron's aircraft capable of being flown departed at 0600 hrs for RAF Hawkinge in Kent. At 0830 hrs those members of the squadron who had not been able to fly out arrived at Dunkirk, whilst on the other side of the English Channel its Lysanders flew on 30 miles north-west, to RAF Detling in Kent. At 1830 hrs the remaining squadron personnel embarked on the Great Western Railway passenger steamer SS *St Helier*, and reached Dover three hours later.

A few hours after this, at 0300 hrs on 23 May 1940, they were on the move again, this time by train to Tidworth in Wiltshire, which they reached at 0830 hrs, and upon arrival were transported to Royal Army Service Corps Perham Down, 1 mile away. After a few hours rest they went back to the station to get on another train at 1530 hrs, this time going towards

Lysander Mk.III, showing air gunner's position (Chris Goss Collection)

Manchester. At 2300 hrs they arrived at Altrincham in Cheshire, and were taken by bus to RAF Ringway, 4 miles away, where they were finally able to regroup.

RAF Ringway was destined only to be a temporary destination, and two weeks later, on 7 June, the squadron relocated to RAF Linton-on-Ouse by bus. Finally at a permanent base, 4 Squadron was able to resume operations, this time performing coastal reconnaissance, weather reconnaissance and flying training sorties such as dive bombing.

On 27 August 1940 the squadron moved again, this time 9 miles south-east to RAF Clifton, just outside of York city centre, and took delivery of the Lysander Mk.III. This aircraft provided Ivor with double the firepower from the rear cockpit, the single Lewis or Vickers gun being replaced by a twin 0.303" Browning installation. There was an increase in training flying as crews became familiar with their new aircraft; dive bombing, and front and rear gunnery practice, supplemented their reconnaissance sorties. In addition, the squadron started to evolve new capabilities such as supply dropping and drogue towing.

Ivor having served as an air gunner for 19 months with 4 Squadron, found his tour of operations drawing to a close on 31 March 1941. The next day he was promoted to F/Sgt and went to study the new breed of four-engine heavy bombers, earning his Lancaster airframe certificate on 17 June 1941. His newly acquired skills led him to his next posting, on 13 October 1941 to 44 Squadron at RAF Waddington. This would shortly become the first operational Lancaster squadron, and Ivor stayed for seven weeks to learn about the Merlin engine. He then went to take an examination at Rolls-Royce on 31 November [*sic*], gaining his Merlin engine certificate on 1 December 1941. From here he returned to 44 Squadron until 23 December 1941, when he was posted to 102 Squadron, where he stayed for a fortnight over Christmas. On 8 January 1942 he took a temporary detachment to 10 Squadron at RAF Leeming, which was already operating the Halifax. At the end of this detachment Ivor would be fully conversant with the Halifax airframe and its Merlin engines, and by the time 102 Squadron had finished converting to the Halifax he would be ready to meet his latest challenge as air engineer.

24 December 1941

Ed Cooke recalled an informal arrangement for Christmas, namely 'we were told that we would not be operating if the other side stayed at home', so after breakfast, when the bar opened at 1000 hrs, they started their celebrations. He takes up the story:

> Someone must have answered the phone about 11.45am as a big shout 'OPS ON, report to the Flights.' We all put on our greatcoats, mounted our trusty steeds and off we went being joined by the officers from their Mess; over a hundred bods cycling through the village singing Christmas Carols. By the time we approached the airfield I think the songs had slowly swung around to Air Force ones (lullabies etc). We all turned left into the camp and there was W/Cdr Bintley standing outside his office. He took one look at us and roared 'You drunken bums – you are not flying my aeroplanes today'. So we all saluted as we went past, did a U-turn on the tarmac and headed back to the Mess.

27 December 1941

Target[100]	Aircraft on target	Types
Düsseldorf	132	66 Wellington 30 Hampden 29 Whitley 7 Manchester
CC29 Boulogne	34	15 Whitley 13 Wellington 6 Hampden
Brest (*Scharnhorst* and *Gneisenau*)	29	23 Wellington 6 Stirling
Soesterberg aerodrome	6	Blenheim
Minelaying off Kiel (Forget-me-nots)	5	Hampden

Nursery Operation

Primary target: Boulogne (docks and shipping).
Alternative: AIP.
Last Resort: AIP.
Operation C.184: 7 aircraft (freshmen), operational call sign QH7.
Bomb load: 12 × 250 lb GP TD 0.025.
Route: Base – Finningley – Orford Ness – Boulogne and return.
Time Off: 1710 hrs.
Weather: 6/10 to 8/10 cloud. Considerable gaps.
Opposition: Negligible.

The last action of the year was a nursery operation to Boulogne. There were so many inexperienced crewmen needing to be brought up to speed that the three novice captains scheduled for the night's freshman operation were supported by two experienced 102 Squadron pilots and two more captains brought in from other squadrons. The crewmen manning the other positions were also noticeably light on experience, but for each crew there was at least one other combat-hardened crewman providing an anchor. There was also a concerted effort to re-introduce crewmen who had been away from operational flying duties for extended periods, many of whom had not logged combat hours on the squadron for months; three of them had not flown operationally for four months. The squadron was making a conspicuous effort to get all of its crewmen current during the limited time remaining on Whitleys.

Crews left in 1-minute intervals from 1707 hrs, led out by Sgt Derrick Riley. Five crews found their primary target, whilst P/O JM Hartley, with a navigator on only his second operation, failed to find it and jettisoned his bombs in the sea. The remaining crew, led by Derrick Riley, bombed Le Touquet-Étaples from only 4,000 ft. This was the same aerodrome that P/O Hartley had mistakenly bombed during his freshman operation on 7 November, but Derrick Riley, an experienced captain, would not have taken such a decision without compelling justification. The fact that he had gone in at such an unusually low level suggests that he had not only seen something relevant, but had gone in sufficiently low to make absolutely sure of his target.

The night was kind to the squadron, and there were no losses to crews, but all were ordered to land away, at RAF Driffield.

5 January 1942

Target[101]	Aircraft on target	Types
Brest:		
(i) *Scharnhorst* and *Gneisenau*	87	48 Wellington 27 Hampden 12 Manchester
(ii) Z498 docks in Port Militaire	67	41 Wellington 17 Whitley 7 Halifax 2 Stirling
CC16 Cherbourg docks	37	19 Whitley 16 Wellington 1 Hampden 1 Stirling
Minelaying in Quiberon Bay (Gorse)	5	Hampden
Nickelling:		
(i) Rennes area	3	Hampden
(ii) Paris area	2	Hampden

NURSERY OPERATION

Primary target: Cherbourg (docks and shipping).
Last Resort: AIP.
Operation C.185:[102] 4 aircraft (freshmen), operational call sign JZ6.
Bomb load: 12 × 250 lb GP TD 0.025.
Route: Base – Cranfield – Bridport – Cherbourg and return.
Time Off: 0420 hrs.
Weather: 10/10 cloud in target area.
Opposition: Slight.

January 1942 started as December 1941 had finished, with another nursery operation to a French port; this time four freshmen were scheduled to attack Cherbourg. Unusually, this would be an early morning start, the crews scheduled to arrive at their primary target 2½ hours before sunrise,[103] their journey being assisted by a full moon: ideal conditions. Their enemy would not have been used to such an attack at this time in the morning, so there would have been the element of surprise.

As the squadron was used to conducting night operations that began on one date and concluded the next, the entry in the ORB reflects the night that the preparation for the operation began, although it would not be conducted until the next day, 6 January.

The captains this time were to comprise three qualifying 2nd pilots and an experienced pilot, Sgt John Barber, from another squadron. Barber did not, however, start, leaving the three novice captains to complete the operation without him.

To arrive over the port at about an hour before dawn, the aircraft left from 0424 hrs at very conservative 5-minute intervals behind Australian Sgt Alex Hollingworth in Z9289. Upon arriving over the port, there was too much cloud cover for the crews to identify the target, and they had been given strict instructions that under such conditions they were to return to base without dropping their bombs. To give the weather a chance they waited for some time, but it soon became evident that it was unlikely to clear and so they set course for home with their bombs still on board. Aboard Z9289, things took a turn for the worse; Sgt Ed Brain later commented:[104] 'Suddenly there was a horrendous noise and the aircraft shook violently. The starboard engine temperature was off the clock and had to be shut down.'

Once they were over the English coast the unmistakable sound of a labouring engine was recognised by a searchlight crew, who realised the aircraft was in trouble and needed to land, so shone their light across the ground in the direction of the nearest aerodrome. Ed Brain recalls Alex Hollingworth saying 'They want us to land, but I want to make it back to base.' No-one on board disagreed with what was to become a fateful decision.

The aircraft struggled on past all the diversionary aerodromes, one by one, in the south of England and made its slow progress northwards on one engine, still carrying a full bomb load. With the sun now risen, Air Gunner Sgt Leonard 'Jacko' Jackson called out the names of the towns they passed, and when they began to lose height too fast over Derbyshire, they jettisoned their bombs over open ground to the south of Sheffield. By the time they reached Barnsley, the loss of height was now so serious that Alex Hollingworth tried to restart the

*Royal British Legion memorial plaque
at Cresswell Street, Barnsley
(Barnsley War Memorials Project)*

defective starboard engine, but it caught fire, as he had feared it would.

Continuing inexorably to lose altitude and now with 15-foot-long flames streaming from the starboard engine, Jacko Jackson and 2nd Pilot Sgt John Hazledine appreciated the seriousness of the situation and baled out. Alex Hollingworth, without his mask and helmet, could not order evacuation, so pushed Navigator Sgt Ed Brain in the arm, directing him to escape. Ed Brain in his turn ordered the aircraft's evacuation, although there were by now only three of them left aboard. As he made for the escape hatch, he grabbed the leg of Canadian Sgt Alexander 'Big Buck' Buchanan, who was busily fixing his wireless, and gestured him to get out. With flames from the defective engine now even longer, Ed Brain took one last look at Alex Hollingworth, observing that he had no parachute and that his face was 'ashen white' as the implications of his decision to return to base struck home, and jumped to safety, as had the other two crewmen before him.

Big Buck left his escape late, and was reported to have been no more than 100 ft above the ground when he jumped. The minimum survivable jump height with the Irvin R24 chest-type parachute from an aircraft flying at around 100 mph being 150 ft, he might have just got away with it, but when he came down in the site of the local refuse incinerator he hit his head on an obstruction and was killed.

With no hope of recovery and no escape, Alex Hollingworth stayed at his post to steer his dying aircraft away from rows of terraced houses as he descended rapidly over the town of Pogmoor. Bystanders looked up to see the death throes of the fated bomber with flames pouring off her starboard wing, as she described a desperate decaying trajectory just over their heads. As they stared, transfixed, few would have even stopped to consider that there might still be a pilot aboard; a 22-year-old Australian fighting a war far from home, known by his brother as Lex, but to his friends as Bruno.

As he ran out of altitude, he ran out of options and steered his doomed aircraft towards a quarry behind Cresswell Street, where he attempted a crash-landing in a clay pit at 1015 hrs. He did not survive.

On the same day, Sgt Ernest de Mattos returned from his two-week detachment to 75 Squadron. During the time he had been there, he would have helped accustom the Wellington air gunners to the four-gun Nash & Thompson rear turret. There is no record of his having done any operational or training flying whilst on this detachment, so it must be assumed that his contribution was limited to ground training. When he returned to 102 Squadron he did not rejoin A Flight, but went instead to B Flight to address an imbalance of air gunnery skills across the squadron.

Also on this date, Whitley and Halifax veteran P/O Wally Lashbrook arrived from 28 Conversion Flight (CF) at RAF Leconfield in Yorkshire to formally set up 102 CF at RAF Dalton, although some conversion flying had already begun back in December.

6 JANUARY 1942

Target[105]	Aircraft on target	Types
Brest (*Scharnhorst* and *Gneisenau*)	31	Wellington
Roving patrols over Emden, Hamburg, Kassel and Aachen	19	Hampden
SN25 Stavanger-Sola aerodrome	11	Whitley
CC16A Cherbourg docks	5	Wellington
Nickelling:		
(i) Northern France	15	10 Whitley 5 Wellington
(ii) Orleans – Bourges area	1	Whitley

NURSERY OPERATION

Dropping area: Nickelling over Paris.
Operation C.186: 4 aircraft (freshmen), operational call sign K3N.
Route: Base – Cranfield – Harwell – Bognor – Quiberville – Compiègne – dropping area and return.
Time Off: 1730 hrs.
Weather: Fine ground haze.
Opposition: Nil.

The squadron was given a break from bombing operations and, for a change, was tasked to drop nickels over Paris. This was classified as a freshman operation, and the squadron called upon two captains who had just qualified on their first operations on 27 December, as well as two experienced captains who had just joined the squadron and had also completed their nursery runs on the same night. Each crew dropped 25 packets of nickels over Paris unopposed, and all returned safely.

7 JANUARY 1942

In the evening, 102 CF received its first dual-control-equipped Halifax, L9565. This was an old B Mk.I sent from 1652 CU. Fitted with Merlin X engines, it lacked engine power and also lacked the mid-upper turret of the prevailing standard B Mk.II aircraft, but was otherwise perfectly adequate for pilot conversion training.

8 JANUARY 1942

The first two pilots to join 102 CF under P/O Wally Lashbrook, both from A Flight, were its new commander, S/Ldr ED Griffiths, and the newly promoted F/Lt Harry Williams. They both received dual instruction and completed their first solo flights in L9565.

The evening marked the arrival of the second aircraft from 1652 CU. This was L9532, which was also a B Mk.I, but this one arrived in an unserviceable condition and could not be put to work immediately, as had been hoped, slowing the conversion programme.

Target[106]	Aircraft on target	Types
Brest:		
(i) *Scharnhorst* and *Gneisenau*	92	45 Wellington 37 Hampden 10 Manchester
(ii) Z498 docks in Port Militaire	59	27 Wellington 27 Whitley 5 Halifax
CC16 Cherbourg	35	18 Wellington 10 Manchester 7 Hampden
Minelaying off the Frisian Islands (Nectarine)	5	Hampden
Nickelling over Paris area	2	Hampden

Main Operation

Primary target: Brest (arsenal and power station area).
Operation C.187: 6 aircraft, operational call sign 7NL.
Bomb load: No.1 or No.3 TD 0.025 to include 1× 250 lb GP MLD.
Route: Base – Cranfield – Bridport – Pointe de Pontusval – Brest and return.
Time Off: 0320 hrs.
Weather: 5/10 to 10/10 cloud over target area.
Opposition: Moderate heavy flak.

Nursery Operation

Primary target: Cherbourg (docks and shipping).
Alternative: AIP.
Last Resort: AIP.
1 aircraft (freshman), operational call sign 1SY (cancelled).
Bomb load: 12× 250 GP TD 0.025.
Route: Base – Cranfield – Bridport – Cherbourg and return.
Time Off: 0340 hrs.

Brest was still home to the battleships *Scharnhorst* and *Gneisenau* as well as the heavy cruiser *Prinz Eugen*, but was also the base for both the 1st and 9th U-Boat Flotillas. The submarines here were afforded protection by a single bunker that was still under construction, but would eventually be 333 m × 192 m when completed, accommodating 10 dry and 5 wet pens that could hold up to 20 submarines.

Six crews were to be involved, and in continuation of the drive to raise experience levels across the squadron, crewmen who had not been involved in combat operations for a while were brought back, so all could be up to scratch for the challenges of conversion. As with the attack on Cherbourg earlier in the week, this was to be an operation scheduled to deliver its payload in the pre-dawn hours,[107] and so the crews departed in 2-minute intervals from 0321 hrs.

Concurrent with this was to be a nursery operation for Sgt John Barber following his not starting on the Cherbourg run three days previously. This was scheduled for Cherbourg once more, but the operation was cancelled and John Barber would have to wait for yet another day.

Meanwhile, four of the crews on the main operation to Brest claimed to have attacked the primary target. One of these crews was led by Sgt Charles Barr, two of whose two bombs had been hung up, and which he was subsequently able to jettison over the Channel. His return journey was complicated further when his aircraft developed a glycol leak and had to divert to RAF Upavon. His aircraft would be repaired and fly again with the squadron, but Sgt Derrick Riley's aircraft suffered heavy flak damage and would not.

10 JANUARY 1942

New Zealander F/Lt Peter Robinson arrived at 102 CF from 35 Squadron to take charge of the Halifax conversion flying that had been set up during the last five days by P/O Wally Lashbrook.

17 JANUARY 1942

Another new starter on 102 Squadron was Pilot Kenneth Bernard Wright, a young man with an impressive portfolio of flying experience belying his age. His father was Herbert Wright, son of an iron moulder from Wellington, Shropshire. By the time Herbert was 17, he had become a grocer's apprentice, and his father John had died leaving his widow as the head of the household. In the same village lived Elizabeth Pountain Turner, daughter of a general dealer of clothing and furniture.

Herbert and Elizabeth met, and when they were both 26 years old were married in Shifnal, Shropshire, in September 1920. About a year later, on 11 August 1921, they had their son Kenneth Bernard Wright. Kenneth attended Solihull School, and had a strong interest in flying, so in 1936 joined the Cadet School and also attended the flying school at Brough. In 1937 he went to work as a clerk for the Beacon Insurance Company in Birmingham, but left to join the RAF as soon as he could.

On 2 September 1939 he accepted a commission as an acting pilot officer on probation (backdated to July 1939) and was posted to No.9 Flying Training School at RAF Hullavington in Wiltshire. After three weeks he was posted to No.11 Service Flying Training School at RAF Shawbury in Shropshire. Whilst there, Kenneth gained experience flying the Hart, Audax and Hind single-engined biplane light bombers. On 18 November 1939 he was issued with his flying brevet, along with a narrative of his performance that stated he had: 'improved from average to above average during ATS in ground subjects. Good average flying ability very keen but does not look around enough. A satisfactory officer.' He had only just turned 18.

Following his time at RAF Shawbury, Kenneth was posted to 12 OTU at RAF Benson in Oxfordshire on 20 April 1940 and was promoted to pilot officer on probation. Whilst on this ten-week course, he was trained to fly serving front line bombers such the Fairey Battle, and twin-engined trainers such as the Anson.

Having gained experience on twin-engined types, he was next posted to 10 OTU on 29 June 1940 where he undertook a one-week conversion course to the Whitley, following which he was posted to 19 OTU in the capacity of instructor. Three days later his appointment as pilot officer was confirmed. He was still only 18 years old.

During March 1941 Kenneth started reporting recurrent eustachian catarrh, an ailment that prevented his eustachian tube from draining and thereby preventing him from equalising the pressure in his ears. This would become a significant problem for him as a flying instructor.

Kenneth was promoted to flying officer on 20 April 1941 and continued instructing at 19 OTU. Sadly, his ear problems became more frequent and he was admitted to the Officers' Hospital, Gleneagles (Gleneagles Hotel) for two weeks in August 1941, then a further four weeks in the Officers' Hospital Torquay (Palace Hotel) during September and October the same year. On 28 October 1941, Kenneth instructed No.31 course at 19 OTU. This was to be his last course, and when he left he had accrued a remarkable 977 flying hours.

On 16 January 1942, he reported to 35 Squadron at RAF Linton-On-Ouse, whereupon he was immediately re-posted to 102 Squadron at RAF Dalton, 10 miles to the north. Upon his arrival, he was assigned to B Flight.

26 January 1942

Target[108]	Aircraft on target	Types
Hanover aim point A (town)	71	51 Wellington 17 Hampden 3 Halifax
Emden aim point A (town)	31	23 Whitley 6 Wellington 2 Manchester
Brest (*Scharnhorst* and *Gneisenau*)	25	22 Wellington 3 Stirling
Minelaying off the Frisian Islands (Nectarine)	6	Hampden
Nickelling:		
(i) Emden	2	Whitley
(ii) Lille area	2	Hampden

Preparing an Anson for a bombing and gunnery training sortie (Chris Goss Collection)

P/O Kenneth Wright at 19 OTU, 16 February 1941 (the National Archive AIR 29/663)

Ju 88 from NJG2 (Deutsches Bundesarchiv, Bild 101I-367-2377-07A / Schilling / CC-BY-SA)

Nursery Operation

Nickelling
Primary / dropping area: Emden (centre of town).
Alternative: AIP.
Last Resort: AIP.
Operation C.188: 3 aircraft (freshmen), operational call sign L7X.
Aircraft Ē Bomb load: 1× 1,000 lb, 3× 500 lb, 1× 250 lb @ TD 0.025, 1× 250 MLD.
Aircraft C̄ and F nickels only, no bombs.
Route: Base – Filey – Norderney – Großes Lake – Emden and return.
Time Off: 1700 hrs.
Weather: Clear, slight ground haze.
Opposition: Considerable light flak.

Sgt John Barber would have his third attempt at a nursery operation tonight, having missed out on both 5 and 8 January 1942. He was to line up for his freshman operation in front of two other aircraft flown by newly qualified captains, all going to Emden. His aircraft took off at 1700 hrs carrying a live bomb load, while the others took off behind him at 1-minute intervals carrying only payloads of nickels.

John Barber returned at 2340 hrs following a successful sortie, followed by one of the nickelling crews an hour later; but the other, led by Sgt John White in Z9283, did not return. Amongst this crew was Sgt John Hazledine, who had only just escaped the Pogmoor crash three weeks previously.

Two crews from NJG2 were to claim victories tonight, both against Whitleys: Oblt Rudolf Schönert 5./NJG2 operating from Leeuwarden claimed his victory at 2050 hrs, whilst Ofw Heinz Strüning of Ergänzungsstaffel (Erg.)/NJG2 from Gilze-Rijen, claimed his at 2235 hrs. Leeuwarden was just below the route taken by the three 102 Squadron crews so was in the area, whilst Gilze-Rijen was 120 miles further away to the south. This suggests strongly that John White was intercepted by Oblt Rudolf Schönert somewhere north of the West Frisian Islands en route to the dropping area.

Operation
C.189 to
Argent,
31 January
1942

RAF Dalton

RAF Oakington

Cranfield

Harwell
Beacon

Quiberville

Bognor

Rouen

Argent

31 January 1942

Reports would have come through bearing the news that the last of the Allied forces had retreated from the Malay mainland for the safety of Singapore, but the optimism of the moniker 'Britain's Impregnable Fortress' now sounded very hollow indeed. None would have received this news with greater feelings of personal loss than Sgt Ernest de Mattos; the Japanese forces had rampaged with consummate efficiency through the country he had known as home, dispelling the defending forces and subjugating the population in less than eight weeks.

Those who had escaped south to Singapore would have bought themselves some time, but although it was defended with 15" naval guns and an aerodrome, Singapore was still ultimately an island not much bigger than the Isle of Wight. As its inhabitants' last refuge was surrounded, and with dwindling resources to sustain their defence, any respite from the Japanese forces could only ever be temporary; the ability of the Allied forces to resist would be measured not in weeks but in days.

Target[109]	Aircraft on target	Types
Brest (*Scharnhorst* and *Gneisenau*)	72	41 Hampden 18 Wellington 11 Manchester 2 Stirling
CC55A St-Nazaire submarine base	31	19 Wellington 7 Manchester 5 Hampden
Le Havre CC24	14	10 Whitley 4 Wellington
Nickelling:		
(i) Dijon, Bourges, Paris	9	Whitley
(ii) Rennes area	4	3 Hampden 1 Manchester

Nickelling

Dropping area: Nickelling over Bourges area.
Operation C.189: 3 aircraft, operational call sign 8YQ.
Route: Base – Cranfield – Harwell Beacon – Bognor – Quiberville – Rouen – Argent and return.
Time Off: 1700 hrs.
Weather: 10/10 cloud.
Opposition: Nil.

Given the fact that conversion to the Halifax was so soon, the recent losses in the old Whitleys had seemed all the more tragic and pointless. Against this backdrop, another nickelling raid was scheduled, this time for three aircraft to go to Argent, but one of these was to be cancelled. This would be the last operation with the Whitley undertaken by 102 Squadron, and to mark the occasion the two crews chosen had experience levels befitting deep target attack operations.

Sgt John Barber took Len and F/Sgt Richard Bradbury, who had not flown combat operations for the last three months as a sizeable part of this time had been spent in hospital. Tonight they were charged not only with dropping 23 packets of nickels but also with carrying a camera to record the accuracy of their nickelling.

Whitley Z6747 (DY-Q)

Argent

Takeoff 1659 hrs.

Released nickels over target area from 10,500 ft.

Landed 0110 hrs at RAF Oakington.

Operational combat time 8 hrs 11 mins.

Sgt JW Barber

Sgt FA Barker

F/Sgt RF Bradbury   9th operation; combat time 72 hrs 7 mins

Sgt L Starbuck   20th operation; combat time 151 hrs 37 mins

Sgt DC Sandall

Sgt A Huddlestone

John Barber took off first, at 1659 hrs, and encountered no opposition as his crew dropped their nickels. On their return, both aircraft were ordered to land away, John Barber being directed to RAF Oakington, landing uneventfully at 0110 hrs.

Throughout this operation their companion, Z6798, captained by Sgt Bill Davies, had been struggling without altimeter or air speed indicator (ASI) and with a bad glycol leak from the starboard engine, which was reported as being 'on the point of catching fire', so the end of their sortie couldn't come soon enough. They were directed to RAF Lakenheath in Suffolk, which had only recently opened. On their approach at about 200 ft the altimeter indicated 1,500 ft, which nearly resulted in a collision with trees. Bill Davies regained height, raised the undercarriage and crash-landed at 0048 hrs.

102 Squadron had been flying operational sorties with Whitleys throughout the war, but now this operation was to mark the passing of the aircraft type as the squadron looked to the future. As Z6747 was the last of the two aircraft to land, Len and Richard Bradbury could lay claim to being on the crew that had flown 102 Squadron's last ever Whitley operation.

This was also Len's 20th operation; he had now accrued 151 combat hours. Confirming his earlier calculations, this meant that he was on track to achieve his 200 hours at the end of his 27th operation. This would have left him on a happy note going into conversion; he was two-thirds of the way through his tour of operations, but more importantly, three-quarters of the way through on hours, and so could at last perhaps afford to think positively of when it would all be over.

Since B Flight had introduced its black-painted bombers on 20 July 1941 it had despatched 122 aircraft on operations, whilst during the same period the larger A Flight had despatched 265 aircraft in the conventional temperate land scheme camouflage pattern. During these six months, each flight had lost five aircraft to night fighters and two to flak, confirming that the loss rate of black bombers shot down had been more than double those presented in the traditional camouflage pattern. The experimental colour scheme had been an initiative born of desperation, an attempt to be seen to be doing something about the mounting loss rate, but there was now sufficient evidence to confirm that it had not worked, and actually appeared to make matters worse. Consequently, as the squadron looked forward, there would be no further experiments with paint schemes – and no perpetuation of the clashing callsigns.

Whilst the Whitley was waning as a front line bomber, it still had an important role to play in training future crews at the OTUs, in addition to which it could operate as a transport and paratroop platform, two features that made it suitable for special operations. Consequently, as 102 Squadron traded in its obsolescent workhorse and looked to the future, there was no shortage of other squadrons and units that would capitalise upon the availability of its well-worn Whitleys.

Endnotre

96 Halpenny, B.B. (1990) Action Stations: 4. Military airfields of Yorkshire, ISBN 0850595320, Patrick Stephens, p 56.

97 forgottenairfields.com/airfield-dalton-971.html.

98 AIR 14/2673

99 AIR 14/2673

100 AIR 14/2673

101 AIR 14/2674

102 An administrative error led to the misnumbering of the squadron's last Whitley ops of 1942; operation numbers C.185–C.189 being accidentally renumbered C.145–C.149 inclusive.

103 Sunrise over Le Havre (nearest datum point to Cherbourg) 0855 + 1 hour correction for BST.

104 Goss, C. (1995) *It's Suicide but It's Fun: The Story of 102 (Ceylon) Squadron 1917–1956*, ISBN 0947554599, Crécy, pp 61–62.

105 AIR 14/2674

106 AIR 14/2674

107 Sunrise over Nantes (nearest datum point to Brest) 0851 + 1 hour correction for BST.

108 AIR 14/2674

109 AIR 14/2674

6

FLYING THE HEAVIES

The third of the new breed of heavy bombers entering service behind the Short Stirling and Avro Manchester was the Handley Page Halifax, which as bomber technology took a huge leap forward, was widely regarded as being the best of the three. Each Halifax took 76,000 man-hours to build,[110] almost 50 per cent more than the 52,000 man-hours to build a Whitley.

In 1936, the Air Ministry issued Specification P.13/36 for a twin-engined medium bomber for 'world-wide use' based on the unproven Rolls-Royce Vulture engine, an X-configured combination of two V12 Kestrel engines. This competition pitted the Handley Page HP56 directly against the Avro Type 679 Manchester. Problems with the development of the Vulture engine soon convinced Handley Page that any aircraft arising from this competition would become tied to the failure of the engine, leading to a loss of reputation and production orders. Consequently, Handley Page withdrew the HP56 to leave the Manchester unopposed, but in so doing left a sense of bad blood with Rolls-Royce.

Released from its commitments to the Vulture engine, Handley Page evolved the HP56 into a four-engined design known as the HP57 Halifax Mk.I, which was accepted under Air Ministry Specification 32/37 in January 1939 straight off the drawing board, even before the first prototype had flown.

The Halifax could be operated by a crew of six, comprising pilot, navigator, WOp/AG, air engineer, rear air gunner and beam air gunner (Halifax B Mk.I Series 1) or mid-upper air gunner (Halifax B Mk.I Series 2 onwards where a mid-upper turret was fitted). The spacious interior allowed for a range of complements, seven, with the inclusion of a dedicated bomb aimer, generally being accepted as the standard. The pilot's position was on the left of the cockpit. The air engineer's instruments were behind the pilot, but he could also take up position to the right of the pilot in a jump seat when needed. When the aircraft was configured for a training role, a second set of flight controls could be installed to the right of the pilot, and the 2nd pilot would then fly from the air engineer's jump seat. The WOp was below and forward of the pilot, whilst the navigator's chart table was further forward, a short distance from the bomb aimer's position in the nose.

The first truly mass-produced version of this bomber would be the HP59 Halifax Mk.II, with enlarged fuel tanks and uprated Merlin XX engines.[111] She could carry a bomb load of 13,000 lb, almost double that of the Whitley: 10,000 lb in the central 22-ft-long bomb bay, with the remaining 3,000 lb in six bomb cells in the wings between the inner engine nacelles and the fuselage. Furthermore, the bomb bay permitted the concurrent carriage of two 4,000 lb Cookie HC bombs.

The Halifax at this stage, however, exhibited two particularly undesirable traits: the first was lack of power, which manifested itself in a low service ceiling that brought aircrew within range of the medium-calibre flak guns. This problem would become noticeably worse from 10 March 1942, due not to any new enemy weapon but to the operational introduction of the higher-flying Avro Lancaster. The lower-flying Halifaxes provided the Lancasters with a shield from the flak guns below, resulting in Halifax crews becoming known in some circles as 'flak bait'. To add insult to injury, Halifaxes could suddenly find themselves in a hail of bombs as the higher-flying Lancasters released their bomb loads from safety above them. This resulted in much higher losses for the Halifax whilst Lancaster losses on the same operations would be disproportionately lower, providing a skewed basis for the statistics which helped build an aura of apparent invincibility around the Lancaster.

The Lancaster at its introduction was equipped with the same Merlin XX engines as the contemporary versions of the Halifax, leading to speculation that both aircraft should have enjoyed similar performance, but it has been postulated[112] that 'Rolls-Royce advised Avro to install the Merlins well forward and below the leading edge of the wing' on the Lancaster, advice apparently not received by Handley Page, who had mounted the engines higher and closer to the wing. This gave the Halifax two distinct disadvantages:

- The thrust line was higher, disturbing the airflow over the wing and reducing lift.
- The propellers were so close to the leading edge as to cause vibration, which in turn led to premature mechanical failures in components such as the reduction gear and radiators, especially on the outer engines.

The second problem trumped even the lack of power; this was a deadly aerodynamic anomaly known as 'rudder overbalance'. Numbers of losses were starting to rise beyond what could be attributed to enemy action. Where unexplained crashes had been witnessed, reports had emerged of aircraft departing controlled flight to impact the ground in either a spin or an inverted dive – but there were never any survivors to explain what had happened. Further, when crash sites were analysed, there was never any evidence of technical failures. It would not be until 1943 that this problem would be first recreated under trials conditions, at A&AEE Boscombe Down, resulting in the redesign of the fin and rudder assembly.

One aspect of the design that had been particularly well thought through was the ease with which crews could exit the aircraft. By the standards of the day there were plenty of hatches of comparatively generous dimensions to permit escape both below by parachute and above following ditching. This foresight became closely coupled with aircrew survival rates compared with other aircraft, and helped to offset the less desirable features of the early Halifaxes.

All crew entered by the main crew door located behind the port wing. Escape was by the following means:

Parachute Drill – Normal Method[113]

- All crew would fit parachutes and evacuate through a trapdoor hatch behind the bomb aimer's position, the pilot exiting last.

Parachute Drill – Emergency Method[114]

- All crew would fit parachutes.
- The cockpit crew, with the exception of the navigator, would evacuate through the front hatch, the pilot exiting last.
- The navigator would climb aft and open the main crew door, and having opened it would be first out, leaving the air gunners to follow along.
- The rear air gunner could instead elect to climb out of his turret, strap on his parachute, re-enter the turret, rotate it through 90 degrees and then fall out backwards.

This drill could be achieved by a well-practised crew in 14 seconds.[115]

Ditching[116]

- All crew would evacuate through one of three hatches:
- A hatch above the pilot's head.
- A hatch forward of the mid-upper turret.
- A hatch further forward of the mid-upper turret, which included access to dinghy stowage.

Testament is borne to the survival rate of Halifax crews in a survey taken in a prisoner of war (pow) camp by RAF Burn's station commander, Gp Capt Nigel Marwood-Elton, amongst his fellow captives[117] following his having been shot down in March 1944:

SUMMARY OF AIRCREW SURVIVAL BY TYPE

Type	Crew position Safest to Worst	Escaped safely
Halifax	Nav, Flt Eng, WOp, Bomb Aimer, Mid-upper AG, Rear AG, Pilot	29.4%
Wellington	Nav, WOp, Beam AG, Pilot, Rear AG	27.5%
Stirling	Nav, WOp, Rear AG, Flt Eng, Mid-upper AG, Bomb Aimer, Pilot	16.9%
Lancaster	Nav, Bomb Aimer, Flt Eng, WOp, Pilot, Mid-upper AG, Rear AG	10.9%

More Halifaxes arrived on 102 Squadron, and conversion training picked up momentum. One thing immediately apparent was this new aircraft's requirement for a larger complement of crewmen to fulfil all the responsibilities on board. Whilst the Whitley had required a crew of four (plus 2nd pilot and 2nd WOp as circumstances dictated), the Halifax required another air gunner, an air engineer and possibly even a bomb aimer as well.

On squadrons where crews had been encouraged to bond from the outset and remain together throughout their tour, this new requirement would have caused interpersonal frictions in terms of introducing not only new personalities but also different levels of experience into established close-knit crews. Conversely, 102 Squadron's established big-family philosophy meant that there was much less interpersonal impact when introducing new crew members, in fact the whole exercise would likely just be swept up as part of the package of converting to the new aircraft.

The promise heralded by the new aircraft was soon put into an operational context as crews gained experience and got to grips with the type. Opinions were mixed; W/Cdr Bill Swetman[118] recalls:

> Among the crews of Bomber Command, the Halifax quickly gained a reputation as a killer. Take the approved evasive action – the corkscrew – and there was every chance that your rudders would lock, completely overpowering the ailerons, and that you would find yourself in an uncontrollable spin.

Colonel Jean Calmel[119] attests to a further potential danger; 'we had learned that when an engine caught fire it produced an air stream behind it which acted as a blow pipe that could cut through a wing longeron in less than a minute', after which the wing would break off.

Based upon experience gained from the Whitleys, veteran crews were well aware that Merlin engines could occasionally fail without any obvious provocation, and sometimes catch fire even before receiving the attentions of hostile enemy action. This was not an entirely happy coincidence.

The Halifax had got off to a bad start. Maybe some crewmen were already starting to wonder whether the old Whitleys had not been so bad after all.

February 1942

During this month, the British colony of Ceylon formally adopted 102 Squadron and paid for its aircraft. Its informal nickname, 'Morecambe's Own', was now superseded by the official name that would endure throughout the rest of the war: 'Ceylon Squadron'.

14 February 1942

The Area Bombing Directive was introduced. This encapsulated a change in strategy, effectively refocusing the aims of Bomber Command. The first change was catalysed by the advent of new technology: targets in Germany within the range of the new TR1335 GEE navigation capability were to be prioritised, whilst those beyond its range, such as Berlin, were secondary targets, to be attacked when the weather over them was more suitable than that over the area of primary targets. The second change was that Bomber Command was now able to employ its forces 'without restriction', removing a limitation, placed on it in November 1941, that had been invoked in response to severe losses at the hands of enemy night fighters. Most controversial was the third change, a clear statement defining a military objective 'to focus attacks on the morale of the enemy civil population'. This would result in a change of targets being supplied to the bomber crews, but more portentously the combination of these three strands laid the foundations for a far grander exercise that would become known as the Thousand Plan.

22 FEBRUARY 1942

To head up the renewed campaign in the wake of the Area Bombing Directive, Air Chief Marshal Charles 'Peter' Portal, chief of the air staff (CAS), himself a firm believer in air power, appointed the like-minded and charismatic Air Marshal Arthur Harris to the post of commander-in-chief of Bomber Command. Known to his friends and colleagues as Butch, short for butcher, he would soon become known to a much wider audience as Bomber Harris.

24 FEBRUARY 1942

Two Halifaxes operated by 1652 CU at RAF Marston Moor in Yorkshire suffered serious damage on take-off, both for the same reason. The two aircraft, both in the hands of ex-Whitley pilots, swung off the runway due to excessive application of rudder, in each case causing undercarriage collapse. The officer commanding wrote in the accident reports: 'Whitley training pilots have a common characteristic of violent use of rudder – Halifax is sensitive to rudder input and it would be an advantage if ex-Whitley pilots had a refresher course on Oxfords before Halifax conversion.'

25 FEBRUARY 1942

Although the 20-year-old squadron newcomer F/O Kenneth Wright had been promoted to acting flight lieutenant, he had yet to fly operationally on the squadron.

1 MARCH 1942

Richard Bradbury was promoted to WO1; he had been promoted to F/Sgt six months previously, and in that time had flown seven operations.

6–7 MARCH 1942

Len went through his Halifax conversion, becoming WO/AG Grade II on 6 March 1942, followed by achieving WO/AG Grade I on the next day.

Tonight saw the first full-scale operation using GEE-enabled bombing. The new equipment was operated exclusively by the navigator under a shroud of secrecy, its workings withheld from even his close colleague, the WOp. The target for this inaugural massed operation was Essen, and 211 aircraft were detailed to take part, 82 of which (39 per cent) were GEE-enabled. Under a concept known as the Shaker Technique, the GEE aircraft would arrive first and drop flares, which would then indicate the target for the following aircraft, which were not equipped with GEE.

However, this did not play out as intended; there was such a long delay between the flares being dropped and the arrival of the bombers that the flares went out, leaving the bombers without GEE to drop their loads over a wide area, mostly short of the target. The result was that there had been no damage to the main target area.[120]

There were also few trained bomb aimers available at this time, so in many cases this legacy responsibility remained with the navigator, who just before the run into target would have to leave his station to squeeze into the bomb aimer's position in the nose. This left the GEE set unmonitored, depriving the navigator of the precision navigation updates he needed during this most crucial part of the bombing run.

As crews got to grips with learning the lessons of this unsuccessful operation, it would only be a matter of weeks before a noticeable increase in accuracy was achieved. On 102 Squadron, the importance of retraining crewmen to fill the position of bomb aimers was recognised, and a number of WOp/AGs and air gunners were recruited into this role. One such was F/Sgt Frank Kuebler, who had been badly injured on 30 August 1941 when his aircraft stalled and crashed near RAF Docking; another was Sgt Clifford Carr, who lived with the memory of crashing on Danby Head on 29 September 1941, when his captain had fallen asleep at the controls.

It would appear that the established 'big family' philosophy exemplified within the squadron was again being exercised, this time to allow existing crewmen who might have suffered a traumatic experience to be eased back gently into an operational role, one that although demanding a very focused skillset required this ability for only a short period. This may have been very helpful to those for whom returning to operations with the demands to remain focused and alert for the entire sortie could have become excessive, providing them with a role in which they were still a highly valued member of the team even if they would be exercising a discipline in which they had not originally been trained.

10 MARCH 1942

Another GEE-enabled attack was to be made on Essen, this time using the new Sampson technique, which involved the GEE-equipped aircraft dropping 250 lb incendiaries instead of flares. The hope was that the fires from the incendiaries would burn longer and therefore provide greater persistence in marking the target for the bombers that followed on. Once again, however, no damage was recorded on the target, the blame being laid principally on the thickness of the industrial haze over Essen, which hampered visual identification.[121]

25 MARCH 1942

The King and Queen paid a visit to RAF Dishforth to meet members of 51 Squadron following the success of the Bruneval Raid on 27/28 February 1942. This had been the inaugural operation of the recently formed Parachute Regiment, some of whose men had been airdropped into a Würzburg installation near Le Havre in northern France and had escaped by sea with vital elements of the German radar system.

The entourage comprised the King's private secretary, Sir Alan Lascelles, the Crown equerry, Colonel Kavanagh, and Lady Spencer from the royal household, accompanied by AVM Roderick Carr, AOC 4 Group, and Baroness de T'Serclaes, Squadron Officer 4 Group. They arrived at 1145 hrs, and witnessed a demonstration featuring nine Whitleys from 51 Squadron dropping a total of 90 paratroops, after which the royal party went on to RAF Topcliffe 4 miles away, arriving at 1300 hrs. The station records attest to their taking luncheon during their visit and subsequently signing the visitors' book, then leaving at 1500 hrs to the accompaniment of three 102 Squadron Halifaxes flying over in Vic formation at 1,000 ft. Ed Cooke, who was flying in one of the three aircraft, takes up the story: 'Afterwards we gained height and as their car was on the other side of the perimeter track, down we came and flew over them as low as we dared.'[122]

6 APRIL 1942

Halifaxes were being received from a variety of sources, including Handley Page at Radlett and other satellite manufacturers as they came online, such as English Electric at Preston. Others came in from MUs and some from other squadrons, and many were sent back out again as RAF Dalton became a hub for heavy aircraft movements. On Monday 6 April 1942 two new aircraft were received: W7653 and W7654. These had been built during late March / early April at Cricklewood and Radlett, and taken on charge as of 5 April, making their way to RAF Dalton via English Electric at Preston.

During March 1942 a Ministry of Information photographer visited the Handley Page works at Cricklewood and Radlett to record a montage of pictures under the heading 'Birth of a Bomber: Aircraft Production in Britain, 1942', depicting the various stages of design, development, production and test flying of the Halifax.

The two pictures here are from this sequence, which shows the two parallel production lines of Halifax B Mk.II Series 1 bombers at the Cricklewood plant. Based upon production throughput, it is believed that the second picture was taken from atop R9539, facing back towards W7650,[123] W7652 and W7654, with W7656 at the back without her wings fitted, out of camera shot.

The specific delivery of W7654 would have been of little significance in itself, given the mêlée of heavy aircraft movements going on, but this one aircraft would come to entwine the destinies of Len with WO1 Richard Bradbury, Sgt Ernest de Mattos, F/Sgt Ivor Lewis, F/Lt Kenneth Wright and an American, Sgt Jack Fernie, who was currently at No.3 PRC Uxbridge having just made the voyage from Halifax, Nova Scotia.

Halifax B Mk.II Series 1 production line at Cricklewood during March 1942: W7656, at the back of the right-hand line, is having her tail surfaces fitted (D 7114 © IWM)

Halifax B Mk.II Series 1 production line at Cricklewood during March 1942, photo taken from the front of the same line (D 7123 © IWM)

At around this time Kenneth Wright undertook his conversion training on the Halifax; he was the second of six pilots to undergo the process during this month.

9 APRIL 1942

In amongst the frequent aircraft movements, one of the most portentous was the transfer of six English Electric-built aircraft (W1047, W1048, W1049, W1050, W1051 and W1053) to 35 Squadron at RAF Linton-on-Ouse, 11 miles away, in return for which 102 Squadron received six Handley Page-built aircraft : R9441 (DY-S), R9442 (DY-R), R9446 (DY-F), R9449 (DY-T), R9488 (DY-G) and R9494 (DY-C). The underlying reason for this apparently administrative exercise was the recent return of *Tirpitz* from her first anti-convoy sortie, Unternehmen Sportpalast (Operation Sports Palace), and subsequent arrival in Fættenfjord, near Drontheim, 800 miles away to the north-east in occupied Norway.

35 Squadron was one of those chosen to mount operations against *Tirpitz*. However, it had recently received six new Handley Page-built aircraft fitted with the new GEE equipment. Since the coverage of the new GEE system did not extend to Norway, it would have served no useful purpose on these operations, but there were also orders not to risk potential compromise of the new equipment.

The prevailing policy was that airborne GEE equipment was to be fed to Bomber Command on a rolling squadron-by-squadron basis rather than spreading the limited numbers of sets thinly across all the squadrons. At this time, 102 Squadron had not been one of those chosen for conversion to GEE, so the opportunity to inherit such a prized capability, even in small numbers, was received eagerly. The exchange was therefore mutually beneficial, as it provided 102 Squadron for the first time with a genuine precision bombing capability; but the implicit warning accompanying this exchange was that there would probably be no more GEE equipment forthcoming in the immediate future, and consequently these aircraft needed to be well looked after.

10 APRIL 1942

On an operation to Essen, 76 Squadron fielded Halifax R9457[124] callsign MP-A, an aircraft with specially modified bomb doors to carry the latest in the growing family of High Capacity bombs. This new 8,000 lb HC bomb was not in fact a single casing with a homogeneous fill, but two 4,000 lb canisters bolted together, with a third section at one end forming a drum-shaped tail, giving rise to the locally adopted name of 'Two by Four'. These were not the same 4,000 lb HC units used by the Cookie bomb, but at 38" in diameter were 8" bigger, and were also filled with the more stable mixture of 85 per cent AMATOL and 15 per cent RDX/TNT. This powerful new bomb would become more widely known as the Blockbuster.

The narrative delivered by the returning crew described the bomb's effect on Essen thus: 'One very large explosion was seen with a momentary glow of dull red and orange colour.'

12 APRIL 1942

On a training flight with 102 CF, F/Lt Peter Robinson approached the runway on three engines, the fourth feathered. He landed his aircraft heavily, one undercarriage leg torn off, but he throttled up and went around again, finally landing on one wheel.

14 APRIL 1942

Target[125]	Aircraft on target	Types
Dortmund aim point B	208	142 Wellington 34 Hampden 20 Stirling 8 Halifax 4 Manchester
Le Havre docks	23	16 Wellington 5 Hampden 2 Halifax
Enemy aerodromes: Leeuwarden, Schiphol and Soesterberg	5	Blenheim
Minelaying off Heligoland	3	Stirling
Nickelling over Lille	1	Stirling

Following a lengthy conversion, 102 Squadron was finally ready for its first operation with the Halifax, and the three crews selected to fly were sent on check flights. This was when they had their first experience of the notorious, rudder overbalance instability, that would blight the early versions of Halifax. This dramatic vice could manifest itself with little provocation, and lock the rudder in its maximum offset position – from which no squadron pilot had so far been able to recover, even with full application of the ailerons. This was brought home to all at 1246 hrs, when R9488, under the command of F/Lt Harry Williams, stalled over Baldersby, 4 miles from the runway at RAF Dalton, spun into the ground and burned out with the loss of all on board. Eyewitnesses stated that he was executing a series of turns, possibly practising corkscrew evasion manoeuvres. His aircraft was carrying not only a full seven-man crew but also an instrument repairer, LAC John Livesey.

Although such a loss was a desperate personal tragedy, the impact on the squadron extended beyond the loss of a crew; this was one of the six precious new GEE-equipped aircraft.

NURSERY OPERATION

Primary target: Le Havre, target code CC24A.
Alternative: AIP.
Operation C.190: 3 aircraft (freshmen, 1 crashed on air test), operational call sign OU3.
Bomb load: 8× 500 lb GP NTD.
Route: Base – Sywell – Bognor – Le Havre and return.
Time Off: 2058 hrs.[126]
Time Over Target: 2300 – 2330 hrs.
Weather: Fair.
Opposition: Slight.

GEE-equipped Halifax R9494 (Chris Goss Collection)

With the number of aircraft reduced from three to two, 102 Squadron undertook its first operation with the Halifax. Experienced Whitley crews would now see themselves reclassified as freshmen as they gained operational experience on the new aircraft; consequently, there would be a lot of freshman operations for some time to come as all crewmen got up to speed.

This historically significant operation would be led by the squadron's CO, W/Cdr Sydney Bintley, flying another of the new GEE-equipped aircraft. He lined up at 2100 hrs, getting the green light and taking off 2 minutes later, thereby projecting the squadron into a new era. On this occasion he was accompanied by F/Sgt Frank Holmes, who took off 4 minutes later. Both aircraft were manned by a crew of seven, comprising captain, 2nd pilot, navigator, WOp/AG, two air gunners and an air engineer.

Frank Holmes returned without incident at 0252 hrs, while Sydney Bintley's aircraft was attacked by a night fighter and landed an hour later.

16 APRIL 1942

Target[127]	Aircraft on target	Types
CC26 Lorient docks	17	9 Whitley 5 Halifax 3 Wellington
CC24 Le Havre docks	4	Wellington
Minelaying:		
(i) Lorient (Artichoke)	10	Hampden
(ii) St-Nazaire (Beech)	6	Wellington
(iii) Verdon, Gironde (Deodar)	5	3 Stirling 2 Manchester
Nickelling:		
(i) Lille	7	5 Hampden 2 Manchester
(ii) Rouen	4	Wellington

NURSERY OPERATION

Primary target: Lorient, target code CC26A.
Operation C.191: 2 aircraft (freshmen), operational call sign AQ6.
Bomb load: 8× 500 lb GP TD 0.025.
Route: Base – Cottesmore – Abingdon – Bridport – Lorient and return.
Time Off: 2117 hrs.
Time Over Target: 2350 – 0020 hrs.
Weather: Thick ground haze.
Opposition: Moderate light and heavy flak.

Two aircraft were detailed to fly an operation to Lorient, home of the Keroman U-Boat base, the largest and most active hub for enemy submarine operations, due principally to its access to the Atlantic. It was home to the 2nd and 10th U-Boat Flotillas, and sported a number of submarine bunkers, including two 80-metre-long Dom (Cathedral) bunkers;

U-Boat pens under construction at Lorient during April 1942 (Deutsches Bundesarchiv, Bild 101II-MW-3935-02A / Dietrich / CC-BY-SA)

but by far the more impressive were two enormous reinforced concrete structures measuring 403 m × 146 m, accommodating 12 dry submarine pens between them, and a third similar building, still under construction, that when completed would hold a further 13 submarines. This operation would also serve as a diversion to Hampdens on gardening duty close by.

Two GEE-equipped aircraft were scheduled for this attack, one led by Sgt B Boothright and the other by A Flight's commander, S/Ldr ED Griffiths, who would be leading the two crews out at 2116 hrs.

S/Ldr Griffiths was unable to find his target, and brought his bombs back. Meanwhile, Sgt Boothright located and attacked his target, but one of his port engines cut out and he landed away at RAF Cottesmore in Rutland. This incident would put R9494 out of action for six weeks, reducing the number of GEE-equipped aircraft on the squadron. Although the squadron had taken charge of six GEE-equipped aircraft only one week earlier, it was down to four already.

22 APRIL 1942

Target[128]	Aircraft on target	Types
Cologne aim point A	69	64 Wellington 5 Stirling
CC24 Le Havre docks	23	17 Wellington 2 Halifax 2 Stirling 2 Whitley
Minelaying:		
(i) Kiel Harbour (Forget-me-nots)	27	11 Stirling 6 Hampden 5 Manchester 5 Wellington

Target	Aircraft on target	Types
(ii) Heligoland (Rosemary)	16	Hampden
(iii) Langeland Belt (Quince)	8	5 Manchester 3 Stirling
(iv) Fehmarn Channel (Radish)	4	2 Manchester 2 Stirling
(v) Southern entrance to Little Belt (Endives)	3	Stirling
(vi) Little Belt and Flensburg Fjord (Wallflower)	3	Stirling
(vii) South entrance to the Sound (Daffodil)	2	Stirling
Nickelling over Rennes	1	Hampden

NURSERY OPERATION

Primary target: Le Havre, target code CC24A.
Operation C.192: 2 aircraft (freshmen), operational call sign TR8.
Bomb load: 8× 500 lb GP NTD.
Route: Base – Sywell – Abingdon – Bognor – Le Havre and return.
Time Off: 2103 hrs.
Time Over Target: 2315 – 2345 hrs.
Weather: Fair, visibility good.
Opposition: Considerable accurate heavy flak.

Two of the more experienced Whitley pilots were to be given their freshman operations on the Halifax, and one of the aircraft was equipped with GEE, as all crews were eager to gain experience with the new equipment. F/Sgt Larry Carr led out F/Sgt Hank Malkin at 2105 hrs, the latter finding his target and making his run up over Docks 6 and 7, but seven of his bombs did not release and he had no choice other than to bring them back. Larry Carr meanwhile dropped his bombs near Docks 11 and 12, but was engaged by 12 searchlights and hit by heavy flak near Cap de la Hève. As luck would have it, this was R9446, the one GEE-equipped aircraft on the operation, and although returning to base, this aircraft would be out of action for repairs for the next month. This reduced the number of GEE-equipped aircraft available on the squadron to three.

24 APRIL 1942

Target[129]	Aircraft on target	Types
Rostock:		
(i) Rostock aim point A	91	73 Wellington 11 Stirling 7 Whitley
(ii) Marienehe; GY4834 Ernst Heinkel Flugzeugwerke GmbH assembly works	34	21 Hampden 8 Manchester 5 Lancaster

(continued)

Target	Aircraft on target	Types
CC25 Dunkirk docks	47	37 Wellington 6 Halifax 3 Stirling 1 Hampden
Z52 Leeuwarden aerodrome	4	Blenheim
Nickelling:		
(i) Rennes	2	Manchester
(ii) Lille	1	Stirling

NURSERY OPERATION

Primary target: Dunkirk (docks), target code CC25A.
Operation C.193: 4 aircraft (freshmen), operational call sign U1N.
Bomb load: 8× 500 lb GP NTD.
Route: Base – Finningley – Orford Ness – Dunkirk and return.
Time Off: 2142 hrs.
Time Over Target: 2330 – 0030 hrs.
Weather: Mist and ground haze.
Opposition: Considerable light and heavy flak with many searchlights, accurate.

Still working through the backlog of recently converted crewmen, the squadron detailed four more former Whitley pilots and their crews to Halifax operations. Aboard the four

Bf 110 of III./NJG3 (Chris Goss Collection)

aircraft were an increasing number of crewmen who had already flown at least one combat operation since conversion. Since the squadron had begun Halifax operations ten nights earlier, it had been the air engineers who had been called upon to fly most repeatedly, but now other disciplines, principally the air gunners, were starting to be seen coming through again.

At the head of the four aircraft departing at 2140 hrs was P/O William Welch, who was unable to identify the target and brought his bombs back, but the three others carried out their attacks successfully. Three of the four crews returned within quarter of an hour of each other, but Sgt Harold 'Batch' Batchelder in R9441, another of the GEE-equipped aircraft, returned an hour after the first of his colleagues had landed. This aircraft had to be referred to Repair On Site procedures and would not re-appear on the squadron for four months, depriving the squadron of another GEE-equipped aircraft. The squadron had taken charge of six GEE-equipped aircraft only two weeks earlier and was down to two already.

26 APRIL 1942

Target[130]	Aircraft on target	Types
Rostock:		
(i) Rostock (town)	52	45 Wellington 5 Whitley 2 Halifax
(ii) Marienehe; GY4834 Ernst Heinkel Flugzeugwerke GmbH factory	55	19 Hampden 18 Wellington 9 Manchester 8 Stirling 1 Lancaster
CC25A Dunkirk docks	24	11 Blenheim 7 Wellington 3 Halifax 2 Whitley 1 Stirling
Enemy aerodromes:		
(i) Z52 Leeuwarden	2	Blenheim
(ii) Z66 Eindhoven	1	Blenheim
Minelaying in Heligoland Bight	4	2 Manchester 1 Hampden 1 Wellington
Nickelling over Lille	7	Whitley

NURSERY OPERATION

Primary target: Dunkirk (docks), target code CC25A.
Operation C.194: 2 aircraft (freshmen), operational call sign 6KF.
Bomb load: 8× 500 lb GP NTD.

Route: Base – Finningley – Orford Ness – Dunkirk and return.
Time Off: 2144 hrs.
Time Over Target: 2330 – 0001 hrs.
Weather: Clear, visibility good.
Opposition: Some heavy flak and many searchlights.

Following a familiar theme, two more aircraft with crews mostly inexperienced in Halifax combat operations were detailed to attack Dunkirk docks, but Sgt John Barber's aircraft had engine trouble and did not start. Consequently, Sgt Edmund Newell found himself flying the only operational sortie for the squadron, and pressed home his attack successfully.

27 April 1942

Target[131]	Aircraft on target	Types
Cologne:		
(i) Aim point A (ii) A small number of Wellingtons from 1 Group was also directed to attack GN3816 Kalk; Humboldt Deutz Motoren AG diesel engine works	92	71 Wellington 19 Stirling 2 Halifax
Trondheim (*Tirpitz*, *Admiral Scheer* and *Prinz Eugen*)	43	31 Halifax 12 Lancaster
CC25A Dunkirk docks	12	7 Wellington 3 Halifax 2 Whitley
Minelaying:		
(i) Heligoland Bight (Rosemary)	8	4 Wellington 2 Hampden 2 Stirling
(ii) Kiel Harbour (Forget-me-nots)	2	Lancaster
(iii) Langeland Belt (Quince)	1	Lancaster
(iv) Horns Reef (Hawthorn)	1	Lancaster
Nickelling in the Lille area	5	Wellington

Main Operation

Primary target: Cologne, target code Trout A.
Operation C.195: 2 aircraft, operational call sign GL7.
Bomb load: 6× 1,000 lb GP.
Route: Base – Orford Ness – Nieuport – Le Cateau – Cologne and return.
Time Off: 2340 hrs.
Time Over Target: 0310 – 0320 hrs to be strictly adhered to.
Weather: Clear, visibility good.
Opposition: Much heavy flak.

NURSERY OPERATION

Primary target: Dunkirk (docks), target code CC25A.
Operation C.196: 1 aircraft (freshman), operational call sign A9B.
Bomb load: 8× 500 lb GP.
Route: Base – Orford Ness – Dunkirk and return.
Time Off: 2210 hrs.
Time Over Target: 2359 – 0030 hrs.

Tonight marked the first deep strike operation to be conducted by 102 Squadron with the Halifax. The target was to be the industrial area of Cologne which provided a rich diversity of strategic targets such as: Ford-Werke, producing military vehicles; Chemische Fabrik Kalk, producing explosives; and Mülheim, which boasted a port servicing a variety of heavy industries including iron foundries, blast furnaces, rolling mills and machine works, in addition to chemical and electrical industries.

The crews for this operation were drawn loosely from those who had already successfully completed a nursery operation together, and were led by Sgt Boothright and F/Sgt Larry Carr. Meanwhile there would also be in parallel a further nursery operation, this time for Sgt John Barber whose aircraft had suffered engine problems the night before, preventing his starting. The aircraft had been repaired during the day, and he was to be given another opportunity against the same target, Dunkirk docks. His crew would be the same as the night before, but with the substitution of Sgt William Nicoll for Sgt Haycock as WOp. This would turn out to be a very lucky break for the ousted Sgt Haycock.

Of the three crews that departed on operations, only Sgt Boothright and his crew were to return. Given the technical teething problems with the type and the heightened awareness of the aircraft's vices, these losses would not have been received well amongst the squadron. It also brought home that the loss of one aircraft meant the loss of seven friends and colleagues rather than just five, as in the old Whitley.

Keith Janes at www.conscript-heroes.com explains the fate of John Barber's crew:

German control post on the French Ligne de Démarcation (Deutsches Bundesarchiv, Bild 101I-017-1065-44A / Becker / CC-BY-SA)

Sgt John W Barber was killed along with his navigator, Sgt George W Butterworth, and wireless operator, Sgt William Nicoll, when R9528 was shot down by flak over Dunkirk.

Four of the crew survived however: Sgt C V Long, the mid-upper air gunner, was captured, but the other three – Sgt Andrew R Evans (836), Sgt Frederick A Barker (856) and Sgt T G Johnson (790) – all evaded successfully.

Sgt Evans was wounded by shrapnel in the aircraft, and then broke a bone in his ankle on landing just west of the village of Bergues, about 7 kms from Dunkirk. Because of his injuries, he went to the first house he saw, and although the occupants were not prepared to hide him, they did provide something to drink and a bottle of beer to take away with him, and Evans continued walking until he found a barn to shelter in for the rest of the night. When an elderly couple came out of their house that morning, Evans asked them for food. He was taken into their home, and their daughter brought a local schoolteacher and her husband to test his claims of being a British airman. Once they were satisfied as to Evans identity, he was taken to a house in nearby Steene where he stayed, recovering from his wounds, for the next month. On 25 May, he was taken by bicycle to stay overnight in Gravelines, and next day to Calais, and the home of a Mme Amedro [query] where he was put in touch with an organisation. Evans doesn't name his first helpers but does say it was a M. Varaghe who took him to Gravelines, and then handed him over to another man in Calais, and Mme Bossart (presumably of Bourbourg) who contacted the organisation.

Two weeks after he arrived in Calais, three men came to visit him – they said they would return in three days and take him to Lille but two days later, one of the men was arrested for helping another British airman, and Evans' departure was delayed for a further month.

On 10 July, Mme Lea Marie Hyssen (of 43 rue du Vauxhall, Calais) took Evans by train to Lille, and next day, a M. Aumont (see also Johnson below) took him to Paris and his home in the Ternes district. On (about) 15 July, Evans was taken to a Metro station where he was passed over to Louis Nouveau of the Pat Line, and a Belgian named Georges Van Laert, and Nouveau took them to Nimes (Gard). While Nouveau returned to his home in Marseille, Evans and Van Laert stayed in Nimes with Gaston Negre for the next five days until being taken to Toulouse. Evans doesn't say where they stayed for their two nights in the city but does mention a man called Joseph (this was Pat O'Leary) bringing a Spanish guide to meet them. Evans and Van Laert arranged to meet up with the guide (who was almost certainly from the Ponzan-Vidal organisation) at the border town of Osseja, and he took them, along with another Englishman and a Belgian, across the Pyrenees to a small Spanish village where they stayed overnight in a hotel before going on to the British consulate in Barcelona.

Sgt Barker landed in a field just west of Fort Mardick, less than five kilometres from the centre of Dunkirk, and as it was too dark to read his escape map, set out in a generally south-westerly direction. He carried on walking for the next twelve days until reaching Soissons (Picardy) on 9 May, and then as the following day was a Sunday, decided to take a break at Rozieres-sur-Crise. The following day, he continued to Chateau-Thierry but then, having decided that he could not, as originally intended, walk all the way to Switzerland, he took a train Paris. That evening, he took another train, this time to Vesoul (Haute-Saône) where he set off walking once more, until he reached Pont de Roide on 17 May. From there, it was simply a question of heading east until reaching the zone interdite which marked the border, and because he arrived there on a Sunday, and was able to mingle with other walkers, he crossed into Switzerland that evening without too much difficulty.

Barker was soon arrested by friendly Swiss border guards and spent three days in a prison at Porrentruy before being sent to Berne. He told the Swiss intelligence officer who interviewed him that he had escaped from a POW camp (a story which was accepted but not believed), and a few days later, was collected from his hotel by SIS station chief, Victor Farrell, who took him to Geneva. Three days later, he and two Yugoslavs were taken across the border into France where they were picked up by a man on a bicycle who took them into Annemasse. From there, a man and his wife took them by train to Marseille where they were sheltered by Louis Nouveau in his luxury apartment on Quai de Rive Neuve, and where they met three more evaders, including Sgt John Prendergast of the Welch Regiment who had been captured on Crete in June 1941 and escaped from Stalag IIID (Steglitz) on 25 April 1942. Two days later, Francis Blanchain took all six men to Toulouse. They stayed at the Hotel de Paris for three nights before being taken (along with eight civilians) to Banyuls-sur-Mer (where they were joined by another evading airman and a French intelligence agent), and two Spanish guides from the Ponzan-Vidal organisation led them on a four-day journey across the mountains to Figueras.

The guides left them about twenty kilometres from Gerona, and the group split into pairs, Barker going with Prendergast. They were arrested by the Guardia Civil on the railway line just short of Gerona, and spent four weeks going through a series of civilian prisons (Gerona, Figueras, Barcelona and Saragossa) before being sent to Miranda del Ebro, for another seven weeks, before finally being repatriated to Gibraltar on 3 September.

Sgt Johnson says he landed some six miles from their target. After walking south for about three hours, he entered a farm near Brouckerque (Nord-Pas-de-Calais) where the farmer gave him civilian clothes and some food before Johnson continued, passing through Les Attaques that evening. He carried on walking through the following day until approached by a local man on a bicycle who took him to hide overnight in a chicken shed in a wood. Next morning, a man named Boule arrived with two bicycles, and took Johnson to Fiennes, where he was sheltered by farmer and local organisation member, Auguste Lelue. M. Lelue sheltered Johnson until 8 May when he took him, again by bicycle, to Ardres where Johnson was introduced to a M. Aumont who took him by train to Lille and his home at 50 rue Meurein. Next day, M. Aumont took Johnson by train to Paris and an apartment where he met a French test pilot, and an evading American Spitfire pilot, and that night, he and the American were taken to be sheltered by Pat Line logeur Amand Leveque at 19 rue d'Orleons. Ten days later, Johnson was moved to M. Leveque's sister-in-law's home (assume Julienne Lassouquere at 20 rue Saint Ferdinand), where he was sheltered for the next seventeen days, and then with a M. Poignant at 43 rue Gambetta, for a further eighteen days.

If Johnson's account of the days is correct then it would have been about 15 June when he left Paris with an ex-legionnaire called Antonio who took him by train via Vierzon-Ville to Saint-Aignan-des-Noyers, where they hoped to cross the demarcation line[132] into the Vichy French zone non-occupée (ZNO). On arrival however, they found that a number of Frenchmen has recently been arrested trying the same thing and so returned to Vierzon.

A few days later, they crossed into the ZNO by swimming across the Loire [sic] at Mars-sur-Allier and walked to Sancoins where they took a train to Villefranche. From there they made their way to Nimes (Gard) and the home of Pat Line agent, Gaston Negre, where Johnson stayed overnight and met two more RAF evaders, Sqn/Ldr Whitney Straight and Sgt Stefan Miniakowski – both of whom had escaped, along with Pte Charles Knight, from the Pasteur hospital in Nice on 22 June. Johnson then spent three nights at the nearby Café du Soleil before returning to Gaston Negre's house for another five nights.

It would have been about 10 July when 'Joseph' [sic] (Alex Wattebled) took Johnson by train to Coursan (Aude), commenting that Lt Anthony Deane-Drummond (who had escaped from a hospital in Florence) and 'F/Sgt Seymour' (SOE agent André Simon) were also on the train with their guide. From Coursan, they walked to the outskirts of Saint-Pierre-la-Mer where they hid for a day and night before walking to Saint-Pierre-Plage. They (and others) were collected from the beach that night by the British Q-ship, HMS Tarana, and taken to Gibraltar.[133]

Meanwhile, Larry Carr and his crew had crossed the French coast at 12,000 ft on the outward journey in W7653 and made the turn at Le Cateau for the run into Cologne. Just before 0030 hrs, they were 60 miles into this leg of the journey, approaching Namur in Belgium, when they were approached by a night fighter piloted by Oblt Reinhold Eckardt of 7./NJG3.

Larry Carr takes up the story:[134]

The nightfighter made a stern attack and with the first burst, hit the rear turret and injured the gunner. I took evasive action but the night fighter closed in and set the port wing, engines and fuselage on fire as well as killing the Mid-Upper Air Gunner and Flight Engineer. I gave the order to abandon aircraft and those who were still alive baled out ... I then started to get out – the Halifax was well and truly on fire as I was leaving, the plane gave a sudden lurch and the port wing and engines broke away from the fuselage.

Sgt 'Dixie' Lee, the rear air gunner, claimed shooting down the night fighter, but only just before the order to evacuate had been given. He was among a total of five crewmen who baled out, but Sgt James Garroway, the WOp, died when his parachute failed to open, leaving four survivors in occupied Belgium.

Larry Carr 'had only just managed to open his parachute when he hit the ground, with the aircraft crashing very close by',[135] and shortly after his arrival met a local man, Maurice Wilmet,[136] in the company of a policeman, Sgt Louis Massinon.[137] Wilmet arranged shelter at a nearby farm and provided civilian clothes, while Massinon reported that there were no survivors from the crash. Next day Massinon returned with a guide, Fernande Pirlot,[138] who took him by train to Brussels, where he was put up in a series of safe houses.

Meanwhile,[139] Sgt Ron Shoebridge and Sgt Bill Ralston had been met by a teacher who had given them civilian clothes and taken them 7 miles west, to an address in Spontin. The next day, relatives of their hosts took them by train to their house in Brussels, where they stayed briefly before being moved between a number of safe houses in area. Dixie Lee was also sheltered by local people, but he was betrayed by a collaborator and captured.

Escape plans had been made to guide a party of fugitive servicemen through France to Spain starting on 5 May, but only Ron Shoebridge and Larry Carr with their guides turned up; the network had been compromised and further groups of Résistance activists, along with the servicemen they were assisting, had been captured. With escape plans postponed, Larry Carr and his two remaining fellow crewmen continued to be moved around safe houses in the Brussels area. Eventually, Ron Shoebridge and Bill Ralston were captured and all the Résistance workers caught with them were tortured and either executed or sent to concentration camps.

One week later, Larry Carr was introduced[140] to Andrée de Jongh,[141] the creator of the Réseau Comète (Comet Line), and the two of them travelled by train via Paris to Bayonne near the Spanish border. On their approach to Bayonne, they received a warning from the local 'Tante GO' network about increased security at the station, so stayed abroad, continuing another 10 miles further on to St-Jean-de-Luz, where they were met by a Basque sympathiser who smuggled Larry Carr out of the station by a goods entrance.

Their guide arrived at midnight on 22 May, and together they crossed the border into Spain on foot, arriving in the town of Errenteria two days later. Once their guide had departed, the two of them took a tram to San Sebastian, where Larry Carr finally arrived at the British Consulate, five weeks after being shot down. From here he was taken south to Gibraltar, and on 18 June he embarked on the aircraft carrier HMS *Argus*, which delivered him to Gourock, near Glasgow, on 22 June 1942.

In spite of the losses experienced by 102 Squadron, clear visibility over Cologne had facilitated accurate targeting; German reports[142] recorded significant damage to industrial premises, public buildings and 1,520 houses hit or damaged. A large amount of ordnance had also fallen outside the city to the east, and almost 400 acres of forest had been destroyed.

28 APRIL 1942

Target[143]	Aircraft on target	Types
Kiel (town)	88	62 Wellington 15 Stirling 10 Hampden 1 Halifax
Trondheim Naval Base	34	23 Halifax 11 Lancaster
Z105 Langerbrugge power station	6	Blenheim
Enemy aerodromes:		
(i) Schiphol	2	Blenheim
(ii) Soesterberg	2	Blenheim
Minelaying:		
(i) Heligoland (Rosemary)	2	1 Manchester 1 Wellington
(ii) Kiel Harbour (Forget-me-nots)	2	Manchester

(continued)

Target	Aircraft on target	Types
(iii) Langeland Belt (Quince)	1	Manchester
(iv) Fehmarn Channel (Radish)	1	Manchester

Primary target: Kiel, target code Minnow A.
Last Resort: S&M.
Operation C.197: 2 aircraft, operational call sign 5NT.
Bomb load: 2× 1,000 lb GP, 13× SBC 8× 30 lb.
Route: Base – Scarborough – Rømø Sonderby – Selenter Lake – Kiel and return.
Time Off: 2235 hrs.
Time Over Target: 0215 – 0245 hrs.
Weather: Clear, visibility good.
Opposition: Medium heavy and light flak. Searchlights effective.

Two crews were scheduled to attack Kiel, where *Scharnhorst* was still undergoing repairs by Deutsche Werke, following mine damage suffered during the Channel Dash on 12 February. This raid would be against the town rather than the ship, and was scheduled to be another of the pre-dawn[144] operations aimed at catching defending forces by surprise.

Leading the squadron's contribution to the night's operation to Kiel was A Flight's commander, S/Ldr Griffiths. Supporting him was to be F/Sgt Stanley Morgan, but his aircraft failed to start due to a defective instrument panel. Consequently, S/Ldr Griffiths took off alone at 0222 hrs, returning safely at 0507 hrs,[145] having successfully completed his attack against the primary target.

Clear skies over Kiel had contributed to accurate bombing; German reports[146] confirmed damage to all three shipyards, in addition to military and public buildings as well as housing.

29 APRIL 1942

Target[147]	Aircraft on target	Types
Paris, Gennevilliers; Z312 Foundry at the Gnome-Rhône engine works	88	73 Wellington 9 Hampden 6 Stirling
CC13 Ostend	20	8 Wellington 7 Halifax 5 Whitley
Enemy aerodromes:		
(i) Leeuwarden	4	Blenheim
(ii) Schiphol	1	Blenheim
(iii) Soesterberg	1	Blenheim
Minelaying:		
(i) Langeland Belt (Quince)	2	Manchester
(ii) Fehmarn Channel (Radish)	1	Manchester
(iii) Kiel Harbour (Forget-me-nots)	1	Manchester
(iv) South entrance to Little Belt (Endives)	1	Manchester

NURSERY OPERATION

Primary target: Ostend (docks), target code CC13A.
Operation C.198: 1 aircraft (freshman), operational call sign AQ6.
Bomb load: 8× 500 lb GP.
Route: Base – Finningley – Orford Ness – Ostend and return.
Time Off: 2128 hrs.
Time Over Target: 2330 – 0001 hrs.
Weather: Clear.
Opposition: Nil.

The next freshman operation took F/Sgt Wickham to Ostend in R9442, one of the last two GEE-equipped aircraft on the squadron, on her first operational sortie since joining from 35 Squadron.

The sortie did not go well as the bomb sight was damaged and the starboard outer engine failed, causing F/Sgt Wickham to jettison his bombs over the sea and return on three engines. This aircraft would be out of action for a month undergoing repairs, now reducing the number of GEE-equipped aircraft on the squadron to just one.

102 Squadron had flown 16 operational sorties since becoming operational on the Halifax two weeks earlier. Of the six GEE-equipped aircraft taken on charge, one had crashed and four were unserviceable due to a mixture of technical faults and enemy action. The final GEE-equipped aircraft, R9449, was wisely, but somewhat belatedly, held back in reserve to ensure that when called upon the squadron could still field at least one aircraft with GEE-enabled capability.

5 MAY 1942

Hitler ordered the withdrawal of searchlights from the Kammhuber Line. Although they had formed an integral part of an intricately devised and highly successful defensive line, Hitler had taken the unilateral decision to withdraw them to the cities. He reasoned that it would boost public morale if the urban populations could actually see more of the night defences in action and bring down aircraft where they could be seen by more people. The impact of this decision was far more limited than it would have been even a few months earlier, because the DuNaJa system had now proven itself and searchlights were no longer the pivotal factor in facilitating successful night fighter intercepts.

Target[148]	Aircraft on target	Types
Stuttgart:		
(i) Aim point A	41	17 Wellington 13 Stirling 11 Halifax
(ii) Feuerbach; GB3280 Robert Bosch works	36	32 Wellington 4 Lancaster
CC33A Nantes	19	14 Wellington 5 Halifax

(continued)

Target	Aircraft on target	Types
Z57 Schiphol aerodrome	4	Blenheim
Nickelling:		
(i) Paris	6	4 Manchester 1 Hampden 1 Lancaster
(ii) Lille, St-Étienne	1	Stirling
(iii) Vichy, Clermont-Ferrand	1	Halifax
(iv) Montpellier, Nimes	1	Lancaster
(v) Marseilles, Toulon	1	Lancaster

MAIN OPERATION

Special nickelling operation
Dropping area: Nickelling over Vichy area (Vichy and Clermont-Ferrand).
Operation C.199: 1 aircraft, operational call sign 5UW.
Route: Base – Abingdon – Worthing – Cabourg – West of Bourges – dropping area and return.
Time Off: 2258 hrs.
Time Over Target: 0210 – 0219 hrs.
Weather: Thick haze.
Opposition: Slight heavy flak.

NURSERY OPERATION

Primary target: Nantes (shipping), target code CC33A.
Operation C.200: 3 aircraft (freshmen), operational call sign J9Z.
Bomb load: 8× 500 lb GP TD 0.025.
Route: Base – Abingdon – Bognor – Isigny – Nantes and return.
Time Off: 2212 hrs.
Time Over Target: 0100 – 0110 hrs.
Weather: Thick haze.
Opposition: Slight heavy flak.

The nickelling sortie to Vichy and Clermont-Ferrand was the strategic target of the night's two operations, and was to be flown by F/Sgt Stanley Morgan, who was allocated W7654 on her first operational sortie since having been delivered one month earlier. This would be the first aircraft on the squadron to wear the DY-Q for Queenie callsign operationally since Whitley Z6747 on 31 January. A total of 42 packets of nickels was to be distributed evenly between both target areas.

There was also to be a nursery operation to Nantes, a little further afield and further inland than the French coastal targets more traditionally favoured in the past for training purposes. Each of the three aircraft in the freshman sorties would be crewed by only six men, the first time the squadron had flown operationally with less than seven crewmen. This reduction arose by removing the position of the 2nd pilots, presumably because they were no longer

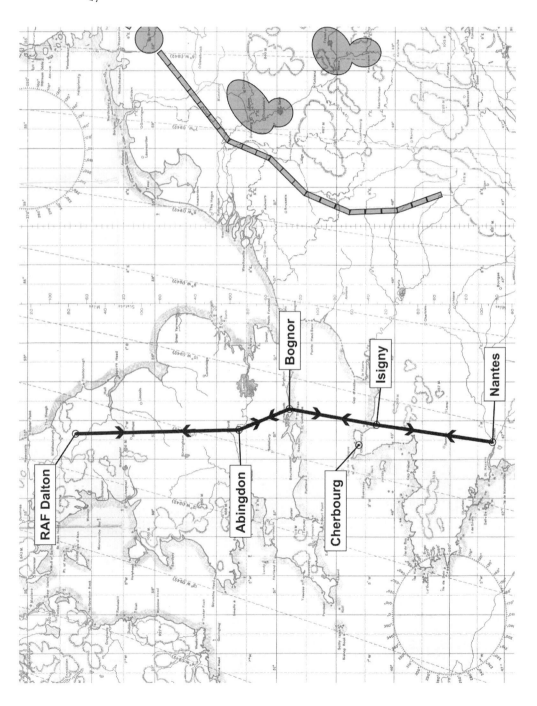

Operation C.200 to Nantes, 5 May 1942

RAF Dalton

Abingdon

Bognor

Cherbourg

Isigny

Nantes

needed given the higher speed of the Halifax and therefore the shorter duration of sorties compared with those of the old Whitleys.

P/O Peter Gaskell would be leading out the three freshman crews, with Sgt Ernest de Mattos in the rear turret for his first operational sortie in the Halifax. Meanwhile F/Sgt Bill Davies would be flying the third of these three aircraft with Air Engineer F/Sgt Ivor Lewis on his first operation with the squadron. The three aircraft bound for Nantes took off from 2207 hrs, whereas Stanley Morgan and his crew had another hour to wait until their departure at 2259 hrs.

The Nantes crews recovered at widely spaced intervals from 0343 to 0509 hrs, having reported bad visibility and time spent trying to locate their targets, none of them completing their attack. Bill Davies diverted on his return journey to bomb Cherbourg, so was last of the three to get back. Finally, Stanley Morgan returned at 0624 hrs following a successful nickelling sortie and completing the quartet of aircraft returning safely from their destinations over France.

Halifax W7652 (DY-P)

Nantes.
Takeoff 2207 hrs.
No attack carried out.
Landed 0343 hrs.
Operational combat time 5 hrs 36 mins.
P/O PR Gaskell
F/Sgt RH Adamson
P/O AJ Graham
Sgt TH May
Sgt ERT DeMattos   6th operation; combat time 42 hrs 3 mins
Sgt DH Craig

Halifax R9530 (DY-J)

Nantes.
Takeoff 2210 hrs.
Released one stick over Cherbourg from 11,000 ft.
Landed 0509 hrs.
Operational combat time 6 hrs 59 mins.
F/Sgt WR Davies
P/O EF Lloyd
F/Sgt JE Sumpton
Sgt BC Sandall
Sgt A Smith
F/Sgt I Lewis   1st operation; combat time 6 hrs 59 mins

6 MAY 1942

Target[149]	Aircraft on target	Types
Stuttgart aim point A	97	55 Wellington 15 Stirling 10 Hampden 10 Lancaster 7 Halifax
CC33A Nantes	19	13 Wellington 2 Hampden 2 Manchester 2 Stirling
Enemy aerodromes:		
(i) Z57 Schiphol	1	Blenheim
(ii) Z52 Leeuwarden	1	Blenheim
(iii) Z53 Soesterberg	1	Blenheim
(iv) Z66 Eindhoven	1	Blenheim
Nickelling:		
(i) Paris, Amiens, Rennes	5	Manchester
(ii) Lyons, St-Étienne, Lille, Lens	2	Stirling
(iii) Vichy, Clermont-Ferrand, Limoges	2	Halifax

MAIN OPERATION

Special nickelling operation
Dropping area: Nickelling over Vichy area (1 aircraft to Montpellier and Toulon, 1 aircraft to Limoges).
Operation C.201: 2 aircraft (1 cancelled[150]), operational call sign 7PM.
Route: Base – Abingdon – Brighton – Cabourg – dropping area and return.
Time Off: 2231 hrs.
Time Over Target: 0150 – 0200 hrs.
Weather: 3/10 to 5/10 cloud, hazy. Visibility moderate.
Opposition: Nil.

With one of the two scheduled aircraft cancelled, F/Sgt Wickham was called upon to conduct a singleton nickelling operation over Vichy. He took W7654 and distributed a total of 60 packets of nickels evenly between both target areas, returning without incident.

7 MAY 1942

Target[151]	Aircraft on target	Types
CC55A St-Nazaire docks	5	4 Wellington 1 Stirling
Minelaying:		
(i) Kiel Harbour (Forget-me-nots)	33	13 Wellington 8 Hampden 8 Stirling 4 Lancaster

(continued)

Target	Aircraft on target	Types
(ii) Great Belt Seiro Revsnes (Broccoli)	18	12 Wellington 3 Lancaster 3 Stirling
(iii) Heligoland (Rosemary)	14	8 Manchester 3 Hampden 3 Wellington
(iv) Little Belt (Carrot)	11	8 Wellington 3 Hampden
(v) North entrance to the Sound (Nasturtium)	3	2 Lancaster 1 Stirling
(vi) Copenhagen (Verbena)	2	Lancaster
Nickelling over Vichy, Clermont-Ferrand	1	Halifax

MAIN OPERATION

Special nickelling operation
Dropping area: Nickelling over Vichy area (Vichy and Clermont-Ferrand).
Operation C.202: 1 aircraft, operational call sign L6G.
Route: Base – Abingdon – Brighton – Cabourg – dropping area and return.
Time Off: 2200 hrs.
Time Over Target: 0127 – 0139 hrs.
Weather: Clear with ground haze.
Opposition: Slight.

This would mark the last of the small-scale operations as the crews built up confidence with the Halifax. Sgt F Williamson was to fly the singleton sortie in W7654, taking on his crew Air Engineer F/Sgt Ivor Lewis and also, for the first time on the squadron, a bomb aimer who was by trade a highly experienced WOp/AG. Although the bomb aimer was not technically vital to the outcome of the operation, as they were only dropping nickels, this sortie would provide the squadron with valuable first-hand experience in the possibilities of vesting a bomb-aiming function in a dedicated crewman as well as in the practicalities of flying with an eight-man crew.

A total of 58½ packets of nickels was to be distributed evenly between both target areas, and the operation was completed without any problems, W7654 having taken three crews to the Vichy area on three consecutive nights without a hitch.

Halifax W7654 (DY-Q)

Vichy area.

Takeoff 2157 hrs.

Nickels dropped as ordered.

Landed 0616 hrs.

Operational combat time 8 hrs 19 mins.

Sgt F Williamson

*Operation
C.202 to Vichy,
7 May 1942*

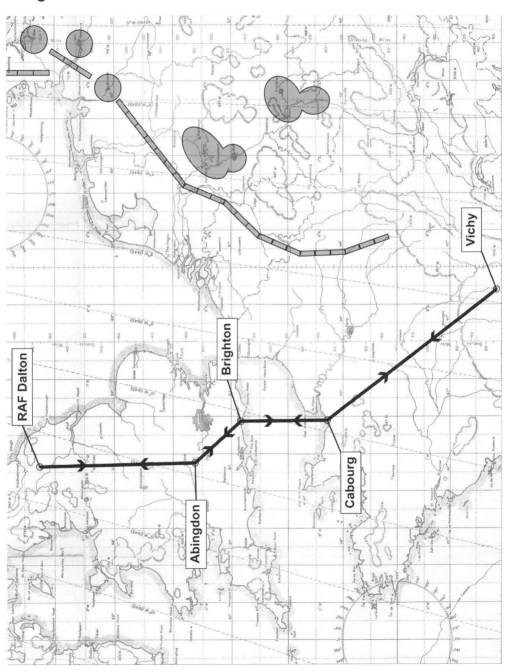

RAF Dalton

Abingdon

Brighton

Cabourg

Vichy

P/O BK Lindsay

Sgt MS Fearnley

Sgt NW Haycock

Sgt TH May

F/Sgt AW Summers

Sgt ER Smith

F/Sgt I Lewis   2nd operation; combat time 15 hrs 18 mins

Ivor Lewis had completed his first operation in Q for Queenie and would henceforth make this aircraft his own, developing a deeper understanding of her idiosyncrasies irrespective of the changes in captains and crewmen going on around him.

11 MAY 1942

S/Ldr Peter Robinson took up a training flight with Canadian pilots F/Sgt Carl Harris and F/Sgt 'Jackie' Towse in V9982 from 102 CF. The exercise called for flying with both port engines feathered. As the weather closed in they tried to restart their engines, but these failed to pick up, resulting in a crash-landing at Pickhill, 7 miles north-west of RAF Dalton at 1630 hrs. Jackie Towse was the only crewman injured and was despatched to the military hospital at Catterick for treatment of concussion and lacerations. Two days later the same crew would go aloft on a check flight with the MO to confirm they were fit to return to flying duties.

Endnotes

110 Hastings, M. FRSL FRHistS (1999) *Bomber Command: The Strategic Bombing Offensive 1939–45*, ISBN 9781509856251, MacMillan, p 139.

111 The first Halifax B Mk.II Series 1 bombers were fitted with legacy Merlin X engines, and some even had beam gun positions.

112 Wheeler, B.C. *Halifax: From Front-Line Bomber to Post-War Transport*, ISBN 9781907426483, Kelsey Publishing Group (www.aeroplanemonthly.com), pp 19–22.

113 AP3001

114 AP3001

115 Calmel, J. DFC Légion d'Honneur (1955) *Night Pilot* (translated by Mervyn Savill), William Kimber, p 161.

116 AP3002

117 Adams, C.W. DFC (1983) 578 Squadron Operations, 1944–45.

118 Dunmore, S. and Carter, W. (1992) *Reap the Whirlwind: The Untold Story of 6 Group, Canada's Bomber Force of World War II*, ISBN 0947554351, Crécy, p 13.

119 Calmel, J. DFC Légion d'Honneur (1955) *Night Pilot* (translated by Mervyn Savill), William Kimber, p 80.

120 Harris, A.T. GCB OBE AFC (1995) *Despatch on War Operations 23rd February 1942 to 8th May 1945*, ISBN 071464692X, Frank Cass, p 77.

121 Harris, A.T. GCB OBE AFC (1995) *Despatch on War Operations 23rd February 1942 to 8th May 1945*, ISBN 071464692X, Frank Cass, p 77.

122 Goss, C. (1995) *It's Suicide but It's Fun: The Story of 102 (Ceylon) Squadron 1917–1956*, ISBN 0947554599, Crécy, p 64.

123 This aircraft uniquely amongst her peers was not to see front-line service, but was instead destined for Contractor's Research and Development (CRD) at Handley Page.

124 Listed erroneously in the ORB as R9487 on this one operation. MP-A is listed in the ORB both before and afterwards until her loss on 3/4 June 1942 as R9457.

125 AIR 14/2674

126 Listed erroneously in the official record as "25.08"; Author has assumed 2058 hrs because it aligns with the actual start time achieved.

127 AIR 14/2674

128 AIR 14/2674

129 AIR 14/2674

130 AIR 14/2674

131 AIR 14/2674

132 The "Zone Libre" or "Free Zone" accounted for roughly half of the area of mainland France and was governed by German consent from Vichy by Maréchal de France Philippe Pétain. It took in south-eastern and central France leaving both the strategically important northern and western coasts under direct German control in the "Zone Occupée". The Ligne de Démarcation was the border between these two sub-states, the integrity of which was enforced by the Germans.

133 Keith Janes at www.conscript-heroes.com

134 Goss, C. (1995) *It's Suicide but It's Fun: The Story of 102 (Ceylon) Squadron 1917–1956*, ISBN 0947554599, Crécy, p 67.

135 Pitchfork, G. MBE (2003) *Shot Down and on the Run: The RCAF and Commonwealth aircrews who got home from behind enemy lines, 1940–1945*, ISBN 1903365538, the national archives, pp 60–64.

136 Hid in his own cellar for two years to avoid capture by the Gestapo.

137 Arrested August 1942 and executed.

138 Arrested and sent to Ravensbrück concentration camp.

139 ww2escapelines.co.uk/sgt-ronald-shoebridge-raf/.

140 cometeline.org/fiche017.html.

141 Arrested January 1943 by the Gestapo, tortured and sent to Bayonne, Fresnes, Ravensbrück and finally Mauthausen concentration camp.

142 Middlebrook, M. and Everitt, C. (1990) *The Bomber Command War Diaries: An Operational Reference Book 1939–1945*, ISBN 0140129367, Penguin, pp 261–262.

143 AIR 14/2674

144 Sunrise over Kiel 0451 + 2 hours correction for BDST.

145 Following the route as laid down in this time would exceed the maximum speed of the Halifax and suggests an error in time recording.

146 Middlebrook, M. and Everitt, C. (1990) *The Bomber Command War Diaries: An Operational Reference Book 1939–1945*, ISBN 0140129367, Penguin, p 262.

147 AIR 14/2674

148 AIR 14/2674

149 AIR 14/2674

150 Analysis of flight times points to the longer-range Montpellier and Toulon sortie having been cancelled.

151 AIR 14/2674

7

A PLAN STARTS TO FORM

17 May 1942

Harris, a keen advocate of air power, believed that the war could be won from the air. In order to demonstrate the effectiveness of such a strategy, he proposed that Bomber Command muster all of its front-line and reserve strengths to focus an attack of such severity on a single German city that the people would rise up against their leadership. This operation, known as the Thousand Plan, was approved by Churchill on this date.

The implicit guidance within the Area Bombing Directive was for the destruction of targets in the Ruhr Valley such as Essen, Duisburg and Düsseldorf. For his *tour de force*, Harris wanted to focus on a target that would vindicate his belief in air power. To this end he wanted to target Hamburg as an important port, it being the centre of submarine production and the second-biggest city in Germany – but Hamburg lay beyond the reach of GEE. Churchill wanted instead to direct this unparalleled destructive force squarely at the heart of Germany's war industry in Essen, but this entire area was typically covered by an industrial haze, compromising navigation and bomb aiming. Impartial advice from Operational Research Section suggested that Cologne would be a good target, because it was a rail and communications hub, not affected by the industrial haze around the Ruhr Valley, and it was within the range of GEE.

Hamburg, however, still remained the preferred target for Harris, and the planning proceeded accordingly:

> Intention: To destroy the port and city of Hamburg.
>
> Code Name: This operation will be known as the 'Thousand Plan'.
>
> Date: The operation will take place on the night of May 27th / 28th or on the first suitable night thereafter until the night of May 31st / June 1st.
>
> Alternative target: If weather conditions are unfavourable in the Hamburg area but favourable in the Ruhr, Cologne will be the target.[152]

The routes were provisionally assigned as follows:[153]

1. Hamburg: Base – position X (54°30'N, 08°00'E) – Hamburg – Hollenstedt (53°22'N, 09°43'E) – position Y (54°00'N, 08°00'E) – Base.

2. Cologne: Base – Ouddorp (51°47'N, 03°50'E) – Bremen – Euskirchen (50°38'N, 06°47'E) – Noordland (51°38'N, 03°36'E) – Base.

The resources were to be directed as follows:[154]

Aircraft involved	Primary Target: Hamburg	Alternative Target: Cologne
1 Group 3 Group 4 Group 5 Group	Dace aim point D	Trout aim point A
91 Group 92 Group	Dace aim point E	Trout aim point X
Coastal Command Flying Training Command Army Co-Operation Command	Dace aim point F	Trout aim point Y
Intruder operations	**Target: Hamburg**	**Target: Cologne**
2 Group (30 Blenheims) and Army Co-Operation Command (16 Blenheims)	Schleswig Stade Ardorf Vechta Twente-Enschede Venlo	Venlo St. Trond Juvincourt Bonn Vechta Twente-Enschede
11 Group (25 Bostons or Havocs)	Schiphol Eindhoven Gilze-Rijen Leeuwarden Soesterberg	Schiphol Eindhoven Gilze-Rijen Leeuwarden Soesterberg
11 Group (12 long range Hurricanes)	To be operated at the discretion of 11 Group during the latter half of the night.	To be operated at the discretion of 11 Group during the latter half of the night.

If crews are unable to identify Cologne they are to set course direct for Essen where the aiming point is Stoat B,[155] with any built-up area seen in the Ruhr as a last resort target. Route home for aircraft attacking Essen or last resort targets is not to be the route home for Cologne, but is to be direct, avoiding as far as possible, heavily defended zones.[156]

The decision as to which target is to be attacked will be communicated to all concerned not later than 1200 hours on the day of the operation.[157]

Meanwhile at RAF Topcliffe, where squadron personnel were oblivious of plans being put in train miles away, the first Halifax landed on the newly completed runway.

19 May 1942

Target[158]	Aircraft on target	Types
Mannheim aim point A	197	105 Wellington 31 Stirling 29 Halifax 15 Hampden 13 Lancaster 4 Manchester
CC55A St-Nazaire	65	46 Wellington 9 Halifax 8 Stirling 2 Manchester
Minelaying:		
(i) Lorient (Artichoke)	6	Wellington
(ii) Heligoland (Rosemary)	3	Hampden
Nickelling:		
(i) Paris	7	6 Wellington 1 Halifax
(ii) Vichy	2	1 Halifax 1 Lancaster
(iii) Rouen	2	Hampden
(iv) Le Mans	2	Manchester

Main Operation

Primary target: Mannheim, target code Chub A.
Alternative: S&M Germany.
Last Resort: S&M Germany.
Operation C.203: 5 aircraft, operational call sign G1Z.
Bomb load: 1× 4,000 lb HC, 6× SBC 90× 4 lb.
Route: Base – Aldeburgh – Knokke – Givet – Mannheim and return.
Time Off: 2224 hrs.
Time Over Target: 0115 – 0155 hrs.
Leeming aircraft to drop green flares 0110 – 0115 hrs. Do not attack until 0115 hrs.
Weather: Visibility good.
Opposition: Moderate heavy flak.

Secondary Operation

Primary target: St-Nazaire, target code CC55A or Le Havre, target code CC24A.
Operation C.204: 1 aircraft, operational call sign 3WV.
Bomb load: 8× 500 lb GP.
Route: Base – Bridport – Bréhat – St-Nazaire and return.
or Base – Abingdon – Brighton – Le Havre and return.
Time Off: 2348 hrs (St-Nazaire),
Time Over Target: 0230 – 0300 hrs.

or 0054 hrs (Le Havre),
Time Over Target: 0300 – 0330 hrs.
Weather: 7/10 cloud. Moderate visibility.
Opposition: Little light and heavy flak.

NURSERY OPERATION

Special nickelling operation[159]
Dropping area: Nickelling over Vichy.
1 aircraft (freshman), operational call sign GQ6.
Route: Base – Abingdon – Brighton – Cabourg – dropping area and return.
Time Off: 2232 hrs.
Time Over Target: 0217 – 0227 hrs.
Weather: Clear.
Opposition: Nil.

NURSERY OPERATION

Special nickelling operation[160]
Dropping area: Nickelling over Paris.
1 aircraft (freshman), operational call sign GQ6.
Route: Base – Abingdon – Brighton – Fécamp – dropping area and return.
Time Off: 0044 hrs.
Time Over Target: 0316 – 0326 hrs.

As crews were becoming accustomed to operating the Halifax, the historically established 'big family' philosophy started to become ever more displaced; there was now becoming a more noticeable drive to establish and retain dedicated crews, as was generally accepted practice on other squadrons.

Further, the role of the bomb aimer was still being worked out on the squadron; A Flight and B Flight were fielding different crewing configurations as they evaluated which was most suited to the way they conducted operations. It was becoming evident that a dedicated bomb aimer could enhance the crews' bombing accuracy by leaving the navigator to operate his TR1335 airborne GEE receiver set unencumbered by other duties. That being the case, a protocol had to be developed to allow the bombs to be dropped either on the mark of the bomb aimer when the target could be confirmed visually, or by the navigator taking his cue from GEE when on a blind bombing run. The system had been developed and promulgated centrally; it flowed down to the squadrons as follows:[161]

a. 'Air bomber calling – target sighted'. The navigator continues to monitor the TR1335 and only steps in if the bomb aimer has misidentified the target.

b. 'Navigator calling. Stand by … Stand by …' The bomb aimer then prepares to release the bombs on the navigator's mark unless he sights the target first. The navigator will continue monitoring his TR1335 'Stand by … Stand by … GO!'

The night's activities were a planning nightmare; eight aircraft were scheduled to four different targets, six conducting attacks and two on nickelling operations. To add to the uncertainty, the choice of port target for the secondary operation had not been announced, and would be advised later.

At the same time, B Flight would be experimenting with different crewing configurations; their three aircraft for tonight each taking a dedicated bomb aimer and two of them taking 2nd pilots, resulting in crews of seven and eight respectively. The requirement for bomb aimers was being fulfilled from the numbers of WOps and/or air gunners on the squadron, this opportunity providing especially a role for those such as Sgt Frank Kuebler and Sgt Clifford Carr who had survived dreadful crashes and had subsequently experienced difficult recoveries. A Flight stuck to the basic six-man crews for all five of their aircraft.

The jumble of different variables settled down as follows:

- The five aircraft bound for Mannheim would be leaving from 2224 hrs, made up of three six-man crews from A Flight, whilst the other two were drawn from B Flight, carrying crews of eight.

- F/Sgt Charles Barr would be leading a six-man crew from A Flight to the Vichy area, departing at 2232 hrs.

- If a late decision came through to attack St-Nazaire instead of Le Havre, Sgt F Williamson would be leading out a crew of seven men from B Flight at 2330 hrs.

- Australian Sgt Brian Treloar would be leading a six-man crew from A Flight to Paris, departing at 0044 hrs.

- If a late decision came through to attack Le Havre instead of St-Nazaire, Sgt Williamson would be leading out a crew of seven men from B Flight at 0054 hrs.

As the events of the evening developed, the target for the secondary operation was notified as St-Nazaire rather than Le Havre. This was the further of the two options and attracted a longer flying time, so in accordance with the plan would be following the later start time.

St-Nazaire was at this time home to the 6th and 7th U-Boat Flotillas, but ten years earlier had seen the construction of the largest and fastest passenger ship of her day, the SS *Normandie*. To support her maintenance requirements, the port was equipped with the specially built Forme-Écluse Louis Joubert (Louis Joubert Lock) to accommodate the liner's impressive size. This also happened to be the only dry dock facility on the Atlantic coast sufficiently large to accommodate battleships the size of *Tirpitz*, and as such presented a significant threat to Allied shipping.

Given the significance of this facility, on 28 March 1942 it had been subject of an audacious RN and Commando raid known as Operation Chariot, which had seen obsolescent destroyer HMS *Campbeltown* packed with explosives and rammed into the lock gates at 0134 hrs. Twenty-four Mk.VII depth charges containing a combined total of 3.1 tons of AMATOL[162] had been placed together underneath the main gun support and wired with delay fuzes that initiated the explosives just after 0930 hrs. Independently calculated assessments suggest that 360–380 German personnel in the vessel and on the quayside were killed in the ensuing explosion, which was so devastating as to render the dry dock inoperative for the duration of the war.

Bombing up on dispersal (Chris Goss Collection)

The main operation was to be centred upon Mannheim's industrial area, which contained targets of key military priority such as military vehicle production by Mercedes-Benz and Heinrich Lanz AG, Motoren-Werke Mannheim AG marine diesel engines, Rudolf Fuchs oil products, and Interessen-Gemeinschaft Farbenindustrie (IG Farben) AG. This latter company produced amongst other chemical products synthetic fuel and oil; they also held the patent for the cyanide-based pesticide Zyklon B, which was being used to facilitate mass exterminations in the gas chambers such as at Auschwitz. Further, the industrial area backed onto the second-largest inland port in Europe, with docks and warehousing servicing the industrial centre.

This operation had been chosen for the squadron's first use of 4,000 lb Cookie HC bombs, each aircraft carrying one of them, accompanied by incendiaries. In order to ensure that each of these unitary HC bombs was placed accurately, it had been decided to mark the target using the Shaker Technique. For this operation, nine aircraft from 10 Squadron were scheduled to be over Mannheim a little before 102 Squadron arrived. Four of the nine had been issued with green flares in addition to full bomb loads, their crews having been instructed to drop the marker flares only when the target had been positively identified, and even then only during the specific 5-minute window of opportunity coinciding with the arrival of 102 Squadron aircraft.

In addition, there would also be two nursery operations: one more experienced Whitley pilot, Charles Barr, bound for Vichy, whilst Brian Treloar, the first of the 2nd pilots who had never made captain on Whitleys, would be flying to Paris.

As the evening approached, preparations on the squadron would have intensified. This was the greatest number of Halifaxes that had been fielded on operations on one night by the squadron so far, and with such a diversity of destinations, payloads and start times, activities would have to run smoothly if all were to get away on time.

The first change to the plan was made for Charles Barr, whose departure to Vichy was brought forward by 10 minutes, placing him at the head of the Mannheim crews instead of behind them as planned. Having accomodated this minor change, the Mannheim aircraft, led out by F/Lt William Welch, followed on 2 minutes later although one of their number, P/O Peter Gaskell, suffered engine trouble and would not start.

An hour after this, at 2338 hrs, Sgt Williamson took off for St-Nazaire, starting 8 minutes late. There should then have been a further gap of an hour before the Paris flight as the last sortie of the night got under way, but before this could happen word was received from RAF Cottesmore that Charles Barr, on the Vichy run in W1099, had crashed on landing at 0025 hrs with an engine on fire. Finally, at the end of the list of the night's departures, Brian Treloar took off for Paris 7 minutes late, at 0051 hrs.

In the event, what had been a planning nightmare had more or less worked out, and the squadron began the long wait for the remaining seven crews to return. The next to be heard from was F/Sgt Hank Malkin, who had been unable to maintain height and airspeed on the Mannheim run and had recovered to RAF Manston at 0330 hrs.

The news from other aerodromes continued to come in; the next to be heard from was Sgt Harold 'Batch' Batchelder in W7677[163] on the Mannheim operation. His troubles had started when the port inner engine failed over Brussels; the No.1 tank was empty but the selector cable for No.2 tank had been severed by flak, so the engine could not be restarted. At 0358 hrs they left behind occupied Belgium at 12,000 ft and headed out over the Channel, whereupon the rear air gunner reported an aircraft, possibly a Bf 110, astern. Immediately both air gunners fired simultaneously and the captain broke to port, enemy tracer passing to starboard. The night fighter passed underneath and made another attack from the port quarter, at which the captain took evasive action to starboard. The engagement continued down to 3,000 ft and ended only when the night fighter was seen breaking away, both air gunners claiming hits.

Their adversary gone, Batch Batchelder then found that the aircraft was difficult to control, as the rudder controls were jammed solid. Flying on ailerons as his only reliable flight control, coupled with rudder and elevator trim tabs, he set course for RAF Horsham St Faith and crossed the English coast at Lowestoft at 1,200 ft at 0440 hrs.

Approaching Norwich they called Horsham, asking them to put on their lights, but the call went unanswered. They tried again, but still to no avail; there was an air raid over Norwich at the time and the Horsham personnel were not going to illuminate themselves as a target unless there was an emergency. With difficulty maintaining height and fuel running dangerously low, Batchelder's next call was a Mayday. This was the cue Horsham needed, and they immediately turned on their lights, accompanied by a searchlight simultaneously pointing the way for the crippled aircraft. Unable to follow the protocol of going into a circuit to land, Batch Batchelder flew straight in and selected undercarriage down – but the night's dramas were not over yet, and no locked-down indications were displayed. Their luck held, however; it was just as they touched down, at 0455 hrs, that the port outer engine cut out.

Batch Batchelder took a look over his aircraft next day:[164]

> On examining the aircraft in daylight, it was found that cannon shells had hit the tail, severing and jamming the rudders and elevators. The port inner engine (the dead one) had been hit by cannon fire and there were numerous holes in the fuselage. An inspection light which was located about 10 inches from the mid-upper gunner's head had been shot

Halifax W7677 port tail fin (Chris Goss Collection)

away and another had entered the fuselage just below the rear turret and must have passed between the gunner's legs! None of us had been hurt.

For his exceptional flying, Batch Batchelder was written up for a DFM.

There had been good visibility over Mannheim; German reports[165] noted that the bombers nevertheless appeared to make repeated passes over the area as if unable to locate their targets. Ultimately, a concentration of around 600 incendiaries did fall on the harbour area, destroying a number of industrial premises, as well as about 10 aircraft-loads of bombs falling on the city.

22 MAY 1942

Target[166]	Aircraft on target	Types
CC55A St-Nazaire docks	27	Halifax
Minelaying:		
(i) St-Nazaire (Beech)	15	Wellington
(ii) Swinemünde (Geranium)	9	Lancaster
(iii) Sassnitz (Willow)	7	Lancaster

NURSERY OPERATION

Primary target: St-Nazaire, target code CC55A.
Operation C.205: 3 aircraft (freshmen), operational call sign 7GA.
Bomb load: 8× 500 lb GP.
Route: Base – Sywell – Bridport – Bréhat – St-Nazaire and return.
Time Off: 0008 hrs.
Time Over Target: 0300 – 0330 hrs.
Weather: 9 to 10/10 cloud.
Opposition: Slight.

Three more aircraft were sent to follow the tracks that had been made by Sgt F Williamson to St-Nazaire three nights earlier. It was now almost two months since the success of Operation Chariot, and Bomber Command wanted to maintain pressure on any attempt to repair the shattered dry dock as well as hindering the operations of the 6th and 7th U-Boat Flotillas stationed there. The U-boats were afforded protection at this base by a single bunker, 291 m × 124 m, accommodating eight dry and six wet pens that could hold 20 submarines.

The time had come for Len to put his Halifax training into practice and kit up for his first operation since 31 January 1942. He would be flying as WOp with B Flight's commander, S/Ldr Richardson, aboard W7654. On the crew were colleagues of his from Whitley days, and also newcomer F/Sgt Ivor Lewis. Uniquely among the three nursery crews, they also carried a bomb aimer, raising their complement to seven. Charles Barr, having suffered an engine fire and crash-landing on his last time out, was to be given another opportunity to complete his nursery operation, and formed another of the crews.

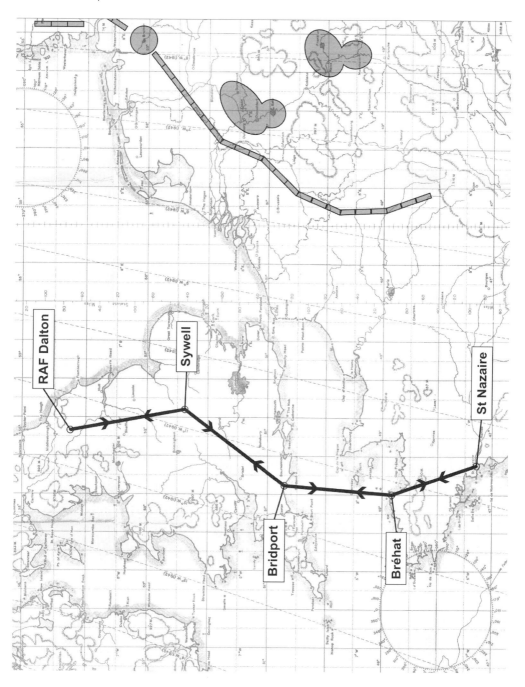

Operation C.205 to St-Nazaire, 22 May 1942

S/Ldr Richardson's crew took off at 0012 hrs, second out of three; but none of the three was able to identify the target through cloud and all brought their bombs back. Richardson's was the first back, and all aircraft were down safely within less than 25 minutes of each other.

Halifax W7654 (DY-Q)

St-Nazaire.

Takeoff 0012 hrs.

Brought bombs back.

Landed 0640 hrs.

Operational combat time 6 hrs 28 mins.

S/Ldr JWB Richardson

F/O AD Dobson

Sgt L Starbuck   21st operation; combat time 158 hrs 5 mins

Sgt BC Sandall

Sgt D Boddy

F/Sgt I Lewis   3rd operation; combat time 21 hrs 46 mins

F/Sgt GM Rowe

Len's first operation on the Halifax had been carried out without incident, but the inability to drop bombs made it a questionable success. The Halifax was much bigger and faster than the Whitley, and this led to an unpleasant discovery: Len's earlier projection of completing his tour had been predicated upon long endurance operations in a slow aircraft, and was consequently skewed in favour of reaching his 200 combat hours before completing the full 30 operations. Now, however, the same distances were being covered in a much shorter time, which meant that the remainder of his tour would have to be counted off by the number of operations instead of on the hours.

23–24 MAY 1942

WO1 Richard Bradbury had last flown operationally on 31 January, nearly four months earlier, and was taken on a check flight by B Flight's incoming commander, S/Ldr John Walkington, on 23 May, who noted that he was a 'very good Air Observer'.

U-Boat operations at St-Nazaire (Deutsches Bundesarchiv, Bild 101I-027-1495-18 / Dinstühler / CC-BY-SA)

The next day, Bradbury accepted a commission to become a pilot officer. He had been promoted to WO1 on 1 March 1942, and now, less than three months later, he was an officer. At this juncture he was given a new service number, J/15512, replacing his old R/58087 number that he had been allocated back in 1939 when starting his military service in the Canadian militia.

25 MAY 1942

Amongst the new starters on the squadron was a 5' 6" air gunner with black hair and dark brown eyes who had enrolled through the RCAF; he was Peter John Fernie, known as Jack, to avoid confusion with a younger cousin of the same name.

His mother was Esther Williams, who had lived on Prince Edward Island in the Gulf of St Lawrence until her family moved across the continent in 1905 to settle in Kitsap County, Washington State. Here she met Harry Fernie, who had been brought up in Great Yarmouth, Norfolk, and who had worked as a telegraph messenger before emigrating to America. They married in 1913 and moved 70 miles north to Victoria, British Columbia, just the other side of the Canadian border, where they had their first son, Harry Jr.

By 1917 Harry, Esther and Harry Jr had moved back into USA and taken up residence 600 miles further south, in Glenn County, California. Here, Harry developed his interest in telegraphy by becoming a telephone pole line foreman employed by Sacramento Valley Telephone Company. On 27 May 1917 the couple had their second son, Peter John (to be known as Jack), in the private Sisters of Mercy hospital in Sacramento, 100 miles further south.

By 1919, they had crossed back into Canada again, and they went to live in Vernon, British Columbia, where they had their third son, William. The family was joined by Harry's younger brother, David, and between them they founded Okanagan Electric in 1920. Six years later they left Vernon behind and moved 50 miles to Kamloops, where they set up Fernie Brothers Electrical Supplies in 1927, and where their fourth child, Patricia, was born.

When the Great Depression hit during the 1930s, young Jack left school at age 17 to go to work, even though he had only spent four years at High School and had not yet matriculated. Whilst his brother William joined the Royal Canadian Navy in 1937, when he was 18, Jack stayed at home to help out with the family business, where he specialised in electric wiring, motors, radio and refrigeration.

However, Jack also wanted to enlist, and so on 17 June 1940 he completed the application form to join the RCAF, listing his occupation as electrician, his hobby as radio repair, and his favoured sports as field and track running, jumping, swimming and football. He also stated his preference to be a pilot. Two weeks later, on 2 July 1940, he was invited to the Vancouver Recruiting Centre, where he was summarised as follows:

Sgt Jack Fernie
(Fernie family)

Clean cut smart bright boy who has not got his Junior Matriculation and is a little short on education. He is a resourceful type however. Quick on the uptake and his natural smartness and keenness would to some extent offset lack of education. Is suited best for work as a WAG [sic] (potential).

With his application for the RCAF still pending, late in 1940 he joined the 2nd Battalion Rocky Mountain Rangers (RMR) under the Non-Permanent Active Militia (NPAM), and was mobilised as part of the Canadian Active Service Force (CASF) on 1 January 1941. He served for one week as a private, from 10 to 17 January 1941, after which he was released to join the RCAF.

On 25 January 1941, Jack enlisted with the RCAF, signing up for training as a W/O (air gunner), and was posted to No.2 MD RCAF Brandon, Manitoba. Immediately upon arrival, on 27 January 1941, he was hospitalised for a week, and after three weeks of training was posted to No.2 MD RCAF Virden, Manitoba, on 24 February 1941. The next day he was posted to No.2 Training Command RCAF Winnipeg, Manitoba, where after a week he was hospitalised for another week before resuming his training. On 16 April 1941 he was posted back to RCAF Brandon, where he finished basic training before being posted to No.2 Wireless School at RCAF Calgary, Alberta, where he joined No.16 course.

Jack struggled with his Morse code and was put back onto No.18 Course, and then No.20 Course, after which his training was discontinued. A report was raised stating: 'Has been set back two entries – cannot get Morse above 14 words per minute. Tries hard.' Jack was interviewed, and the summary read: 'Wants to stay in Aircrew – likes Pilot – if can't get this would like to go back to his trade electrician (6 years' experience).' On 7 November 1941 Jack was posted to the Composite Training School, RCAF Trenton, Ontario, whilst his future was being decided.

Ten days later the Reselection Board commented that although Jack had again made clear his aspiration to be a pilot, he '[h]as insufficient education to enlist as pilot', a legacy from his not having matriculated. However, he clearly had personal qualities that the RCAF wanted to retain, and he was described as being:

Honest, straightforward – anxious to be in air crew in some capacity – not so keen on serving in a ground job – has had considerable training in service life – 6 years in NPAM – RMR 176 – should be suitable fellow for air crew duties in some capacity, is bright and alert and ready with answers.

So it was decided that since he had enlisted as a WOp/AG and his gunnery skills had not so far been evaluated, he was to proceed with air gunner training. Consequently, Jack's next posting, on 20 December 1941, was to No.3 B&GS at RCAF MacDonald, Manitoba, where he joined Course No.23.

During his air gunner training Jack accrued 6 hours 20 minutes in a Fairey Battle and a further 2 hours 20 minutes as a passenger, giving a total of 8 hours 40 minutes. In that time, he managed to score (i) Beam test 13 per cent, (ii) Beam relative speed test 9 per cent, (iii) Under tail test 13 per cent. He scored 67.8 per cent for his air gunnery and 68.4 per cent for his character and leadership, earning him a pass as an average air gunner, and graduating fourth in his class of 37. On 19 January 1942 he was awarded his air gunner brevet and promoted to sergeant.

Now qualified, his next step was onto a troop transport to England, but before he left, he took 10 days' leave to say his goodbyes. He immediately made the journey westwards to see his family and show them his hard-earned new stripes and air gunner's brevet, and on 22 January 1942 arrived at the American border crossing at Blaine, Washington. Here he applied for a two-day pass to visit his Uncle Harry Tench in Seattle, but was debarred because he did not have a visa.

A memorandum from the president of the Officers Selection Board on 3 February 1942 reviewed the results from No.3 B&GS, noted that Jack had graduated fourth in class with a score of 505/700, and recommended him for a commission. This would have come as such a boost following the uncertainty he had experienced with his flying career only a few short months earlier; it was clearly as an air gunner that he had found his niche.

When Jack returned from leave, he joined the muster at No.1 Y Depot Halifax, from where he embarked on a troop ship for England on 10 February 1942. Nine days later the cohort disembarked, and he reported to No.3 PRC, RAF Uxbridge. Soon after his arrival, Jack was posted to No.1 Air Armament School, RAF Manby in Lincolnshire, on 28 March 1942, for a seven-week course. From here he was posted to No.7 Air Gunnery School RAF Stormy Down on 16 May 1942 for a further week, and then on 23 May 1942 to 1484 Target Towing (TT) Flight, RAF Driffield. Finally ready for combat, Jack was posted to 102 Squadron on 25 May 1942, where he was assigned to B Flight.

27 MAY 1942

Initial planning had identified on 17 May 1942 that this evening would mark the start of the moon period that would support the Thousand Plan, but the weather had closed in on both the primary target of Hamburg and the secondary target of Cologne. Indeed, the weather looked set bad for some time to come. For now, Harris would have to be content with playing a waiting game.

29 MAY 1942

Target[167]	Aircraft on target	Types
Paris, Gennevilliers; Z312 Foundry at the Gnome-Rhône engine works	77	31 Wellington 20 Halifax 14 Lancaster 9 Stirling 3 Hampden
CC16A Cherbourg	31	14 Wellington 12 Stirling 5 Hampden
CC31A Dieppe	17	Wellington
Minelaying:		
(i) Frisian Islands (Nectarine)	18	15 Stirling 3 Wellington

(continued)

Target	Aircraft on target	Types
(ii) North entrance to the Sound (Nasturtium)	3	Lancaster
(iii) Copenhagen (Verbena)	3	Lancaster
Nickelling over Rouen	3	Manchester

Primary target: Paris (Gennevilliers Gnome-Rhône aluminium foundry and engine works).
Operation C.206: 3 aircraft, operational call sign J1S.
Bomb load: 2× 4,000 lb HC fuzed instantaneous.
Route: Base – Abingdon – Brighton – St-Valery – Paris and return.
Bomb from 4,000–6,000 ft attack from northeast to southwest along river.
Time Off: 0022 hrs.
Time Over Target: 0250–0310 hrs must be rigidly adhered to.
Weather: Cloudy conditions.
Opposition: Moderate light flak.

The Gennevilliers plant in northern Paris produced the Gnome et Rhône aircraft engines used on a variety of commandeered French aircraft and even on some German-designed types. Because these engines were regarded as underpowered, they would find their way into only a few front line aircraft, such as the ground attack Henschel Hs 129, in addition to the Gotha Go 244 and Messerschmitt Me 323 transports. Of more immediate concern to the Allies was the company having been ordered to produce the highly successful BMW 801 engine, which was used in a variety of front-line aircraft, including the Ju 88 and now the Fw 190.

Three aircraft were called forward for this operation; two were crewed by A Flight, both of which for the first time increased the basic crew of six men to seven with the introduction of 2nd pilots, whilst the third, from B Flight, carried a crew of eight including a 2nd pilot and a bomb aimer. Each aircraft was to carry two 4,000 lb HC bombs, referenced in station documentation as Highball,[168] even though it was more widely known as Cookie.

This would be a very challenging operation, as the target was located in a built-up area and crews would be dropping area-effect HC bombs, so in order to minimise collateral damage specific instructions were issued for the direction of approach and altitude. Further, it had been decided that all aircraft on the operation would be delivering their ordnance to a tight schedule, adding to the pressure faced by the crews.

Two of the crews released their bombs from 5,000 ft and 6,000 ft respectively as ordered, but the third, led by Sgt Edmund Newell, the least experienced of the three captains in Halifaxes and flying without a bomb aimer, had difficulty locating the target through the cloud and flew lower to secure a positive identification. By the time he had found the target, he was at 2,500 ft, which was too low to bomb, given the nature of the 4,000 lb Cookie HC bombs and their instantaneous fuzing. Having only a tight window of opportunity to make his attack, he had no time to make another run and had to turn for home, jettisoning his bombs in the sea on his way back.

Cloud over Paris had compromised the operation; local reports[169] confirmed negligible damage to the factory, but that a number of houses in the vicinity had been destroyed.

30 MAY 1942

During the spring of 1942 careful analysis of the Würzburg equipment seized during the Bruneval Raid on 27/28 February had guided British intelligence as to how the radar worked and, from this, how the German GCI system worked. Frustrated German night fighter crews were already well aware that the system was flawed. It was totally inflexible: if there were no contacts in a predefined area known as a *Raum*, the night fighter on patrol there would not be permitted to move into an adjacent Raum, even if it contained more contacts than the night fighter allocated to that area could cope with. Therefore, even if his immediate neighbour was overwhelmed with contacts, a pilot without contacts in his Raum would have to retire to circling round his beacon until a contact strayed into it. This flaw would unwittingly ensure the survival of a large number of RAF bomber crews.

The solution was elegant in its simplicity. The forthcoming Thousand Plan would call for an aerial armada on a scale never seen before, which could be potentially rich pickings for the night fighters; on a simple numerical basis the losses would be intolerable. Previous operational briefings had issued crews with planned waypoints, but latitude had been given to each of the crews as to how they executed their orders, and thus individual crews had undertaken their own sorties. Tonight, however, Bomber Command would be able to use the Kammhuber Line's rigid Raum limitation to its own advantage by introducing a system under which all the aircraft would fly consecutively along a tightly defined path. This would swamp one or two Räume at most whilst leaving all the other night fighters performing an endless holding circuit round their respective beacons as the bombers surged ahead, unchecked, past them. Thus was the concept of the bomber stream born.

In preparation for the raid on Hamburg, Harris had drafted the following speech to be included as part of the briefing:

> The Force of which you form a part to-night is at least twice the size and has more than four times the carrying capacity of the largest Air Force ever before concentrated on one objective.
>
> You have an opportunity, therefore, to strike a blow at the enemy which will resound, not only throughout Germany, but throughout the world.
>
> Next to London, New York and Liverpool, Hamburg is the most important commercial and industrial port in the world. It is, moreover, the main centre of Germany's submarine building and manning activities, the very focus of German nautical tradition, and a vast hive of general war industry.
>
> In your hands lies the means of destroying a major part of the resources by which the enemy's war effort is maintained. It depends, however, upon each individual crew whether full concentration is achieved.
>
> Press home your attack to your precise objective with the utmost determination and resolution, in the fore-knowledge that if you individually succeed the most shattering and devastating blow will have been delivered against the very vitals of the enemy.
>
> Let him have it – right on the chin.[170]

The bad weather that had been persisting over northern Germany seemed set to continue. The meteorologists advised that once again the Hamburg area would be covered in cloud, whereas a different picture was emerging 250 miles further to the south-west, in the Ruhr; there was a 50:50 chance that Cologne would be under clear skies. They were already four nights into the five-night moon period and, although the real prize of Hamburg still eluded them, passing up this opportunity to wait for better weather, even for the secondary target, could have precluded the Thousand Plan from ever happening. The die was cast.

With Cologne now identified as the primary target, the secondary target was confirmed to be Essen, aiming point Stoat B,[171] the Krupp works.

Primary target: Cologne (aiming point X).
Alternative: Essen (aiming point B).
Last Resort: Any built up area in the Ruhr.
Operation C.207: 20 aircraft (1 cancelled), operational call sign 9PM.
Bomb load:
    18 aircraft: 3× 1,000 lb GP TD 0.025, 8× SBC 90× 4 lb, 4× SBC 8× 30 lb.
    2 aircraft: 8× 1,000 lb GP.
Route: Base – Orford Ness – Ouddorp – Cologne – Euskirchen – Noordland – Base.
    If secondary target attacked head home by the shortest route avoiding defended areas.
Time Off: 2350 hrs.
Time Over Target: 0205 – 0215 hrs.
Aircraft not having found target must S/C [set course] not later than 0240 hrs wherever they may be.
Weather: Clear visibility, good.
Opposition: Considerable heavy accurate flak co-operating with searchlights.

Harris had originally counted on greater support from Coastal Command, but this was not to materialise, and so the number of bombers was made up from any and all available aircraft, including those with pupil and instructor crews. The Thousand Plan was ordered, and in response 1,096 bombers were to be despatched, 1,046 of them heading for Cologne.

102 Squadron received the request for maximum effort, and in response detailed 20 aircraft. At their briefing, crews were advised not only as to the unprecedented scale of the operation, but also that they would be flying as part of the bomber stream which would be compacted tightly together, all the 1,046 aircraft scheduled to clear the target within 90 minutes. To orchestrate this feat of aerial logistics, a finely structured plan was flowed down to squadrons all over the country, each being given start times synchronised to a carefully co-ordinated master plan. This precision planning also extended to maximising the chances of a safe return, and crews were briefed that any aircraft that had not found their target must, wherever they might be, set course for home not later than 0240 hrs, to ensure that there would be no stragglers to be picked off by the German air defences.

Given that most crews would be reliant upon dead reckoning, an initial wave of Stirlings and Wellingtons equipped with GEE were to arrive 15 minutes before the main bomber stream and drop target markers one mile to the north and south of Neumarkt, the city's old town. Incendiaries would then be dropped on these markers, creating readily identifiable beacons for the subsequent arrival of the main force, ensuring that all following aircraft, whether fitted with GEE or not, would be able to release their bombs on target.

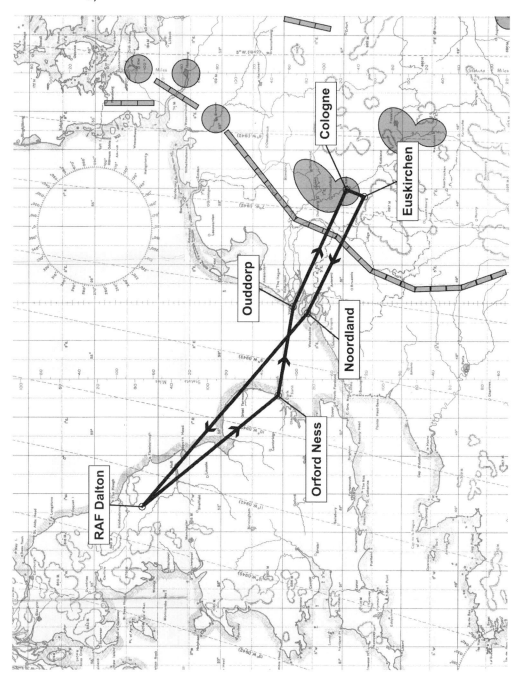

Operation
C.207 to
Cologne,
30 May 1942

Cologne

Euskirchen

Ouddorp

Noordland

Orford Ness

RAF Dalton

102 Squadron's usual cadre of aircraft, with callsigns taken from the sequence DY-A to DY-R, was reduced to 15. No replacement had yet been given the callsign DY-O following the loss of W7677 on 19 May 1942, so to bring the numbers back up two additional aircraft were introduced to operations; W7712 as DY-S and R9449 as DY-T, the sixth and final one of the GEE-equipped aircraft received from 35 Squadron on 9 April. Two more were drafted in from 102 CF: V9987 as DY-U, a B Mk.II Series 1 (Special) without a mid-upper turret, and R9423 as DY-V, an early B Mk.II Series 1. This would only make 19, but it was the best that could be done.

B Flight's commander, S/Ldr Richardson, was to lead a seven-man crew in W7654, including Len, Sgt Ernest de Mattos, F/Sgt Ivor Lewis and newly arrived Sgt Jack Fernie on his first operation. Meanwhile Kenneth Wright, now confirmed in appointment as F/Lt, was allocated to fly as 2nd pilot supporting P/O Peter Gaskell.

At bomber bases across the country, squadrons complying with the maximum effort directive were lining up their aircraft at staggered times, ready for the signal to go. All would shortly be gone, meeting up with fellow travellers from other aerodromes, and all of them then moving onwards together towards the same target in an awesome spectacle of air power such as had never before been seen; a seemingly unending procession of bombers in a single choreographed line.

At RAF Dalton, the imposing spectacle of 19 aircraft was held back as the full moon completed the first hour of its climb above the horizon.[172] One particular aircraft stood out from the rest in having no mid-upper turret: V9987, a B Mk.II Series 1 (Special), which consequently required one less crewman and was fielding only a five-man crew. F/Sgt WJ Weller brought this aircraft into position, second in the line.

Tonight, for the first time, the scheduled Time Off would not be the time when the signal was given to the first aircraft to lead the others out, but the time when the last of the aircraft should be on her way. Planning 1-minute intervals between the aircraft, Sgt Edmund Newell led out 130 men to face their destiny at 2330 hrs; 18 of the aircraft took off without any difficulty, but Peter Gaskell was slightly delayed, and started almost 20 minutes after the others. Three returned early, two of them fitted with GEE, due to technical issues, but 16 aircraft went on to the primary target.

The bomber stream flew above cloud from Holland to the German border, where the cloud disappeared, just as had been forecast. By the time the first bomber arrived over Cologne, the moon was giving near-perfect visibility. The response on the ground was slow. Tragically, this would cost the civilian population dearly, as they were thus caught unprepared when the first bombs started to fall. Fire took hold within minutes of the first bombs landing, and it was soon clear that there was going to be little defence against this unprecedented onslaught. The intensity of the attack was such that the incoming bombers would be able to see the glow of the burning city from the point where they crossed the Dutch coast,[173] 145 miles away.

AVM Baldwin, AOC 3 Group, flying as 2nd pilot in a Stirling from 218 Squadron, is quoted as saying:[174]

I caught sight of the twin towers of Cologne cathedral, silhouetted against the light of three huge fires that looked as though they were streaming from open blast furnaces.

Within nine minutes of the coast, we circled to take a last look. The fires then resembled distant volcanoes.

102 Squadron old boy S/Ldr Leonard Cheshire, who was flying a Halifax from 1652 CU on this operation, was drawn to comment:[175]

Against this pale, duck-egg blue and greyish mauve were silhouetted a number of small black shapes: all of them bombers, and all of them moving the same way. One hundred and thirty-four miles ahead, and directly in their path, stretched a crimson-red glow; Cologne was on fire. Already, only twenty-three minutes after the attack had started, Cologne was ablaze from end to end, and the main force of the attack was still to come.

SUMMARY OF 102 SQUADRON OPERATIONS 30/31 MAY 1942

Number	GEE	Callsign	T/O	Land	Notes
R9529		H	2330	0534	Attacked primary target
V9987		U	2332	0543	Attacked primary target
R9423		V	2334	0549	Attacked primary target
R9494	✓	C	2336	0058	RTB with electrical trouble
R9498		L	2337	0507	Attacked primary target
R9491		N	2340	0515	Attacked primary target
W1142		A	2342	0556	Attacked primary target
R9533		B	2343	0547	Attacked primary target
W1066[176]		G	2344	0510	Attacked primary target
R9531		E	2345	0531	Attacked primary target
W7712		S	2347	0541	Attacked primary target
R9446	✓	F	2348	0046	RTB with ailerons and artificial horizon U/S
R9532		D	2349	0537	Attacked primary target
R9449	✓	T	2350	0525	Attacked primary target
R9530		J	2352	0519	Attacked primary target
W7654		Q	2353	0525	Attacked primary target
R9442	✓	R	2354	0459	Attacked primary target
W7651		M	2355	0326	RTB as aircraft would not climb
W7652		P	0014	0528	Attacked primary target

Three aircraft from 102 Squadron reported encountering night fighters; of these only S/Ldr Griffiths recorded any serious attention from the enemy, R9533 having been hit by flak and attacked twice by enemy aircraft. Sgt Thomas 'Mac' McIlquham, the rear air gunner, claimed one night fighter destroyed and another damaged.

ORDER OF BATTLE FOR 30/31 MAY 1942 [177]

	Group	Type	Sorties	Missing
Cologne		Wellington Mk.Ic	24*	1
		Wellington Mk.II	36*	3
	1 Group	Wellington Mk.III	18	
		Wellington Mk.IV	68*	2
		Wellington 423	5*	
		Whitley	3*	
	91 Group attached to 1 Group	Wellington Mk.II	26*	1
		Wellington Mk.IV	1*	
		Wellington Mk.Ic	36*	1
	3 Group	Wellington Mk.III	91	5
		Wellington 423	6	1
		Stirling	69 + 19*	2
	Flying Training Command attached to 3 Group	Wellington Mk.Ia	4*	1
	91 Group attached to 3 Group	Wellington Mk.Ic	17*	
	92 Group attached to 3 Group	Wellington Mk.Ic	20*	3
		Whitley	7*	1
	4 Group	Wellington Mk.II	9*	2
		Halifax	99 + 32*	3
		Hampden	34*	
	5 Group	Manchester	46*	4
		Lancaster	59 + 14*	1
	91 Group	Whitley	21*	
		Wellington	194*	7
	92 Group	Whitley	45*	1
		Wellington	43*	1
	SUBTOTAL		1046	40
Juvincourt		Blenheim	9*	1
St. Trond	2 Group and Army Co-operation Command	Blenheim	8*	
Venlo		Blenheim	6*	
Twente		Blenheim	10*	
Vechta		Blenheim	9*	1
Bonn		Blenheim	8*	
	TOTAL		1096	42

* Not fitted with TR 1335

Because the smoke rising from the shattered city was so thick, it was not until five days later that a proper assessment of the damage could finally be undertaken. When the photographs had been analysed, they showed that the total amount of destruction visited upon the city from this one attack was equivalent to 2,904,000 square yards.[178] Just as St Paul's Cathedral had seemingly miraculously survived the Blitz, so too Cologne Cathedral, rising resolutely above the desolation all around, had suffered nothing but minor damage to its windows.

> According to local records 3,330 buildings were destroyed, 2,090 seriously damaged and 7,240 lightly damaged, almost all by fire ... The conflagration devoured 13,010 homes, mostly apartments, and seriously damaged 6,360 more.[179]

One mystery widely reported by returning crews was the apparently sporadic nature of the German defences; at one point some of the searchlights were reported as having been switched off and the flak guns having gone silent, only for the searchlights to resume later – but without the flak that would generally herald the approach of a night fighter. One reason postulated was disorganisation amongst the night fighter controllers, whilst another was that the flak gunners had simply run out of ammunition, never expecting to have provided continuous fire for such an extended period. Whatever the reason, many RAF bomber crews benefited from this lull in retaliation.

In the wake of this attack, Churchill wrote to Harris: 'This proof of the growing power of the British bomber force is also the herald of what Germany will receive, city by city, from now on.'

Halifax W7654 (DY-Q)

Cologne.

Takeoff 2353 hrs.

Released one stick over primary target from 12,000 ft.

Landed 0525 hrs.

Operational combat time 5 hrs 32 mins.

S/Ldr JWB Richardson

F/O AD Dobson

Sgt L Starbuck   22nd operation; combat time 163 hrs 37 mins

Sgt PJ Fernie   1st operation; combat time 5 hrs 32 mins

Sgt ERT DeMattos   7th operation; combat time 47 hrs 35 mins

F/Sgt I Lewis   4th operation; combat time 27 hrs 18 mins

F/Sgt JH Rowe

Halifax W7652 (DY-P)

Cologne.

Takeoff 0014 hrs.

Released one stick over primary target from 13,700 ft.

Landed 0528 hrs.

Operational combat time 5 hrs 14 mins.

P/O PR Gaskell

F/Lt KB Wright   1st operation; combat time 5 hrs 14 mins

F/Sgt RH Adamson

Sgt SH Jackson

Sgt TH May

Sgt A Huddlestone

Sgt DH Craig

The new tactics had worked well. The target had been devastated, mainly due to prevailing good weather; but the GEE technology had also played a contributory role, principally in the Stirlings and Wellingtons that had marked the target in advance of the arrival of the main bomber stream. The good visibility experienced over the target had rendered superfluous the need for subsequent aircraft to rely upon the GEE equipment, but this could so easily not have been the case. More importantly, losses had been less than anticipated; while Churchill had been prepared to accept a loss rate of 10 per cent, just under 4 per cent had been recorded. The bomber stream concept had worked, overwhelming enemy defences as hoped, and all 102 Squadron aircraft and crews had returned safely.

31 May 1942

Even as the smoke was clearing over Cologne, Harris still believed that Hamburg had slipped through his grasp. However, there was still one more night in that moon period. This gave him one last chance, and that chance was tonight. If the weather over northern Germany remained unfavourable, his secondary target would once more be the Krupp works at Essen, which had been the secondary target the night before.

With the plans for both primary and secondary targets in place, Harris wrote as a prelude to the night's operation:

> Before the Thousand Plan Force disperses, a final attack of great magnitude will be made tonight in the area where weather conditions are likely to be most favourable.[180]

The initial plan to attack the Krupp works at Essen read as follows:[181]

> Shaker attack on Stoat.
> Intention: To completely destroy an industrial area.
> Z = 0050 hrs
> Primary target Stoat E or any built up area on the Ruhr:
> 20 TR equipped Wellingtons from 3 Group illuminate target from Z to Z +23 minutes.
> 125 TR equipped heavies drop loads from Z +2 minutes to Z +15 minutes.
> Remaining aircraft drop loads from Z +15 minutes to Z +90 minutes.

Targets:

1 Group and 3 Group: Stoat D Main Post Office (195 deg 300 yards from B).

4 Group + 92 Group Stoat C large shed in Krupp works (300 deg 1,000 yards from B).

5 Group + 91 Group Stoat E crossroads (198 deg 1,100 yards from B).

As Harris waited for favourable weather reports, he drafted another morale-boosting speech to be relayed to the crews during the briefing:

By your skill, determination and courage in last night's operation you have undoubtedly struck the enemy a stunning blow. All and more than was expected of you you have achieved.

I now ask you for one additional effort tonight against an even more vital objective before the Thousand Plan force disperses and while the weather yet holds.

You all know the value of a right and left, and I am confident that you will bring it off.[182]

He waited, frustrated, for news of a break in the weather over northern Germany, but it did not come, and so at 1830 hrs he cancelled the second outing of his Thousand Bomber force. Hamburg was saved – for now. This marked the last opportunity in the moon period specified on 17 May, after which the moon had been considered to be rising too late to provide the necessary illumination over the target. Harris, however, felt he was within an ace of realising his goal of annihilating Hamburg, and so instead of standing his crews down gave himself one more night's grace, as he had the benefit of momentum behind him.

Postponing for one further night would mean that the moon would not even be rising over Hamburg until 0047 hrs the following morning, and not reaching apogee until 0512 hrs.[183] Consequently, the outward journey would have to be undertaken in darkness, which would place a heavy reliance on navigation. Furthermore, Hamburg lay beyond the reach of GEE, which meant that the last part of the outward journey would have to be flown on dead reckoning, and secondly that moonlight would be essential to illuminate the target area.

The advent of moonrise would not of itself provide adequate illumination to support targeting, so the bombers would have to wait for it to rise high enough before the first bombs could be dropped with any accuracy. If the start of the bombing was rushed, then the risk would be that the first bombers would misidentify their targets and the subsequent waves of bombers would use the earlier fires to cue their own aim points, compounding the error and compromising the operation.

Furthermore, the bomber stream on the last Thousand Plan operation to Cologne had been compressed into 90 minutes in conditions whereby crews could maintain safe visual separation with the benefit of a full moon. Consequently, this time serious consideration would need to be given to ensuring safe separation between aircraft, especially during the early part of the outward journey, which would be conducted in darkness, increasing the risk of collisions.

Allowing only an hour for the moon to rise obliquely over Hamburg and assuming the same 90 minutes for the procession of the bomber stream over the target, the last few aircraft should be bombing Hamburg at 0317 hrs before commencing their return journeys. The sun would rise over Hamburg at 0558 hrs[184] the following morning, but crucially the proposed route for the bomber stream was to return to base from position Y (54°00'N, 08°00'E), which would then lead them on a westerly heading just to the north of the German and Dutch coasts. Assuming departure from Hamburg at 0317 hrs, the last aircraft in the bomber stream should pass closest to the night fighter base at Leeuwarden as the skies began to lighten around 0500 hrs, around an hour before sunrise there at 0616 hrs.[185]

Consequently, whilst delaying the start of the operation would improve the illumination from the moon over the target, and extending the duration of the bomber stream would reduce the risk of collisions, the corollary of either action would be to delay the time at which the crews would return. This would mean their being increasingly within range of the day fighter stations as dawn approached, leaving them desperately exposed. Further, as the sky grew brighter towards sunrise any later stragglers would not stand a chance.

If Hamburg was to be considered seriously as a target under these conditions, then significant losses could be expected on both the outgoing and return journeys – but that may yet have been a price Harris was willing for his men to pay. Certainly, planning assumptions to attack Hamburg on this scale could not be stretched any further during this moon period. Essen, on the other hand, was a shorter flight time and within the range of GEE, which supported both navigation and targeting, thereby facilitating departure times that would allow the aircraft to return under the cover of night. Essen therefore presented the more logistically workable of the two operations. But Hamburg still remained the first choice.

There would be just one last chance to reconvene the Thousand Plan, or it would have to be stood down with no idea of when, or indeed if, it could ever be pulled together again.

1 June 1942

The weather reports over northern Germany were bad once more. There was also cloud over Essen, adding to the constant industrial smoke and haze that persisted irrespective of the weather. These were not the best conditions under which to mount an attack, but the alternative was to stand the crews down. Harris decided: the Thousand Plan would have one more outing – to Essen.

Primary target: Essen (large shed in Krupp works, 300° 1,000 yards from aiming point B).
Alternative: Any built up area in the Ruhr.
Last Resort: Any built up area in the Ruhr.
Operation C.208: 20 aircraft, operational call sign GL5.
Bomb load: 3× 1,000 lb GP TD 0.025, 8× SBC 90× 4 lb, 4× SBC 8× 30 lb.
Route: Base – Finningley – North of Hague – Essen – Krefeld – South of Hague – Base.
5 aircraft (Initial Force) Set Course: 2302 hrs, Time Over Target: 0052 – 0105 hrs.
15 aircraft (Main Force) Set Course: 2355 hrs, Time Over Target: 0125 – 0145 hrs.
Weather: 8/10 to 10/10 cloud at 8,000 ft dispersing later, but thick haze and smoke which obscured visibility.
Opposition: Moderate intense heavy flak bursting through clouds. Numerous searchlights in cones but hampered by haze and cloud.

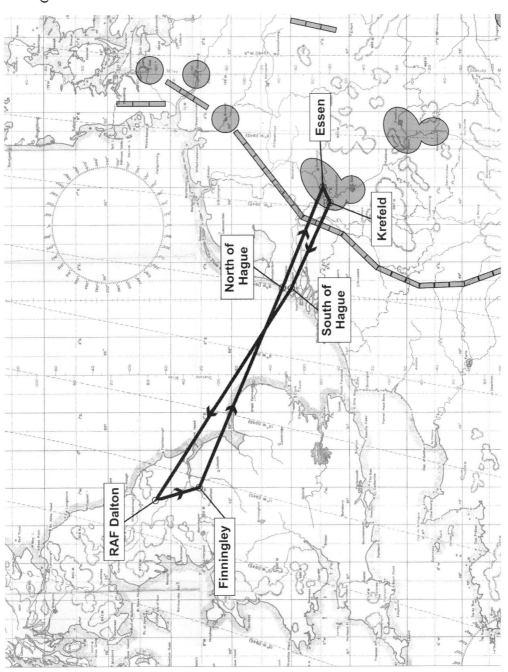

*Operation
C.208 to Essen,
1 June 1942*

So it was that two days after the success of the Thousand Plan against Cologne the aircrews were brought back to repeat the feat whilst the new technology and tactics still gave them the element of surprise. This put pressure on the ground crews, as this most recent request for maximum effort had come just two days after the last, and not all aircraft would be available; on 102 Squadron for example, R9533 was undergoing repairs following engagement with enemy night fighters, and R9491 was unserviceable and would also not be ready in time. One new aircraft was to be brought on charge; W7706 was to join as the new DY-O, but this still only brought the number up to 16.

102 CF stepped in with the two aircraft it had loaned to support the previous operation to Cologne:

- V9987 (DY-U), a B Mk.II Series 1 (Special) without a mid-upper turret.
- R9423 (DY-V), an early-build B Mk.II Series 1.

The squadron was also able to find two more aircraft to bring itself up to strength:

- R9426 (DY-W) an early-build B Mk.II Series 1.
- L9532 (DY-Y) a B Mk.I with no mid-upper turret, but two very draughty beam positions with fitments for twin Vickers K 0.303" guns in the rear fuselage, and the underpowered Merlin Mk.X engines.

W7654 would be in action again, with Len, Sgt Ernest de Mattos, F/Sgt Ivor Lewis and Sgt Jack Fernie, but this time under the captaincy of S/Ldr Peter Robinson from 102 CF. F/Lt Kenneth Wright would also be flying once more, as 2nd pilot in P/O Peter Gaskell's crew, which remained otherwise unaltered from the Cologne operation two nights earlier.

A new term, 'Set Course', was added to the departure routine for the first time tonight. This meant that once each crew became airborne, instead of immediately assuming a heading to take them to their first waypoint, they would perform a circuit over the aerodrome so that it could be used as their first navigational fix This allowed the navigator to calculate the drift experienced between the aerodrome and his next fix, to improve the accuracy of his navigational calculations throughout the rest of the sortie. To ensure that crews were not delayed by incorporating this additional manoeuvre, the aircraft were scheduled to be in the air a few minutes before the set course time.

When the set course time was applied to more than one aircraft, it was taken as applying to the last aircraft airborne, from which the take-off time for the first aircraft had to be back-calculated, including a margin for safety; unsurprisingly, the more aircraft that were involved the more challenging it became to get this exercise right.

The squadron was split into an initial force of five aircraft, with the remainder scheduled to follow in the main force shortly after. This time it fell to Sgt F Williamson to lead the initial force out, taking off at 2252 hrs. The last of the five took off at 2258 hrs, hitting the set course time of 2302 hrs. The remaining 15 aircraft lined up under a moonless sky,[186] the fifth and the eighth standing out without mid-upper turrets. After a pause of only 20 minutes following the departure of Peter Gaskell, the last of those in the initial force, the aircraft of the main force were led out by W/Cdr Sydney Bintley at 2318 hrs.

A planning assumption had been made to allow over 2 minutes' gap between each of the remaining aircraft to ensure that the last of them would be able to set course by 2355 hrs as scheduled – but as it happened, the crews halved the spacings to just over 1 minute each, with the result that F/Lt William Welch, captaining the last aircaft out, took off no less than 19 minutes before the scheduled set course time; nobody wanted to be the last man in the bomber stream.

As with the first Thousand Plan operation, crews were briefed to 'turn for home by 0235 hrs whether having bombed or not'; this was to ensure that the bomber stream departed in a synchronised manner and that there would consequently be only a minimum of stragglers for the night fighters to pick off.

Further, crews were advised to 'gain speed and lose height on their return to under 1,000 ft when over the Dutch border'. This served two purposes; firstly it was addressing the vulnerability of bombers to attack from beneath, and secondly it was responding to wireless intercepts from frustrated German night fighter controllers who had routinely been overheard abandoning radar-guided intercepts below 3,000 ft with words similar to 'British bomber too low'.[187]

Three of the squadron's aircraft returned with various issues; two of them had technical problems and in the third case the captain was unwell. For the remaining 17, the outward journey was cloudy, and although the cloud cleared over the target, the expected industrial haze was so thick as to obscure visibility.

SUMMARY OF 102 SQUADRON OPERATIONS 1ST/2ND JUNE 1942

Number	GEE	Callsign	Force Element	T/O	Land	Notes
R9498		L	Initial Force	2252	0338	Attacked primary target
W7712		S	Initial Force	2253	0414	Attacked primary target
W7651		M	Initial Force	2255	0430	Attacked primary target
R9442[188]	✓	R	Initial Force	2257	0353	Attacked primary target
W7652		P	Initial Force	2258	0440	Attacked primary target
W1066		G	Main Force	2318	0437	Attacked primary target
R9529		H	Main Force	2320	MIA	
R9494	✓	C	Main Force	2321	0500	Attacked primary target
R9530		J	Main Force	2322	0415	Attacked primary target
L9532		Y	Main Force	2323	0547	Attacked primary target
R9532		D	Main Force	2325	0445	Attacked primary target
R9446	✓	F	Main Force	2327	0511	Attacked primary target
V9987		U	Main Force	2328	0515	Attacked primary target
R9449	✓	T	Main Force	2329	0405	Attacked primary target
W7654		Q	Main Force	2330	0440	Attacked primary target

(continued)

Number	GEE	Callsign	Force Element	T/O	Land	Notes
R9531		E	Main Force	2331	0507	Attacked primary target
W9426		W	Main Force	2333	0532	Attacked primary target
W1142		A	Main Force	2334	0147	RTB unable to maintain height
W7706		O	Main Force	2335	0345	RTB with intercom failure
R9423		V	Main Force	2336	0123	RTB Captain sick

Halifax W7654 (DY-Q)

Essen.

Takeoff 2330 hrs.

One stick released over primary target from 13,000 ft.

Landed 0440 hrs.

Operational combat time 5 hrs 10 mins.

S/Ldr PB Robinson

F/O AD Dobson

Sgt L Starbuck   23rd operation; combat time 168 hrs 47 mins

Sgt PJ Fernie   2nd operation; combat time 10 hrs 42 mins

Sgt ERT DeMattos   8th operation; combat time 52 hrs 45 mins

F/Sgt I Lewis   5th operation; combat time 32 hrs 28 mins

Halifax W7652 (DY-P)

Essen.

Takeoff 2258 hrs.

One stick released over primary target through 10/10 cloud from 15,000 ft.

Landed 0440 hrs.

Operational combat time 5 hrs 42 mins.

P/O PR Gaskell

F/Lt KB Wright   2nd operation; combat time 10 hrs 56 mins

F/Sgt RH Adamson

Sgt SH Jackson

Sgt TH May

Sgt A Huddlestone

Sgt GH Craig

This time, the squadron was not as lucky as before, and lost Sgt Edmund Newell, who had led out crews for the first Thousand Plan operation only two nights previously; his R9529 crashed near Düsseldorf with the loss of all crew.

Overall, the loss rate had remained within 'acceptable' limits, at just over 3 per cent. Photographs taken at the time by the returning crews were inconclusive, but photographic reconnaissance soon showed the extent of the damage. Given the success of the Thousand Plan on Cologne, Harris could have reasonably expected the focused concentration of such lethal capacity onto a much smaller area to have rendered the armaments manufacturer unable to recover for the duration of the war. However, such was not the case; no damage at all appeared to have been caused to the primary target of the Krupp works. This news would have shaken Harris to the core.

The industrial haze predicted as being bad had militated to compromise bombing accuracy to a degree unexpected, even given the availability of GEE. Further, crews unable to locate the primary target would have chosen alternative targets in the area, resulting in the bombs being more widely spread and so their effect less concentrated. This vexed Harris on two scores: first, the enemy's principal armaments factory was still in production; and secondly, since the results were so much less satisfactory than had been experienced two nights previously, he did not want Essen to be the catalyst that could shut down the Thousand Plan in which he had invested such personal capital, and for which he still harboured further plans.

ORDER OF BATTLE FOR 1/2 JUNE 1942 [281]

	Group	Type	Sorties	Missing
Essen	1 Group	Wellington Mk.Ic	21*	
		Wellington Mk.II	34*	
		Wellington Mk.III	14	
		Wellington Mk.IV	66*	3
		Whitley	2*	
	91 Group attached to 1 Group	Wellington Mk.Ic	27*	
	3 Group	Wellington Mk.Ic	8 + 24*	1
		Wellington Mk.III	90	1
		Stirling	68 + 9*	1
	Flying Training Command attached to 3 Group	Wellington Mk.Ic	2*	
	91 Group attached to 3 Group	Wellington Mk.Ic	14*	1
	92 Group attached to 3 Group	Wellington Mk.Ic	15*	1
	4 Group	Whitley	5*	
		Wellington Mk.II	6*	
		Halifax	89 + 38*	8

(continued)

215

ORBAT 1/2 June 1942[189]	Group	Type	Sorties	Missing
Essen	5 Group	Hampden	26*	1
		Manchester	33*	1
		Lancaster	49 + 25*	4
	91 Group	Whitley	22*	1
		Wellington Mk.Ic	181*	6
	92 Group	Hampden	45*	
		Wellington Mk.Ic	43*	2
	SUBTOTAL		956	31
Juvincourt	2 Group and Army Co-operation Command	Blenheim	3*	
St. Trond		Blenheim	8*	
Venlo		Blenheim	8*	1
Twente		Blenheim	8*	
Rheine		Blenheim	4*	
Vechta		Blenheim	9*	
Bonn		Blenheim	8*	2
	TOTAL		1004	34

* Not fitted with TR 1335

Endnotes

152 AIR 14/276

153 AIR 14/276

154 AIR 14/276

155 The codeword 'Stoat' identified the target as the Krupp works in Essen, not the city itself, which had been allocated the codeword 'Bullhead'.

156 AIR 14/276

157 AIR 14/276

158 AIR 14/2674

159 Operation number not allocated.

160 Operation number not allocated.

161 AVIA 7/1250

162 Lyman, R. (2013) *Into the Jaws of Death: The True Story of the Legendary Raid on Saint-Nazaire*, ISBN 9781782064442, Quercus, p 126.

163 Goss, C. (1995) *It's Suicide but It's Fun: The Story of 102 (Ceylon) Squadron 1917–1956*, ISBN 0947554599, Crécy, pp 68–69.

164 Goss, C. (1995) *It's Suicide but It's Fun: The Story of 102 (Ceylon) Squadron 1917–1956*, ISBN 0947554599, Crécy, pp 69–70.

165 Middlebrook, M. and Everitt, C. (1990) *The Bomber Command War Diaries: An Operational Reference Book 1939–1945*, ISBN 0140129367, Penguin, p 267.

166 AIR 14/2674

167 AIR 14/2674

168 The same codename was used later in 1942 to describe the spherical anti-ship 'Bouncing Bomb', smaller sibling to

the 'Upkeep' bomb used in Operation Chastise against the Ruhr dams on 16/17 May 1943.

169 Middlebrook, M. and Everitt, C. (1990) *The Bomber Command War Diaries: An Operational Reference Book 1939–1945*, ISBN 0140129367, Penguin, p 268.

170 AIR 14/2024

171 AIR 14/276

172 Moonrise over York (nearest datum point to RAF Dalton) 2028 + 2 hours correction for BDST.

173 Taylor, E. (2004) *Operation Millennium: 'Bomber' Harris's Raid on Cologne, May 1942*, ISBN 1862272301, Spellmount, p 112.

174 Ministry of Information (1942) *Bomber Command Continues*, His Majesty's Stationery Office, p 50.

175 Cheshire, L. VC OM DSO DFC (1988) *Bomber Pilot*, ISBN 0907579108, Goodall (Crécy Publishing) p 158.

176 Listed erroneously in the ORB as W7706. W7706 was on the squadron at this time, and would be flying her first operation two nights later with callsign DY-O. Author makes the assumption that the ORB compiler would have been more likely to misread the serial number in small print than the callsign on the side of the aircraft.

177 AIR 14/3408

178 Ministry of Information (1942) *Bomber Command Continues*, His Majesty's Stationery Office, p 51.

179 Bishop, P. (2007) *Bomber Boys: Fighting Back 1940–1945*, ISBN 9780007189861, HarperCollins, p 98.

180 AIR 14/2024

181 AIR 14/2024

182 AIR 14/2024

183 Moonrise over Hamburg 2247 + 2 hours correction for BDST, moonset 0738 + 2 hours correction for BDST on 2 June.

184 Sunrise over Hamburg 0358 + 2 hours correction for BDST on 2 June.

185 Sunrise over Leeuwarden 0416 + 2 hours correction for BDST on 2 June.

186 Moonrise over York (nearest datum point to RAF Dalton) 2234 + 2 hours correction for BDST.

187 AIR 40/1135, Paragraph 25 of Enemy Night Fighter Defence (Report of Operational Research Committee Sub-Committee) TC29 dated November 1942.

188 Listed erroneously in the ORB as R9942. R9942 was not a Halifax, it was an Anson.

189 AIR 14/3408

8

IN SEARCH OF A KNOCKOUT BLOW

2 June 1942

Target[190]	Aircraft on target	Types
Essen and area	195	97 Wellington 38 Halifax 27 Lancaster 21 Stirling 12 Hampden
Dieppe docks	6	Wellington
Minelaying:		
(i) St-Nazaire (Beech)	6	Wellington
(ii) Lorient (Artichoke)	4	Hampden
Nickelling over Rennes area	4	Hampden

Primary target: Essen (aiming point B).
Alternative: Cologne (aiming point A).
Operation C.209: 8 aircraft, operational call sign 6JR.
Bomb load: 3× 1,000 lb GP TD 0.025, 8× SBC 90× 4 lb, 4× SBC 8× 30 lb.
Route: Base – Mablethorpe – Leiden – Essen – South of Krefeld – Ouddorp – Orford Ness – Base.
Bomb from 14,000 – 15,000 ft. Aircraft advised to lose height and gain speed keeping as low as possible until Dutch coast is crossed.
Time Off: 2335 hrs.
Set Course: 2342 hrs.
Time Over Target: 0132 – 0200 hrs.
15× 3 Group Wellingtons will drop flares between 0130 – 0148 hrs.
Weather: Thick haze in target area prevented recognition of aiming point. Crew were able to pinpoint Rhine and in some cases Dortmund-Ems Canal from which point runs were made.
Opposition: Heavy flak in target area, numerous cones of searchlights working in co-operation, two lanes of searchlight lines between Essen-Krefeld. All aircraft reported large number of dummies in area but were easily picked out.

Frustrated by the lack of success, Harris wanted to hit the same target again, but crews needed recuperation; they had supported two maximum effort operations in the last three nights and were exhausted. Nevertheless, before the tempo could be allowed to reduce, crews would be directed to attack Essen once more. This would be a significantly less intense operation than the night before, requiring 102 Squadron to provide only eight aircraft. All the aircraft detailed for this operation had supported at least one of the previous Thousand Plan operations; most had flown both, and were consequently surviving on the minimum of maintenance. With the call for maximum effort behind them, at least for a while, the Time Off measure reverted to being the time at which the operational crews would be led out.

F/Sgt Bill Davies was scheduled to fly this operation in W7712, but was unable to start due to a glycol leak. The ORB implies that the operation proceeded with seven remaining aircraft, but a standby crew led by Sgt Brian Treloar in R9532 was drafted in to make the number back up to eight. During the operation this aircraft was 'severely damaged by flak', and Brian Treloar lost control on final approach, landing heavily. As the aircraft was in the act of turning over[191] her back broke and she fell back, allowing all inside to escape. Squadron Commanding Officer W/Cdr Sydney Bintley had been watching from the control tower and, fearing there may have been crewmen trapped, ran the quarter-mile to the wrecked aircraft to get the crew out.

Worse was to befall F/Sgt Frank Holmes and his crew in R9491, who were intercepted over the North Sea by either Hptm Horst Patuschka Erg./NJG2 at 0250 hrs or Oblt Alois Lechner Erg./NJG2 at 0300 hrs. The bomber was shot down 30 miles east of Southwold at around 0257 hrs, with the loss of all crew. Only one body was found, that of the rear air gunner, Sgt David Boddy, recovered 5 miles east of Harwich.

The results of this operation were still not considered to have been satisfactory, as even after two attacks on consecutive nights the Krupp works was still not showing the signs of destruction that had been hoped for, given the level of devastation meted out to Cologne less than a week earlier. This would have been most unwelcome to Harris, who must have begun to wonder what more he could do to deal a knock-out blow to the principal German armaments supplier as it continued to stand in defiance.

3 June 1942

Harris went before the cameras to deliver a speech outlining his views about the bombing initiative. This was to become one of his most famous speeches:

> The Nazis entered this war under the rather childish delusion that they were going to bomb everybody else and nobody was going to bomb them. At Rotterdam, London, Warsaw, and half a hundred other places, they put that rather naive theory into operation. They sowed the wind and now they are going to reap the whirlwind.

> Cologne, Lubeck, Rostock – those are only just the beginning. We cannot send a thousand bombers a time over Germany every time, as yet. But the time will come when we can do so.

It is interesting to note the exclusion of Essen, the target of the previous two nights, from this list of successes, as if he considered the job yet to be completed.

Operation C.210 to Bremen, 3 June 1942

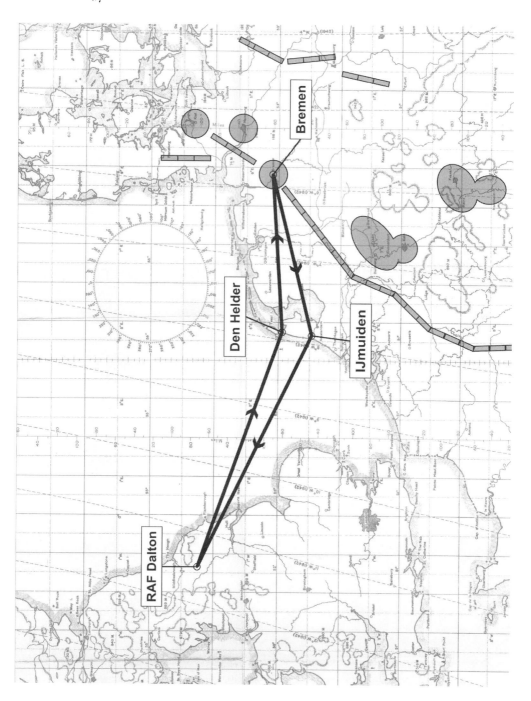

Target[192]	Aircraft on target	Types
Bremen aim point A	170	88 Wellington 37 Halifax 15 Lancaster 15 Stirling 9 Hampden 6 Manchester
CC31A Dieppe docks	4	2 Stirling 2 Wellington
Enemy aerodromes:		
(i) Stade	3	Blenheim
(ii) Vechta	3	Blenheim
(iii) Ardorf	2	Blenheim
(iv) Leeuwarden	1	Blenheim
Minelaying:		
(i) Verdon, Gironde (Deodar)	4	Lancaster
(ii) St-Nazaire (Beech)	3	Hampden
Nickelling:		
(i) Le Mans	2	Manchester
(ii) Lille	2	Manchester
(iii) Rennes	1	Hampden

Primary target: Bremen (318° 600 yards from aiming point A).
Alternative: S&M Germany.
Operation C.210: 8 aircraft, operational call sign A8U.
Bomb load: 3× 1,000 lb GP TD 0.025, 8× SBC 90× 4 lb, 4× SBC 8× 30 lb.
Route: Base – Den Helder – Bremen – IJmuiden – Base.
Bombing height at Captain's discretion.
Time Off: 2255 hrs.[193]
Set Course: 2306 hrs.
Time Over Target: 0117 – 0145 hrs.
15× 3 Group Wellingtons will drop flares at eight second intervals over the TR release point between 0115 – 0133 hrs.
Weather: Thick haze in target area made visual identification difficult.
Opposition: Intense heavy and light flak in area. Numerous searchlights, cones north and south of Bremen.

Eight crews were detailed to attack Bremen, including F/Lt Kenneth Wright who continued as 2nd pilot, this time flying with F/Sgt Wickham as part of an eight-man crew.

Sgt Batch Batchelder arrived back at 0143 hrs with a defective intercom, having elected to jettison his bombs but to bring the incendiaries back. The remaining seven crews went on to complete their attacks, but Brian Treloar was attacked by a night fighter and was forced to bomb early. The only other noteworthy event was that the precious GEE equipment in R9449 flown by Sgt 'Robbie' Robinson went unserviceable.

Halifax W7652 (DY-P)

Bremen.

Takeoff 2256 hrs.

Released one stick over primary target from 17,000 ft.

Landed 0418 hrs.

Operational combat time 5 hrs 22 mins.

F/Sgt HW Wickham

F/Lt KB Wright   3rd operation; combat time 16 hrs 18 mins

F/Sgt DL Boyd

Sgt GR Davidson

Sgt D Carroll

F/Sgt WA Gillies

Sgt R Levente

F/Sgt FG Kuebler

Although visibility over Bremen had been compromised by thick haze, German reports[194] confirmed significant damage to housing, with serious fires on six streets. Concurrently, the harbour area had sustained damage to a pier, warehousing and destroyer Z-25.

Halifax starting up at its dispersal at RAF Dalton (Chris Goss Collection)

5 JUNE 1942

Target[195]	Aircraft on target	Types
Essen aim point B	180	98 Wellington 33 Halifax 25 Stirling 13 Lancaster 11 Hampden
Minelaying:		
(i) Frisian Islands (Nectarine)	12	7 Wellington 3 Hampden 2 Lancaster
(ii) Quiberon Bay (Gorse)	3	Manchester
Nickelling:		
(i) Paris	2	Wellington
(ii) Rennes	1	Manchester

Primary target: Essen (aiming point B), target code Stoat B.
Last resort Cologne (aiming point B).
Operation C.210A: 11 aircraft, operational call sign 7VR.
Bomb load: 3× 1,000 lb GP TD 0.025, 8× SBC 90× 4 lb, 4× SBC 8× 30 lb.
Route: Base – Alkmaar– Essen – South of Bonn – Valenciennes – Nieuport – Orford Ness – Base.
Set Course: 2308 hrs.
Time Over Target: 0117 – 0145 hrs.
15× 3 Group Wellingtons will drop flares at eight second intervals over the TR release point between 0115 – 0135 hrs.
Weather: Good weather throughout trip. Visibility at target area impaired by ground haze.
Opposition: Considerable accurate heavy flak in area. Searchlights very active along Rhine south of Bonn.

As the Krupp works remained seemingly steadfast against the onslaught of the whirlwind re-leased by Bomber Command, it became an athame pointing to the wisdom of the belief that war could be won from the air. Consequently, with a better weather forecast, Harris sent his force back once more.

For this operation, P/O Richard Bradbury would be flying with F/Sgt Bill Davies, whilst Sgt Jack Fernie was allocated to a crew led by F/O Peter Gaskell, promoted since his last sortie, on 3 June.

Two of the 11 did not start, and a further aircraft returned early with an engine failure, but the remaining eight went on to attack their primary target.

Halifax W7706 (DY-O)

Essen.

Takeoff 2306 hrs.

Released one stick over the primary target from 16,000 ft.

Landed 0430 hrs.

Operational combat time 5 hrs 24 mins.

F/Sgt WR Davies

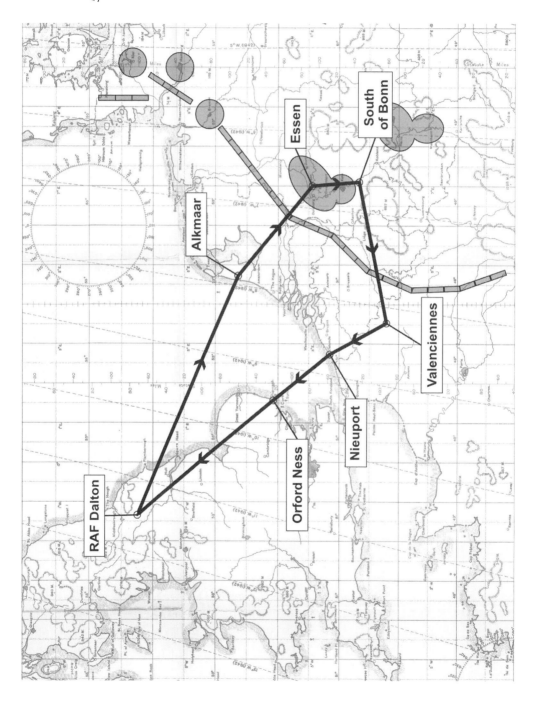

Operation C.210A to Essen, 5 June 1942

Essen

South of Bonn

Alkmaar

Valenciennes

Nieuport

Orford Ness

RAF Dalton

P/O[196] RF Bradbury   10th operation; combat time 77 hrs 31 mins

Sgt BC Sandall

Sgt LH Cailes

Sgt CM Bowring

Sgt J Whitfield

F/Sgt GH Rowe

Halifax W7652 (DY-P)

Essen.

Takeoff 2300 hrs.

Released one stick over primary target from 17,500 ft.

Landed 0422 hrs.

Operational combat time 5 hrs 22 mins.

F/O PR Gaskell

F/Sgt RH Adamson

P/O AJ Graham

Sgt PJ Fernie   3rd operation; combat time 16 hrs 4 mins

Sgt DK Breary

Sgt D Craig

Sgt A Huddlestone

All aircraft returned, but in an astonishing twist of fate one of the crewmen went missing. R9498, commanded by Sgt F Williamson, was hit by flak on the return journey, and she entered a dive that he felt he would be unable to control. He gave the order to bale out, and with the aircraft continuing to fall out of control the WOp, Sgt Haycock, whose post was nearest to the nose escape hatch, promptly did so. Shortly thereafter, however, Sgt Williamson was able to regain control of the aircraft and fly home, now with a bit of a draught from the nose escape hatch. Sgt Haycock, meanwhile, landed safely and was captured.

6 JUNE 1942

Target[197]	Aircraft on target	Types
Emden	233	124 Wellington 40 Stirling 27 Halifax 20 Lancaster 15 Hampden 7 Manchester
Enemy aerodromes:		
(i) GU4182 Ardorf	3	Blenheim
(ii) Z52 Leeuwarden	3	Blenheim

Nursery Operation

Primary target: Emden (aiming point A).
Operation C.211: 3 aircraft (freshmen), operational call sign 1YR.
Bomb load: 3× 1,000 lb GP TD 0.025, 8× SBC 90× 4 lb, 4× SBC 8× 30 lb.
Route: Base – Flamborough – Schiermonnikoog – Emden – Rottumeroog – Base.
Set Course: 2329 hrs.
Time Over Target: 0117–0155 hrs.
15× 3 Group Wellingtons will drop flares at eight second intervals over the TR release point between 0115–0135 hrs.
Weather: Clear excellent conditions in target area.
Opposition: Little heavy flak mostly to north and northwest of town. Searchlights few and ineffective.

Of the three freshmen flying this nursery operation to Emden, F/Lt Kenneth Wright, due to his impressive portfolio of flying experience, would be using only his fourth operation on the squadron as his opportunity to qualify as captain. Supporting him in W7654 would be a number of crewmen with whom he had never flown before, but who were coalescing and becoming established as the nucleus of a crew, including Len, P/O Richard Bradbury, Sgt Ernest de Mattos and F/Sgt Ivor Lewis. Tonight's operation would also call upon the crew to drop nickels.

All three crews took off at regular 2-minute intervals and all returned 4¼ hours later after an unremarkable operation, landing in the same sequence at regular 5-minute intervals.

Halifax W7654 (DY-Q)

Emden.

Takeoff 2329 hrs.

One stick released over primary target from 16,500 ft.

Landed 0347 hrs.

Operational combat time 4 hrs 18 mins.

F/Lt KB Wright	4th operation; combat time 20 hrs 36 mins
P/O RF Bradbury	11th operation; combat time 81 hrs 49 mins
Sgt L Starbuck	24th operation; combat time 173 hrs 5 mins
Sgt GF Fargher	
Sgt ERT DeMattos	9th operation; combat time 57 hrs 3 mins
F/Sgt I Lewis	6th operation; combat time 36 hrs 46 mins

Clear skies over Emden supported accurate bombing; German reports[198] confirmed damage to the docks in addition to 500 houses having been damaged or destroyed.

This would be the last operation undertaken by the squadron from RAF Dalton, as the paved runways at RAF Topcliffe were now ready.

7–10 June 1942

On the first day of the move, the HQ and A Flight returned to RAF Topcliffe. In the time they had been gone, the bombing circle had been replaced by new paved runways, the main 1,975-

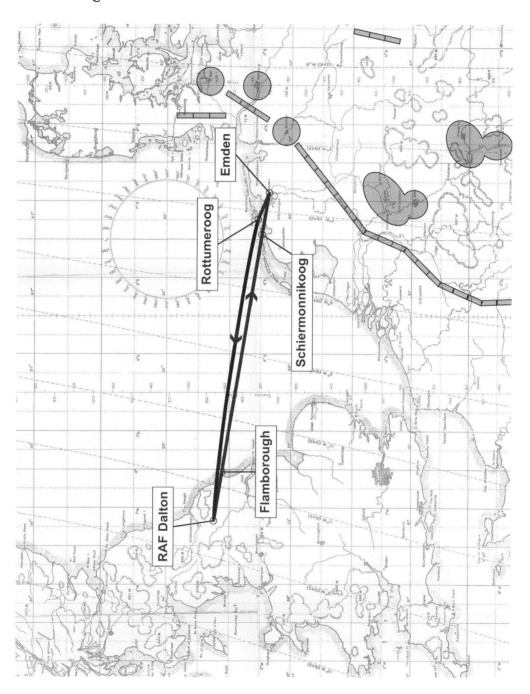

Operation C.211 to Emden, 6 June 1942

yard runway aligned 03/21, whilst the secondary runways, 1,380 yards and 1,153 yards long, had been arranged in a standard triangular pattern, aligned 13/31 and 08/26.[199,200] The main runway had originally been shorter but was lengthened before the station was re-opened.

Although the squadron was now operating from RAF Topcliffe once more, Ed Cooke adds a surprising footnote: 'We flew the aircraft and all our flying kit back to our previous rooms, but we still remained in our huts back at Dalton and used to bus in', so the men fell into the unusual routine of sleeping at Dalton and living at Topcliffe.

The second day of the move saw the return of B Flight and Maintenance Flight, whilst two days later the move was completed when 102 CF joined them.

13 JUNE 1942

Although the Thousand Plan had run its course, Churchill was under increasing political pressure to make a further significant push. Stalin was accusing him of cowardice, making comparisons with what the Russians had inflicted on the German forces in pushing them back from Moscow, whilst there were claims in America that the British were sitting back to let others do their fighting for them.[201]

With both the country's key allies openly questioning British resolve, Churchill found himself in conversation in Harris,[202] the one man who was capable of mounting the demonstration he needed to silence his critics. As expected, he was pushing on an open door, the only concern expressed by Harris being whether he could secure the support of Coastal Command in sufficient numbers to achieve the necessary concentration of attack. In spite of the willingness of Air Chief Marshal Philip Joubert de la Ferté, AOC in C Coastal Command, the final approval to release these aircraft would reside with Admiral of the Fleet Dudley Pound, Chief of Naval Staff (CNS). Churchill took this on board and agreed to talk to the Admiralty accordingly.

14 JUNE 1942

Buoyed up by his conversation with Churchill, Harris wrote to Portal[203] proposing to 'lay on another Thousand Plan during this moon period'.
He continued:

> I hope you will succeed in persuading the CNS, if necessary with the assistance of the PM, to allow Coastal Command to come in on this occasion. I am not asking for help from Training Command because, although they were the most willing, they have nothing ponderable to offer.

15 JUNE 1942

Churchill wrote to Portal[204] to reference his recent conversation with Harris two days previously and expressed his firm support for 'Arabian Nights', a codeword representing the continuation of the Thousand Plan. He also followed up on his promise to clear the way for the support of Coastal Command: 'I have asked the Admiralty to make sure they do not prevent Coastal Command from playing its part. I understand Joubert had 250 machines ready, but that the Admiralty stopped their use.'

16 June 1942

Approached by both Churchill and Portal, and with the obvious willingness of Joubert,[205] CNS agreed to release 'all the East Coast Hudsons, numbering about 100'. This amounted to the smallest token of support that could have been offered without openly snubbing Churchill, and was significantly less than the 250 aircraft that had been hoped for. The bitterness of the timbre of this offer was further reinforced by the following statement, quoted by Portal:[206] 'He also offers the Polish Wellington Squadron on the understanding that we will exchange it after the Operation for another Wellington squadron, as he thinks the Poles are too wild for Coastal Command work.' Goodwill was clearly in short supply at the higher echelons of the Admiralty.

Target[207]	Aircraft on target	Types
Essen aim point B	106	40 Wellington 39 Halifax 15 Lancaster 12 Stirling
Minelaying off Lorient (Artichoke)	12	Hampden
Nickelling over Le Mans and Seine Valley	9	5 Stirling 4 Wellington

Main Operation

Primary target: Essen (aiming point B), target code Stoat B.
Alternative: Bonn or any built up area outside area of Ruhr.
Operation C.212: 9 aircraft, operational call sign FJ1.
Bomb load: 3× 1,000 lb GP TD 0.025, 8× SBC 90× 4 lb, 4× SBC 8× 30 lb.
Route: Base – Orford Ness – Blankenberge – Givet – South of Bonn – Essen – Katwijk – Mablethorpe – Base.
Set Course: 2302 hrs.
Time Over Target: 0150 – 0220 hrs (endeavour to concentrate on target at 0200 hrs at 19,000 – 20,000 ft). Attack to concentrate at 0200 hrs to confuse flak control.
Weather: Insufficient cloud [sic] to attack primary. Aircraft acting on instructions attacked Bonn on TR fix.
Opposition: Little flak and searchlights, ineffective through clouds.

Nursery Operation

Primary target: Lorient (docks).
Alternative: Cherbourg (docks).
3 aircraft (freshmen), operational call sign A70 (cancelled).
Bomb load: 8× 500 lb GP.
Route: Base – Sywell – Bridport – Pleubian – Lorient and return.
Set Course: 2325 hrs.
Time Over Target: 0155 – 0220 hrs to be strictly adhered to.

U-67 in a dry U-Boat pen at Lorient (Deutsches Bundesarchiv, Bild 101II-MW-5335-30 / Dietrich / CC-BY-SA)

To signal their return to operational status back at RAF Topcliffe, the squadron detailed nine aircraft to attack the Krupp works at Essen once again, whilst a nursery operation was scheduled to Lorient as a diversion for 5 Group, which was sending 13 Hampdens gardening off that coastline between 0200 and 0220 hrs. The nursery operation was subsequently cancelled, but the main attack on Essen went ahead as scheduled. Len was not called upon to fly, which was lucky for him as this was to be a disastrous operation.

F/Sgt Hank Malkin did not start, due to an unserviceable rear turret, but the remaining eight aircraft left from 2257 hrs at 1-minute intervals. Amongst the eight crews to continue was Sgt Batch Batchelder in W7652, who had only just been gazetted for his DFM, earned a month earlier when he had safely landed his crippled Halifax at RAF Horsham St Faith; all but one of his crew tonight having also served with him on that occasion. It was with bitter irony, then, that a message was received from W7652 at 0230 hrs reporting an engine failed and having been hit by flak just after completing the bombing run, and the crew abandoning the aircraft.

Whilst on their bombing run, they had been coned by four of the blue radar-guided master searchlights and all their supporting white searchlights; as their bombs were released, the heavy-calibre flak had begun. As soon as possible, Batch Batchelder initiated violent evasive manoeuvres and dived steeply. At this point, the engines started malfunctioning; the starboard inner stopped after heavy vibration, and they sent the signal reporting their situation at 0230 hrs. Shortly thereafter, the port inner and the starboard outer engines also failed and, at 5,000 ft over Hamminkeln, he ordered evacuation. All the crew baled out successfully and were captured.

At 0440 hrs, RAF Topcliffe received back the first of the aircraft from the Essen run; at 0512 hrs they received the fourth and last that would be returning that night. This landing was undertaken by F/Sgt Weller, but his aircraft had been damaged by flak on the port wing and landed heavily, bursting the starboard tyre. At around the same time, word would have been received that F/Sgt Boothright had diverted to RAF Coltishall in Norfolk with a flak-damaged starboard outer engine, but nothing would be heard from two more aircraft:

- W/O Charles Barr, shot down with a crew of six in R9530 by Hptm Herbert Bönsch of Erg.St./NJG2 over the sea 60 km west of Walcheren, Middelburg at 0025 hrs.

- W/O Bill Davies, shot down with a crew of eight in W7651 by Oblt Wilhelm Dormann of III./NJG1 over Radewijk, Hardenberg, at 0300 hrs.

Cloud over Essen prevented all but 16 of the 106 crews from identifying the target; German reports[208] recorded that only 3 HE bombs and 400 incendiaries had fallen on the city. More than half the crews diverted to bomb secondary targets, principally Bonn.

Of more pressing immediacy to those serving on the squadron was the fact that three of the eight aircraft they had fielded had not returned from this operation. This amounted to a 38 per cent loss rate or, in more human terms, 20 crewmen missing.

17 JUNE 1942

Disappointed by the lack of support from CNS, Harris wrote to Portal,[209] opining a requirement for a greater level of support from Coastal Command than had been so far offered, stating that Joubert had willingly offered 250 aircraft on the last occasion 'before the Admiralty put the embargo on'. As Churchill's intervention would again be needed to free up more aircraft, planning for the third Thousand Plan operation proceeded accordingly:[210]

> Intention: To destroy the port and city of Bremen, or alternatively Duisburg.
>
> Code Name: This operation will be known by the code name "Millennium Two".
>
> Date: The operation will take place on the night of 25th / 26th June or on the first suitable night thereafter until the night of 29th / 30th June.

The routes were provisionally assigned as follows:[211]

> 1. Bremen: Base – Egmond aan Zee – Bremen – Osterholz-Scharmbeck – 54°15'N 05°00'E – Base.
>
> 2. Duisburg: Base – Ouddorp (51°47'N 03°50'E) – Duisburg – Viersen (51°16'N 06°33'E) – Noordland (51°38'N 03°36'E) – Base.

The reasoning behind this choice of target was encapsulated in the following Intelligence brief, dated 15 June 1942:

> The Deschimag yards are capable of building warships of all classes – except battleships. There are more submarines being built at the present time than any other single yard in Germany with the exception of Blohm und Voss at Hamburg; they are also busily engaged in the construction of destroyers and the 8" cruiser Seydlitz is fitting out there. To the south of town there are the main Focker [sic] Wulf works where Fw 200s and Fw 190s are under construction, both of which types are exceptionally successful and of the greatest value to the Germans. Components for the aircraft are made at works within the town itself and there is a useful Ju 88 factory close to the Deschimag yards.

To frame the target into context for the crews, he added the following analogy:

When attacking Bremen it would be well to remember Bristol, a very similar town with its docks and aircraft factories. Bristol has taken much punishment but survives. Bremen must be obliterated for the duration.

In the event of weather being unsuitable to attack Bremen, the force would be directed instead to Duisburg. The reasoning supporting this choice was contained in the following Intelligence brief, dated 17 June 1942:

It is difficult to over-emphasize the value of this area round Duisburg to the enemy's war machine. Steelworks, armaments, synthetic oil products, metallurgical works, coking plants and chemical works are to be found in profusion and a large proportion of them lie close round the town which is bounded on the north by the great inland port. The raw materials to these works and the finalised products from them as well as for other adjacent industrial areas all pass through this port and its associated, vast and complex network of railways.

To bring home the significance of the target to the crews it was described thus:

Duisburg is the Sheffield of Germany and about the same size, it is however with its port and railway system the core of a far greater industrial area than Sheffield. Its activities form an integral part of the whole industrial Ruhr in which the elimination of Duisburg would have the most serious consequences for the duration of the war however long.

At this stage in the planning process, the operation was scheduled against targets in Bremen or Duisburg as follows,[212,213] Z hour to be allocated according to the phase of the moon on the night chosen:

First draft of Millennium Two against Bremen or Duisburg

Aircraft involved	Target: Bremen			Target: Duisburg		
	Aim Point	Time over Target		Aim Point	Time over Target	
		From	To		From	To
1 Group All TR aircraft	Salmon Aim Point X	Z + 10	Z + 20	Cod Aim Point D	Z + 10	Z + 25
1 Group All remaining aircraft	Salmon Aim Point C	Z + 20	Z + 55	Cod Aim Point X	Z + 20	Z + 65
3 Group 50 best TR Stirlings	Salmon Aim Point X	Z	Z + 10	Cod Aim Point D	Z	Z + 10
3 Group All remaining Stirlings	Salmon Aim Point X	Z + 45	Z + 65	Cod Aim Point D	Z + 55	Z + 75
3 Group All TR Wellingtons	Salmon Aim Point X	Z + 10	Z + 20	Cod Aim Point D	Z + 10	Z + 25

Aircraft involved	Target: Bremen			Target: Duisburg		
	Aim Point	Time over Target		Aim Point	Time over Target	
		From	To		From	To
3 Group All remaining Wellingtons	Salmon Aim Point X	Z + 20	Z + 55	Cod Aim Point D	Z + 20	Z + 65
4 Group 50 best TR Halifaxes	Salmon Aim Point X	Z	Z + 10	Cod Aim Point D	Z	Z + 10
4 Group Half remaining Halifaxes	Salmon Aim Point C	Z + 45	Z + 65	Cod Aim Point X	Z + 55	Z + 75
4 Group All remaining Halifaxes	Salmon Aim Point Y	Z + 45	Z + 65	Cod Aim Point Y	Z + 55	Z + 75
5 Group All aircraft	Cobra (GY4772: Focke-Wulf factory)	Z + 20	Z + 55	Cod Aim Point Y	Z + 20	Z + 65
91 Group All aircraft*	Salmon Aim Point Y	Z + 20	Z + 55	Cod Aim Point Y	Z + 20	Z + 65
92 Group All aircraft	Salmon Aim Point C	Z + 20	Z + 55	Cod Aim Point X	Z + 20	Z + 65
Coastal Command All aircraft	GR3586 (Deschimag submarine building yards)	Z + 30	Z + 50	GF2229 (Thyssen steel works)	Z + 30	Z + 50

* Aircraft of 91 Group operating from stations in 1 Group and 3 Group are to be considered as belonging to the Group to which they are attached.

19 JUNE 1942

Churchill wrote to Portal[214] to confirm that he had been exercising his influence with CNS to secure the support of Coastal Command in the forthcoming Thousand Plan operation to Bremen / Duisburg, the result of which was a short statement advising: 'I am sure he will not be any obstacle to the use of Coastal Command.'

Harris now had what he wanted.

Target[215]	Aircraft on target	Types
Emden aim point A	194	112 Wellington 37 Halifax 26 Stirling 11 Hampden 9 Lancaster
Enemy aerodromes:		
(i) GU4182 Ardorf	2	Blenheim

(continued)

Target	Aircraft on target	Types
(ii) Z52 Leeuwarden	2	Blenheim
(iii) GU4159 Vechta	2	Blenheim
Nickelling:		
(i) Albert area	2	Stirling
(ii) Rouen	1	Halifax
(iii) Chartres	1	Halifax
(iv) Le Mans	1	Halifax

MAIN OPERATION

Primary target: Area I Emden, Area II Osnabrück.
Alternative: S&M in Germany.
Operation C.213: 5 aircraft, operational call sign A70.
Bomb load: 3× 1,000 lb GP TD 0.025, 8× SBC 90× 4 lb, 4× SBC 8× 30 lb.
Area I Route: Base – Flamborough – Schiermonnikoog – Emden – Rottumeroog – Base.
Area II Route: Base – Flamborough – Alkmaar – Osnabrück and return.
Area I Time Off: 2350 hrs.
Area II Time Off: 2334 hrs.
Time Over Target: 0130 – 0200 hrs (concentrate if possible between 0130 – 0140 hrs and bomb from
   14,000 – 15,000 ft).
15× 3 Group Wellingtons will drop flares at eight second intervals over the TR release point between 0130 – 0155 hrs.
Weather: 8/10 to 10/10 cloud in target area. One aircraft which continued to Osnabrück reported clear skies but
   considerable ground haze.
Opposition: Moderate heavy and light flak, searchlights ineffective.

NURSERY OPERATION

Nickelling
Dropping area: Nickelling over Rouen, Le Mans and Chartres.
Operation C.214: 3 aircraft (freshmen), operational call sign NT5.
Aircraft D to Rouen; Time Over Target: 0024 – 0034 hrs.
Aircraft R to Le Mans; Time Over Target: 0054 – 0100 hrs.
Aircraft Q to Chartres; Time Over Target: 0044 – 0054 hrs.
Route: Base – Abingdon – Brighton – St-Valery – dropping areas and return.
Time Off: 2245 hrs.
Weather: 10/10 cloud on French coast clearing inland but ground haze.
Opposition: Uneventful trip.

The squadron was detailed to support two operations; five aircraft to attack Emden / Osna-brück, and three nursery operations to drop nickels over three separate locations in northern France: Rouen, Le Mans and Chartres. All crews would be carrying cameras. Although Emden had been a destination flown previously by freshmen on nursery operations, tonight it was reclassified as the main operation.

Meanwhile on nickelling duty to Chartres, a crew comprising Len, P/O Richard Bradbury, Sgt Ernest de Mattos, F/Sgt Ivor Lewis and Sgt Jack Fernie would be flying in W7654 with B Flight's new commander, S/Ldr John Walkington, supporting him on his first operational sortie since joining from 405 Squadron RCAF.

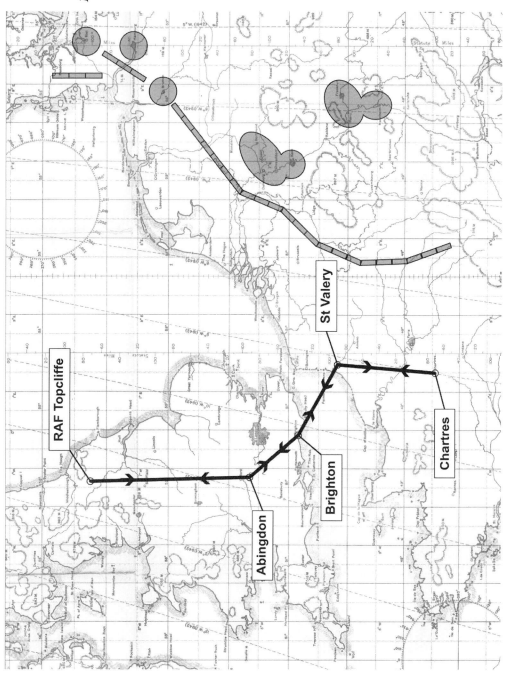

Operation
C.214 to
Chartres,
19 June 1942

RAF Topcliffe

St Valery

Abingdon

Brighton

Chartres

The nickelling crews took off from 2242 hrs, and then there was a wait of 45 minutes until the Emden crews went out. John Walkington may have been the last of the nickelling crews to take off, but was the first of the three to return. As the night wore on, the two other nickelling crews returned successfully, as did the crews supporting the main operation, only W/O Hank Malkin having flown beyond Emden and attacked the Area II target of Osnabrück.

Halifax W7654 (DY-Q)

Chartres.

Takeoff 2245 hrs.

Nickels released over primary target from 12,000 ft.

Landed 0338 hrs.

Operational combat time 4 hrs 53 mins

S/Ldr JG Walkington

P/O RF Bradbury	12th operation; combat time 86 hrs 42 mins
Sgt L Starbuck	25th operation; combat time 177 hrs 58 mins
Sgt PJ Fernie	4th operation; combat time 20 hrs 57 mins
Sgt ERT DeMattos	10th operation; combat time 61 hrs 56 mins
F/Sgt I Lewis	7th operation; combat time 41 hrs 39 mins

20 JUNE 1942

With the planning for the next Thousand Plan operation safely in hand, Harris looked to the future, and wrote to Portal[216] to outline his desire to ramp up four Thousand Plan operations

Halifax on dispersal (Chris Goss Collection)

every month with routine operations being conducted on fine nights in between, principally to provide experience to training crews. He went on the compare this proposal against what he saw as the weaker approach of 'one Thousand Plan a month plus ordinary every day humdrum operations in the interim'.

Given the rate at which targets would be required service the prospect of four Thousand Plan operations a month, he went on:

> Perhaps you would therefore ask Intelligence to produce a list of say twenty or thirty best targets for such a programme. I assume that they would be Kiel, Hamburg, Bremen, the major Ruhr towns, half-a-dozen of the towns further down the Rhine, with Berlin, Nürnberg, Munich, and Kassel, etc., as make-weights.

Target[217]	Aircraft on target	Types
Emden aim point A	185	91 Wellington 37 Halifax 24 Lancaster 21 Stirling 12 Hampden
Enemy aerodromes:		
(i) Leeuwarden	3	Blenheim
(ii) Ardorf	1	Blenheim
(iii) Twente	1	Blenheim
Nickelling:		
(i) Lille	2	Hampden
(ii) Tours	1	Halifax

MAIN OPERATION

Primary target: Emden, target code Herring.
Alternative: S&M Germany.
Last Resort: S&M Germany.
Operation C.215: 5 aircraft, operational call sign B9R.
Bomb load: 3× 1,000 lb GP TD 0.025, 8× SBC 90× 4 lb, 4× SBC 8× 30 lb.
Route: Base – Flamborough – Schiermonnikoog – Emden – Urk – Alkmaar – Base.
Set Course: 2335 hrs.
Time Over Target: 0115 – 0145 hrs (concentrate 0130 hrs if possible).
15× 3 Group Wellingtons will drop flares at eight second intervals over the TR release point between 0115 – 0125 hrs.
Weather: Haze or mist and a thin layer of cloud made observation of results difficult.
Opposition: Large amount of light flak, little heavy and very few searchlights.

NURSERY OPERATION

Nickelling
Dropping area: Nickelling over Tours.
Operation C.216: 1 aircraft (freshman), operational call sign 1JG.
Route: Base – Abingdon – Brighton – St-Valery – dropping point and return.
Time Off: 2250 hrs.

Time Over Target: 0130 – 0140 hrs.
Weather: Good visibility and no cloud.
Opposition: Nil. Uneventful trip.

A further five aircraft were scheduled to support another massed operation against Emden; and all sorties were conducted without any incident.

The scheduled nursery operation to Tours was penetrating even further down into France than those to Rouen, Le Mans and Chartres the night before, and starting to stretch what could be defined as a nursery run.

Poor visibility over Emden had limited the effectiveness of this attack; German reports[218] confirmed that about 100 houses had been damaged.

22 June 1942

Portal received a letter from Assistant Chief of the Air Staff (Intelligence) (ACAS(I)), AVM Charles Medhurst[219] in response to the request for targets for future Thousand Plan operations made to him by Harris on 20 June. In this letter ACAS(I) had indeed selected 20 targets in accordance with this request, but observed that 'the economic, burnability and moral factors will require discussion'.

The list catalogued in no specific order enemy towns by range from a nominal base at RAF Mildenhall in Suffolk, referencing the size of the population each supported, along with the number of Thousand Plan operations they believed would be required to 'knock them out'; the X category. Berlin, Nürnberg, Munich and Leipzig were considered, but 'owing to their size, the long distance and strong defences [would] probably not prove such profitable targets' and were thus excluded. The list comprised:

Towns shortlisted as Thousand Plan targets

Town	Population	Miles from Base	Category
Hamburg	1,700,000	400	5X
Bremen	325,000	350	2X
Kiel	220,000	420	X
Hanover	450,000	380	2X
Kassel	200,000	380	X
Stuttgart	420,000	450	2X
Magdeburg	300,000	470	X
Brunswick	170,000	420	X
Frankfurt	550,000	380	X
Mannheim-Ludwigshafen	385,000	400	2X
Düsseldorf	500,000	280	2X
Duisburg	450,000	270	2X

Town		Population	Miles from Base	Category
Mainz		150,000	370	X
Stettin		275,000	590	2X
Saarbrücken		130,000	350	X
Karlsruhe		160,000	410	X
Eisenach *	50,000			
Erfurt *	150,000			
Jena *	60,000	360,000	Average 450	2X
Weimar *	50,000			
Gotha *	50,000			
Osnabrück		100,000	320	X
Dessau		100,000	500	X
Schweinfurt		50,000	440	X

'This group of five towns is of great industrial importance particularly for the aircraft industry, and although non of them are big enough in themselves to warrant a 1,000 bomber attack, and all would individually be difficult to identify, they have been included as a group as they lie close together and are likely to be less well defended than other industrial areas.'

Target[220]	Aircraft on target	Types
Emden aim point A	227	144 Wellington 38 Stirling 26 Halifax 11 Lancaster 8 Hampden
Enemy aerodromes:		
(i) Z52 Leeuwarden	6	Blenheim
(ii) GU4182 Ardorf	4	Blenheim
Nickelling over Laon and Les Andelys	2	Stirling

Primary target: Emden
Operation C.217: 5 aircraft, operational call sign GP3.
Bomb load: 3× 1,000 lb GP TD 0.025, 8× SBC 90× 4 lb, 4× SBC 8× 30 lb.
Route: Base – Flamborough – 53°50'N 05°00'E - Schiermonnikoog – Emden – Rottumeroog – 53°50'N 05°00'E – Base.
Set Course: 2342 hrs.
Time Over Target: 0115 – 0145 hrs (endeavour to concentrate over target at 0130 hrs) bomb at or below 15,000 ft. lose height rapidly be under 1,000 ft over Rottumeroog in order to prevent fighter a chance to follow up aircraft flying northwest into the afterglow.
15× 3 Group Wellingtons will drop flares at eight second intervals over the TR release point between 0115 – 0135 hrs.
Weather: Light haze, visibility good.
Opposition: Intense light flak in target area, little heavy to north of town, searchlights ineffective.

This would be the last familiarisation operation to Emden. A final selection of five crews would support this massed operation in the same way as those conducted twice before in the last three nights. This was not a coincidence, neither was the use of different crews; this was a familiarisation run for an operation that was to come very shortly.

Operation C.217 to Emden, 22 June 1942

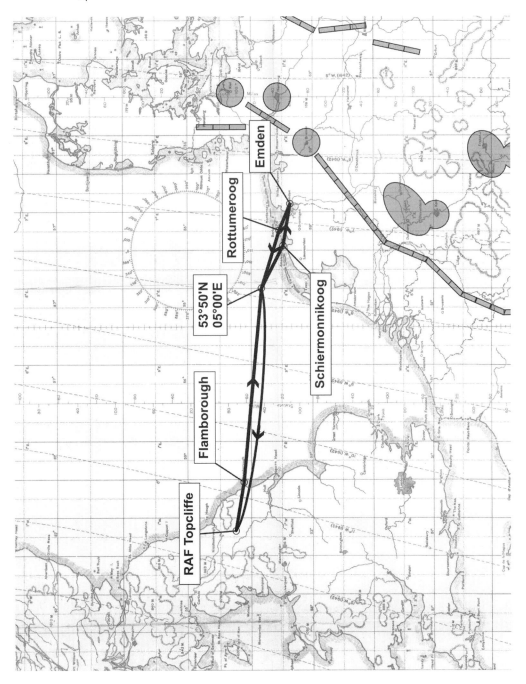

Emden

Rottumeroog

53°50'N
05°00'E

Schiermonnikoog

Flamborough

RAF Topcliffe

P/O Richard Bradbury was scheduled to fly with F/Sgt RF Stone, who was operating a six-man crew.

Halifax R9442 (DY-R)

Emden.

Takeoff 2341 hrs.

One stick released over primary target from 15,000 ft.

Landed 0410 hrs.

Operational combat time 4 hrs 29 mins.

F/Sgt RF Stone

P/O RF Bradbury   13th operation; combat time 91 hrs 11 mins

Sgt EH Williams

Sgt B Carroll

Sgt VH Twining

Sgt MA Barratt

All five aircraft left within 5 minutes from 2339 hrs, and all returned in a 35-minute spread between 0345 hrs and 0420 hrs; all sorties having been completed without incident. The training and familiarisation was over.

25 June 1942

Rumours were spreading among the crews that the Thousand Plan was back and, sure enough, serviceability on the squadron was high. As with the previous Thousand Plan operations the squadron was once again making up numbers by bringing in three aircraft from 102 CF:

- V9987 (DY-U), a B Mk.II Series 1 (Special) without a mid-upper turret.
- R9426 (DY-W), an early-build B Mk.II Series 1.
- L9532 (DY-Y), a B Mk.I with beam air gunner positions and underpowered Merlin Mk.X engines.

Primary target: Bremen.
Alternative: any built up area of Wilhelmshaven, Emden, Vegesack or Bremerhaven.
Operation C.218: 20 aircraft, operational call sign 8FH.
Bomb load: 3× 1,000 lb GP TD 0.025, 8× SBC 90× 4 lb, 4× SBC 8× 30 lb.
Route: Base – Egmond aan Zee – Bremen – Osterholz-Scharmbeck – 54°15'N 05°00'E – Base.
First Wave (8 aircraft)
Aiming point X Set Course: 2310 hrs, Time Over Target: 0120–0130 hrs.
Attack between 14,000–15,000 ft unless target obscured in which case aircraft to descend below cloud to ensure incendiaries drop in town. The minimum bombing height to be 8,000 ft.
Rear Force (12 aircraft)
Aiming point C Set Course: 2355 hrs, Time Over Target: 0205 – 0225 hrs.
Attack between 13,000 – 14,000 ft.
All aircraft are to turn for home not later than 0230 hrs wherever they may be, whether they have dropped their bombs or not.
Immediately after bombing, all aircraft to gain speed and lose height to come over the sea homeward at less than 1,000 ft.
Weather: Cloud conditions were experienced all the way en-route and target area was covered with 8/10 to 10/10 cloud.
Opposition: Considerable light and moderate heavy flak over Bremen. Searchlights ineffective and hampered by cloud.

Len may have been feeling that the end of his tour was in sight. He had 25 operations under his belt now, so tonight's would be his 26th; it would finish on 26 June and he was 26 years old. A good omen or a bad one? Only time would tell.

The day had started cloudy at RAF Topcliffe, and had become fair as the day wore on. There was good visibility and a 10–15 mph northerly wind; conversely, the weather over northern Germany was described as cloudy with the possibility of thunderstorms. The chance of less than 5/10 cloud was 50:50 over Bremen, and a strong wind in the area would help move along the stratocumulus clouds over the target. Reconnaissance flights had confirmed that the target was covered in cloud, but that prospects were good: only small amounts of cloud, providing that there was no shift in the wind. The prospect of the strong wind also meant that below the cloud-base the sea would be stormy, offering little hope for survival or recovery in the event of ditching.

The waxing moon was three nights away from full, and consequently classified as being at 91 per cent, rising over York at 1841 hrs[221] and over Bremen at 1859 hrs, setting again at 0439 hrs.[222] There would also be sightings of the northern lights.

To maximise the numbers, Harris mustered every type of aircraft available to Bomber Command, including squadron reserves and inexperienced crews from the OTUs; he also took Wellingtons and Hudsons from Coastal Command, Blenheims from Army Co-operation Command and even Bostons and Mosquitos from 2 Group, which had so far only been used for day operations and would be operating for the first time at night.

The night's offensive would begin with intruder operations from dusk onwards, aimed at keeping the night fighters on the ground. With air defences suppressed, the bomber force would follow in a condensed 65-minute stream – less than three quarters of the time allocated to the previous Thousand Plan operations.

First Wave (0120–0140 hrs)

0120–0130 hrs:

- 50 GEE-equipped Stirlings and 50 GEE-equipped Halifaxes to attack the town centre.

0130–0140 hrs

- All the GEE-equipped Wellingtons of 1 and 3 Groups to attack the town centre.

Main Force (0140–0215 hrs)

0140–0215 hrs:

- All remaining aircraft of 1 Group to attack the south end of the docks.
- All remaining Wellingtons of 3 Group to attack the town centre.
- All aircraft of 5 Group to attack the Focke-Wulf aircraft works.
- All aircraft of 91 Group to attack the south east end of town.
- All aircraft of 92 Group to attack the south end of the docks.

0150–0210 hrs:

- All Coastal Command aircraft to attack the Deschimag submarine building yards.

Rear Force (0215–0225 hrs)

0215–0225 hrs:

- All remaining Stirlings to attack the town centre.
- All remaining Halifaxes to divide evenly between the south end of the docks and the south-east of the town.

To record the damage and support post-operation analysis, all 102 Squadron aircraft in the rear force would be carrying cameras and were instructed to take photographs between 0210 and 0225 hrs. This order excluded the three aircraft drafted in from 102 CF.

Further, as a safeguard against enemy wireless spoofing, the usual recall code-group BBA was not to be used; instead different recall code-groups were allocated as follows:[223]

NEW RECALL CODE-GROUPS

Group	Recall code-group
1 Group	STY
2 Group	KUT
3 Group	YAT
4 Group	HAT
5 Group	ARC
OTUs in 91 Group	PUB
OTUs in 92 Group	NUT

The route was to comprise five legs:

  i. Base to Egmond aan Zee (271 miles)

 ii. Egmond aan Zee to Bremen (175 miles)

iii. Bremen to Osterholz-Scharmbeck (8 miles)

 iv. Osterholz-Scharmbeck to 54°15'N 05°00'E (a point directly north of Vlieland and due east of Scarborough – 175 miles)

  v. 54°15'N 05°00'E to base (250 miles)

The previous Thousand Plan operations against Cologne and Essen had both taken the bomber stream directly over the Kammhuber Line on both the outward and the return legs, but for the attack on Bremen the bombers would not be crossing it again. Instead, their route would be taking them into KoNaJa zone Roland, which provided night fighter and flak

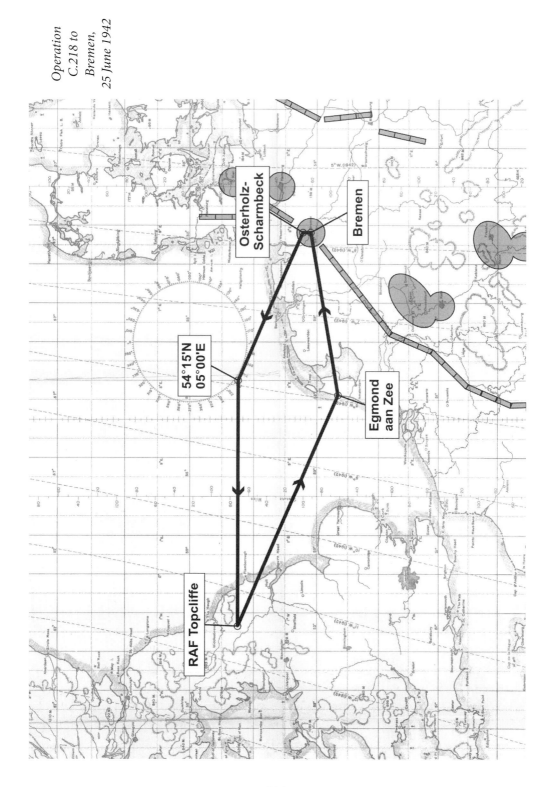

Operation C.218 to Bremen, 25 June 1942

Osterholz-Scharmbeck

Bremen

54°15'N 05°00'E

Egmond aan Zee

RAF Topcliffe

coverage to a depth of 14–23 miles from the centre of the city. Roland was broken into three roughly equal Räume: Roland A covering approximately 240° to 360°, Roland B covering 000° to 120° and Roland C covering 120° to 240°. Within each of these Räume, night fighters would be waiting, flying their individual racetrack holding patterns.

The bomber stream was directed to fly towards the target on a bearing of roughly 080 degrees, almost exactly between Roland A and Roland C, creating conditions of uncertainty amongst the defenders as to which of those two Räume should send night fighters to intercept. The bombers would then head due north, between Roland A to the west and Roland B to the east, hopefully causing further interception ambiguities between the two Räume. The next turn, towards 54°15'N 05°00'E on a bearing of 300 degrees, would begin over Osterholz-Scharmbeck before the bomber stream was clear of the KoNaJa, and route them through the north-eastern extent of Roland A. Penetrating KoNaJa Roland would be unavoidable, but every effort was to be made to overload the night fighters on patrol in Roland A and create confusion within the others, thereby minimising the risk to the bombers.

Halifax W7654, identified as DY-Q for Queenie, would be flown tonight by a six-man crew with an average age of 23 years:

Captain F/Lt Kenneth Wright, age 20
Navigator P/O Richard Bradbury, RCAF, age 21
WOp/AG Sgt Leonard Starbuck, age 26
Mid-Upper Air Gunner Sgt Jack Fernie RCAF, age 25
Rear Air Gunner Sgt Ernest de Mattos, age 22
Air Engineer F/Sgt Ivor Lewis, age 26

Since joining the squadron, Len had flown operationally on eight different Whitleys, but since conversion had only ever flown operationally on Halifax W7654, Q for Queenie. Tonight he would be flying with the same crew with whom he had flown the last time, the only difference being that F/Lt Kenneth Wright would now be their captain.

Q for Queenie had been delivered to 102 Squadron with three sisters, W7651, W7652 and W7653, which had all been shot down on operations already, so she appeared to be lucky. Lucky or not, this was the aircraft with which the men were all best acquainted and which had served them so faithfully over her career of nine operational sorties to date.

The aircraft destined for the first wave lined up under an almost full moon as it approached apogee. In near-perfect conditions, these eight aircraft took turns in 1-minute intervals to throttle up and follow each other into the night sky. They were led out by F/Sgt Stanley Morgan at 2258 hrs; the procession concluding at 2307 hrs, just in time to meet the Set Course deadline. The 12 aircraft of the rear force would have to wait a further 40 minutes before they could follow on.

The crews in the rear force had an additional concern to contend with; they would be the last aircraft in the bomber stream, and therefore at most risk of being picked off by night fighters. Nobody wanted to be last, so nobody wanted to be delayed.

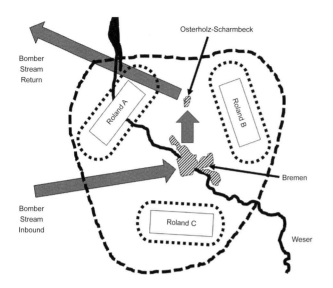

Osterholz-Scharmbeck

Bomber
Stream
Return

Roland A

Roland B

Bremen

Bomber
Stream
Inbound

Roland C

Weser

*KoNaJa Roland, showing
the positions of the three
Räume, their respective
holding circuits and the
path of the bomber stream
(Author)*

(gyges.dk/Himmelbett.htm)

(luchtoorlog.net/hoofdstuk1.html)

By the time their earlier departing crewmates were over the North Sea, halfway to the first turning point at Egmond aan Zee, the rear force was led out at 2345 hrs by F/Sgt RF Stone R9442, the only remaining GEE-equipped aircraft from the squadron to be on the rear force. The flow of crews eager to get airborne was interrupted, however, when P/O BGH Smith caught his tail wheel in a hole inside the perimeter track, breaking off the wheel and an inner portion of the fuselage; the tension would have risen among the remaining crews, eager to ensure that this diversion did not delay their departure. Q for Queenie lined up eighth out of eleven, and finally took off at 2355 hrs. They were now late. The last crew to depart should have already set course by this time.

The moderate to strong northerly winds that had been expected to blow the cloud away from the target area with clear air from Heligoland Bight suddenly slackened to moderate around 2200 hrs and then veered north-easterly, drawing in cloud from over Denmark. In a pivotal turn of events, the projected 50:50 odds forecast for reasonable visibility over the target area had just been lost.

By the time the crews were scheduled to fly, the northerly winds had started to pick up again and were increasing from the east as the isobars bunched up; however, it had come too late to clear the target area. The Operational Research Section report[224] states:

> Owing to a change of wind the weather over Bremen did not clear and throughout the raid the target was covered by thin layer cloud, in which there were only occasional small breaks. Similar conditions were experienced en route.

Worse, reports identified that night fighters were 'out in force'; crews reported seeing their colleagues being shot down around them, the losses due to enemy action being in the ratio 5:1 for the outward journey compared with the return. Intercepted wireless transmissions identified interceptions being carried out by the following night fighter units:[225,226]

Wireless intercepts of night fighter activity

Time	Night Fighter Unit	No of aircraft active	Operating from
0012 – 0531 hrs	I./NJG2, II./NJG2, III./NJG2	16	Gilze-Rijen Leeuwarden Eindhoven Ardorf Wittmundhaven
0054 – 0514 hrs	I./NJG1, III./NJG1	8	Twente-Enschede Rheine Venlo
0147 – 0455 hrs	I./NJG3, II./NJG3, III./NJG3	9	Vechta Schleswig-Land Stade Rheine Westerland-Sylt

The official report laid part of the blame for the defensive forces being in a position to mount such a spirited defence on the fact that the intruders tasked with attacking night fighter aerodromes had not been as successful as intended prior to the arrival of the bomber stream: 'Many intruder operations did not find their targets in the dark.'[227]

Much of this was down to the lack of experience amongst Boston and Mosquito crews flying at night; of the seven targets given to the Boston crews, it was reported that 'In only two cases Valkenburg and Ardorf did the whole formation find and bomb the target'[228] and of the two targets given to the four Mosquito crews, it was reported that '1 attacking Schleswig-Jagel was successful, but the others all failed to find their primary owing to the darkness.'[229]

When the main and rear forces arrived the target area was well alight, but Bremen was still covered with 8/10–10/10 cloud. The official report reinforces the significance of GEE in this operation in facilitating what success would ultimately be achieved:

> In view of the fact that the glow on the clouds from fires started by aircraft bombing blind on GEE fixes was the chief means used by later aircraft to identify the target, it may be said that the results achieved on this raid were mainly due to the use of GEE as a blind bombing device.[230]

Whilst the first wave of bombers, comprising 124 Wellingtons, 50 Stirlings and 50 Halifaxes, were all supposed to be bombing with the benefit of GEE, only one in seven of those following on behind would have this advantage. The subsequent main force and rear force of bombers would therefore be finding their targets in large part by looking for fires through the cloud. Despite the directive to bomb from a minimum of 8,000 ft, one Halifax even dropped down below the cloudbase at 3,000 ft over Bremen, to make a more accurate bombing run. Crews employing this tactic were able to report two key observations; firstly, tethered balloons had been deployed, one concentration of 24 being in two lines at 6/7000 ft[231] whilst others were deployed up to 10,000 ft, and secondly a number of dummy fires were seen to have been started away from the target areas.

Some crews diverted to their secondary targets in the hope of being able to see them better and also avoid the risk of collision in the skies above Bremen as the tightly packed concentration of aircraft jostled to make their bombing runs against a variety of real and imaginary targets. All the secondary targets were attacked, in addition to further attacks being made on targets of opportunity as they could be glimpsed through the prevailing cloud, notably Oldenburg, Cuxhaven and Hamburg. The danger with attacking any of these secondary targets was that once away from the collective safety of the bomber stream, the individual aircraft would stand out, inviting attention from the night fighters.

Crews at the end of the bomber stream had another issue to contend with. As they approached Bremen with their narrow 10-minute window of opportunity drawing to an end at 0225 hrs, they would have had to weigh up how they should interpret their directive 'to turn for home not later than 0230 hrs wherever they may be, whether they have dropped their bombs or not'. This dilemma would result in difficult decisions being taken, some of the last crews to arrive choosing to continue with their bombing runs even past the 0230 hrs deadline. Kenneth Wright would have been among those facing this dilema, along with the other 102 squadron crews that had got away late.

There was considerable light and moderate heavy flak over Bremen, although the cloud that had so confounded the crews in their bombing now worked to their advantage in rendering ineffective the batteries of searchlights. The crews had been briefed that once they were free of land-based flak they were to return over the sea at less than 1,000 ft; but unfortunately this then placed them within reach of flak ships, some of which happened to be in locations where they would be gifted with targets they could not miss, especially with their short-range fast-firing 2 cm cannons.

SUMMARY OF 102 SQUADRON OPERATIONS, 25/26 JUNE 1942

Number	GEE	Callsign	Force Element	T/O	Land	Notes
R9446	✓	F	First Wave	2258	MIA	
R9533		B	First Wave	2259	0458	Attacked Bremerhaven
R9494	✓	C	First Wave	2300	0430	Attacked primary target
R9531		E	First Wave	2300	0515	Attacked Emden
W1153		H	First Wave	2301	0427	Attacked Wilhelmshaven
W1158		P	First Wave	2302	0441	Attacked primary target
W1167		J	First Wave	2305	0436	Attacked primary target
W7712		S	First Wave	2307	0410	Attacked primary target
R9442	✓	R	Rear Force	2345	0510	Attacked primary target
W1142		A	Rear Force	2346	0530	Attacked primary target
W7706		O	Rear Force	2349	0506	Attacked primary target
L9532		Y	Rear Force	2350	0450	Attacked primary target
W1107		D	Rear Force	2350	0520	Attacked primary target

Number	GEE	Callsign	Force Element	T/O	Land	Notes
W7752[232]		M	Rear Force	2351	0535	Attacked primary target
V9987		U	Rear Force	2354	MIA	
W7654		Q	Rear Force	2355	MIA	
W1066		G	Rear Force	2356	0114	RTB with No.3 engine U/S
W7759		L	Rear Force	2359	MIA	
R9426[233]		W	Rear Force	0002	0341	RTB with engine trouble
W7746		N	Rear Force	n/a		U/S with broken tail wheel

Even aside from well-prepared defences, there was something else at work to sinister effect; the wind had veered from NE to NNW and was increasing, almost head-on to the returning bombers, which now had no landfall until Yorkshire. As the official report acknowledges: 'Weather conditions were very bad and the wind experienced differed from that forecast.'[234]

Some would run out of fuel on the return journey; those nearest to shore had a hope of being rescued as dawn broke, but for those ditching further away the chances of recovery were slight, and they would simply be listed as missing.

Although the full facts surrounding the fate of W7654 Q for Queenie and her crew may never be known, the following fits all the known facts:

Some of 102 Squadron's aircraft in the initial wave had been unable to press home their attacks on the primary target and had instead gone on to secondary targets, possibly because of the shortage of airborne GEE sets available on the squadron. By the time the rear force arrived, Bremen was well alight and all the 102 Squadron crews in this wave that filed reports confirmed that they had attacked their primary targets. The crew of Q for Queenie had completed their attack on Bremen and had turned north, away from the fiery maelstrom below, providing Ernest de Mattos in the rear turret with his first view of the devastation lighting up the sky. A few short minutes later they would have turned to port over Osterholz-Scharmbeck, aiming for a point over the North Sea due east of their home base.

The return leg from Osterholz-Scharmbeck directed the bomber stream to the north of the town of Norden, an area which was right in the middle of DuNaJa Languste. In keeping with the philosophy employed by the KoNaJa zones whereby the code name of a night fighter zone should bear a similarity to the name of the local area and also have a local connection. This DuNaJa was named after the local lobsters, a word conveniently similar to the name of the island of Langeooge, upon which it was based.

Inside the night fighter control station at the heart of DuNaJa Languste, personnel on duty had been witnessing a continuous stream of contacts for over an hour. This procession had been counterpointed only by those bombers that had not attacked their primary target but whose crews had instead pressed home their attack against a secondary target such as Cuxhaven; aircraft from this destination stood out clearly as they made their solitary way home westwards, well to the north of the returning bomber stream. By 0300 hrs, the tempo of contacts had started to reduce to a level whereby individual targets in the bomber stream could be more readily identified and selected for interception. Such was the case when Q for Queenie passed unwittingly into the DuNaJa.

They were on their way home. The crew, so keyed up for the attack, would now have started to unwind subconsciously just a little, as each minute took them nearer home. Q for Queenie was thundering along on a heading of 300 degrees, descending towards an altitude of around 1,000 ft as she passed to the north of the town of Norden on the way to the German coast, aiming for the gap between the islands of Juist and Norderney to the North Sea beyond, after which there would be no further landfall until Scarborough. The moon was shining obliquely at them from the west as it descended towards the horizon[235] and it would have set by the time they returned home,[236] but was still providing them with enough light by which they could see – and be seen.

At that precise moment and completely unbeknownst to them, they were being represented as a red spot on a radar screen on the island of Langeooge, from where their progress was being observed.

Converging onto the red spot at that same moment was a green spot signifying a Bf 110 from 5./NJG3 closing on an intercept vector.

Unlike the journey to the target when the bombers flew at altitude with plenty of room underneath to make an approach unseen, the bomber crews were now running for home at a much lower level, making it more hazardous for a night fighter to entertain such an approach.

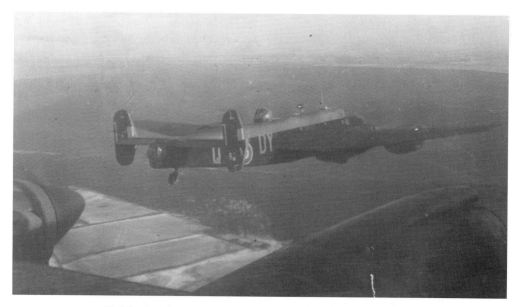

Halifax B Mk.II Series 1 DY-Q for Queenie over Bridlington
(Yorkshire Air Museum and Allied Air Forces Memorial)

This picture is identified on the reverse as "Jackie Towse Bridlington". Sgt, and subsequently F/Sgt Jackie Towse, served on 102 Squadron during the period when there were three separate Halifaxes identified as Q for Queenie flying operations; W7654, W7677 and DT 512. The serial number cannot be seen on this picture.

Perhaps there was just enough space to spare under the returning bomber as she continued her descent, or perhaps the hunter had a heightened understanding of how to blend in with his background, or possibly a measure of both, but somehow the night fighter was able to close in.

Unlike the bomber crew, three hours into their sortie, the night fighter was just starting his task and so was at the peak of his alertness. He would have been vectored into his target by Languste control and closed in, to identify his target as a four-engined aircraft.

The night fighter's twin aims were to inflict critical damage, with minimum exposure to personal risk. If he had room to manoeuvre under the bomber, an attack from underneath would have been preferred; if not, then he would have chosen another approach that minimised his exposure to the bomber's defensive firepower. In the final phases of stalking his unknowing prey, the pilot would have released the safety catch with his right thumb and seen six red lamps flash, indicating his guns and cannons to be ready. Then on his own cue, he centred the oblivious bomber in his sight and pressed the button that sent shockwaves of recoil through his own aircraft.

The shock of cannon fire tearing into Q for Queenie would have reverberated throughout the fuselage as she flew onward through the night sky. Len would have known immediately what this meant, since he had survived attacks from night fighters twice before; others with less experience might not have realised quite so readily the immediacy of their situation. Their nemesis was out there in the darkness, close by. F/Lt Kenneth Wright would have been very alert to any change of feel in the aircraft that had for the last three hours been an extension of himself, and given their altitude would have manoeuvred as much as he dared, whilst listening hard for commands from the air gunners, to give them a better view of their attacker.

There might have been some return of fire from Jack Fernie in the mid-upper turret if he had been able to glimpse their attacker from his position high on the fuselage, but given the weather into which they were descending, this may not have been possible. Ernest de Mattos in the rear turret may have had a less obstructed view and would also have been returning fire if he was still able. However, the night fighter pilot would have been standing off from his prey just far enough to ensure that he could avoid any last desperate retaliation whilst remaining sufficiently close to be in a position to confirm his imminent victory.

The Halifax, with its inbuilt tendencies towards instability from the design of the tail section and spar weakness in the event of fire, could fail aerodynamically or structurally at short notice. Given sufficient warning of impending failure, Kenneth Wright would have had no choice other than to give the order to bale out, even though they were at low altitude over a stormy sea. In response, the crew would have left their stations to put on parachutes and followed the rehearsed escape drill, although unlike during practice the aircraft would have probably been behaving in ways they had never expected in their worst nightmares, throwing them around and pinning them down under unnatural forces.

Len's journey to the front escape hatch was the shortest of all, due to the proximity of the wireless and front turret where he served. He would have got quickly to the front hatch to open it for himself, and for and Ivor Lewis and Kenneth Wright to follow, whilst Richard

Bradbury would have taken a much longer journey back over the spar to open the rear crew door for himself, Jack Fernie and Ernest de Mattos. Len would have got the front hatch open and slid away into the cold blast of the airflow, probably unaware of how high he was above the sea below him.

As they were so low, there would have probably been little time to have conducted a complete evacuation; even Len, as the crewman with the easiest route, would have had to work fast, since his very life depended on it. Kenneth Wright would have kept aloft as best as he could for as long as possible to buy time for his crew to escape, but the odds were against him: Q for Queenie was mortally wounded.

Although the East Frisian Islands stand distinctly separated to the north of the Lower Saxony coast, the Wattensee between them and the German mainland is comprised of tidal mudflats, and even when covered by the tide remains very shallow in places. However, in a cruel twist of fate, at that time the tide was out,[237] presenting the mudflats at their most exposed and most unyielding.

This would very shortly become Q for Queenie's final resting place.

The air gunners may have left their posts as ordered to bale out, or kept firing at their attacker until they could no more in one final act of heroic defiance; Kenneth Wright would certainly have been drawing on all of his considerable experience to maintain, and then attempt to regain, control as the damage inflicted gradually took control away from him.

Len got out, but his year-long run of luck had finally deserted him. By the time he was able to escape, they were just too low.

It was 0308 hrs.

Endnotes

190 AIR 14/2674

191 Goss, C. (1995) *It's Suicide but It's Fun: The Story of 102 (Ceylon) Squadron 1917–1956*, ISBN 0947554599, Crécy, pp 70–71.

192 AIR 14/2674

193 Listed erroneously in the official record as "21.55"; Author has assumed 2255 hrs because it aligns with the set course time and the actual start time achieved.

194 Middlebrook, M. and Everitt, C. (1990) *The Bomber Command War Diaries: An Operational Reference Book 1939–1945*, ISBN 0140129367, Penguin, p 275.

195 AIR 14/2674

196 Richard Bradbury had been commissioned as a P/O on 24 May 1942. The ORB would continue to reflect incorrectly his rank as W/O and would never recognise that he had been commissioned.

197 AIR 14/2674

198 Middlebrook, M. and Everitt, C. (1990) *The Bomber Command War Diaries: An Operational Reference Book 1939–1945*, ISBN 0140129367, Penguin, p 276.

199 Halpenny, B.B. (1990) *Action Stations: 4. Military airfields of Yorkshire*, ISBN 0850595320, Patrick Stephens, p 189.

200 ukairfieldguide.net/airfields/Topcliffe.

201 New York Times, 20 May 1942.

202 AIR 8/864, ref M.258/2

203 AIR 8/864, ref ATH/DO/6

204 AIR 8/864, ref M.258/2

205 AIR 8/864, ref ATH/DO/6

206 AIR 8/864, ref ATH/DO/6

207 AIR 14/2674

208 Middlebrook, M. and Everitt, C. (1990) *The Bomber Command War Diaries: An Operational Reference Book 1939–1945*, ISBN 0140129367, Penguin, p 277.

209 AIR 8/864, ref ATH/DO/6

210 -217 AIR 14/2332

212 AIR 14/2332 (targeting data)

213 AIR 14/693 (codewords)

214 AIR 8/864, ref M.194/2

215 AIR 14/2674

216 AIR 8/864, ref ATH/DO/6

217 AIR 14/2674

218 Middlebrook, M. and Everitt, C. (1990) *The Bomber Command War Diaries: An Operational Reference Book 1939–1945*, ISBN 0140129367, Penguin, p 278.

219 AIR 8/864

220 AIR 14/2674

221 Moonrise over York (nearest datum point to RAF Topcliffe) 1641 + 2 hours correction for BDST.

222 Moonrise over Bremen 1659 + 2 hours correction for BDST, Moonset over Bremen 0239 + 2 hours correction for BDST on 26 June.

223 AIR 14/2332

224 BC/S. 26342/2/ORS dated 15 August 1942.

225 AIR 14/3802 Chapter 8 Wireless Intelligence.

226 A large number of reported sightings by bomber crews of single-engined night fighters have subsequently been put down to misidentification.

227 AIR 14/3802

228 AIR 14/3408

229 AIR 14/3408

230 AIR 14/3802

231 AIR 14/3802 Chapter 7 Flak/Searchlights/Other Aids to Defence.

232 Listed erroneously in the ORB as W7751. W7751 was a 158 Squadron Halifax allocated callsign NP-F which coincidentally flew her first operation on this date.

233 Listed erroneously in the ORB as W9426. W9426 was not a Halifax, the number appears never to have been allocated.

234 AIR 14/3802

235 Moonset over Groningen (nearest datum point to Norden) 0247 + 2 hours correction for BDST/MESZ.

236 Moonset over York (nearest datum point to RAF Topcliffe) 0216 + 2 hours correction for BDST.

237 Low tide at Norderney (Riffgat) (53°42'N 7°09'E) had been at 0241.

EPILOGUE

ORDER OF BATTLE FOR 25/26 JUNE 1942 [238, 239]

	Group	Type	Sorties	Missing
Bremen	1 Group	Wellington Mk.Ic	18*	1
		Wellington Mk.II	28*	
		Wellington Mk.III	19 + 2*	
		Wellington Mk.IV	49*	1
		Whitley	2*	
	91 Group attached to 1 Group	Wellington Mk.Ic	11*	1
	2 Group	Blenheim	15*	
	Army Co-operation Command	Blenheim	5*	
	3 Group	Wellington Mk.Ic	9*	
		Wellington Mk.III	105 + 10*	1
		Stirling	52 + 20*	3
	4 Group	Halifax	88 + 36*	8
	91 Group	Whitley	32*	4
		Wellington Mk.Ic	155*	17
	92 Group	Hampden	24*	1
		Whitley	16*	3
		Wellington Mk.Ic	66*	2
	5 Group	Hampden	26*	
		Manchester	20*	1
		Lancaster	69 + 27*	1
	Coastal Command	Hudson	88*	4
		Wellington	14*	1
	SUBTOTAL		1006	49

(continued)

	Group	Type	Sorties	Missing
St. Trond		Blenheim	6*	1
Haamstede		Boston	3*	
Gilze-Rijen		Boston	3*	
Venlo		Blenheim	5*	1
Valkenburg		Boston	3*	
Twente		Blenheim	5*	
Alkmaar	2 Group	Boston	3*	
Leeuwarden	and	Blenheim	7*	
Leeuwarden	Army Co-operation	Boston	6*	
Jever	Command	Boston	3*	
Ardorf		Blenheim	4*	
Ardorf		Boston	3*	
Vechta		Blenheim	4*	
Stade		Mosquito	2*	
Schleswig-Jagel		Mosquito	2*	
	TOTAL		1065	51

* Not fitted with TR 1335

From the combined force of 1,065 bombers sent, 51 were lost; this was under a 5 per cent loss rate, and so was still 'acceptable'. The heaviest casualties were suffered by the OTUs of 91 Group, which lost 22 of the 198 Whitleys and Wellingtons it had fielded, an 11 per cent loss rate. This sacrifice of inexperienced aircrews was acknowledged in the official report, which stated: 'The loss rate was very high amongst 91 Group from inexperienced pupil crews blamed on poor navigation in bad weather.'[240]

It had been a bad night, too, for 102 Squadron, losing 4 of the 19 aircraft it had got airborne, a 21 per cent loss rate. The rear force was particularly badly affected, with none of the last five into the air completing their mission. *Nobody had wanted to be last in the bomber stream.*

Results were not as good had been hoped; the destructive force unleashed on Cologne had once more failed to be repeated. Further operations were mounted against Bremen on 27 June, 29 June and 2 July to generate the sought-after annihilation, but it was not to be.

The Thousand Plan was over. The body of Sgt Len Starbuck from Burton on Trent, WOp aboard W7654 Q for Queenie, was recovered 18 days later from the vicinity of buoy Tonne H off Cuxhaven by Patrol Boat No. 457, on 14 July 1942. This was one year to the day since he had flown his first operational sortie, which by coincidence had also been to Bremen.

No trace of the rest of the crew was ever found.

Endnotes

238 AIR 14/3408 (excepting Coastal Command data).
239 AIR 14/3408 (excepting Coastal Command data).
240 AIR 14/3802

ANNEX A

ANALYSIS OF HALIFAX LOSSES
25/26 JUNE 1942

German Claims (Western Front) 25/26 June 1942

The following compilation of claimed victories against British bombers has been researched as far as possible by the author at the Bundesarchiv-Militärarchiv (BA-MA), Freiburg. At the end of the war, many of the original paper records were destroyed, but a number of salvaged records were taken to the United States, where they were preserved on microfilm and copies issued back to the German authorities for their subsequent reference. It is important to recognise that BA-MA have no records other than these microfilms, which are now classed as 'originals'. Some of the source records were originally typed, but most have been handwritten in a flowing cursive script unique to the individual who wrote them, and even under ideal conditions can be hard to decipher. Sadly, over time the script has faded and in many cases is now the same colour as the background, rendering interpretation impossible. Any exercise to interrogate these records today will enable the researcher to merely glimpse a picture of the past that is in itself incomplete, and with the passage of time this picture willinevitably fade further in spite of the efforts of BA-MA staff to preserve them.

I am indebted to Theo Boiten for his support in filling in the gaps of my personal research to realise the following tables of claimed victories against British bombers for the night of 25/26 June 1942:

German Flak claims for 25/26 June 1942

Flak Unit(s)	Type	Time	Location
Flak Abt. 265 and Flak Regt. 46.	Wellington	0120	Between Kieselhorst and Winkelsett, Harpstedt
Flak Abt. 988 and Marine Flak.	Halifax	0131/51[241]	Near Juist, in the sea
Flak Abt. 162.	Hudson	0155	NE Hamburg, near Farmsen/ Hinschenfelde

(continued)

Flak Unit(s)	Type	Time	Location
Flak Abt. 611, Flak Abt. 222 and Flak Abt. 334.	Wellington	0205	Bremen-Sebaldsbrück, in the Schlosspark
Flak Abt. 531, Flak Abt. 231, Flak Regt. 46 and Flak Abt. 265.	Lancaster	0208	Kirchseelte, Muna (ammunition dump)
Flak Abt. 117, Flak Abt. 265, Flak Abt. 334 and Flak Abt. 231.	Halifax	0221	Near Colmar II-Nordmentzhausen
Flak Abt. 922, Flak Abt. 879, Flak Abt. 531 and Flak Abt. 615.	Manchester	0225/27[242]	Grambke, Bremen
Flak Abt. 611, Flak Abt. 606, Flak Abt. 879 and Flak Abt. 117.	Wellington	0230	Bad Zwischenahn, near Aschhauserfeld
Flak Abt. 231, Flak Abt. 265 and Flak Regt. 46.	Halifax	0230	Near Delmenhorst-Dwoberg
Marine Flak Abt. 226 and Flak Abt. 988.	Wellington	0230	Near Juist
Flak Abt. 222, Flak Abt. 262 and Flak Abt. 872.	Wellington	0240	Between 2 km NW Westeraccumersiel and Baltrum in the Wattensee
Flak Abt. 988, Marine Flak Abt. 216 and Vorpostenboot H630.	Hampden	0331	Borkum Island, seaplane base
Flak Abt. 306.	Wellington	0500	Lollum, near Bolsward

German night fighter claims for 25/26 June 1942

Unit	Pilot	Type	Time	Location
9./NJG3	Oblt Hans-Joachim Jabs	Stirling	nk	nk
6./NJG2	Oblt Ludwig Becker	Stirling	0039	Oude Zeug, near Wieringermeer
5./NJG2	Uffz Heinz Vinke	Halifax	0042	IJsselmeer near Molkwerum
4./NJG2	Ltn Kaiser	Stirling	0052	40 km N Juist, in the sea.
8./NJG1	Oblt Herbert Lütje	Wellington	0058	10 km NE Nordhorn, near Wietmarschen
5./NJG2	Oblt Egmont Prinz zur Lippe-Weißenfeld	Wellington	0105	Terschelling
Erg./NJG2	Ofw Heinz Strüning	Liberator	0113	Hoek van Holland-Rotterdam
8./NJG1	Ltn August Geiger	Wellington	0120	20 km NE Rheine, near Schale
1./NJG3	Uffz Wolfgang Heymann	Wellington	0120	Nk
8./NJG1	Ltn August Geiger	Whitley	0130	10 km NW Lingen, near Dalum

Unit	Pilot	Type	Time	Location
Stab III./ NJG2	Hptm Herbert Bönsch	Boston	0132	1 km S Ouddorp, in the sea
5./NJG2	Ltn Lothar Linke	Stirling	0132	NE Wieringen, in the Wattensee
6./NJG1	Oblt Eckart-Wilhelm von Bonin	Blenheim	0138	NW Houwaart, N Tirlemont
Stab II./ NJG2	Oblt Rudolf Sigmund	Halifax	0150	Assen
5./NJG2	Oblt Egmont Prinz zur Lippe-Weißenfeld	Wellington	0152	E De Kooy airfield
8./NJG1	Ltn August Geiger	Stirling	0158	6 km NW Nordhorn, near Bimolten
9./NJG1	Hptm Alfred Haesler	Halifax	0205	8 km NW Eldenzaal, near Weerselo
7./NJG1	Oblt Fritz Carstens	Halifax	0209	1½ km N Luttenberg
6./NJG3	Ltn Paul Szameitat	Halifax	0211	Cuxhaven
8./NJG3	Ltn Hans-Heinrich König	Hudson	0214	S Fehmarn, in the sea
5./NJG3	Oblt Werner Hoffmann	Hudson	0226	6 km SE Heide, near Fiel
6./NJG2	Ltn Robert Denzel	Wellington	0232	5 km E De Kooy airfield
Stab II./ NJG2	Hptm Helmut Lent	Wellington	0237	6 km NW Enkhuizen, near Andijk
3./NJG3	Ltn Armin Hubmann	Whitley	0250	Meppen
Stab III./ NJG4, det. II./NJG2	Maj Kurt Holler	Whitley	0254	N Vlieland, in the sea
Stab II./ NJG2	Hptm Helmut Lent	Whitley	0256	Wervershoof
8./NJG1	Oblt Werner Rowlin	Wellington	0256	3 km SW Borne, NW Hengelo
Erg./NJG2	Oblt Heinrich Prinz zu Sayn-Wittgenstein	Wellington	0307	nk
5./NJG3	Unknown crew	nk	0308	nk
Erg./NJG2	Hptm Erich Simon	Blenheim	0318	25 km WNW Walcheren
5./NJG3	Oblt Werner Hoffmann	Whitley	0324	6 km NW Büsum, on the beach
Stab III./ NJG4, det. II./NJG2	Maj Kurt Holler	Wellington	0327	NW Terschelling, in the sea
Erg./NJG2	Ltn Hans-Hermann Müller	Wellington	0358	20 km W Den Haag, in the sea
II./NJG2	Oblt Franz Buschmann	Wellington	0402	W Terschelling, in the sea

(continued)

Unit	Pilot	Type	Time	Location
5./NJG2	Ltn Günther Löwa	Whitley	0426	10 km SW Den Helder, in the sea
6./NJG2	Ltn Hans-Georg Bötel	Wellington	0429	10 km NW Terschelling, in the sea
6./NJG2	Ltn Hans-Georg Bötel	Wellington	0438	15 km NW Vlieland, in the sea
II./NJG2	Oblt Hermann Greiner	Wellington	0600	Ijsselmeer near S Harlingen

ANALYSIS OF HALIFAX LOSSES

In total, nine Halifaxes were lost on this operation in a ddition to a further three in the build-up and during preparation. Some of these nine can be readily identified from records taken from the crash sites where they occurred on land, and/or crewmen were captured, and these can be cross-referenced against the German claims. However, four aircraft were lost with no survivors and no uniquely identifiable wreckage:

- R9446 DY-F
- W7747 MP-G
- W7654 DY-Q
- W7759 DY-L.

Equivalent ground speeds were estimated for each of the different legs on the operation by plotting the position at which each Halifax was lost along the route against its flight time to that point, taking into account the aircraft's known laden and unladen cruising speeds and the synoptic working chart. Reasonable deviations were calculated by reviewing the differences between overall sortie times of those Halifaxes that returned to base. When added onto the respective start times and locations, these data provide a reasonably accurate position for each individual aircraft at any given time.

Next, time defined routes were plotted for each of the four missing aircraft and cross referenced against unsatisfied claims from the flak units and night fighters for potential Halifax interceptions:

0113	Liberator	Hoek van Holland-Rotterdam	Ofw Heinz Strüning	Erg./NJG2
0131/51	Halifax	Near Juist, in the sea	Flak Abt. 988 and Marine Flak	
0150	Halifax	Assen	Oblt Rudolf Sigmund	Stab II./NJG2
0205	Halifax	Weersalo, Eldenzaal	Hptm Alfred Haesler	9./NJG1
0211	Halifax	Cuxhaven	Ltn Paul Szameitat	6./NJG3
0308	nk	nk	Unknown crew	5./NJG3

Note: There were no Liberators flying on this operation, but the high tailplane configuration is sufficiently similar to a Halifax to consider possible misidentification.

R9446 AND W7654

Both R9446 and W7654 had bodies of crewmen recovered from the North German coast. As the bomber stream crossed the Dutch coast on the outward journey and only crossed the German coast on the return journey, then it is a safe assumption that they were both returning when they were lost.

Based on the flight time recorded for W1105, which was shot down by flak over Colmar II-Nordmentzhausen at 0221 hrs:

- R9446 would have been on the overland part of the fourth leg at around 0223 hrs. The only claim that comes near to matching this is that made by Ltn Paul Szameitat of 6./NJG3 over Cuxhaven at 0211 hrs.

- W7654 would have been on the overland part of the fourth leg at 0320 hrs, around an hour later. The only claim that comes near to matching this is that made by an unknown crew from 5./NJG3 at 0308 hrs.

W7747 AND W7759

No identifiable remains were found of either W7747 or W7759, but a Halifax was confirmed shot down over Weerselo, Eldenzaal by Hptm Alfred Haesler of 9./NJG1 at 0205 hrs.

Based on the flight time recorded for V9993, which was shot down by Oblt Carstens of 7./NJG1 over Luttenberg, Raalte at 0209 hrs:

- W7759 would have been in the Luttenberg region at around ~0215 hrs
- W7747 would have been in the Luttenberg region at around ~0157 hrs

Whilst both aircraft would have been in the same area at roughly the same time, one approximately eight minutes before the recorded interception over Weerselo at 0205 hrs and the other ten minutes after, it is considered that the later of the two is the more likely. This is because an aircraft is probably less likely to be exceeding the speed of the others, but could conceivably be flying marginally slower, but this is by no means conclusive. This suggests that W7759 was the aircraft that crashed at Weerselo.

If this is taken as correct, then W7747 must be assumed to have been lost at sea, probably trying to return home following having been intercepted. Given her start time, this aircraft could have been expected to be at the following claimed interception points around the following approximate times:

- Hoek van Holland-Rotterdam around ~0126 hrs
- Assen around ~0143 hrs
- Juist around ~0244 hrs

This discounts the flak claim near Juist, and although the misidentified claim made by Ofw Heinz Strüning of Erg./NJG2 over Rotterdam at 0113 hrs cannot be discounted, the claim made by Oblt Rudolf Sigmund of Stab II./NJG2 over Assen at 0150 hrs is the better fit in terms of both time and recognition, and is therefore considered to be the more likely.

RECONSTRUCTION OF LOSSES

W1155 (ZA-U)

10 Squadron

Air test.

Crashed at RAF Leeming with crossed elevator trim tab controls 1445 hrs.

Sgt WJW Wiseman	†
Sgt JA Carter	†
F/O JG Mutter	†
Sgt SV Duvall	†
F/Sgt DR Stewart RCAF	†
P/O DA Street RCAF	†

R9482 (MP-D)

76 Squadron

Air test.

Stalled and crashed RAF Middleton St George following engine failure on takeoff 1530 hrs.

Sgt A Aston	†
Sgt HR Smith	†
Sgt CD Barnett	†
P/O WJ Cole	†
Sgt LD Richardson	†
P/O HR Higgins	inj

R9378 (MP-K)

76 Conversion Flight

Caught fire on dispersal at RAF Middleton St George after incendiaries fell onto the ground 2000 hrs.

W1067 (EY-P)

F/O John Whittingham had either benefited from a very strong tailwind or cut the corner at the Egmond aan Zee turn point when he was intercepted by a night fighter, piloted by Uffz Heinz Vinke, over the Ijsselmeer south of Stavoren. Although the bomber was mortally damaged, John Whittingham headed for land and once near Mirns ordered the crew to bale out; four of the crew escaped, but the fifth crewman, Sgt Harold Dronfield, was not so lucky. Next, there was an explosion in the bomb bay, which John Whittingham took as his cue to escape. However, by this time his aircraft was very low, skimming over the dyke between

Stavoren and Molkwerum and still on a north-westerly heading. He jumped, but was too low and his parachute did not have time to open; meanwhile his aircraft impacted the water a few hundred yards from the coast.

The last moments of this aircraft were recorded on a sighting report:

> Egmond 0039 hours 12000 feet aircraft at 13000 feet seen shot down by fighter (tracer seen). Fell in flames and later exploded. Exploded again after hitting ground.[243]
>
> 78 Squadron
>
> Shot down by Uffz Heinz Vinke of 5./NJG2 over Molkwerum, IJsselmeer 0042 hrs.

F/O JA Whittingham	†
P/O G Gibson	pow
Sgt H Dronfield	†
Sgt RA Brown	pow
Sgt AG Springthorpe	pow
Sgt DB Donaldson	pow

W7747 (MP-G)

Officially recorded as lost without trace, it is probable that this aircraft was intercepted over Assen at 0150 hrs by Oblt Rudolf Sigmund of Stab II./NJG2. It is proposed that following interception the aircraft turned for home but succumbed to damage received during the engagement and was lost at sea.

It is possible that a sighting in accordance with these parameters was recorded in the vicinity of Assen, lending credence to the claim by Oblt Rudolf Sigmund:

> Meppel area 0140 hours 13,000 ft. aircraft seen falling in flames. No flak or searchlights, but believed tracer.[244]
>
> 76 Squadron
>
> Possibly shot down by Oblt Rudolf Sigmund Stab II./NJG2 over Assen 0150 hrs.[245]

Sgt JE Meyer RCAF	†
Sgt JS Almond	†
Sgt J McDonald Cameron	†
Sgt WC Francoeur RCAF	†
Sgt AC Gasson	†
Sgt WJ Mills	†
Sgt A Wearmouth	†

W7759 (DY-L)

This was probably the aircraft intercepted by Hptm Alfred Haesler over Weersefo, Eldenzaal, and is reported as having crashed near Dulder at 0205 hrs with 'such a big explosion that nor the airmen nor the aircraft could be identified', so the five bodies recovered were buried in the cemetery as 'known unto god'.

*Halifax losses
25/26 June
1942*

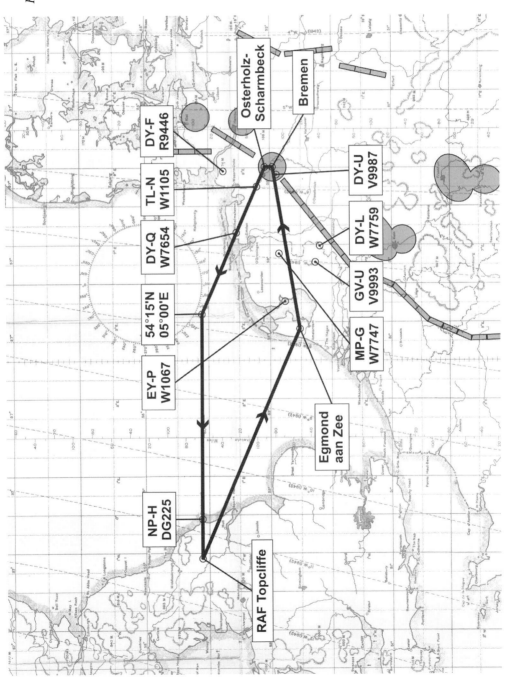

DY-F
R9446

Osterholz-
Scharmbeck

Bremen

DY-U
V9987

TL-N
W1105

DY-Q
W7654

DY-L
W7759

GV-U
V9993

54°15'N
05°00'E

MP-G
W7747

EY-P
W1067

Egmond
aan Zee

NP-H
DG225

RAF Topcliffe

102 Squadron

Probably shot down by Hptm Alfred Haesler of III./NJG1 over Weerselo, Eldenzaal 0205 hrs.[246]

F/Sgt CC Harris RCAF	†
Sgt VJF Bicat	†
Sgt TH May	†
Sgt JB Smith	†
Sgt JP Hankin	†
Sgt GC Pratt †	†

V9993 (GV-U)

1652 CU had responded to the latest call for maximum effort by fielding 12 aircraft, including a number of former 102 Squadron pilots: S/Ldr Leonard Cheshire, F/Sgt Eric Borsberry, F/O William Welch and F/O Kenneth Whisken.

With the inquiry surrounding the damage to Halifax R9377 still hanging over him from 24 June, Kenneth Whisken stood ready to take the same crew into combat in response to the most recent demand for maximum effort. He was allocated V9993, a Halifax B Mk.II Series 1 (Special) which was not equipped with a mid-upper turret. This would not have been a first choice to take on such an operation when the presence of enemy night fighters could be predicted and the requirement for self-defence would have been at a premium. His crew would contain only one air gunner, but would be made up to a complement of seven with the inclusion of a 2nd pilot and a bomb aimer.

They were intercepted over Holland by a night fighter piloted by Oblt Fritz Carstens, killing Sgt James Watson, the inexperienced American rear air gunner. Kenneth Whisken recognised the severity of the damage suffered by his aircraft and so he ordered the crew to bale out. Once the remaining crew were all safely out, he dropped his bombs and then jumped out himself, near Lemelerveld, but his parachute did not open. His aircraft flew on for about 5 miles before crashing near Raalte, close to Luttenberg.

1652 Conversion Unit

Shot down by Oblt Carstens of 7./NJG1 over Luttenberg, Raalte 0209 hrs.

F/O KD Whisken	†
F/Sgt HF Spratt RCAF	pow
P/O WH Andrews RCAF	pow
Sgt RW Wagstaff RCAF	pow
Sgt J Watson RCAF	†
Sgt VA Martin	pow
F/O DM McKenzie RCAF	pow

R9446 (DY-F)

The bodies of both Navigator P/O Patrick Robinson and Air Engineer Sgt Jack Southern are reported as having been washed ashore on the German North Sea coast. Given the escape sequence from the aircraft, this points to at least a successful partial evacuation having taken place, with other crewmen having escaped, but the sea in the Heligoland Bight was stormy and unforgiving.

Sightings that may correlate with this incident quote:

> (i) 'Ardorf 0212 hours 12000 feet exchange of tracer seen and starboard engine of bomber observed to catch fire and the aircraft fell in flames through cloud.'[247,248]

> (ii) 'Bremen 30 miles N. of, 0215 hours 6,000 ft. Ju.88 seen attacking 4-engined A/C at 250 yards range closing to 250 yards and firing long bursts cannon shell. No return fire from bomber which fell away with sparks flying round from fuselage. Large red glow seen from ground at approx. point where aircraft fell.'[249]

102 Squadron
Most likely shot down by Ltn Paul Szameitat of 6./NJG3 over Cuxhaven 0211 hrs.[250]

F/Sgt SEH Morgan	†
P/O PJN Robinson	†
Sgt JA Fraser	†
Sgt RH Brett	†
F/Sgt DG Williamson	†
Sgt JJ Southern	†

W1105 (TL-N)

The last moments of this aircraft may have been captured in the following sighting:

> Bremen 40 miles N/W 0225 hours 10000 feet large flash in sky at same height some distance dead astern. Looked like aircraft on fire not seen to crash.[251]

35 Squadron
Shot down by flak over Colmar II-Nordmentzhausen 0221 hrs.

F/O HGB Mays	†
Sgt SJ Harding	pow
Sgt RG Gumbley	†
P/O RH Birch	pow
P/O SF Hazleton	†
Sgt AJ Selby	†
Sgt RW Fisher	†

V9987 (DY-U)

This aircraft was shot down by flak over Delmenhorst-Dwoberg on the approach to Bremen at 0230 hrs. It is possible that the last moments of this aircraft may have been captured in the following sighting:

Bremen area 0225 hours 12,500 ft. A/C seen shot down in flames.[252]

102 Conversion Flight
Shot down by flak over Delmenhorst-Dwoberg 0230 hrs.

F/Sgt FF Duff RCAF	†
Sgt JR Shellard	pow
F/Sgt A Hartley	pow
Sgt W Weightman	†
Sgt GA Losh	pow

W7654 (DY-Q)

This aircraft is most likely to have been lost in the Wattensee shortly after crossing the German coast near Norden: any sooner, and identifiable wreckage would have been found on the German mainland; any later, and the body of Sgt Len Starbuck would have been swept out to sea. The Wattensee is an area epitomised by tidal mudflats[253] with tidal current and residual eddies. Consequently anything floating in this region would not be driven by any current but more by the prevailing wind, which during the summer months is dominated by a strong westerly to WNW wind.[254] The body of Sgt Len Starbuck was eventually recovered off Cuxhaven on 14 July 1942, having taken almost three weeks to get there from the postulated crash site in the Wattensee, around 60 miles away. This suggests its having made steady progress eastwards under the prevailing summer winds at an average of 3 miles per day before it was recovered, which is perfectly feasible for the region and provides further evidence for the location of the final resting place of Q for Queenie and her crew.

102 Squadron
Most likely shot down by unidentified crew from 5./NJG3[255] over the Wattensee near Juist/Norderney at 0308 hrs.[256]

F/Lt KB Wright	†
W/O RF Bradbury RCAF	†
Sgt L Starbuck	†
Sgt PJ Fernie RCAF	†
Sgt ERT De Mattos	†
F/Sgt I Lewis	†

DG225 (NP-H)

This crew ran out of fuel on their return journey and ditched on the sea less than a mile off Scarborough Pier, all crew being recovered safely.

158 Squadron
Ran out of fuel and ditched off Scarborough Pier 0530 hrs.
P/O LE Bradbury

Sgt R Edlington

Sgt AJ Fromings

Sgt WJ Smart RCAF

Sgt W Walton

Sgt RW Brindley RAAF

Sgt RA Petherbridge

Endnotes

241 Could not clearly identify whether time recorded was 0131 or 0151 hrs.

242 Could not clearly identify whether time recorded was 0225 or 0227 hrs.

243 AIR 14/2601 Chapter K Other Observations (A) A/C Seen Shot Down or Falling, Ref 27.

244 AIR 14/3802 Chapter 9 Own Observations, 3 Group Ref (vi).

245 Author's assessment.

246 Author's assessment.

247 AIR 14/2601 Chapter K Other Observations (A) A/C Seen Shot Down or Falling, Ref 26.

248 AIR 14/3802 Chapter 9 Own Observations, 92 Group Ref (xi).

249 AIR 14/3802 Chapter 9 Own Observations, 1 Group Ref (v).

250 Author's assessment.

251 AIR 14/2601 Chapter K Other Observations (A) A/C Seen Shot Down or Falling, Ref 32.

252 AIR 14/3802 Chapter 9 Own Observations, 4 Group Ref (vi).

253 Admiralty Charts and Publications (2010) Admiralty Sailing Directions – North Sea (East) Pilot, ISBN 9780707742366, United Kingdom Hydrographic Office, pp126.

254 Admiralty Charts and Publications (2010) Admiralty Sailing Directions – North Sea (East) Pilot, ISBN 9780707742366, United Kingdom Hydrographic Office, pp44.

255 On the night of 25/26 June 1942, Hptm Werner Hoffmann (5./NJG3) shot down two RAF twin-engined bombers during the Thousand Bomber Raid on Bremen to record his first victories at night. The name of his contemporary who recorded this victory cannot be read on the original Luftwaffe records.

256 Author's assessment.

ANNEX B

DEVELOPMENT OF EARLY GERMAN
NIGHT ANTI-AIR DEFENCES

In the first year of the air war, German night anti-air defences relied upon acoustic aircraft sound locaters to cue the nearby searchlights, which would then seek to cone their target for the flak batteries close by. These defences were initially concentrated around cities, but the strategic importance of the industrial centres in the Ruhr drove the creation of a protective echelon to the north and west of the region.

This barrier was extended progressively to make it deeper, increasing the time that the bombers had to fly through the defences. However, the demand for ever-greater protection for the German industrial heartland had to be offset by reducing the defences available to the other towns and cities. This approach was not only incoherent but also unsustainable.

The introduction of short-range Würzburg precision radar sets in May 1940 was quickly seized upon to complement the existing long-range early warning Freya radar, to create a GCI system capable of integrating the searchlights not only with flak but also with night fighters. This system, known as Helle Nachtjagd Verfahren (HeNaJa, bright night fighting), became operational in September 1940, and prominently featured the newly created Nachtjagd (Luftwaffe night fighter capability), which had been formed only three months previously.

The Freya long-range radar, although limited by its inability to determine altitude, could nevertheless detect the target at long range, giving time for the other elements of the system to be placed into readiness. Once the target was closer, it would be passed to the first of two Würzburgs which, although lacking the range of the Freya, could pinpoint the contact in both azimuth and elevation. The Würzburg receiving the contact was identified as *Rot* (red), and cued a group of radar-controlled searchlights that it updated constantly with intercept vector data. Crucially, the searchlights remained switched off as the system tracked the target unerringly into the trap. Meanwhile, a second Würzburg, identified as *Blau* (blue), tracked the intercepting night fighter.

Inside the Flugmeldemess-Stellung (night fighter control station), the red and blue tracks were received from the operators of the two separate Würzburg systems, and were projected

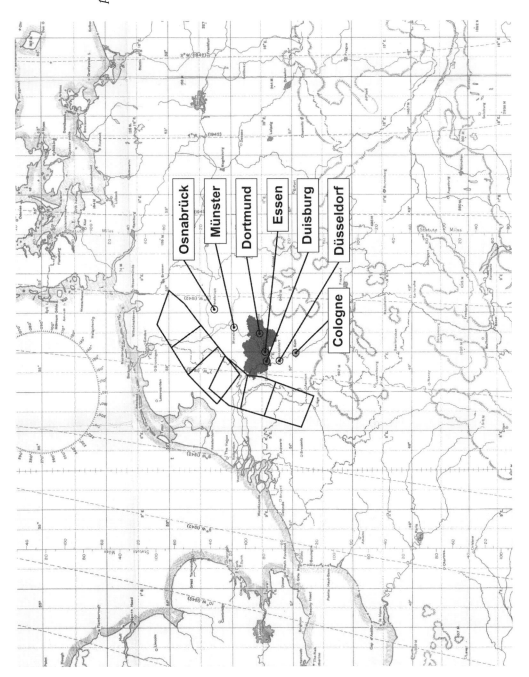

Early searchlight defences protecting the Ruhr

Osnabrück

Münster

Dortmund

Essen

Duisburg

Düsseldorf

Cologne

concurrently onto an *Auswerte Tisch* (plotting board). (The term 'blue' referred to the Würzburg equipment; the track was actually projected onto the glass screen of the Auswerte Tisch as a green light.[257])

Meanwhile, the night fighter would be flying a holding pattern at combat height, waiting to be issued with intercept commands from the JLO (Jägerleitoffizier/Fighter Control Officer), based upon his interpretation of the display on the Auswerte Tisch.

The night fighter would then be commanded onto an intercept vector by the JLO, who would fine-tune the interception as it proceeded by issuing coded commands from a comprehensive lexicon, key, amongst which were the following directions:[258,259]

- Rolf[260]   Turn to starboard by 10°; for 20° or 30°, 2× or 3× respectively.
- Lisa[261]   Turn to port by 10°; for 20° or 30°, 2× or 3× respectively.
- Siegfried   Climb by 100 m; for 200 m or 300 m, 2× or 3× respectively.
- Frieda   Descend by 100 m; for 200 m or 300 m, 2× or 3× respectively.
- Marie   Distance to intercept in km; 'Marie 5' being 5 km to target.

Provided the JLO's calculations had been correct, the bomber should be within optimal range of the searchlights just as the night fighter got into position. At this point, the radar-controlled searchlights would have switched on, illuminating the bomber, and on this cue an array of manually controlled searchlights would also be switched on and rotated towards the target, which they would proceed to cone for the night fighter.

Not only was this integrated system seen to be effective, but it could also be easily replicated in self-contained sections, and this led to an ambitious plan to construct an unbroken defensive screen from Denmark down into France. The first step towards achieving this goal was to rationalise the existing Ruhr defences into a baseline configuration that was then capable of being extended to meet this bold ambition.

This re-invented searchlight belt would come to present a psychological barrier that would soon be extended over such a long distance that there would be no way of making detour round it. It would be known in Germany as the Helle Riegel (bright bolt), but bomber crews would come to know it as the Kammhuber Line.

Whilst recognising the potential of this proposed searchlight belt, Gen.Maj Kammhuber acknowledged that it would take time to come to fruition, and that the largest German cities were in immediate need of better protection. Consequently, he embarked upon the radical plan of creating extended searchlight zones around the cities within which *the combined operations of both night fighters and flak would be permitted to operate concurrently.*

This system, known as the Kombinierte Nachtjagd (KoNaJa, combined night fighting) was to be made possible by the introduction of a new Identification Friend or Foe (IFF) system, intended to identify night fighters clearly from the ground. It would therefore be incumbent upon the flak units to make sure that the targets they were firing at were not friendly, and to observe the appropriate restraint whilst their own night fighters were flying overhead. As a failsafe, night fighters could also fire flares of pre-arranged colours should they find

Introduction of the KoNaJa zones and rationalisation of the Ruhr's searchlight defences

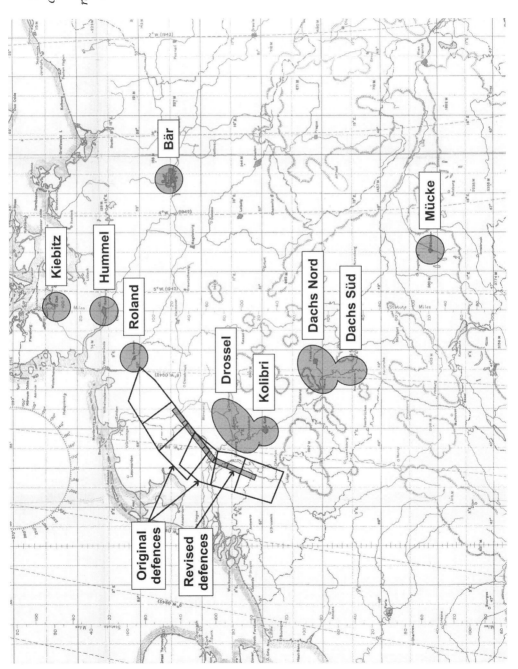

Bär

Mücke

Kiebitz

Hummel

Roland

Dachs Nord

Dachs Süd

Drossel

Kolibri

Original defences

Revised defences

Layout of
completed
Kammhuber
Line

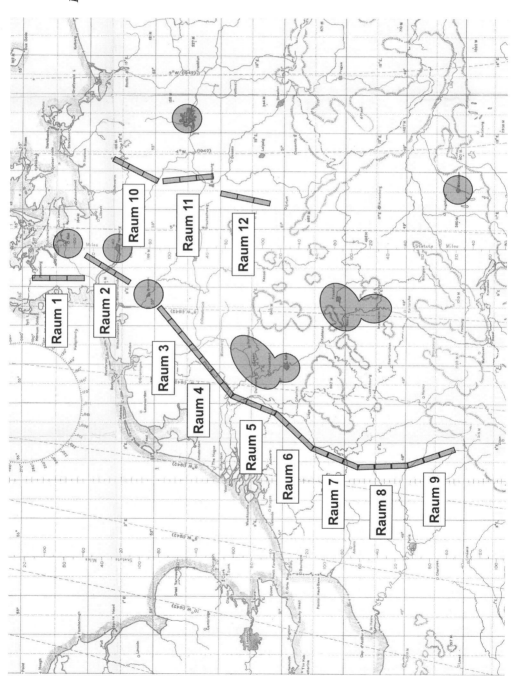

Raum 1

Raum 2

Raum 3

Raum 4

Raum 5

Raum 6

Raum 7

Raum 8

Raum 9

Raum 10

Raum 11

Raum 12

themselves being fired on. The potential of doubling the success of an intercept through using units both in the air and on the ground concurrently was considered worth the risk to the night fighters, but in practice there was a sudden increase in their loss rate.

Colonel Jean Calmel recounts having been attacked under such conditions whilst holding steady on his bombing run:[262]

> With a courage worthy of respect the German fighter sought us out in the middle of the flak barrage. Against the red background of fires or the milky-white curtain of the searchlights one caught a glimpse of a fast black snub nose lit up by bursts of spurting flames. At that moment it was impossible to take evasive action.

The first KoNaJa Raum was set up around Berlin in May 1941, and it was followed by similar arrangements for other cities in key target areas. They were given code names,[263,264,265] especially those of birds and other animals beginning with the same letter or letters as the city they protected. In many cases the name would reflect a traditional or contemporary connection:

- Berlin: KoNaJa 'Bär' (Bear – the city's symbol).
- Bremen: KoNaJa 'Roland' (a Roland statue is a symbol of freedom and law in a German city).
- Darmstadt: KoNaJa 'Dachs' (Badger – the nocturnal predator), comprising Mannheim in Dachs Süd / Frankfurt and Mainz in Dachs Nord.
- Düsseldorf: KoNaJa 'Drossel' (Thrush – possibly after the popular contemporary nursery rhyme 'Alle Vögel sind schon da',[266] or a reference born of dark humour among locals that the air in this region was so polluted that the song of a thrush would never be heard), extending to cover the main industrial area of the Ruhrgebiet, including Duisburg, Essen, Wuppertal and Dortmund.
- Hamburg: KoNaJa 'Hummel' (Bumblebee – after Hans Hummel,[267] an eccentric local personality).
- Kiel: KoNaJa 'Kiebitz' (Lapwing – Kiel hosted/hosts breeding colonies of lapwings).
- Köln: KoNaJa 'Kolibri' (Hummingbird – the name of a famous cabaret venue in the city).
- München: KoNaJa 'Mücke' (Mosquito – Munich suffers from mosquitoes in the summer).

Meanwhile, work continued on the Kammhuber Line, the new capability being brigaded as follows:[268]

- A Zug (squad) comprised three manually controlled searchlights 3 km apart, arrayed to face the approach of the bombers.
- A Batterie comprised three Züge in rows 5 km directly behind each other.

- An Abteilung (Battalion) comprised three Batterien all arrayed side by side, presenting a 30 km front facing the approach of the bombers. There were three radar-guided searchlights in front of each Abteilung, which would in turn cue the manually controlled searchlights behind it. In addition, there was also a Funkfeuer (radio beacon) and Leuchtfeuer (visual beacon) for the night fighters.

- A Regiment comprised three Abteilungen, presenting a front 90 km across. This whole area constituted a Nachtjagdraum (night fighting box).

The Nachtjagdräume were renumbered in a new sequence, with each regiment being allocated a number running from north to south. Each Abteilung within its Raum was allocated a suffix letter – A, B or C – again numbered from north to south. Coincident with the radar upgrades, the cumbersome Auswerte Tisch plotting table was replaced with the new Seeburg Tisch comprising a glass plate etched with a map view of the area covered by the radar installations. The hostile and friendly tracks were now back-projected onto this screen by red and green lights articulated on a new turntable arrangement.

These defences would be restructured during June and early July 1941, starting with Raum 5, which replaced the western stretch of the old Ruhr defences, whilst Raum 4 replaced the northern stretch. During this restructuring, Raum 4 exceeded the 90 km standard length used elsewhere, and was constructed comprising four Abteilungen: A, B, C and D.

Whilst the location of the defences can be established by reference to existing sources,[269,270,271,272,273] further research by the author suggests that 90 km stretches were capable of being constructed and commissioned in three weeks. This has been determined by examining the routes flown during operational sorties, which can be seen to have skirted around the latest extent of the defences.

Extension of the Kammhuber Line defences during 1941

Week commencing	20 Jul	27 Jul	3 Aug	10 Aug	17 Aug	24 Aug	31 Aug	7 Sep	14 Sep	21 Sep	28 Sep	5 Oct	12 Oct	19 Oct	26 Oct	2 Nov	9 Nov	16 Nov	23 Nov
Abteilung (30 km)	3C	3B	3A	6A	6B	6C	1C		1B			1A		7A	7B	7C	2A	2B	2C

The sequence of development from July to November 1941 extended the Ruhr defences alternately north-easterly and south-westerly until there was an unbroken line from the Danish border to the Ardennes. Following a lull in construction, possibly due to the harsh winter or a focus on other work, construction reconvened in early 1942, pushing down deeper into France.

Endnotes

257 Hinchliffe, P. OBE (1997) *The Other Battle: Luftwaffe Night Aces versus Bomber Command*, ISBN 1853105473, Airlife, p 95.

258 Aders, G. (1980) *History of the German Night Fighter Force 1917–1945*, ISBN 0354012479, Fakenham Press, pp 274–278.

259 Hinchliffe, P. OBE (1997) The Other Battle: Luftwaffe Night Aces versus Bomber Command, ISBN 1853105473, Airlife, pp 95–97.

260 Popular contemporary boy's name beginning with R for Recht (right).

261 Short for Liselotte, popular contemporary girl's name beginning with L for Links (left).

262 Calmel, J. DFC Légion d'Honneur (1955) *Night Pilot* (translated by Mervyn Savill), William Kimber, p 152.

263 Aders, G. (1980) *History of the German Night Fighter Force 1917–1945*, ISBN 0354012479, Fakenham Press, p 37.

264 gyges.dk/Himmelbett.htm.

265 luchtoorlog.net/hoofdstuk1.html

266 The popular German nursery rhyme "Alle Vögel sind schon da" references this bird in the second verse.

It was written by August Heinrich Hoffmann von Fallersleben, who had studied at the university in nearby Bonn, but who had also come to endear himself unwittingly to the ruling regime by penning his evocative later work ‚Das Lied der Deutschen', the German national anthem.

267 Real name Johann Wilhelm Bentz, 1787–1854. Local legend, confirmed with the Museum for Homburgs Schacht.

268 Jones, R.V. (1978) *Most Secret War: British Scientific Intelligence 1939–1945*, ISBN 0241897467, Hamish Hamilton, p 267.

269 MPI 1/467

270 Aders, G. (1980) *History of the German Night Fighter Force 1917–1945*, ISBN 0354012479, Fakenham Press, pp 32–54.

271 Jones, R.V. (1978) *Most Secret War: British Scientific Intelligence 1939–1945*, ISBN 0241897467, Hamish Hamilton, pp 264–279.

272 luchtoorlog.net/hoofdstuk2.0.html.

273 gyges.dk/Himmelbett.htm.

ANNEX C

GEE NAVIGATIONAL EQUIPMENT

GEE (G for Grid) was a triangulation-based navigation system employing a series of three geographically distant but tightly synchronised transmitters; one master (A) and two slaves (B and C).

When A and B transmitted at precisely the same time, the signal from each would arrive at a remote receiver with a small but measurable time difference. That difference would place the receiver anywhere along a line described by a hyperbola on a chart. Similarly, the time difference between A and C would describe another hyperbola, and where the two intersected would triangulate the position of the receiver.

During the system's development, the master station was located at Daventry in Northamptonshire (A) with the slaves at RAF Stenigot in Lincolnshire (B) and RAF Ventnor on the Isle of Wight (C). To enable discrimination between AB and AC pulses, RAF Stenigot transmitted a double pulse for B, and to ensure that the phase and frequency being transmitted from all three stations was correct, a monitoring station was placed at RAF Bromley in Essex. All locations had been chosen as far as possible to be on existing Chain Home radar sites, where installing new aerials would be less likely to attract attention.

The three transmitting stations were positioned in an arc focused in a direction south of east, from which position the greatest separation between A–B and A–C could be viewed concurrently. This generated the greatest density of intersecting hyperbolae and thereby the best possible accuracy from the system in a direction south of east, which happened to point directly out over the Ruhr Valley.

The range of the system was predicted to be ~450 miles from the most remote ground station to a receiver at 10,000 ft, and the accuracy at this distance was denoted by a diamond shape (generated by the intersection of the hyperbolic lattices) of ~3 miles. Furthermore, as the closer the aircraft was to the transmitters the better the system's accuracy, it was postulated that GEE could also be used to guide the returning aircraft back to their home bases.

This system finally provided Bomber Command with the navigational accuracy it needed, irrespective of visibility. Also, unlike contemporary German beam guidance systems, it did

Revised transmitter locations for Eastern GEE chain from early 1942

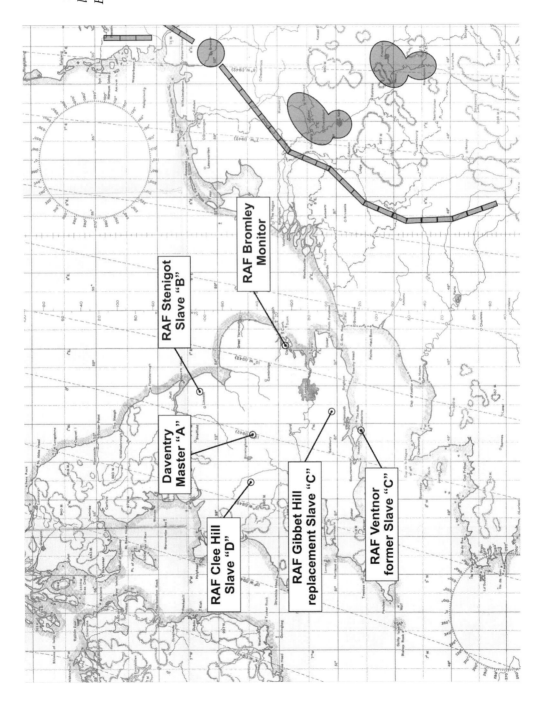

RAF Stenigot
Slave "B"

RAF Bromley
Monitor

Daventry
Master "A"

RAF Clee Hill
Slave "D"

RAF Gibbet Hill
replacement Slave "C"

RAF Ventnor
former Slave "C"

not betray where the bombers were headed – and crucially it was passive, so it would not betray the position of the aircraft.

To support system trials, the Telecommunications Research Establishment (TRE) was tasked with producing a total of 24 prototype airborne units. Following this, the plan was for an 'initial phase' of 300 single-frequency Mk.I receivers (TR1335[274]) to be hand-built by Cossors, with the first 50 to be delivered by 31 October 1941; the 'final phase' would be for all Bomber Command and Coastal Command aircraft to be fitted with variable-frequency Mk.II receivers capable of working from several chains of ground stations.

Excluded from the list of bomber types to receive this equipment were the Whitley and Hampden, as the fit in these aircraft was deemed to be 'exceedingly difficult if not impossible'. The aircraft chosen as being most suitable for these trials was the Wellington, and by 1 August 1941 a total of six TRE receivers had been delivered to 115 Squadron at RAF Marham. None of these was fitted with detonators, so they were only deemed suitable for flight over friendly territory in the event of loss.

Feedback from trials with these early receivers over the British Isles and the Irish Sea had delivered very positive results, and so once the TRE-built receivers with detonators fitted started to be received there was a strong desire to see how well the system performed over Germany. Operational trials 11/12 August 1941 supported the earlier findings, but following the loss of Wellington Z8835 the next night all further GEE trials over enemy territory were suspended.

On 11 October 1941, proposals were submitted for GEE coverage around the British Isles:

- Eastern GEE chain (Germany)
- Southern GEE chain (France)
- Western GEE chain (SW Approaches)
- Northern GEE chain (North Sea).

Although only three transmitter stations were required to provide the necessary navigational coverage on operations, the Eastern GEE chain uniquely was modified to include a fourth. This was because whilst the three stations in this chain had been optimised to present maximum separation over the Ruhr, they showed very obliquely from Yorkshire and Lincolnshire, preventing returning aircraft from being able to rely on GEE to navigate back to their home bases. To overcome this problem, a further slave station, D, would be placed on the rear radiation line near Shrewsbury, which, in conjunction with the existing A and B stations, would provide navigational coverage over the bombers' home bases.

By 10 January 1942 almost all the infrastructure to support the operational use of the Eastern GEE chain was in position. This included relocating Slave Station C from RAF Ventnor, which was seen to be too vulnerable to attack, to RAF Gibbet Hill in Surrey. It had also been decided that the monitoring station at RAF Bromley would be moved, but the new location had not yet been announced.[275] Further, RAF Clee Hill in Shropshire had been chosen to be the location for the new Slave Station D.

By 14 February 1942, the airborne receivers originally ordered back in July 1941 had finally become available in sufficient numbers to support a massed operation. On 8/9 March 1942 the first full-scale operation using GEE-enabled bombing was undertaken.

Endnotes

274 In a strange quirk of fate, when the Mk.II GEE airborne equipment was introduced in February 1943 with a range of frequencies and better anti-jamming capability, it was allocated the number TR1355, only one digit different and hence the cause of some subsequent confusion.

275 This function would eventually be relocated to RAF Barkway in Hertfordshire.

ANNEX D

RAF TARGETING CODES

Locations for Gardening operations

From the beginning of the RAF's sea-mining operations from the air in the Second World War, target areas for dropping the mines were referred to by single-letter codes. On 11 April 1940 AVM Norman Bottomley, senior air staff officer at HQ Bomber Command, wrote a memorandum which was promulgated under No.5 Group Operation Order No. B.57,[276] in which he explained that henceforth there would be new terms allocated to these activities; from that point on, dropping the sea mines from the air would be referred to as Gardening, whilst the mines themselves would be referred to as Vegetables. He continued:

> The areas in which Vegetables are emplaced are at present designated alphabetically, and when a 'lay' is made the name of a vegetable commencing with the same alphabetical letter as the area in which it is dropped will be used in reporting.

The point was illustrated by the following examples:

A	Asparagus	Great Belt Eastern Channel
B	Broccoli	Great Belt Western Channel
C	Carrots	Little Belt
D	Damsons*	The Sound

* This was soon changed to Daffodils.

This system was adopted formally, and a degree of credulity had to be stretched once the code letters rose to X, Y and Z. There also remained a slight degree of confusion as to whether these plants should appear in the singular or the plural; official documentation seemed to hold no fixed view on the subject, as subsequent orders regularly alternated between both variants when they were issued. Further, it soon became clear that there were not enough different types of vegetable to satisfy operational needs, and so all manner of flowers, shrubs, trees and even marine animals were added to the list of code names as the need dictated, although this did defocus from the concept of gardening in its truest sense.

Many different bomber types were called upon to perform minelaying operations, much of the responsibility during the early campaign of sea mining from the air being shouldered exclusively by Hampdens, which could carry only one mine apiece. As larger aircraft became deployed in this role the number of mines carried increased, the Manchester showing particularly well in this regard by being able to carry four mines; however, it would be the Lancaster, with its payload of six, that would underscore the bomber's capability in this role.

The list of gardening targets in the domain of northern Europe and Scandinavia is as follows:[277]

LOCATION CODES FOR GARDENING OPERATIONS

Alder	South of Bodø	Gorse	Belle Île	Quinces	Langeland Belt
Anemone	Le Havre	Greengage	Cherbourg	Radish	Fehmarn Belt
Artichokes	Lorient	Hawthorn I	Fanø Island	Rosemary	Heligoland
Asparagus	Great Belt	Hawthorn II	Mouth of Limfjord	Scallops	Rouen
Barnacle	Zeebrugge	Hollyhocks	Lübeck	Silverthorne	Areas in Kattegat
Beech	St-Nazaire	Hyacinth	St-Malo	Smelt	Vaagso
Bottle	Haugesund	Jasmine	Warnemünde	Spinach	Gdynia
Broccoli	Great Belt	Jellyfish	Brest	Stickleback	N. of Stadland (Åramsund)
Calabash	South of Harstad	Juniper	Antwerp	Stingray	N. of Stadland (Roresund)
Campion	North of Harstad	Kraut	Off Aalborg – Limfjord	Sweet Peas	Cadet Channel
Carrots	Little Belt	Lettuce	Kiel Canal	Tangerine	Pillau
Cinnamon	La Rochelle	Limpets	Den Helder	Tomato	Frederickstad
Cypress	Dunkirk	Melon	Eckernförde	Trefoil	Texel (south)
Daffodils	Copenhagen	Mussels	Frisian Islands	Turbot	Ostend
Daffodils II	Copenhagen area	Nasturtiums	The Sound	Undergrowth	Frederikshavn Harbour
Dandelion	South of Tromsø	Nectarines	Frisian Islands	Upastree	Morlaix
Deodar	Gironde Estuary	Newt I	Mouth of River Maas	Verbena	Copenhagen Approaches
Dewberry	Boulogne	Newt II	River Maas and E.Scheldt	Vineleaf	Dieppe

Eglantine	Heligoland Approaches	Newt III	East Scheldt	Wallflower	Little Belt
Elderberry	Bayonne	Onions	Oslo	Whelk	Zuider Zee
Endive	Little Belt	Oysters	Rotterdam	Willow	Sassnitz
Flounder	East Scheldt	Persimmon	Tromsø	Xeranthe-mums	Frisian Islands
Forget-me-not	Kiel	Pollock	Bornholm Island	Yams	Heligoland Approaches
Furze	St-Jean-de-Luz	Prawns	Calais	Yew Tree	Skagerrak
Geranium	Swinemünde	Privet	Danzig	Zinnias	Frisian Islands
		Pumpkins	Sejrø Deep		

Notes

The Danish Straits:

1. The Little Belt (Danish: Lillebælt) is the strait between the island of Funen (Danish: Fyn) and the Jutland peninsula.

2. The Great Belt (Danish: Storebælt) is the strait between the Danish islands of Funen and Zealand (Danish: Sjæland).

3. Langeland Belt (Langelandsbælt) is the strait at the southern end of the Great Belt, which separates the Danish islands of Langeland and Lolland.

4. The Sound (Danish: Øresund, Swedish: Öresund) is the strait that separates the Danish island of Zealand from the Swedish Province of Scania.

Strategic Target Codes

In the early days of the Second World War, Bomber Command referred to its individual targets by an alphanumeric code. This took the form of a single-letter prefix followed by a number of between one and four digits long; the letter categorised the class of target, whilst the numbers identified a specific target. This system was replaced in September 1940[278] with a different alphanumeric code, that which applied to Germany comprising two letters followed by a new number between one and four digits long. Examples of these codes include GB3280 for the Bosch works in Stuttgart, GY4772 for the Focke-Wulf factory in Bremen and GR3587 for the Blohm & Voss shipbuilding yards in Hamburg. A booklet providing a look-up guide between old and new codes was issued in November 1940.[279]

ALPHANUMERIC TARGET CODE GROUPS

Early target codes	Target codes from 09/1940	Group
C	GS	Chemical and explosive
M	GH	Transportation
B	GO	Power
A	GQ	Fuel
L	GF	Mining and metallurgy
P	GA	Tele-communication factories
	GL	Aircraft components
G	GZ	General engineering
	GB	Electrical engineering
D	GR	Naval armament
E	GN	Land armaments
H	GU	Aerodromes
N	GK	Foodstuffs
F	GY	Air armaments
K	GW	Aircraft stores
-	GD	Inland waterways

In parallel with the system devised for the many and varied targets across Germany, targets in France and the occupied Low Countries were allocated bands of numbers in the range 1–999 prefixed with the letter Z, examples being Leeuwarden aerodrome in Holland, which was represented by Z52, whilst the Abbeville railway marshalling yards in France were Z440. Other countries were allocated their own distinct numerical systems, such as the targets in occupied Norway being prefixed with an SN code. Further, enemy or enemy-occupied ports were prefixed by a CC code, such as Bremerhaven in Germany being represented by CC5 whilst Ostend in Belgium was CC13.

The Fish codes

Following the lead from AVM Bottomley, who had introduced the gardening codes over a year before, keen fisherman Air Commodore Robert Saundby devised the Fish Codes[280] in 1941 as a system for providing code names for the principal cities destined to be the primary bomber targets in Germany and Italy.

The list of cities represented by the names of fish soon grew quite long, but Saundby was determined to limit them exclusively to fish, unlike the defocusing of code names in the gardening codes. However, even in its embryonic form some of the 64 fish names were at best obscure to all but the most enthusiastic and knowledgeable of his fellow fishermen. Indeed, the level of aquatic discrimination required to operate this code successfully appears to have eluded many, including those responsible for issuing the official directives, and so spelling mistakes in the names of relatively obscure piscine sub-species, even in official correspondence, were not uncommon. This raised the potential for ambiguity when accurate targeting information was so vital for those tasked with organising and flying the operations.

Some of the established code names would be re-used; for example, Char would be reallocated from Turin to Worms, Gudgeon would be reallocated from Milan to Hamm, and Shark would be reallocated from Genoa to Bonn.

The early Fish codes

Anchovy	Gotha	Finnock	Hildesheim	Rainbow	Hagen
Barbel	Stuttgart	Gillaroo	Oberhausen	Redfin	Aschersleben
Bass	Bielefeld	Goldfish	Regensburg	Roach	Bremerhaven
Blackfin	Chemnitz	Grayling	Nürnberg	Rudd	Münster
Bleak	Würzburg	Grilse	Magdeburg	Salmon	Bremen
Blenny	Königsberg	Haddock	Leipzig	Sardine	Halberstadt
Bloater	Breslau	Herring	Emden	Sewin	Stettin
Bluefin	Leverkusen	Jack	Mönchen-gladbach	Shad	Dessau
Bream	Kassel	Kelt	Danzig	Skate	Brunswick
Bullhead	Essen	Kipper	Wilhelmshaven	Smolt	Osnabrück
Carp	Rostock	Luce	Darmstadt	Sole	Frankfurt AM
Catfish	Munich	Mackerel	Lübeck	Sprat	Dortmund
Chavendar	Remscheid	Mahseer	Krefeld	Sprod	Wuppertal
Chevin	Dresden	Minnow	Kiel	Steelhead	Mülheim
Chub	Mannheim	Parr	Mainz	Tope	Wiesbaden
Cod	Duisburg	Peal	Saarbrücken	Trout	Cologne
Dace	Hamburg	Perch	Düsseldorf	Truff	Solingen
Eel	Hanover	Pickerel	Halle	Tuna	Bernburg
Elver	Aachen	Pike	Karlsruhe	Whitebait	Berlin
Ferox	Gelsenkirchen	Pollan	Schweinfurt	Whiting	Augsburg
		Quinnat	Bochum		
Char	Turin	Gudgeon	Milan	Shark	Genoa

The list of code names was supplemented by a subset of specific critical targets such as key factories, shipyards, submarine bases and even individual marshalling yards; these were given the names of dangerous animals. Foremost amongst these was the use of Stoat for the Krupp factory in Essen, rather than the city of Essen, which was denoted by Bullhead.

Some early supplements to the Fish codes

Cobra	Focke-Wulf factory, Bremen	Mantis	Vulkanwerft, Hamburg
Mamba	Deschimag shipyards, Bremen	Stoat	Friedrich Krupp AG, Essen

Endnotes

276 AIR 14/796

277 AIR 14/2064 supported by AIR 2/7976, AIR 14/796 and AIR 14/797

278 AIR 10/3993 for Germany, AP SD159 for most other countries; Part 1: AIR 10/3951 and Part 2: AIR 10/3952.

279 AIR 10/3994

280 AIR 40/1517

281 AIR 14/3408

ANNEX E

GERMAN TIME VS BRITISH TIME

Although British and German forces clashed in the skies over the British Isles and Occupied Europe, they operated from bases operating under different time zones. This gives rise to the possibility that aerial engagements could be reported at different times in British and German records.

1. Great Britain operated British Summer Time (BST), so in springtime the clocks went forward by one hour (GMT+1) and in autumn they went back one hour (GMT). However, in the autumn of 1940 the clocks were not put back, and thus the winter of 1940 was conducted under BST (GMT+1). Then in spring 1941 the clocks went forward another hour, creating the phenomenon of British Double Summer Time (BDST, GMT+2).

2. Germany operated Mitteleuropäischen Zeit (MEZ, Middle European Time) which was one hour ahead of GMT (GMT+1). In the spring of 1940, they moved their clocks forward to Mitteleuropäischen Sommerzeit (MESZ, Middle European Summer Time) two hours ahead of GMT (GMT+2), and did not lose the extra hour again until the winter of 1942.

BRITISH AND GERMAN TIME ZONES AND OFFSETS

	Spring 1939	Autumn 1939	Spring 1940	Autumn 1940	Spring 1941	Autumn 1941	Spring 1942	Autumn 1942
British Forces	16 Apr	19 Nov	25 Feb		4 May	10 Aug	5 Apr	9 Aug
	BST (GMT+1)	GMT	BST (GMT+1)	BST (GMT+1)	BDST (GMT+2)	BST (GMT+1)	BDST (GMT+2)	BST (GMT+1)
German Forces			1 Apr					2 Nov
	MEZ (GMT+1)	MEZ (GMT+1)	MESZ (GMT+2)	MESZ (GMT+2)	MESZ (GMT+2)	MESZ (GMT+2)	MESZ (GMT+2)	MEZ (GMT+1)

Consequently, when analysing corresponding timings it is important to be aware of the time differences:

- 3 September 1939–19 November 1939 → no adjustment.
- 19 November 1939–25 February 1940 → +1 hour (German time one hour ahead).
- 25 February 1940–1 April 1940 → no adjustment.
- 1 April 1940–4 May 1941 → +1 hour (German time one hour ahead).
- 4 May 1941–10 August 1941 → no adjustment.
- 10 August 1941–5 April 1942 → +1 hour (German time one hour ahead).
- 5 April 1942–9 August 1942 → no adjustment.

ANNEX F

COMPARISON BETWEEN RAF AND LUFTWAFFE PERSONNEL STRUCTURES

RAF rank	Short form	Luftwaffe rank	Short form
Group Captain	Gp Capt	Oberst	Oberst
Wing Commander	W/Cdr	Oberstleutnant	Obstlt
Squadron Leader	S/Ldr	Major	Maj
Flight Lieutenant	F/Lt	Hauptmann	Hptm
Flying Officer	F/O	Oberleutnant	Oblt
Pilot Officer	P/O	Leutnant	Ltn
Warrant Officer	W/O	Stabsfeldwebel	Sfw
Flight Sergeant	F/Sgt	Oberfeldwebel	Ofw
Sergeant	Sgt	Feldwebel	Fw
Corporal	Cpl	Unteroffizier	Uffz

Comparison between RAF and Luftwaffe ranks

Unlike in the RAF, the rank held in the Luftwaffe did not dictate the role or function in which the holder could serve. The roles of, for example, Staffelkapitän, Gruppenkommandeure and Geschwaderkommodore were not in themselves ranks and could be fulfilled by personnel at a variety of different levels. Typically, these roles could be expected to be filled by the following ranks:

- **Staffelkapitän**: Oberleutnant or Hauptmann.
- **Gruppenkommandeure**: Hauptmann or Major.
- **Geschwaderkommodore**: Major, Oberstleutnant or Oberst.

.

ANNEX G

102 SQUADRON AIRCRAFT SERIAL NUMBERS BY CALLSIGN

The following lists of aircraft serial numbers cross-referenced against their operational callsigns have been derived by cross-referencing a number of documents, principally the Squadron Operations Record Books (AIR 27/808) against the Station Operations Record Books for RAF Topcliffe (AIR 28/851, AIR 28/854 and AIR 28/855). They may contain inaccuracies due to typographical errors on the original documents, and also possible failures of administration in adjusting records to reflect last-minute substitutions on operations.

Further complications arose due to:

(i) Some damaged aircraft being withdrawn for repair and their callsigns allocated to replacement aircraft. In such circumstances the eventual return to service of a repaired aircraft would have to be managed by a new callsign being allocated.

(ii) Aircraft subject to the B Flight clashing callsigns initiative started on 20 July 1941.

LIST OF WHITLEYS ON 102 SQUADRON OPERATIONS FROM JULY 1941 TO WITHDRAWAL

Established 102 Squadron callsigns and A Flight system from 20 July 1941		B Flight system from 20 July 1941	
DY-A	Z6795 Z6871 Z6820	DY- Ā	Z6842 Z6959
DY-B	Z6796	DY- B̄	Z6574 Z6973
DY-C	T4330	DY- C̄	Z6862 Z6951 Z9128 Z9312
DY-D	Z6821 Z6868 Z9222	DY- D̄	
DY-E	Z6876 Z6761 Z9219	DY- Ē	Z6798 Z9167 Z9362 Z9310
DY-F	Z6653 Z6829 Z6958 Z9283	DY- F̄	
DY-G	Z6830 Z9289	DY- Ḡ	
DY-J	P5014 Z6755 Z6761 Z6572* Z6653	DY- J̄	

Established 102 Squadron callsigns and A Flight system from 20 July 1941		B Flight system from 20 July 1941	
DY-K	Z6820 Z6755	DY- K̄	
DY-L	Z6572 Z6800 Z9421	DY- L̄	
DY-M	Z6494 Z6945	DY- M̄	
DY-N	Z6573 Z6863 Z6812	DY- N̄	Z6866 Z6837 Z6974
DY-O	Z6562 Z6762* Z9201	DY- Ō	Z9212
DY-P	Z6748 Z6875	DY- P̄	Z6870 Z6798
DY-Q	Z6749 Z6747	DY- Q̄	
DY-R	Z6746 Z6970 Z6494 Z9281	DY- R̄	
DY-S	Z6574 Z6749 Z6875	DY- S̄	
DY-T	Z6798 Z6940	DY- T̄	
DY-U		DY- Ū	Z6949 Z6414
DY-V	Z6576 Z6935 Z9282	DY- V̄	
DY-X		DY- X̄	Z6946
DY-Y		DY- Ȳ	Z6877

Note: Entries marked with an asterisk, although featuring in the appropriate Operations Record Books, are considered highly likely to be erroneous.

List of Halifaxes on 102 Squadron operations
from introduction to 25 June 1942

DY-A	R9528 W1099 W1142		DY-N	R9491 W7746
DY-B	R9533		DY-O	W7677 W7706
DY-C	R9494		DY-P	W7652 W1158
DY-D	R9532 W1107		DY-Q	W7654
DY-E	R9531		DY-R	R9442
DY-F	R9446		DY-S	R9441 W7712
DY-G	R9488 W1066		DY-T	R9449
DY-H	R9529 W1153		DY-U	V9987
DY-J	R9530 W1167		DY-V	R9423
DY-L	R9498 W7759		DY-W	R9426
DY-M	W7653 W7651 W7751		DY-Y	L9532

GLOSSARY OF GERMAN WORDS

Abteilung / Abteilungen (pl)	Battalion. In the context of the Kammhuber Line, this comprised a 30 km subset of a Nachtjagdraum identified as a suffix letter, typically A, B or C.
Auswerte Tisch	Plotting board (employed in the early days of the Kammhuber Line)
Batterie	In the context of the Kammhuber Line, this comprised three Züge of manually controlled searchlights, nine in all.
Blau	Blue
Breslau	Former Prussian town, now Wrocław, in Poland
Danzig	Former Prussian town, now Gdańsk, in Poland
Dom	Cathedral
Drontheim	Trondheimduring the German occupation
Ergänzungsstaffel / Ergänzungsstaffeln (pl)	Staffel covering the various roles of providing reserves, supplements and training
Fliegerabwehrkanone(n)	Anti-aircraft gun(s)
Flugmeldemess-Stellung	Night fighter control station
Frieda	Order to descend
Freya	Long-range radar
Funkfeuer	Radio beacon
Geschwader (s/pl)	Translated variously as Wing or Group, but not strictly comparable with either in contemporary RAF terminology. It comprised a complement of between 100 and 180 aircraft.
Geschwaderkommodore	Commander of a Geschwader
Geschwaderstab	Geschwader headquarters
Gruppe / Gruppen (pl)	Translated as Group, but not comparable with a contemporary RAF Group. It comprised a complement of typically 30 aircraft.
Gruppenkommandeure	Commander of a Gruppe
Gruppenstab	Gruppe headquarters
Hannover	Hanover
Helle Riegel	Bright Bolt: line of anti-aircraft defences underpinned by searchlights, known by the British as the Kammhuber Line.
Jagdgeschwader	Fighter Geschwader
Jägerleitoffizier	Fighter Control Officer
Kampfgeschwader	Bomber Geschwader
Köln	Cologne
Kriegsmarine	German Navy (1935–1945)
Leuchtfeuer	Visual beacon
Lichtenstein	Early German AI radar

Lisa	Order to turn to port
Mitteleuropäischen Sommerzeit	Middle European Summer Time
Mitteleuropäischen Zeit	Middle European Time
München	Munich
Nacht	Night
Nachtjagd	German night fighter force
Nachtjagdgeschwader	Night fighter Geschwader
Nachtjagdraum / Nachtjagdräume (pl)	Night fighter interception area extending typically along a 90 km stretch of the Kammhuber Line. It would be identified by a single-digit number and typically divided into three Abteilungen.
Nürnberg	Nuremberg
Pillau	Former Prussian town, now Baltiysk, in Russia
Raum / Räume (pl)	Room or area
Reichsluftfahrtministerium	German Air Ministry
Rolf	Order to turn to starboard
Rot	Red
Seeburg Tisch	Plotting board (refined design)
Siegfried	Order to climb
St. Trond Sint-	Truiden during the German occupation
Stab	Headquarters
Staffel / Staffeln (pl)	Lowest level of operational flying unit, similar to an RAF squadron, but with a complement of typically only nine aircraft.
Staffelkapitän	Leader of a Staffel
Stettin	Former Prussian town, now Szczecin. in Poland
Unterseeboot	Submarine
Vorpostenboot / Vorpostenboote (pl)	Outpost boat(s) / improvised flak ship(s)
Würzburg	Flak-guiding radar deployed to guide night fighters
Würzburg Riese / Riesen (pl)	Giant Würzburg (larger and longer-range Würzburg)
Zug / Züge (pl)	Squad. In the context of the Kammhuber Line this comprised a row of three manually controlled searchlights.

ABBREVIATIONS

A/C	Aircraft
A&AEE	The Aeroplane and Armament Experimental Establishment
AC1	Aircraftsman First Class
ACH	Aircraft Hand
AG	Air Gunner
AI	Airborne Intercept (radar)
AIP	Any Invasion Port
ALG	Advanced Landing Ground
AMATOL	AMmonium nitrate And (trinitro)TOLuene
ASI	Air Speed Indicator
ASV	Air to Surface Vessel (Radar)
AUW	All Up Weight
BDST	British Double Summer Time
BSA	Birmingham Small Arms Company Ltd
BST	British Summer Time
CF	Conversion Flight
CRD	Contractor's Research and Development
CU	Conversion Unit
Deschimag	Deutsche Schiff und Maschinenbau AG
DF	Direction Finding
DuNaJa	Dunkel Nachtjagd
Erg	Ergänzungsstaffel
ETA	Estimated Time of Arrival
evd	Evaded capture
Flak	Fliegerabwehrkanone(n)
GCI	Ground Control Interception
GEE	G for Grid
GMT	Greenwich Mean Time
GO	Gas Operated
GP	General Purpose
HC	High Capacity
HE	High Explosive
HeNaJa	Helle Nachtjagd
IAS	Indicated Air Speed
IFF	Identification Friend or Foe
IG Farben	Interessen-Gemeinschaft Farbenindustrie AG
JG	Jagdgeschwader
JLO	Jägerleitoffizier
KG	Kampfgeschwader
KoNaJa	Kombinierte Nachtjagd
LAC	Leading Aircraftsman
LMS	London, Midland and Scottish (Railway)

MESZ	Mitteleuropäischen Sommerzeit
MEZ	Mitteleuropäischen Zeit
MLD	Mixed Long Delay
MU	Maintenance Unit
NJG	Nachtjagdgeschwader
ORB	Operations Record Book
ORBAT	Order of Battle
OTU	Operational Training Unit
PAO	Pat O'Leary Line
pow	prisoner of war
PRC	Personnel Reception Centre
RDF	Radio Direction Finding
RDX	Research Development Explosive
RLM	Reichsluftfahrtministerium
rpm	revs per minute
RTB	Return to Base
S&M	Strategic and Military
SAP	Semi-Armour Piercing
SBC	Small Bomb Container
TD	Time Delay
TNT	Trinitrotoluene
TORPEX	TORPedo EXplosive
TR	Transmitter Receiver
TRE	The Telecommunications Research Establishment
U-Boat	(U-Boot) Unterseeboot
ut	Under Training
WOp	Wireless Operator [2]
WO/AG	Wireless Operator / Air Gunner [2]
WOp/AG	Wireless Operator / Air Gunner [2]
wpm	words per minute

Note:

1. A wide variety of abbreviations was used in official correspondence to represent the term for a wireless operator. The choice of abbreviation appears to have been one of personal preference, but all parties understood what was meant and no single cohesive abbreviation emerged during this period.

REFERENCES AND BIBLIOGRAPHY

1. National Archive AIR series references

German night air defence capabilities

AIR 2/5070	Operations: Combat Reports (Code B, 55/3): Bomber Command reports: phenomena connected with enemy night defensive tactics: 1940–1942.
AIR 20/4725	Phenomena connected with enemy night defence tactics: Dec 1940–Apr 1942.
AIR 40/1135	Operational Research Committee: tactical counter measures to combat enemy night fighter defence systems: 1 August 1941–31 August 1943.
MPI 1/467	3 items extracted from AIR 40/1135. Europe. 'German Night Fighters Areas and Controls': maps covering parts of Denmark, Germany, Sweden, Norway, northern France, Netherlands and Belgium showing approximate limits of main belt sectors, location of GCI stations, night fighter aerodromes and areas of GCI cover.

RAF bombing operations; planning and reports

AIR 2/7976	*Operations: Sea Areas (Code B, 55/2/11): Gardening operations and results (1941–1944).*
AIR 8/864	*Operation Arabian Nights.*
AIR 10/3951	*Operational Nos: Countries other than Germany, Austria, Czechoslovakia and Poland (1943).*
AIR 10/3952	*Operational Nos: Countries other than Germany and Italy (1940).*
AIR 10/3993	*Operational numbers of bomb targets in Germany (1940).*
AIR 10/3994	*Bomb targets in Germany: conversion table, Air Ministry number to new operational number (1940).*
AIR 14/276	*Thousand Plan: operation orders and correspondence.*
AIR 14/693	*Operation Millennium.*
AIR 14/796	*Gardening Operations (Apr 1940–Apr 1941.)*
AIR 14/797	*Gardening Operations (May 1941–Aug 1942).*
AIR 14/1218	*Operational Research.*
AIR 14/2024	*Operation Thousand.*
AIR 14/2064	*Operation Gardening (Mar 1940–Dec 1943).*
AIR 14/2332	*Operation Millennium Two.*
AIR 14/2601	*Summary of night operations target: Bremen June 1942.*
AIR 14/2664	*Night Bomb raid sheets Vol.I. (Sep 1939–Apr 1940).*
AIR 14/2673	*Night Bomb raid sheets Vol.X. (Jun–Dec 1941).*
AIR 14/2674	*Night Bomb raid sheets Vol.XI. (Jan–Jun 1942).*
AIR 14/3256	*Navigation aids: Gee (Dec 1940–Nov 1942).*
AIR 14/3363	*Day bomb raid sheets Vol.IV. (Jun–Dec 1941).*
AIR 14/3364	*Day bomb raid sheets Vol.V. (1942).*

AIR 14/3408	*Operational Research Section: final reports on operations, night raids, Nos 1–164 Vol.I. (Feb 1942–Sep 1942).*
AIR 14/3802	*Operation Millennium 2.*
AIR 20/5542	*Gee and Oboe: development and production (Jul 1941–Dec 1942).*
AIR 40/1517	*Target Code Names for Bombing Operations Fish Code Names.*

Operations Record Books (AIR 27 series)

4 Squadron

| AIR 27/47 | 1929–1940 |
| AIR 27/48 | 1941–1943 |

10 Squadron

| AIR 27/143 | 1942 |

22 Squadron

| AIR 27/278 | Aug 1915–Dec 1941 |

35 Squadron

| AIR 27/379 | Mar 1929–Oct 1942 |

75 Squadron

| AIR 27/645 | Oct 1916–Dec 1941 |
| AIR 27/646 | 1942–1943 |

76 Squadron

| AIR 27/650 | Sep 1916–Sep 1942 |

77 Squadron

| AIR 27/655 | Oct 1916–Dec 1941 |
| AIR 27/659B | Appendices 1939–1945 |

78 Squadron

| AIR 27/660 | Nov 1916–Dec 1943 |
| AIR 27/663 | Appendices Sep 1939–Feb 1943 |

102 Squadron

| AIR 27/808 | Jan 1941–Nov 1942 |
| AIR 27/809 | 1943 |

115 Squadron

| AIR 27/888 | 1941 |

158 Squadron

| AIR 27/1048 | Feb 1942–Dec 1943 |

218 Squadron

| AIR 27/1350 | 1942 |

301 Squadron

| AIR 27/1660 | Jul 1940–Dec 1946 |

RAF Stations (AIR 28 series)

RAF Leeming

AIR 28/450	Jun 1940–Dec 1942
AIR 28/455	Jun 1941–Aug 1943
AIR 28/456	Aug 1941–Jul 1942

RAF Marston Moor
AIR 28/524   Sep 1941–Oct 1945

RAF Middleton St George
AIR 28/541   Jan 1941–Sep 1945
AIR 28/542   Apr 1941–Jan 1942

RAF St Eval
AIR 28/739   Aug 1942–Oct 1942

RAF Topcliffe
AIR 28/851   Sep 1940–Dec 1943
AIR 28/854   Oct 1940–Dec 1941
AIR 28/855   Jan 1942–Feb 1943

Operational Training Units (AIR 29 series)
10 OTU
AIR 29/638   Apr 1940–Dec 1943
AIR 29/640   Jul 1940–Oct 1946
12 OTU
AIR 29/638   Apr 1940–Dec 1943
19 OTU
AIR 29/662   Apr 1940–Jun 1945
AIR 29/663   Appendices. Contains 239 photographs depicting: Training course for pilots, observers and air gunners (named) 1940–1945.

1652 CU
AIR 29/612   Jan 1942–Feb 1944

2. Air Publications

Air Ministry, *Air Publication 1522E, Pilot's Notes: The Whitley V Aeroplane Two Merlin X Engines.*
Air Ministry, *Air Publication 1719B, Pilot's Notes: Halifax II Aeroplane Four Merlin XX Engines.*
Air Ministry, *Air Publication 3001, Halifax II & V Parachute Drill.*
Air Ministry, *Air Publication 3002, Emergency Equipment & Exits – Halifax II.*
AVIA 7/1250, *GEE Manual* (1941–1944)

3. RLM records

C 2031 Abschuβ Teil I (fighter and flak claims)

4. RAF disclosures

AM Form 1406 42668
AM Form 1406 J.15512
Form 543 566355
Form 543 968101
Form 543A 1325482

5. Imperial War Museum collections

Birth of a Bomber: Aircraft Production in Britain, 1942.

6. Books

Adams, C.W. DFC (1983) *578 Squadron Operations, 1944–45.*

Aders, G. (1980) *History of the German Night Fighter Force 1917–1945*, ISBN 0354012479, Fakenham Press.

Admiralty Charts and Publications (2010) *Admiralty Sailing Directions–North Sea (East) Pilot*, ISBN 9780707742366, United Kingdom Hydrographic Office.

Baber, D. (1954) *Where Eagles Gather*, Viking Press.

Bishop, P. (2007) *Bomber Boys: Fighting Back 1940–1945*, ISBN 9780007189861, HarperCollins.

Boiten, T. (1997) *Nachtjagd: The Night Fighter versus Bomber War over the Third Reich*, ISBN 9781861260864, Crowood Press.

Boiten, T. (1999) *Night Airwar: Personal Recollections of the Conflict over Europe 1939–45*, ISBN 9781861262981, Crowood Press.

Calmel, J. DFC Légion d'Honneur (1955) *Night Pilot* (translated by Mervyn Savill), William Kimber.

Cassidy, James J. Jr (ed.) (1995) *Through Indian Eyes: The Untold Story of Native American Peoples*, ISBN 089577819X, Reader's Digest.

Cheshire, L. VC OM DSO DFC (1988) *Bomber Pilot*, ISBN 0907579108, Goodall.

Chorley, W.R. (1992) *Royal Air Force Bomber Command Losses of the Second World War: Volume 1 1939–40*, ISBN 9780904597851, Midland.

Chorley, W.R. (2006) *Royal Air Force Bomber Command Losses of the Second World War: Volume 2 1941*, ISBN 9780904597875, Midland.

Chorley, W.R. (2006) *Royal Air Force Bomber Command Losses of the Second World War: Volume 3 1942*, ISBN 9780904597899, Midland.

Chorley, W.R. (2002) *Royal Air Force Bomber Command Losses: Volume 7 Operational Training Units 1940–1947*, ISBN 9781857801323, Midland.

Cooper, A.W. (2009) *Air Gunner: The Men Who Manned the Turrets*, ISBN 9781844158256, Pen and Sword.

Dunmore, S. and Carter, W. (1992) *Reap the Whirlwind: The Untold Story of 6 Group, Canada's Bomber Force of World War II*, ISBN 0947554351, Crécy.

Goss, C. (1995) *It's Suicide but It's Fun: The Story of 102 (Ceylon) Squadron 1917–1956*, ISBN 0947554599, Crécy.

Green, W. (1960) *Famous Bombers of the Second World War*, MacDonald.

Halpenny, B.B. (1990) *Action Stations: 4. Military airfields of Yorkshire*, ISBN 0850595320, Patrick Stephens.

Harris, A.T. GCB OBE AFC (1995) *Despatch on War Operations 23rd February 1942 to 8th May 1945*, ISBN 071464692X, Frank Cass.

Hastings, M. FRSL FRHistS (1999) *Bomber Command: The Strategic Bombing Offensive 1939–45*, ISBN 9781509856251, MacMillan.

Hinchliffe, P. OBE (1997) *The Other Battle: Luftwaffe Night Aces versus Bomber Command*, ISBN 1853105473, Airlife.

Johnen, W. Ritterkreuz des Eisernen Kreuzes (1994) *Duel Under the Stars*, ISBN 9780947554422, Crécy.

Jones, R.V. (1978) *Most Secret War: British Scientific Intelligence 1939–1945*, ISBN 0241897467, Hamish Hamilton.

Lake, J. (1999) *Halifax Squadrons of World War 2*, ISBN 9781855328921, Osprey.

Lyman, R. (2013) *Into the Jaws of Death: The True Story of the Legendary Raid on Saint-Nazaire*, ISBN 9781782064442, Quercus.

Middlebrook, M. and Everitt, C. (1990) *The Bomber Command War Diaries: An Operational Reference Book 1939–1945*, ISBN 0140129367, Penguin.

Ministry of Information (1941) *Bomber Command: The Air Ministry Account of Bomber Command's Offensive Against the Axis September 1939–July 1941*, His Majesty's Stationery Office.

Ministry of Information (1942) *Bomber Command Continues*, His Majesty's Stationery Office.

Pitchfork, G. MBE (2003) *Shot Down and on the Run: The RCAF and Commonwealth Aircrews Who Got Home from Behind Enemy Lines, 1940–1945*, ISBN 1903365538, the national archives.

Rasmussen, N. (2008) *On Speed: The Many Lives of Amphetamine*, ISBN 0814776019, New York University Press.

Sweetman, J. (2005) *Bomber Crew: Taking on the Reich*, ISBN 0349117969, Abacus.

Taylor, E. (2004) *Operation Millennium: 'Bomber' Harris's Raid on Cologne, May 1942*, ISBN 1862272301, Spellmount.

Ward, C. (2012) *4 Group Bomber Command: An Operational Record*, ISBN 9781848848849, Pen & Sword.

Wheeler, B.C. *Halifax: From Front-Line Bomber to Post-War Transport*, ISBN 9781907426483, Kelsey Publishing Group (www.aeroplanemonthly.com).

7. Newspapers

1915–1916 Alaska-Yukon Gazetteer and Business Directory.
New York Times, 20 May 1942.
The London Gazette, 16 June 1942.
Seattle Times, 3 February 2008.

8. Public records

British records

1911 England and Wales Census
1901 England and Wales Census
1891 England and Wales Census
1881 England and Wales Census
England and Wales Birth Index
England and Wales Marriage Index
England and Wales Death Index
UK Incoming Passenger Lists
UK Outward Passenger Lists

American records

1930 United States Federal Census
1920 United States Federal Census
1910 United States Federal Census
1900 United States Federal Census
US Indian Census Roles 1885–1940
US World War 1 Draft Registration Cards 1917–1918
California, Voter Registers, 1866–1898
Washington Marriage Records 1865–2004
Border Crossings: from Canada to US 1895–1956
Alaska Passenger and Crew Manifests 1906–1981
Washington, Passenger and Crew Lists 1882–1961

Canadian records

Library and Archives of Canada
1921 Census of Canada
1911 Census of Canada
1901 Census of Canada
Canadian Passenger Lists 1865–1935

9. Websites

Electronic references being subject to change, the content of some sites listed here may not be the same as when it was first referenced.
Alaska Marriages 1745–1950, *alaskaweb.org/marrs/marrs-a.html.*
Belgian Aviation History Association, *luchtvaartgeschiedenis.be.*
British Columbia City Directories 1860–1955, *vpl.ca/bccd/index.php.*
De Studiegroep Luchtoorlog 1939–1945 (SGLO), *airwar39-45.nl.*

Flute, D. *ukairfieldguide.net.*
Janes, K. *conscript-heroes.com.*
Juneau AKGenWeb, *sites.rootsweb.com/~akcjunea/cemeteries/evergreena.htm.*
Layne, D. *wallyswar.wordpress.com.*
Ligne d'Évasion Comète, *cometeline.org.*
Marr, C.J. *content.lib.washington.edu/aipnw/marr.html.*
Nederlandse Federatie voor Luchtvaart Archeologie (NFLA), *nfla.nl.*
Ronald, V. *forgottenairfields.com.*
Svejgaard, M. *gyges.dk.*
The WW2 Escape Lines Memorial Society, *ww2escapelines.co.uk.*
The Commonwealth War Graves Commission, *cwgc.org.*
Voulon, R. *luchtoorlog.net.*